Mining Imperfect Data

Mining Imperfect Data

Dealing with Contamination and Incomplete Records

Ronald K. Pearson

ProSanos Corporation
Harrisburg, Pennsylvania
and
Thomas Jefferson University
Philadelphia, Pennsylvania

Society for Industrial and Applied Mathematics
Philadelphia

Copyright © 2005 by the Society for Industrial and Applied Mathematics.

10 9 8 7 6 5 4 3 2 1

Excel is a trademark of Microsoft Corporation in the United States and/or other countries.

Mathematica is a registered trademark of Wolfram Research, Inc.

S-PLUS is a registered trademark of Insightful Corporation.

Library of Congress Cataloging-in-Publication Data

Pearson, Ronald K., 1952-
    Mining imperfect data : dealing with contamination and incomplete records / Ronald K. Pearson.
        p. cm.
    Includes bibliographical references and index.
    ISBN 0-89871-582-2 (pbk.)
    1. Data mining. I. Title.

    QA76.9.D343P43 2005
    006.3–dc22   2004065395

 is a registered trademark.

Contents

Preface   **ix**

1   Introduction   **1**
   1.1   Data anomalies   2
      1.1.1   Outliers   2
      1.1.2   Boxplots: A useful comparison tool   4
      1.1.3   Missing data   7
      1.1.4   Misalignments   9
      1.1.5   Unexpected structure   11
   1.2   Data anomalies need not be bad   13
      1.2.1   Materials with anomalous properties   13
      1.2.2   Product design: Looking for "good" anomalies   14
      1.2.3   "Niches" in business data records   16
   1.3   Conversely, data anomalies can be very bad   16
      1.3.1   The CAMDA'02 normal mouse dataset   16
      1.3.2   The influence of outliers on kurtosis   18
   1.4   Dealing with data anomalies   19
      1.4.1   Outlier-resistant analysis procedures   20
      1.4.2   Outlier detection procedures   23
      1.4.3   Preprocessing for anomaly detection   24
   1.5   GSA   25
   1.6   Organization of this book   31

2   Imperfect Datasets: Character, Consequences, and Causes   **33**
   2.1   Outliers   34
      2.1.1   Univariate outliers   34
      2.1.2   Multivariate outliers   37
      2.1.3   Time-series outliers   40
   2.2   Consequences of outliers   41
      2.2.1   Moments versus order statistics   41
      2.2.2   The effect of outliers on volcano plots   45
      2.2.3   Product-moment correlations   47
      2.2.4   Spearman rank correlations   50
   2.3   Sources of data anomalies   52
      2.3.1   Gross measurement errors and outliers   52

	2.3.2	Misalignments and software errors	54
	2.3.3	Constraints and hidden symmetries	58
2.4	Missing data		60
	2.4.1	Nonignorable missing data and sampling bias	60
	2.4.2	Special codes, nulls, and disguises	61
	2.4.3	Idempotent data transformations	63
	2.4.4	Missing data from file merging	66

3 Univariate Outlier Detection   69

3.1	Univariate outlier models	70
3.2	Three outlier detection procedures	73
	3.2.1	The 3σ edit rule	74
	3.2.2	The Hampel identifier	76
	3.2.3	Quartile-based detection and boxplots	77
3.3	Performance comparison	78
	3.3.1	Formulation of the case study	79
	3.3.2	The uncontaminated reference case	79
	3.3.3	Results for 1% contamination	80
	3.3.4	Results for 5% contamination	82
	3.3.5	Results for 15% contamination	84
	3.3.6	Brief summary of the results	86
3.4	Application to real datasets	86
	3.4.1	The catalyst dataset	87
	3.4.2	The flow rate dataset	88
	3.4.3	The industrial pressure dataset	90

4 Data Pretreatment   93

4.1	Noninformative variables	93
	4.1.1	Classes of noninformative variables	94
	4.1.2	A microarray dataset	95
	4.1.3	Noise variables	96
	4.1.4	Occam's hatchet and omission bias	98
4.2	Handling missing data	102
	4.2.1	Omission of missing values	102
	4.2.2	Single imputation strategies	103
	4.2.3	Multiple imputation strategies	105
	4.2.4	Unmeasured and unmeasurable variables	108
4.3	Cleaning time-series	110
	4.3.1	The nature of the problem	110
	4.3.2	Data-cleaning filters	115
	4.3.3	The center-weighted median filter	118
	4.3.4	The Hampel filter	122
4.4	Multivariate outlier detection	124
	4.4.1	Visual inspection	125
	4.4.2	Covariance-based detection	127

	4.4.3	Regression-based detection	131
	4.4.4	Depth-based detection	134
4.5	Preliminary analyses and auxiliary knowledge		138

5 What Is a "Good" Data Characterization?   **141**

5.1	A motivating example		142
5.2	Characterization via functional equations		143
	5.2.1	A brief introduction to functional equations	144
	5.2.2	Homogeneity and its extensions	147
	5.2.3	Location-invariance and related conditions	149
	5.2.4	Outlier detection procedures	152
	5.2.5	Quasi-linear means	154
	5.2.6	Results for positive-breakdown estimators	155
5.3	Characterization via inequalities		159
	5.3.1	Inequalities as aids to interpretation	159
	5.3.2	Relations between data characterizations	161
	5.3.3	Bounds on means and standard deviations	163
	5.3.4	Inequalities as uncertainty descriptions	166
5.4	Coda: What is a "good" data characterization?		172

6 GSA   **177**

6.1	The GSA metaheuristic		177
6.2	The notion of exchangeability		179
6.3	Choosing scenarios		180
	6.3.1	Some general guidelines	181
	6.3.2	Managing subscenarios	186
	6.3.3	Experimental design and scenario selection	188
6.4	Sampling schemes		190
6.5	Selecting a descriptor $d(\cdot)$		192
6.6	Displaying and interpreting the results		193
	6.6.1	Normal Q-Q plots	194
	6.6.2	Direct comparisons across scenarios	195
6.7	The model approximation case study		197
6.8	Extensions of the basic GSA framework		201
	6.8.1	Iterative analysis procedures	201
	6.8.2	Multivariable descriptors	204

7 Sampling Schemes for a Fixed Dataset   **207**

7.1	Four general strategies		207
	7.1.1	Strategy 1: Random selection	208
	7.1.2	Correlation and overlap	212
	7.1.3	Strategy 2: Subset deletion	213
	7.1.4	Strategy 3: Comparisons	217
	7.1.5	Strategy 4: Partially systematic sampling	222
7.2	Random selection examples		231
	7.2.1	Variability of kurtosis estimates	232
	7.2.2	The industrial pressure datasets	235

	7.3	Subset deletion examples	237
	7.3.1	The storage tank dataset	237
	7.3.2	Dynamic correlation analysis	240
	7.4	Comparison-based examples	244
	7.4.1	Correlation-destroying permutations	245
	7.4.2	Rank-based dynamic analysis	248
	7.5	Two systematic selection examples	251
	7.5.1	Moving-window data characterizations	252
	7.5.2	The Michigan lung cancer dataset	263

8 Concluding Remarks and Open Questions   269

	8.1	Analyzing large datasets	269
	8.2	Prior knowledge, auxiliary data, and assumptions	272
	8.3	Some open questions	274
	8.3.1	How prevalent are different types of data anomalies?	274
	8.3.2	How should outliers be modelled?	276
	8.3.3	How should asymmetry be handled?	277
	8.3.4	How should misalignments be detected?	283

Bibliography   287

Index   301

Preface

Data mining may be defined broadly as the use of automated procedures to extract useful information and insight from large datasets. In practice, these datasets contain various types of anomalous records that significantly complicate the analysis problem. In particular, the prevalence of *outliers, missing* or *incomplete data*, and other more subtle phenomena such as *misalignments* can completely invalidate the results obtained with standard analysis procedures, often with no indication that anything is wrong. This book is concerned with the problems of detecting these data anomalies and overcoming their deleterious effects.

Two ideas that are central to this book are *data pretreatment* and *analytical validation*. Data pretreatment is concerned with the issues of detecting outliers of various types, treatment strategies once we have found them, the closely allied problem of missing data, the detection of noninformative variables that should be excluded from subsequent analyses, and the use of simple preliminary analyses to detect other types of data anomalies such as misalignments. The essential idea behind pretreatment is the too often overlooked early computer axiom garbage in, garbage out. Analytical validation is concerned with the assessment of results once we have them in hand to determine whether they are garbage, gold, or something in between. The essential idea here is the use of systematic and, to the degree possible, extensive comparison to assess the quality of these results. This idea is formalized here as generalized sensitivity analysis (GSA), based on the following idea:

> A "good" data analysis result should be insensitive to small changes in either
> the methods or the datasets on which the analysis is based.

Although this statement sounds very much like the definition of *resistance* in robust statistics, the GSA formulation differs in two important respects, both of which are particularly relevant to the data-mining problem. First, the GSA formulation is broader since the notion of "small changes in a dataset" considered here is based on the concept of *exchangeability* as defined by Draper et al. (1993), whereas resistance usually involves either small changes in all of the data values or large changes in a few of the values. The difference is important since exchangeable datasets can include either of these data modifications, together with many others, such as randomly selected subsets of a larger dataset, subsets obtained by deleting observations, or subsets obtained by stratification based on auxiliary variables. The second important difference is that the GSA formulation is informal, based ultimately on graphical data summaries, although formal extensions are possible, as in the case of the comparison-based GSA strategies discussed in Chapter 7. This informality does cost us in terms of the power of the statements we can make about the data, but this loss is offset by the tremendous flexibility of the GSA framework. For example, this framework is applicable to any of the popular data-mining methods discussed by Cios, Pedrycz, and Swiniarski (1998) without modification.

This book grew from the presentation materials for a two-hour tutorial that I gave at the 2002 SIAM International Conference on Data Mining in Arlington, Virginia. I am indebted to Joydeep Ghosh, who organized the tutorial sessions and offered a number of practical suggestions concerning the scope and level of the tutorial, and Linda Thiel, the SIAM editor who suggested this extension of the original course notes and who has been very patient and supportive during the process of transforming those notes into this book. The material presented here has been drawn from many sources beyond the obvious ones cited in the bibliography. Some of the ideas originated in discussions with my former colleagues at the DuPont Company, especially Tunde Ogunnaike (now at the University of Delaware), Martin Pottmann, and the late W. David Smith, Jr. Another source of ideas and insight is the four years I spent at the Institut für Automatik at ETH, Zürich; particular thanks go to Prof. Manfred Morari, director of the Institute; Prof. Frank Allgöwer and his group, Eric Bullinger, Rolf Findeisen, and Patrick Menold, currently all at Universität Stuttgart; and the ETH students in the data analysis courses I taught there. It is said that the best way to learn a subject is to teach it, and I learned much from my students. Special thanks also to Prof. Emeritus Janos Aczél, University of Waterloo, whose visit to the ETH helped introduce me to the intriguing world of functional equations.

Work on this book began while I was a Visiting Professor at the Tampere International Center for Signal Processing in Tampere, Finland, where I was able to focus on two primary topics: nonlinear digital filtering, a small amount of which appears here in the discussions of time-series data cleaning in Chapter 4, and the analysis of microarray data. This last problem has occupied much of my effort in my recent position with the Daniel Baugh Institute for Functional Genomics in the Department of Pathology, Anatomy, and Cell Biology at Thomas Jefferson University. There again, I am indebted to my colleagues, especially Jim Schwaber, director of the Institute, and Profs. Greg Gonye and Jan Hoek, with whom I have worked closely. In addition, I am indebted to Ausra Milano and Egle Juskeviciute for providing me with the microarray data examples presented here and helping me to understand what the analysis objectives are for these large, challenging datasets. Similarly, I owe a debt of gratitude to Reed Hendershot and Jochen Lauterbach of the University of Delaware, Department of Chemical Engineering, for providing me with the catalyst dataset discussed here. Finally, useful insight into the analysis of contaminated data has also come from my current employer, ProSanos Corporation, particularly Alan Hochberg, Andrew Lebeau, and Bob Kingan. To all of you, thanks very much for making this a better book. Conversely, to those of you whom I have omitted and should have thanked, please accept my apologies and smile smugly in the certain knowledge that there are other errors of omission or commission sprinkled here and there throughout the book. To everyone, my sincerest apologies for those.

Ronald K. Pearson

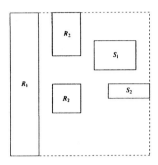

Chapter 1

Introduction

The term *data mining* usually refers to the exploratory analysis of datasets that are large enough to require a significant degree of automation in their analysis. For example, English et al. (1998) describe an automated fault diagnosis system developed to monitor an industrial polymerization unit. The computer-based data collection system for this process measured 522 variables every 2 seconds, generating approximately 22.5 million numbers per day. A second representative example is the cDNA microarray dataset discussed in various chapters of this book: there, every microarray generates a 32-number summary for each of 9,120 genes in a biological tissue sample, and each gene is replicated twice on the microarray. The overall dataset contains results for 48 microarrays, for a total of about 28 million numbers.

One of the key points of this book is that datasets this large almost always contain *anomalous records* of various types, including unusually small or large values, individual cases that violate the nominal relationship between specific variables, and missing data values. Another key point of this book is that the presence of even a few of these anomalies in a large dataset can have a disproportionate influence on analytical results. In some cases, even a preliminary understanding of the nature and source of these few anomalies can be more valuable than a more complete understanding of the rest of the dataset, a point discussed further in Sec. 1.2. Conversely, in cases where these anomalies are of no inherent interest (e.g., anomalies caused by gross measurement or data conversion errors), it is important not to allow them to dominate our analysis results.

This book is concerned with the practical problems of analyzing large datasets containing various types of anomalies. Detailed discussions of the character, sources, and influence of these anomalies are presented, along with procedures for detecting them and for analyzing datasets that may (or may not) contain them. A general strategy emphasized throughout is the use of comparisons, particularly between results obtained by procedures that are known to be sensitive to anomalies and those that are known to be anomaly-resistant. This notion is formalized as *generalized sensitivity analysis (GSA)*, a framework introduced in Sec. 1.5, illustrated by example in Chapters 2, 3, and 4, and discussed in more detail in Chapters 6 and 7.

1.1   Data anomalies

Data anomalies can take a number of different forms, each with a different range of analytical consequences. The following discussion considers four different classes of data anomalies: outliers, missing data, misalignments, and unexpected structure. Further, each of these classes may be subdivided into distinct types, each with its own distinctive characteristics and consequences. All of the topics introduced here are discussed in more detail in Chapter 2, but the following discussions provide a useful introduction to a number of important practical distinctions among these different types of data anomalies.

1.1.1   Outliers

Outliers are perhaps the simplest and best-known type of data anomaly. It is important to bear in mind that outliers, often viewed as another term for "gross measurement errors," can arise from many different sources, and some may be more interesting than the rest of the data values. This crucial point is discussed further in Sec. 1.2. Here, we adopt the following data-based working definition of outliers, offered by Barnett and Lewis (1994, p. 4):

> An outlier *is an entry in a dataset that is anomalous with respect to the behavior seen in the majority of the other entries in the dataset.*

To turn this definition into a procedure for deciding whether a specific entry in a dataset is an outlier or not, two things are required:

1. a characterization of the *nominal* (i.e., "nonanomalous") part of the dataset;

2. a quantitative criterion for deciding whether the entry in question is in significant conflict with this nominal characterization.

The existence of different nominal behavior classes of practical importance leads to the existence of different types of outliers, and the existence of different criteria for evaluating deviations from nominal behavior leads to a range of different outlier detection algorithms. Both of these factors are extremely important in practice, ultimately providing the basis for deciding which outlier detection procedure or outlier-resistant analysis procedure to use. Detailed discussions of outlier detection procedures are deferred to Chapters 3 and 4, but the following paragraphs introduce a few key ideas, focusing primarily on some of the different types of nominal data characterizations that lead to different classes of outliers.

The simplest class of outliers is the class of *univariate outliers* in a sequence $\{x_k\}$ of real numbers. Here, the nominal model is that the observations are all approximately equal, and observations are declared anomalous if they lie too far from the majority of the others in the data sequence. The following example, based on a small collection of cDNA microarray results, illustrates this idea. Essentially, microarray experiments measure expression level changes in several thousand genes simultaneously. The microarray experiments considered here attempt to measure the changes in gene expression levels in the brainstem in rats exposed to ethanol. Results for one specific gene are shown in Figure 1.1, with eight results from control animals shown to the left of the vertical dashed line and eight results from ethanol-treated animals shown to the right of this line. All but one of these values lies in the range from about -1.5 to 1, but one is anomalously large, at approximately 4.5.

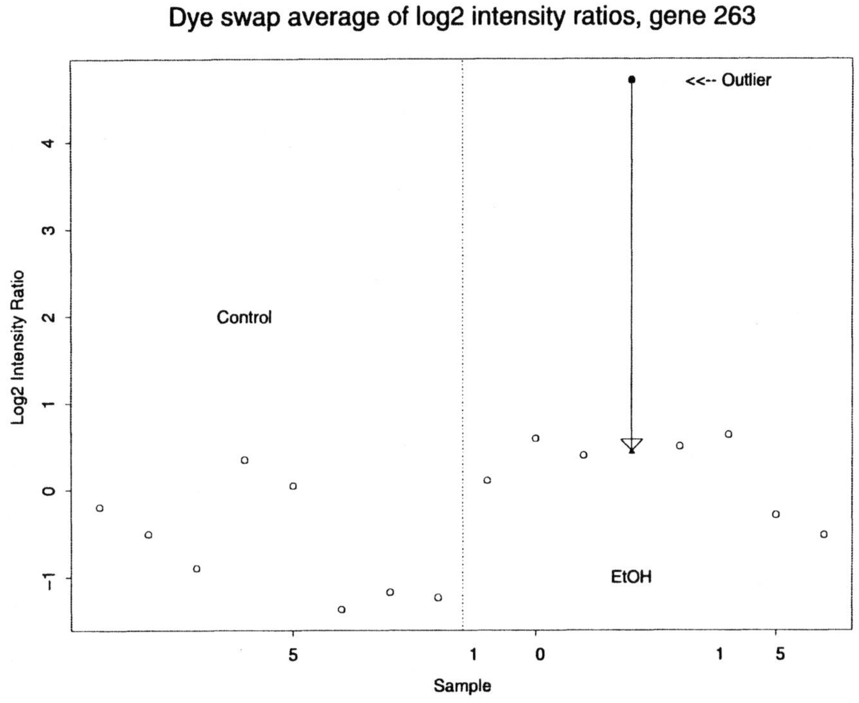
Dye swap average of log2 intensity ratios, gene 263
<<-- Outlier
Control
EtOH
Log2 Intensity Ratio
Sample
-1
0
1
2
3
4
5
1 0
1 5

Figure 1.1. *An outlier in a sequence of microarray results.*

This example is revisited in Chapter 3 in connection with the problem of automated outlier detection, but it is clear from a visual examination of Figure 1.1 that this point satisfies the working definition of an outlier given above: it lies well outside the range of variation of the other 15 points in this data sequence.

The standard working assumption for univariate outliers is that the nominal data values are statistically independent random samples, drawn from some well-behaved distribution. Historically, *well-behaved* has most often been taken to mean Gaussian, but a less restrictive alternative is to assume a symmetric distribution with finite mean and variance. Under this assumption, outliers correspond to data values that are unusually far from the center of the cluster of data values. Probably the best-known criterion for declaring a data value x_j in the sequence $\{x_k\}$ to be an outlier is the 3σ *edit rule*, which declares any point lying farther than three standard deviations from the mean an outlier. Unfortunately, this procedure tends to perform poorly in practice, a point discussed at some length in Chapter 3, where some more effective alternatives are also described. Regardless of the specific criterion chosen, however, an important characteristic of univariate outliers is that they are extreme values in the data sequence. That is, if x^o is an outlier lying above the center of the data cluster and x^* is a data value lying above x^o (i.e., if $x^* > x^o$), then x^* is necessarily also an outlier. Similarly, if x_o is an outlier lying below the center of the data cluster and $x_* < x_o$, then x_* is also an outlier.

This last observation is important in part because it does not extend to other classes of outliers. In particular, a *multivariate outlier* in a sequence $\{\mathbf{x}_k\}$ of vectors corresponds to a

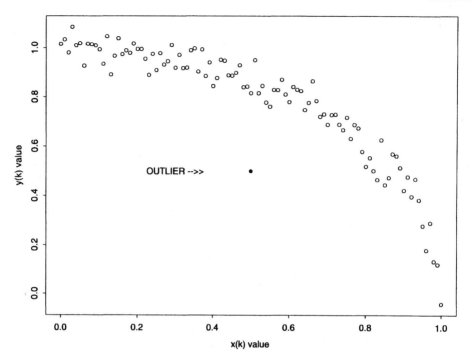

Figure 1.2. *A simple bivariate outlier example. Note that the outlier (solid circle) is not extreme with respect to either its x- or y-component values.*

vector $\mathbf{x}_j$ whose individual components are significantly discordant with the intercomponent relations exhibited by the majority of the other data values. This point is illustrated in Figure 1.2, which shows a bivariate example where most of the observations, indicated by open circles, satisfy the intercomponent relationship $y_k \simeq \sqrt{1 - x_k^2}$. The single glaring exception to this relationship is the point in the center of the plot, marked with a solid circle. Note that all of the x and y values for this example lie within the approximate range $0 \lesssim x, y \lesssim 1$, *including the bivariate outlier, which has both components in the center of this range.* One practical significance of this observation is that multivariate outliers are usually more difficult to detect than univariate outliers are. In particular, note the necessity of considering the x and y components together in Figure 1.2 to detect the outlier seen there.

This last example illustrates an important general point: as the complexity of the nominal data model increases, so generally does the effort required to detect outliers. This point is discussed further in Chapter 2, where additional classes of outliers are introduced, and in Chapter 4, where algorithms for detecting outliers in these more difficult settings are discussed.

1.1.2 Boxplots: A useful comparison tool

The following example introduces the construction of *boxplots* (Hoaglin, Mosteller, and Tukey, 1991, p. 44), an extremely useful graphical technique for summarizing and comparing datasets. These summaries are based on the *order statistics* of a data sequence $\{x_k\}$ of length N, defined as the rank-ordered sequence

$$x_{(1)} \leq x_{(2)} \leq \cdots \leq x_{(N-1)} \leq x_{(N)}. \tag{1.1}$$

These order statistics define a corresponding set of *empirical quantiles* denoted $x_{(q)}$, where $q = (i-1)/(N-1)$. Thus, the sample minimum $x_{(1)}$ corresponds to the zero quantile $x_{(0)}$ and the sample maximum $x_{(N)}$ corresponds to the unit quantile $x_{(1)}$. Quantiles for arbitrary values of q between 0 and 1 may then be defined by linearly interpolating the sample quantiles defined by the rank-ordered values $x_{(i)}$ in (1.1). That is, for an arbitrary value of q between 0 and 1, we select the values of i and $i+1$ such that $(i-1)/(N-1) \leq q \leq i/(N-1)$ and compute $x_{(q)}$ as

$$x_{(q)} = x_{(i)} + [(N-1)q - i + 1][x_{(i+1)} - x_{(i)}], \tag{1.2}$$

which lies between $x_{(i)}$ and $x_{(i+1)}$. As a specific example, the *sample median* corresponds to $x_{(0.5)}$, which is equal to the order statistic $x_{([N+1]/2)}$ if N is odd and the average of the two central order statistics if N is even, since 0.5 lies midway between $(N/2 - 1)/(N-1)$ and $(N/2)/(N-1)$ for any even integer N.

The simplest boxplots are based on the following five-number summary, easily computable for any sequence $\{x_k\}$ of real numbers:

1. the *sample maximum*, $x_{(N)} = x_{(1.00)}$;

2. the *upper quartile*, $x_{(0.75)}$;

3. the *median*, $x_{(0.50)}$;

4. the *lower quartile*, $x_{(0.25)}$; and

5. the *sample minimum*, $x_{(1)} = x_{(0.00)}$.

The basic construction of the boxplot is illustrated nicely in Figure 1.3, which compares the results obtained from 100 repeated kurtosis calculations obtained from statistically independent data sequences drawn from 2 different distributions. Kurtosis is a historically important distributional characterization discussed further in Sec. 1.3.2 and defined as the normalized fourth moment

$$\kappa = \frac{E\{(x - E\{x\})^4\}}{[\text{var}\{x\}]^2} - 3. \tag{1.3}$$

The basis for this particular definition, which is also sometimes known as the *excess of kurtosis*, is that for a Gaussian random variable x, $E\{(x - E\{x\})^4\} = 3[\text{var}\{x\}]^2$, meaning that $\kappa = 0$ for any Gaussian random variable. It is easy to demonstrate that κ is invariant under arbitrary linear transformations of the form $x \rightarrow ax + b$. As a consequence, κ is sometimes taken as a measure of deviation from Gaussianity. Replacing the expectations appearing in the definition of κ with averages leads to the computable estimator

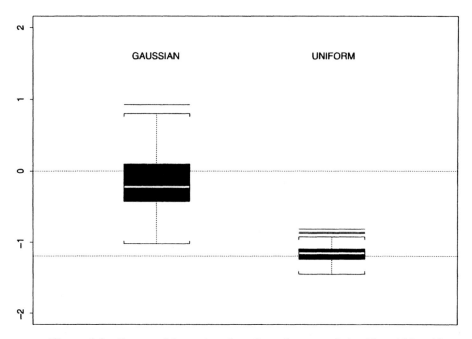

Figure 1.3. *Computed kurtosis values from datasets of size $N = 100$, with normally and uniformly distributed data.*

$$\hat{\kappa} = \frac{\sum_{k=1}^{N} (x_k - \bar{x})^4}{\left[\sum_{k=1}^{N} (x_k - \bar{x})^2\right]^2} - 3,$$

$$\bar{x} = \frac{1}{N} \sum_{k=1}^{N} x_k. \tag{1.4}$$

The results shown in Figure 1.3 illustrate some of the significant influences of the underlying data distribution on the estimated kurtosis values $\hat{\kappa}$.

More specifically, each of the two boxplots shown in Figure 1.3 summarizes the results of 100 kurtosis computations from statistically independent data sequences, each of length $N = 100$ and drawn from one of two specified distributions. The boxplot on the left summarizes the results obtained for a zero-mean, unit-variance Gaussian sequence, and the boxplot on the right summarizes the results obtained for a uniformly distributed sequence on the unit interval [0, 1]. The horizontal white line at the center of each plot corresponds to the median kurtosis value computed for these 100 sequences, and the upper and lower limits of the black box in the center of each plot correspond to the upper and lower quartiles defined above. In the simplest boxplot construction, extreme values (i.e., maximum and minimum data values) are marked with thin horizontal lines connected to the upper and lower ends of the central black box by dashed vertical lines. In Figure 1.3, the minimum kurtosis values are indicated this way for both data distributions.

The maximum kurtosis value computed from the Gaussian data sequences is shown as a thin horizontal line in the left-hand plot in Figure 1.3, but this line is not connected to the central black box by the dashed vertical line, in contrast to the sample minimum. Instead, the dashed vertical line extending from the top of the central box terminates at a horizontal line drawn at a smaller value than the sample maximum. This line indicates the largest *nonanomalous* value in the dataset, a determination made from the sample median and the interquartile distance (IQD) (i.e., the difference between the upper and lower quartiles). A detailed discussion of this outlier detection strategy is given in Chapter 3, but the key points here are that this procedure is simple, systematic, and reasonably popular. For the kurtosis values computed from the Gaussian data sequences, the left-hand boxplot indicates that the largest observed value is declared an outlier by this detection strategy. Similarly, the right-hand boxplot shows that this procedure declares several of the largest kurtosis values outliers for the uniformly distributed data sequences.

One of the primary advantages of boxplots is that they provide a simple basis for making effective graphical comparisons of two datasets. Here, this comparison is between a dataset of 100 kurtosis values computed from Gaussian data sequences and a dataset of those computed from uniformly distributed data sequences. It is immediately clear from these plots that there is a pronounced distributional dependence: the Gaussian kurtosis values span a much wider range than the uniform kurtosis values do. Also, the dashed horizontal lines in Figure 1.3 indicate the correct values of κ for each of the two distributions: $\kappa = 0$ for Gaussian data, as noted earlier, and $\kappa = -1.2$ for uniformly distributed data. It is clear that κ is underestimated somewhat, on average, when $\hat{\kappa}$ is computed from Gaussian data, but it is overestimated slightly when it is computed from uniformly distributed data. Also, the range of variation is much wider for the Gaussian case than for the uniformly distributed case. An expanded version of this example is considered in Sec. 1.3.2, where a third distribution is considered, as are the (profound) influences of outliers on the standard kurtosis estimator.

1.1.3 Missing data

An extremely common anomaly in large datasets is *missing data,* corresponding to data values that *should* be present in a dataset but that, for various reasons, are absent. One common source of missing data is measurement system failures, which can occur in either manual or automated data collection systems. For example, power failures in computerized data collection systems can result in the loss of data values that would normally be recorded. Further, *partial system failures* will generally mean that, at given measurement times, some data values are recorded but other data values are not. In manual data collection systems, certain types of data tend to be more frequently missing than others. As a specific example, Adriaans and Zantinge (1996) note that certain variables, such as "client age," are quite likely to be missing from business databases.

The practical consequences of missing data depend both on what fraction of data values is missing and on the *type* of missing data. *Ignorable missing data* generally corresponds to the omission of a randomly selected subset of data values from a dataset. Since the variability of results computed from N data values normally decreases with increasing N, the effect of ignorable missing data is generally an increase in this variability relative to the results we would obtain from a complete dataset. Conversely, *nonignorable missing data* generally correspond to *systematically missing* data values from a dataset. The consequence of nonignorable missing values is more severe, since it often introduces significant biases into our analysis results. As a specific example, Rubin (1987) discusses a survey of schools conducted for the Educational Testing Service (ETS) intended to evaluate the performance of a special program in the school system: certain schools expecting criticism for poor performance in implementing this program refused to respond to the ETS survey. In such cases, since the missing data values are not representative of the values that are available in the dataset, simply ignoring them and proceeding with our analysis can lead to significantly biased results. This problem is potentially much more severe than the increase in variability that typically results from ignorable missing data.

The following mathematical example provides a simple illustration of the difference between ignorable and nonignorable missing data. An important characterization of time-series is the *sample autocorrelation function*, which may be defined by the following formula for a data sequence $\{x_k\}$ that contains missing values:

$$\hat{R}_{xx}(m) = \frac{1}{|S_m|} \sum_{k \in S_m} x_k x_{k+m},$$

$$S_m = \{k \mid x_k, x_{k+m} \in \mathcal{D}\}. \tag{1.5}$$

Here, S_m corresponds to the subset of the data sequence $\{x_k\}$ for which the required products $x_k x_{k+m}$ are available, and $|S_m|$ denotes the size of this subset. As noted in the preceding discussion, if some fraction α of the data values $\{x_k\}$ is missing at random, the size of the subset S_m will be on the order of $(1 - \alpha)(N - m)$, resulting in an increase in the variance of $\hat{R}_{xx}(m)$ by a factor of approximately $1/(1 - \alpha)$. This case corresponds to one of ignorable missing data and illustrates the increase in the variability of computed results noted in the preceding discussion.

Next, suppose that m is an odd number and suppose that x_k is missing for every odd integer k. In this case, the product $x_k x_{k+m}$ always involves one even index and one odd index (i.e., if k is even, $k + m$ is odd and vice versa), so the set S_m is empty. Consequently, the quantity $\hat{R}_{xx}(m)$ defined in (1.5) cannot be computed at all from the available data for this case. This example illustrates the notion of nonignorable missing data, since its loss has much more serious consequences than the *nonsystematic* loss of the equivalent amount of data. That is, note that the loss of all odd-indexed data values x_k represents a 50% data loss: although a loss of 50% of the data *at random* would cause a substantial increase in the variability of $\hat{R}_{xx}(m)$ for odd integers m, it would still be possible to compute this quantity from the available data.

Finally, it is worth noting that in certain cases, missing data values may actually appear in disguised form in a dataset. Ironically, this problem frequently arises as a direct consequence of rigid validation procedures that are built into the data collection system. This point is important and is discussed in some detail in Chapter 2, but the following example from Adriaans and Zantinge (1996, p. 84) provides a typical illustration:

> Recently a colleague rented a car in the USA. Since he was Dutch, his post code did not fit into the fields of the computer program. The car hire representative suggested that she use the zip code of the rental office instead.

In extremely rigid, forms-based data entry systems, it may not be possible to complete the required paperwork without filling in all parts of the electronic form. In examples like the preceding one, since *formally valid data must be provided*, the most commonly adopted practical alternative is to provide responses that are *formally valid but factually erroneous*. This problem is a direct consequence of data collection systems that include *idempotent processing elements* in the front end, which effectively disguise missing data values as something else. (The term *idempotent* refers to a mathematical transformation that has the same effect when applied repeatedly as it has when applied once; a detailed discussion of these transformations and the way they arise in data acquisition systems is given at the end of Chapter 2.) Unfortunately, this conversion is often insidious because the requirement of formal validity imposed by the data collection process greatly reduces the likelihood of the erroneous values being anomalous with respect to any of the entered data variables. If it is necessary to detect these outliers after they have been entered into the data collection system, it is usually necessary to apply multivariable outlier detection procedures that look for anomalies with respect to the relationships between different variables. The significance of this observation lies in the fact, noted previously, that multivariate outlier detection is inherently more difficult than univariate outlier detection.

1.1.4 Misalignments

An extremely important class of data anomaly that is of particular concern in the analysis of large datasets is the class of *misalignments*, defined as follows. Suppose $\{x_k\}$ and $\{y_k\}$ represent two sequences of measurements of the variables x and y, respectively, ordered by the strictly increasing index sequence k, taking values from 1 to N inclusively. The identity of the index variable k is often of little or no importance, but the fact that x_k and y_k have the *same* subscript value k means that these two data observations represent values of x and y measured under the same conditions. In other words, the data values x_k and y_k may be regarded as two distinct measurable attributes of the same physical (or biological, chemical, financial, etc.) entity. In cases where the data sequences $\{x_k\}$ and $\{y_k\}$ occupy distinct data files at some point in the data collection process, it is possible to misalign them, effectively replacing $\{y_k\}$ with $\{y_{k'}\}$, where $\{k'\}$ is any sequence other than the desired index sequence $\{k\}$. The CAMDA normal mouse dataset discussed in Sec. 1.3.1 provides an important real-world illustration of this type of data anomaly, which can have profound consequences in cases where it is undetected.

It is important to emphasize that misalignment anomalies can take many different forms, as the following examples illustrate:

0. (correct sequence) $\{k\} = \{1, 2, 3, 4, 5, 6, 7, 8, 9, 10\}$;

1. (permutation) $\{k'\} = \{2, 7, 4, 5, 1, 9, 3, 6, 10, 8\}$;

2. (missing values with extension) $\{k'\} = \{1, 2, 3, 4, 7, 8, 9, 10, 11, 12\}$;

3. (duplication) $\{k'\} = \{1, 1, 2, 2, 3, 3, 4, 4, 5, 5\}$;

4. (shift with duplication) $\{k'\} = \{1, 2, 3, 3, 4, 5, 6, 7, 8, 9\}$.

The consequences of misalignment types 1, 2, and 3 are illustrated graphically in Figure 1.4. The upper left plot shows the y values plotted against the x values in the absence of misalignment. In this case, the two variables are highly correlated Gaussian random sequences

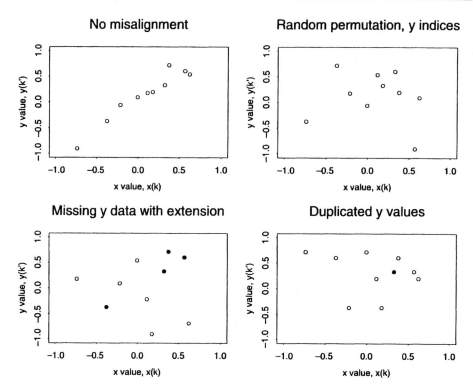

Figure 1.4. *The influence of misalignments on the relationship between variables.*

(correlation $\rho = 0.98$), and the existence of a strong linear relationship between them is clearly evident in this plot. The most popular measure of association between two variables is the product-moment correlation coefficient $\hat{\rho}$, discussed in detail in Chapter 2, a computable estimator of the distributional parameter ρ. For this group of 10 data points, this estimated correlation value is $\hat{\rho} = 0.96$, quite close to the correct value of ρ and giving strong evidence in support of the linear association between these variables. The upper right plot shows the result of a random permutation applied to the y values, which destroys virtually all visual evidence of this linear relationship and changes the product-moment correlation from $\hat{\rho} = 0.96$ to $\hat{\rho} = -0.11$.

Since a random permutation of the data labels may perhaps be regarded as the most severe mislabelling error possible, it is fair to ask about the influence of less severe alternatives. The effect of missing samples 5 and 6 from the y data sequence and extending it with elements 11 and 12 is shown in the lower left plot. As a result of this misalignment, only the first four x and y values are aligned correctly, and these values are indicated with solid circles in the plot. Comparison with the upper left plot shows that these four points are indeed the only ones that coincide with points in the correctly labelled plot. The effect of this misalignment error is to reduce the product-moment correlation estimates from 0.96 to 0.03. Finally, the lower right plot shows the effect of erroneously duplicating the first five y values and plotting them against the first ten x values. Here, only the first y value is correctly aligned with the sequence of x values, and this point is marked with a solid circle. Again, the pattern seen in the original data plot is completely obscured and the product-moment correlation estimate is reduced from 0.96 to -0.22.

It should be clear from these examples that misalignment errors can be extremely serious because they disrupt any true relationship that may exist between different variables. As the CAMDA normal mouse example discussed in Sec. 1.3.1 demonstrates, such misalignment errors do occur in practice, often as the result of simple errors in data conversion software. Because of its extreme practical importance, this anomaly generation mechanism is discussed in some detail in Chapter 2.

1.1.5 Unexpected structure

As noted in Sec. 1.1.1, it is important to distinguish between simple univariate outliers and outliers in more complex settings. For example, outliers in a bivariate data sequence $\{(x_k, y_k)\}$, where the nominal data observations satisfy some approximate constraint $f(x, y) \simeq 0$, correspond to individual observations for which $|f(x_j, y_j)|$ is "unusually large," as in the example shown in Figure 1.2.

It is important to emphasize that the opposite situation can also occur: two variables x and y in a dataset can approximately satisfy an *unsuspected* relationship of the form $f(x_k, y_k) \simeq 0$. As a particularly simple but important special case, the problem of *collinearity*, which has been discussed at some length in the statistics literature (Belsley, 1991; Jobson, 1991), corresponds to the existence of an approximate linear relationship between two or more potential explanatory variables in a multiple linear regression model. This problem and its consequences are discussed in more detail in Chapters 2 and 4, but it is worth emphasizing that these consequences can be quite significant. Specifically, attempts to build prediction models for some third variable, say z, involving both x and y can lead to model parameter estimation problems that are extremely ill-conditioned numerically if an unsuspected relationship exists between these variables.

This point is illustrated in Figure 1.5, which presents boxplot summaries for 6 collections of 50 statistically independent simulation-based regression model parameters. In each case, data values were generated according to the model

$$
\begin{aligned}
y_k &= Au_k + Bv_k + \epsilon_k, \\
u_k &= ax_k + (1-a)z_k, \\
v_k &= bx_k + (1-b)z_k,
\end{aligned}
\tag{1.6}
$$

where $\{e_k\}$, $\{x_k\}$, and $\{z_k\}$ each represent statistically independent sequences of independent, identically distributed (i.i.d.) Gaussian random variables. All of these variables have mean zero, the variables x_k and z_k have unit variance, and the variable ϵ_k has standard deviation 0.1. The constants A and B are unknown model parameters to be determined by fitting a model of the correct form (i.e., $y \simeq Au + Bv$) to the observed data triples (u_k, v_k, y_k). The constants a and b both lie in the interval $(0, 1)$ and they jointly determine the correlation between the sequences $\{u_k\}$ and $\{v_k\}$. In particular, it is not difficult to show that the correlation coefficient between these two sequences is given by

$$
\rho_{uv} = \frac{1 - a - b + 2ab}{\sqrt{(1 - 2a + 2a^2)(1 - 2b + 2b^2)}}.
\tag{1.7}
$$

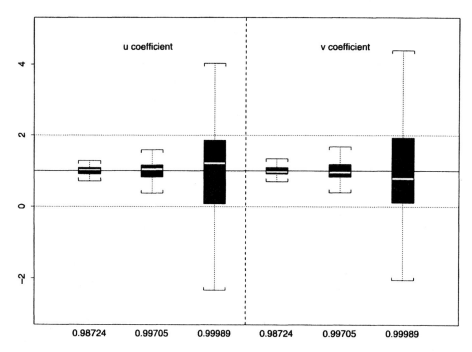

Figure 1.5. *The influence of collinearity on computed regression coefficients: boxplot summaries of the estimated coefficient values (vertical axis) against the correlation between explanatory variables (horizontal axis).*

Note that when a and b are approximately equal, the correlation between the sequences $\{u_k\}$ and $\{v_k\}$ becomes quite large. In the examples considered here, $a = 0.8$ and b has been taken as 0.7, 0.75, and 0.79, implying that $\rho = 0.98724, 0.99705$, and 0.99989. Although these correlations are somewhat extreme, they provide a very compelling illustration of just how severe the collinearity problem can be.

Specifically, the boxplots shown in Figure 1.5 summarize the A and B parameter values obtained from 50 statistically independent repetitions of the regression-modelling problem just described, with the parameters a and b chosen to yield the high correlations between $\{u_k\}$ and $\{v_k\}$ noted on the horizontal axis labels. The solid horizontal line at 1 corresponds to the correct value for both parameters, and the dashed horizontal lines at 0 and 2 represent $\pm 100\%$ error bounds for these parameter estimates. These results illustrate that, if the correlation between explanatory variables such as $\{u_k\}$ and $\{v_k\}$ becomes large enough, including both of them in an ordinary least squares (OLS) regression model results in enormous amplification of small data differences. This problem is well recognized in the statistics literature and has led to the development of diagnostic techniques to search for collinearity and modelling techniques such as *ridge regression* (Jobson, 1991), which attempt to obtain reasonable model parameter estimates even in the presence of significant correlations between explanatory variables. These ideas are discussed further in Chapter 4, along with some other related concepts.

1.2   Data anomalies need not be bad

Although the term "outlier" often has a pejorative connotation, it is worth emphasizing that this view is misguided. In particular, the investigation of data anomalies can lead to important discoveries that far outweigh a detailed understanding of the nominal behavior of a data sequence. This point is illustrated nicely by Lord Rayleigh's analysis of a set of nitrogen atomic weight measurements, discussed by Tukey (1977, p. 49). This dataset consisted of 15 measured weights for a fixed volume of a gas that was believed to be nitrogen. Small but systematic differences between these weights were observed, depending on whether the nitrogen was obtained by removing oxygen from air or by the decomposition of nitrogen-containing compounds. Lord Rayleigh's careful investigation of these differences led ultimately to his discovery of argon, a previously unknown component of air and the first known inert gas. For this discovery, he was awarded the 1904 Nobel Prize in Physics.

1.2.1   Materials with anomalous properties

In the context of chemistry, physics, and materials science, the discovery of materials with anomalous chemical or physical characteristics can lead to entirely new applications. One important example is that of *giant magnetostriction*, which is an unusually strong form of the phenomenon of magnetostriction discovered by Joule in the mid-19th century. Specifically, Joule found that certain materials would change their dimensions in the presence of a magnetic field, but in materials that exhibit giant magnetostriction, these dimension changes are one or two orders of magnitude larger than those of traditional magentostrictive materials. A commercially available material exhibiting magnetostrictive strains almost 40 times larger than nickel alloys is TERFENOL-D, an alloy of terbium, iron, and dysprosium; the name is an acronym that somewhat loosely combines the chemical symbols for these elements (TER for terbium, whose symbol is Tb; FE, which is approximately the symbol (Fe) for iron; and D for dysprosium, whose symbol is Dy) with the abbreviation NOL for the U.S. Naval Ordinance Labs, where the material was developed. In addition to large room temperature magnetic–field-induced strains, TERFENOL-D exhibits a response time in the milliseconds and can apply significant forces (hundreds of newtons). The development of this novel material, based on the unexpected discovery of anomalously large magnetostrictive effects in dysprosium/terbium alloys, represents an extremely constructive use of an outlier in physical properties data.

   Many material parameters are constrained by thermodynamics or other physical constraints to be positive; others are almost always positive but can exhibit negative values in unusual circumstances. As an example, for most compressible solids, such as rubber, if we apply a compressive force in one direction, the material expands perpendicular to the direction of the compression, as shown in the left-hand diagram in Figure 1.6. *Poisson's ratio* is defined as the ratio of this lateral expansion to the axial compression and, for most materials, it is positive, corresponding to the left-hand diagram in Figure 1.6. It is possible, however, for materials to exhibit a *negative* Poisson ratio, as shown in the right-hand diagram: applying a compressive force results in a lateral *contraction*. Poisson himself demonstrated theoretically that this behavior was possible and he sought in vain for materials that actually exhibited it. Such materials were ultimately discovered, but they were also found to exhibit highly unusual reentrant structures and other unusual characteristics such as anomalously

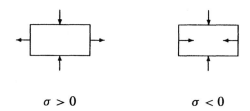

$$\sigma > 0 \qquad\qquad\qquad \sigma < 0$$

Figure 1.6. *Positive and negative Poisson's ratio.*

large fracture resistance (Ranganath, 1992). The key point here is that the discovery of such anomalies can have unexpected benefits.

Finally, another example of a material that is useful because of its anomalous physical properties is boron nitride, a solid that exhibits a high thermal conductivity but a low electrical conductivity. This behavior is unusual because materials with high thermal conductivity typically also have high electrical conductivity. In particular, for metals, the thermal conductivity κ is related to the electrical conductivity σ via the Wiedermann–Franz law:

$$\kappa = \frac{k^2 \pi^2}{3e^2} \sigma T, \qquad\qquad (1.8)$$

where T is the absolute temperature of the material, k is Boltzmann's constant, and e is the charge on the electron. Although boron nitride is not a metal, it does violate our expectations that good thermal conductors are also good electrical conductors. Relative to these expectations, boron nitride provides a nice illustration of a multivariable outlier: individual characteristics are not unusual, but their relationship is. A practical consequence of this anomalous behavior is that boron nitride may be used to construct electrically insulating heat sinks to carry heat away from electrical circuitry in, for example, low-temperature electrical characterization experiments.

1.2.2   Product design: Looking for "good" anomalies

An area that has been receiving increasing attention recently in chemical engineering is that of *product design*, which attempts to apply chemical engineering process design ideas to the systematic design of new products. Often, the objectives of product design are closely related to the search for "good outliers." As a specific example, Baker (2002) notes that sales of membrane-based separation equipment have grown from initial product introductions in 1980 to about \$150 million per year. Two critical operating parameters for these membranes are permeability and selectivity, which generally exhibit a strong trade-off: highly selective membranes have low permeability and highly permeable membranes have low selectivity. In practice, it is desirable to have large values for both of these parameters, motivating the search for materials that represent outliers with respect to this bivariate relationship. Baker (2002) presents a plot analogous to Figure 1.7 showing this trade-off for glass and rubber membranes, where the lines with negative slopes illustrate overall material performance bounds in 1980 and 1991. In addition, Baker (2002) discusses a new class of materials called Co(3-MeOsaltmen) facilitated transport membranes (FTMs). Relative to all of the other membrane examples considered, these materials represent the

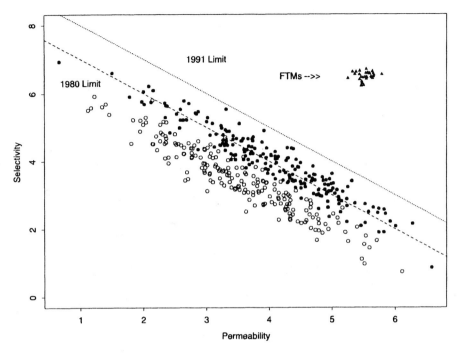

Figure 1.7. *Behavior of membrane selectivity versus permeability, after Baker (2002, Figure 7), showing typical behavior, trade-off lines for 1980 and 1991, and the anomalous behavior of the FTM material class.*

desired bivariate outliers, simultaneously exhibiting selectivities and permeabilities near the maximum values seen for all known glass and rubber membranes.

A class of materials with enormously greater economic importance than gas separation membranes is the class of catalysts, used to increase chemical reaction rates. According to Senkan (2001), catalysts are used in the manufacture of over 7,000 products worldwide, with an annual net worth of over $3 trillion. Potential formulations have been historically developed largely through trial and error, and their number is astronomical. In particular, Senkan (2001) notes that there are 50 useful, stable elements in the periodic table, so the number of possible binary combinations is 1,225 even if we neglect the range of possible compositions for these compounds. This number grows exponentially as we consider combinations of more elements; for example, there are 230,300 possible 4-element combinations. Recent advances in automation and miniaturization have led to the development of high-throughput synthesis and screening procedures for the rapid screening of potential catalyst formulations, but the number of possible formulations is so large that an exhaustive search will never be feasible. Hence, the development of *guided* search strategies, based on both fundamental chemical understanding and extensive analysis of experimental data, is an area of significant research interest (Eriksson et al., 2002). The key point here is that the most interesting materials to emerge from these searches are usually outliers with respect to important properties or property combinations.

1.2.3   "Niches" in business data records

An example of the constructive use of data anomalies that lies entirely in the domain of data mining is the search for "niches" in customer records described by Dong and Deshpande (2001). These authors offer the following definition:

> *Niches are surprising rules that contradict set routines; they capture significant, representative client sectors that deserve new, targeted, more profitable treatments.*

They illustrate this point with the example of Farmers' Insurance Company, which discovered an unrecognized niche: married "baby boomers" with families which owned both a family car (e.g., a minivan) and a sports car. Since insurance companies historically associated sports car ownership with high-risk, young, unmarried male drivers, insurance rates on these cars were typically quite high. By identifying a lower-risk group of sports car owners, Farmers' Insurance was able to offer lower rates to this target group in order to gain market share. Like the boron nitride example discussed previously, this example is unusual because it violates the expected relationship between two different data attributes (i.e., electrical and thermal conductivity for boron nitride; car type and perceived risk in the Farmers' Insurance example).

1.3   Conversely, data anomalies can be very bad

The preceding examples made the important point that the discovery of data anomalies can be highly beneficial, leading to valuable new discoveries. Conversely, it is also important to emphasize that undetected data anomalies can arise from gross measurement errors and other highly undesirable sources, and that the effects of these data anomalies can be catastrophic. As a specific example, the $125-million Mars Climate Orbiter was lost in 1999 because certain data values were provided in the wrong units (pounds versus newtons). The first of the following two discussions describes a more typical but still quite serious real-world data anomaly (Sec. 1.3.1), and the second discussion illustrates the severe consequences that even a small number of outliers can have on a simple data characterization (Sec. 1.3.2).

1.3.1   The CAMDA'02 normal mouse dataset

It was shown in Sec. 1.1.4 that misalignments between related variables can be extremely damaging to subsequent analysis efforts, greatly obscuring important relationships between variables. The examples used to illustrate this point in Sec. 1.1.4 were simulation-based, but the following example is an instructive illustration of how this situation can arise in practice.

An increasingly important source of large datasets is the recently developed "high-throughput" analysis methods in biology, including both cDNA microarrays (Schena et al., 1995) and high-density oligonucleotide arrays (Lipshutz et al., 1995). Both of these approaches provide the basis for measuring thousands of gene expression levels simultaneously in biological tissue samples, and in a typical microarray experiment the results give an indication of the difference in gene expression levels for this set of genes under two different biological conditions (e.g., different tissue samples from the same animal, differences in the same type of tissue sample between different animals, differences between treated animals and control animals, or differences between tumor cells and normal cells). The question of how best to analyze and interpret the datasets that result from these experiments is one of active research, and one recent survey concludes, after noting a number of important practical difficulties, that "data from microarray analysis need to be interpreted cautiously" (Kothapalli et al., 2002). Motivated by such concerns, a series of conferences on Critical Assessment of Microarray Data Analysis (CAMDA) has been held, taking the form of an analysis competition based on datasets that are made available to the public. For the 2002 CAMDA competition, one of these datasets was based on a collection of cDNA microarray experiments designed to assess the normal variability of gene expression levels in three organs in mice.

A detailed analysis of this collection of microarray experiments was published by Pritchard et al. (2001) based on seventy-two microarrays, representing four arrays each for liver, kidney, and testes in six untreated mice. In these experiments, material extracted from each individual mouse tissue sample was labelled with one fluorescent dye, and a control mix obtained from tissue samples for all eighteen mouse organ samples was labelled with a second fluorescent dye. The four arrays for each organ from each mouse correspond to pairs of duplicate slides for each of the two possible dye labellings. In the dataset provided for the CAMDA competition, all of these results were placed in three data files, one for each organ. One of the participating groups began with a preliminary validation experiment using principal components analysis (PCA), plotting the first principal component against the second (Stivers et al., 2003). The expected outcome of this analysis was four reasonably well-separated clusters: one for each organ and one for the common control mix. Instead, it was found that although the three individual organ responses showed roughly the expected clustering, the control mix results exhibited a nonphysical association with the individual organ results. A subsequent examination of auxiliary information provided in the datasets (specifically, location information for the spots on the microarray) revealed a discrepancy between the numbers recorded in the three data files. Reordering the data files to make this auxiliary information consistent then led to more consistent PCA results. A careful examination of these results led to the conjecture that a misalignment had occurred between the different data files; it was ultimately confirmed, both by further analysis of this dataset and by contacting the providers of the dataset, that 1,932 genes had been incorrectly labelled in the creation of the 3 data files.

This example is important primarily because it illuminates the nature of the difficulties that can arise from subtle errors in the necessary data management operations when working with large datasets. In particular, Stivers et al. (2003) make the following observation:

> The data used here was assembled into packages, probably manually using an ad hoc database, spreadsheet, or perl script. Under these conditions, it is remarkably easy for the row order to be changed accidentally; for example, by sorting the rows based on the values in an arbitrarily chosen column.

In this particular case, a simple error in the process of creating the three data files provided to the CAMDA participants resulted in the misalignment of approximately 36% of the data values. The key point here is that small errors in these data management operations can cause large errors in the final dataset, and these errors can require careful analysis to detect. The nature of this important practical problem is discussed further in Chapter 2.

1.3.2 The influence of outliers on kurtosis

Historically, kurtosis (the normalized fourth moment κ defined in Sec. 1.1.2) and skewness (the corresponding normalized third moment) have been used as a basis for selecting data distributions (Johnson, Kotz, and Balakrishnan, 1994, p. 23). In fact, the *method of moments*, introduced by Karl Pearson at the end of the 19th century, uses estimates of the first four moments—mean, variance, skewness, and kurtosis—as a basis for fitting one of seven families of distributions to a sequence of data observations. More recently, estimated kurtosis values have been used in characterizing noise in microwave devices (Mantegna, Ferrante, and Principato, 1999a,b). Despite its conceptual appeal, however, the distributional characterization of kurtosis estimates is difficult even in simple cases (see, for example, the discussion of the Gaussian case given by Anscombe and Glynn (1983)). Even worse, the outlier-sensitivity of the standard kurtosis estimate is extreme, as the following example demonstrates.

Figure 1.8 presents a boxplot summary of kurtosis estimates computed from data sequences having one of three different distributions and one of three different outlier contamination levels. The three distributions are the standard Gaussian (mean 0, standard deviation $\sigma = 1$), for which the kurtosis is $\kappa = 0$; the uniform distribution on $[0, 1]$, for which $\sigma = 1/\sqrt{12} \simeq 0.289$ and $\kappa = -1.2$; and the Student's t-distribution with 9 degrees of freedom and a standard deviation of $\sigma = \sqrt{9/7} \simeq 1.134$, chosen because it has a kurtosis of $\kappa = +1.2$. The three contamination scenarios considered are 0% contamination, a contamination level of 1% (a single outlying value of $+8\sigma$ in a sequence of length $N = 100$), and a contamination level of 5% (5 outliers, all with the value $+8\sigma$, in a sequence of length $N = 100$). Each boxplot in Figure 1.8 summarizes the kurtosis estimates $\hat{\kappa}$ defined by (1.4) computed from one hundred statistically independent data sequences generated under one of the six scenarios just described. The horizontal dashed lines on the plot correspond to the correct values for the three distributions, $\kappa = -1.2$, 0, and $+1.2$. It is immediately clear from these boxplots that the effects of outliers on the kurtosis estimates are completely overwhelming: the *smallest* kurtosis estimate obtained from any of the contaminated data sequences is $\hat{\kappa} \simeq +2.9$, and the largest kurtosis estimates obtained are greater than 20.

Another potentially more significant point is also illustrated by this example: the severity of the outlier influence is *not* a monotonic function of the contamination level. That is, for all three of the distributions considered here, the effects of contamination by a single outlier are worse, on average, than the effects of contamination by five outliers, and in the case of the Gaussian and Student's t-distribution, the single outlier effects are substantially worse. This counterintuitive result has to do with the nature of the kurtosis itself. Specifically, the smallest possible kurtosis value is $\kappa = -2$, achievable for a symmetric binary distribution (Rohatgi and Szekely, 1989). More generally, bimodal distributions commonly exhibit negative kurtosis values. (Indeed, it can be shown that any symmetric, unimodal distribution has a kurtosis value of at least $-6/5$ (Rohatgi and Szekely, 1989), so symmetric distributions with kurtosis values between $-6/5$ and -2 are necessarily multimodal.) Now, suppose we consider a narrow nominal data distribution heavily contaminated by a narrow outlier distribution: as the contamination level approaches 50%, the distribution looks increasingly like a symmetric, bimodal distribution, exhibiting a negative kurtosis value. Hence, as the contamination level increases, the estimated kurtosis value will tend to decrease, although

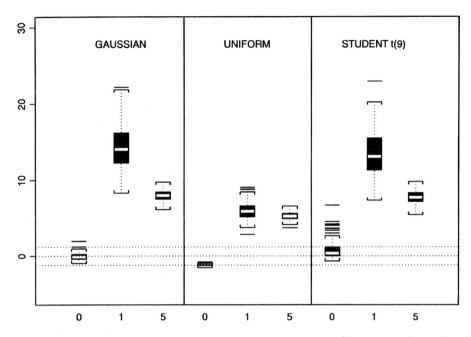

Figure 1.8. *Influence of contamination on computed kurtosis values, plotted against the number of outliers in a dataset of size $N = 100$.*

as the results shown here suggest, the outlier effects can be expected to remain dominant. These results serve to emphasize that the effects of outliers are difficult to predict, even for a fairly simple data characterization like the kurtosis estimate $\hat{\kappa}$.

1.4 Dealing with data anomalies

The preceding examples have illustrated that data anomalies do arise in practice and that their influence is disproportionate to their concentration or *contamination level*, defined as the fraction of contaminating anomalies in the dataset. These observations lead naturally to two questions: first, how common are these data anomalies in practice, and, second, how do we deal with them in our analysis? Concerning the first point, Huber (1993) offers the following advice:

> *Contaminations between 1% and 10% are sufficiently common that a blind application of procedures with a breakdown point of less than 10% must be considered outright dangerous.*

The *breakdown point* mentioned here is defined as the fraction of arbitrarily extreme outliers required to make arbitrarily large changes in the computed result. The largest achievable breakdown point is 50%, corresponding to a procedure that is insensitive to any fraction of outliers less than 50%. The best-known procedure with a 50% breakdown point is the sample median, discussed further in Sec. 1.4.1. Unfortunately, many of the most popular data characterization procedures exhibit a 0% breakdown point, meaning that a single outlier of sufficient magnitude can completely determine the computed results obtained from an arbitrarily large dataset. In fact, this problem is seen clearly in the kurtosis example discussed in Sec. 1.3.2, which illustrates the practical consequences of the 0% breakdown point of the standard kurtosis estimator $\hat{\kappa}$. More common data characterizations with 0% breakdown points include the sample mean, the standard deviation, and OLS regression models, among many, many others.

In dealing with data anomalies, one of two approaches is commonly taken. The first is to develop and use anomaly-resistant analysis methods, an idea that forms the basis for the field of *robust statistics* (Huber, 1981). Perhaps the best-known example of this approach is the use of the median as an outlier-resistant alternative to the mean as a *location estimator*, giving us an idea of the "typical" value of a sequence of numbers. The other common approach is to first detect the data anomalies and then either omit them or replace them with alternative data values that are judged to be more reasonable and apply standard analysis procedures to the cleaned result. Although it has been argued that this latter approach is inherently less effective (Huber, 1981, p. 4), it is much easier to apply and can be used in a wide variety of data analysis and data-mining applications where outlier-resistant procedures are not yet available and where the development of such procedures remains a research topic (e.g., outlier-resistant artificial neural networks or self-organizing map classifiers). Both approaches are related, however, because the effective detection of data anomalies is often based on outlier-resistant data characterizations such as the median. Because the data-cleaning approach is much more broadly applicable, it is the primary focus of this book rather than the development of outlier-resistant methods. In particular, the data-cleaning and data validation procedures discussed here should be useful in conjunction with a wide range of data-mining procedures, such as those described by Cios, Pedrycz, and Swiniarski (1998).

1.4.1 Outlier-resistant analysis procedures

Although the primary focus of this book is anomaly detection and rejection procedures, it is important to say something about outlier-resistant procedures for at least two reasons. First, any consideration of these procedures necessarily focuses at least partially on the question of *why* many standard procedures exhibit the extreme outlier-sensitivity that they do. An understanding of this point is useful in better understanding the nature and severity of the data anomaly problem in data-mining applications. Second, ironically, these procedures lie at the heart of many outlier detection procedures.

Without question, the most common outlier-resistant data characterization is the sample median. For symmetrically distributed random variables, the median represents a logical alternative to the sample mean, which is known for its extreme outlier-sensitivity. For example, in his concluding remarks in the Princeton Robustness Study, F.R. Hampel notes (Andrews et al., 1972, p. 243):

> *As everybody familiar with robust estimation knows, the mean is a horrible estimator, except under the strict normal distribution; it gets rapidly worse, even under very mild deviations from normality, and at some distance from the Gaussian distribution, it is totally disastrous.*

Conversely, Hampel also characterizes the mean as *the* location estimator of choice on the basis of various theoretical considerations, and he resolves this apparently strong conflict by

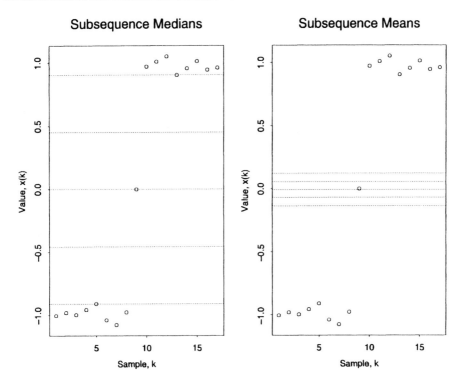

Figure 1.9. *A subset-based comparison of the mean and the median.*

noting that "a good statistician (or research worker) never uses the mean, even though he may honestly claim to do so." Instead, Hampel notes the importance of detecting and removing outliers from a data sequence before computing the mean. This necessity follows from the mean's 0% breakdown point: a single outlier of sufficient magnitude in any fixed dataset, no matter how large, can make the mean assume arbitrarily large values. In contrast, it was noted that the median exhibits a 50% breakdown point, meaning that the median remains bounded when anything less than 50% of the data values become arbitrarily large.

Despite its excellent outlier-resistance, the median is not always the best alternative to the mean, however. For example, the median can be extremely sensitive to deletions of a few points from some datasets. This behavior is illustrated in the left-hand plot in Figure 1.9, which shows a 17-point dataset, where the first 8 points are uniformly distributed over the interval $[-1.1, -0.9]$, the 9th point has the value 0, and the last 8 points are uniformly distributed over the interval $[0.9, 1.1]$. The points are marked with open circles, and the five dashed lines shown in this plot indicate the values of the median computed from the following five subsequences:

1. The line at -0.91 is the median of points 1 through 15.

2. The line at -0.46 is the median of points 1 through 16.

3. The line at 0.0 is the median of the complete sequence, points 1 through 17.

4. The line at 0.45 is the median of points 2 through 17.

5. The line at 0.91 is the median of points 3 through 17.

The very substantial differences in these median values reflect the fact that the median does not depend *smoothly* on the data values from which it is computed. Consequently, although it exhibits excellent outlier-resistance, the median is undesirably sensitive to certain types of "conceptually small changes" in a data sequence.

For comparison, the right-hand plot in Figure 1.9 shows the corresponding results for the *means* of the same data subsequences. Again, the points are marked with open circles and the mean values computed from the same data subsequences as in the left-hand plot are indicated with dashed lines. The range of these mean values is dramatically smaller than the range of the median values: the mean values span the range -0.14 to 0.12, while the median values span the range -0.91 to 0.91. This example illustrates one of the prices we must pay for the extreme outlier-resistance of the median. Another price is computational: although medians are not difficult to compute in practice, they do involve sorting the data sequence, which requires greater computation time than averaging does for long data sequences. More generally, for more complex extensions of the sample median, such as the *least median of squares (LMS)* regression procedures discussed briefly in Chapters 4 and 8, computational issues can become dominant.

For both of these reasons—the nonsmooth behavior of the median and its increased computational complexity—many alternatives have been proposed. Further, these extensions can also provide the basis for practical approaches to other, more complicated, data characterization problems. The Princeton Robustness Study (Andrews et al., 1972) summarizes an extensive comparison of 68 different location estimators, including both the mean and the median, comparing their outlier-resistance under a number of different scenarios for simulation-based datasets ranging in size from $N = 5$ to $N = 40$. The two basic requirements for all of the estimators compared were, first, that they be explicitly computable for these datasets, and, second, that they be location- and scale-invariant, meaning that if the data values are transformed as $x_k \rightarrow ax_k + b$ for fixed constants a and b, the computed location estimates should exhibit the same scaling behavior; this important notion is discussed further in Chapter 5. Although the mean emerged as the "worst" estimator of the 68 considered in terms of its outlier-sensitivity, no single alternative emerged as "best" under all of the different circumstances considered. The results of this survey are discussed further in Chapter 2, but the key points here are, first, that "good" outlier-resistant procedures tend to be highly problem-specific, and, second, that the development of these procedures typically represents a significant research undertaking rather than a simple modification of standard procedures. Hence, despite their recognized limitations, data-cleaning procedures are extremely practical because they can be used as a preprocessing step ahead of essentially any standard data analysis procedure. That is, provided we use an *effective* data-cleaning procedure, the subsequent results we obtain from standard data analysis procedures will usually be much better than those we obtain without data cleaning, as Hampel notes in his discussion of the mean, quoted above. The keys to the development of effective data-cleaning procedures lie, first, in the use of effective outlier detection procedures, and, second, in the use of reasonable replacement strategies for outliers once they have been detected. Since the detection of an outlier in data-cleaning applications essentially creates a *missing* data value, the problem of computing a suitable replacement value is closely related to that of *missing value imputation*, a topic discussed further in Chapter 4.

1.4.2 Outlier detection procedures

The basic notion behind outlier detection is simple, but, as with many things, "the devil is in the details." That is, automated outlier detection procedures are all based on some specific interpretation of our basic working definition of an outlier, repeated here for convenience (Barnett and Lewis, 1994, p. 4):

> *An outlier is an entry in a dataset that is anomalous with respect to the behavior seen in the majority of the other entries in the dataset.*

To turn this idea into a specific outlier detection procedure, we require two things:

1. a quantitative characterization of *nominal* data values;

2. a quantitative measure of "unusually large" deviations from this nominal value.

The simplest case is that of *univariate outliers*, discussed in detail in Chapter 3; there, the dataset consists of a sequence $\{y_k\}$ of real numbers, and each observation y_k in this dataset may be represented as

$$y_k = y_{nom} + e_k, \tag{1.9}$$

where y_{nom} represents the nominal value for this data sequence and the sequence $\{e_k\}$ measures how far each individual observation lies from this nominal value. Univariate outlier detection then proceeds by defining, first, a way of computing y_{nom} from the original data sequence $\{y_k\}$, and, second, a criterion for deciding whether each deviation e_k is "unusually large" or not.

The simplest approach to univariate outlier detection is the 3σ edit rule, which takes the sample mean $\bar{y}$ as the reference value for the data sequence and assesses the distance from this reference value to the sample standard deviation $\hat{\sigma}$. Under the historically popular assumption that the nominal data sequence exhibits an approximately Gaussian distribution, we are unlikely to observe data values y_k farther than about three standard deviations from the mean. Hence, an apparently reasonable data-cleaning strategy is to declare any point y_k farther than three sample standard deviations $\hat{\sigma}$ from the sample mean $\bar{y}$ as an outlier. Unfortunately, despite the widespread popularity of this approach, it often fails to detect outliers when they are present. A more detailed discussion, including examples and an explanation of the underlying reasons for this failure, is given in Chapter 3. The basic problem is that both the sample mean and the sample standard deviation are highly outlier-sensitive estimators of the corresponding population values. In particular, outliers often cause the standard deviation to be greatly overestimated, decreasing the likelihood of finding any outliers that may be in the data sequence.

To obtain a more effective outlier detection procedure, it is necessary to replace the mean and standard deviation with alternative location and scale estimators that have lower outlier-sensitivity. As discussed previously, the median $y^{\dagger}$ represents an outlier-resistant alternative to the mean, and two alternatives to the standard deviation are the (median absolute deviation) MAD and IQD scale estimates, defined as follows. The MAD scale estimate is defined as a scaled version of the median of the absolute deviations from the sample median:

$$S = 1.4826 \text{ median } \{|y_k - y^\dagger|\}. \tag{1.10}$$

Here, the sequence $\{|y_k - y^\dagger|\}$ measures the distance of each data observation from the reference value $y^\dagger$, so the median indicated in (1.10) provides an indication of how far these points "typically" lie from $y^\dagger$; the mysterious factor $1.4826 = 1/0.6745$ was chosen to make S an unbiased estimate of the standard deviation σ when $\{y_k\}$ has a Gaussian nominal distribution (Huber, 1981, p. 108).

Replacing the mean with the median and the usual standard deviation estimate with the MAD scale estimate S in the 3σ edit rule leads to an outlier detection procedure called the *Hampel identifier* (Davies and Gather, 1993). This procedure is generally much more effective in detecting outliers than the 3σ edit rule is, but it is sometimes too aggressive, declaring nominal data values as outliers. A more detailed discussion of the Hampel identifier is given in Chapter 3, and a further discussion of the MAD scale estimator on which it is based in given in Sec. 1.5.

Another alternative outlier detection procedure is to again replace the mean with the median, and to replace the standard deviation with the IQD, defined as the distance between

L, the *lower quartile*, $y_{(0.25)}$, and

U, the *upper quartile*, $y_{(0.75)}$.

The outlier detection limits used in constructing the boxplots discussed in Sec. 1.1.2 are based on IQD = U − L. As with the MAD scale estimate, to make the IQD an unbiased estimator of the standard deviation for Gaussian data, it is necessary to rescale it, dividing by 1.35 (Venables and Ripley, 2002, p. 122).

Finally, it is worth reiterating that outlier detection becomes more complicated as the nominal data model becomes more complicated. In particular, *multivariate outliers* are based on an assumed *relationship* between the different components of a sequence of vector-valued observations. The nature and origin of some of these more complex outlier types is discussed in Chapter 2, and some procedures for dealing with outliers in these more complex settings are discussed in Chapter 4.

1.4.3 Preprocessing for anomaly detection

The CAMDA'02 normal mouse dataset discussed in Sec. 1.3.1 provides a nice illustration of the use of data preprocessing as a method of detecting other types of data anomalies. The essential idea is to compute one or more simple characterizations of a dataset for which expected outcomes are known. Large deviations from these expectations suggest the possibility of data anomalies and should be investigated to determine their origin. In the CAMDA'02 normal mouse data example, a preliminary PCA was performed and plots were constructed of the first principal component versus the second. The expected outcome was that the four distinct data sources—liver, heart, testes, and control mix—should exhibit four distinct clusters in this plot, corresponding to their biologically distinct characters. The fact that the control mix samples did *not* cluster as expected provided preliminary evidence of possible data anomalies.

The results of the preliminary analysis just described led to a second preliminary analysis step, based on comparing ancillary variables that should be the same in the three datasets considered. Specifically, since all microarrays had the same configuration, the location of each gene *should* have been the same on each slide. The fact that these locations differed between datasets suggested that something was wrong. As in the case of the PCA results, this comparison represented a simple preprocessing step, further supporting the PCA-based evidence of a problem. Making the gene positions consistent between the three datasets— instead of the gene labels—gave PCA results that were more consistent with expectations.

This example illustrates the use of simple preliminary analysis in finding misalignment errors such as those discussed in Sec. 1.3.1. Other data anomalies that can be detected by simple preliminary examination include outliers, as noted previously and discussed further in Chapters 3 and 4; unexpected structure such as the collinearity problem discussed in Sec. 1.1.5; and the presence of *extraneous* or *noninformative variables*. The utility of eliminating extraneous variables in cluster analysis is illustrated nicely by Gordon (1999, p. 24), who considers a simulated collection of eight-dimensional vectors. Three well-defined clusters are clearly evident in a scatterplot of the first two of these components, but the other six components are unrelated Gaussian random variables. Applying a simple clustering procedure to these vectors resulted in significant misclassification, despite the fact that two of the eight simulated attribute variables provided the basis for a perfect classification and the other six attributes were completely noninformative. These important concepts are discussed further in Chapter 4, which is concerned with data pretreatment to improve the quality and reliability of subsequent analytical results.

1.5   GSA

Chapter 6 is devoted to a detailed discussion of *GSA*, a systematic procedure for assessing the sensitivity of analytical results to changes in the problem formulation that are expected to be "small." The basis for this procedure is the following informal statement:

> A "good" data analysis result should be insensitive to small changes in either the methods or the datasets on which the analysis is based.

This idea is closely related to the notion of *resistance* or *robustness* on which robust statistics is based (Huber, 1981), but the interpretation considered here is much broader. In particular, a data analysis procedure is generally called *resistant* if it is insensitive to either small changes in all of the data values or large changes in a small fraction of the data values. Here, a somewhat more general notion of "small changes in the datasets" is adopted based on the concept of *exchangeability* discussed by Draper et al. (1993). A detailed discussion of this concept is given in Chapter 6, but, informally, the idea is that two datasets are exchangeable if we should obtain "essentially the same result" on applying the same analysis method or characterization procedure to both datasets. The basic idea behind GSA is to develop a systematic approach to evaluating the exchangeability of datasets that we believe *should* or *could* be exchangeable. More specifically, the basic GSA procedure consists of the following four steps:

1. Select a collection $\{\Sigma_\ell\}$ of *scenarios* to be compared, corresponding to different choices of data sources, analysis methods, or both.

2. Select a *sampling scheme* that generates, for each scenario Σ_ℓ, a collection $\{S_j\}$ of datasets, each of which is expected to give comparable analysis results.

3. Select a common real-valued *descriptor* $d(\cdot)$ that may be used to compare analysis results, both within and across scenarios.

4. Construct a boxplot summary of the descriptor values for each scenario.

In this procedure, scenarios are chosen on the basis of problem-specific analysis objectives. For example, in a biological application, typical scenarios might correspond to different animals, tissue types, or treatments. In mining business transaction data, scenarios might include different merchandise categories, different stores in a chain, or different geographical regions, and in evaluating computational procedures, different scenarios might correspond to different benchmark problems. Alternatively, different choices of analysis methods or, in cases where these methods have adjustable parameters or other options, different choices of these parameters or options may be taken as different analysis scenarios to be considered.

Given a collection of scenarios to be considered, the sampling scheme required in the second step specifies a well-defined procedure for obtaining data from each scenario. Ideally, the sampling scheme should be the same for each scenario compared and it should generate a collection of M distinct but exchangeable datasets. Possible sampling schemes include either systematic or random subset selection from a fixed dataset $\mathcal{D}$, an experimental protocol for obtaining "replicate" experimental results from the same scenario, or a simulation procedure that generates either deterministic or random data sequences that exhibit "the same character" (e.g., have the same distribution of values or the same "true" power spectral density). The fundamental idea of the GSA approach is that if we apply either the same method to "equivalent" datasets or "equivalent" methods to the same dataset, we should obtain results that are "almost the same." To provide an informal basis for assessing "sameness," the GSA method uses a *descriptor* $d(\cdot)$ that represents some useful real-valued characterization of our analysis results. In cases where the analysis results are themselves real numbers (e.g., means, standard deviations, etc.), the descriptor can be as simple as $d(x) = x$ for all $x \in R$. More generally, however, analysis methods return more extensive results, such as regression models, estimated power spectral densities, or data clusterings. In these cases, the GSA approach requires a real-valued descriptor that permits us to compare the results obtained, either from different analysis methods (e.g., classical versus maximum entropy spectral estimation procedures) or from different datasets. In its simplest implementation, the GSA procedure generates a collection of boxplots, one for each scenario, permitting a graphical assessment of differences between different scenarios.

These ideas are perhaps best illustrated with a simple example. Figure 1.10 shows four simulation-based data sequences, each of length $N = 17$, that will be used as the basis for GSA comparisons of four different location estimators and three different scale estimators. The data sequence shown in the upper left plot (Sequence 0) consists of 17 points uniformly distributed over the range $[-1.1, 1.1]$. The data sequence (Sequence 1) shown in the upper right plot is the one previously considered in Sec. 1.4.1 to illustrate the sometimes unexpected behavior of the median. Sequence 2, shown in the lower left plot, is a modification of Sequence 0, obtained by setting the middle five samples to zero, corresponding to one possible model for missing data values. Finally, Sequence 3, shown in

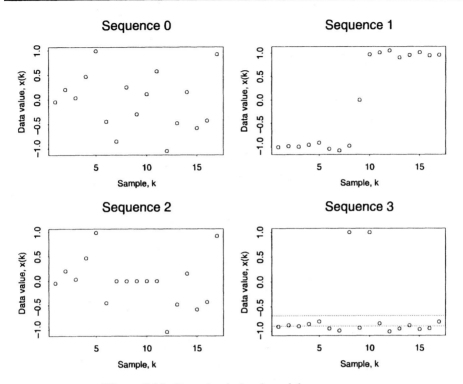

Figure 1.10. *Four simulation-based data sequences.*

the lower right plot, consists of a shifted and scaled version of Sequence 0 with two outliers in the center of the data sequence. Note that this behavior is precisely what would result if a contaminated data sequence were scaled to fit into the range $[-1, 1]$, analogous to what is commonly done in preparing data for subsequent processing by artificial neural networks. The 2 dashed lines shown in this plot represent the mean (the upper line) and the median (the lower line) computed from this sequence of 17 numbers. Note that while the median line passes through the center of the 15 nonoutlying observations, the mean is shifted upward toward the 2 outliers and lies entirely outside the nominal range of variation.

The location estimates considered here all represent special cases of the *trimmed mean*, an idea that dates back to at least Mendeleev at the end of the 19th century (Barnett and Lewis, 1994, p. 23). More specifically, the symmetric α-trimmed mean is defined as the mean of the data values that remain after the fraction α of largest values and the fraction α of smallest values have been removed from the sample. Note that the class of symmetric α-trimmed means includes both the standard arithmetic mean ($\alpha = 0$) and the sample median (the limit as $\alpha \to 0.5$). The first of the two applications of the GSA framework considered here compares the following four symmetric α-trimmed means for the four data sequences shown in Figure 1.10:

A: $\alpha = 0$, corresponding to the standard arithmetic mean;

B: $\alpha = 0.125$, approximately the value recommended by Lehmann (1983, p. 366);

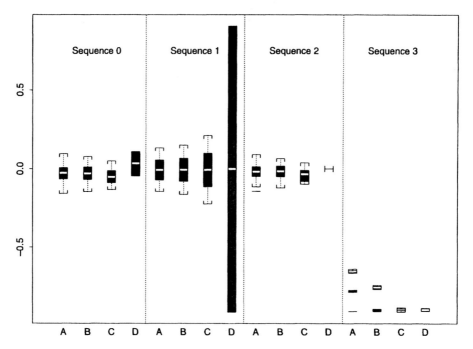

Figure 1.11. *Symmetric trimmed mean comparisons for the* 4 *simulation-based sequences shown in Figure* 1.10: *boxplot summaries of the* 136 *two-point deletion subsets for each sequence, as a function of the trimming percentage, designated as* A ($\alpha = 0$), B ($\alpha = 0.125$), C ($\alpha = 0.25$), and D ($\alpha = 0.5$).

C: $\alpha = 0.25$, the *midmean*, one of the favorite estimators to emerge from the Princeton Robustness Study (Andrews et al., 1972);

D: $\alpha = 0.5$, corresponding to the sample median.

The scenarios Σ_ℓ considered in this comparison correspond to the four data sequences shown in Figure 1.10, and the four methods compared here may be regarded as *subscenarios*, well defined and consistent for each scenario. The sampling scheme considered here is a simple deletion-based procedure, applicable to any dataset $\mathcal{D}$: for each of the 17-point data sequences, the sampling scheme generates all possible subsequences of length 15 obtained from the original data sequence by deleting 2 points. This procedure generates 136 subsequences for each data sequence, and the results obtained by applying the 4 analysis procedures, A through D listed above, to each of these 15-point subsequences are summarized in Figure 1.11.

For Sequence 0, the correct location estimate is 0, and all four of the trimmed means considered here are generally consistent with this result, although the median exhibits a value that appears to be somewhat biased (i.e., consistently larger than the other three trimmed means) and different in distributional character: specifically, its interquartile range coincides with the entire data range, suggesting a bimodal distribution of values. A much more dramatic difference between the median and the other three trimmed means is seen

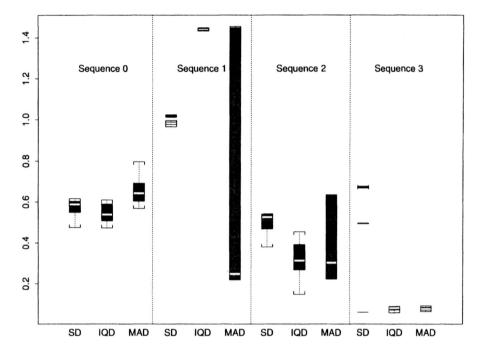

Figure 1.12. *Scale estimate comparisons for the* 4 *simulation-based sequences shown in Figure* 1.10: *boxplot summaries of the* 136 *two-point deletion subsets for each sequence, as a function of the estimator, designated SD for the standard deviation, IQD for the IQD, and MAD for the MAD scale estimator.*

for Sequence 1; in fact, this behavior corresponds exactly to that described in Sec. 1.4.1 for the median: deletion of two points from this data sequence is enough to shift the median value from approximately -1.1 to approximately $+1.1$. In marked contrast, note that for Sequence 2, the median value is *always exactly zero*, corresponding to the fact that five of the seventeen data values are equal to zero, six of these data values are strictly negative, and six are strictly positive. Hence, the median value is zero for *any* subset of fifteen points chosen from this data sequence. Finally, the results shown for Sequence 3 illustrate the point made earlier concerning the outlier-sensitivity of the mean and the outlier-resistance of the median. In addition, these results illustrate the intermediate outlier-sensitivities of the trimmed means for $\alpha = 0.125$, which is somewhat better behaved than the standard mean but not as good as the median, and $\alpha = 0.25$, which exhibits comparable behavior to the median here. This latter observation corresponds to the fact that, if we make the trimming percentage α large enough, we are guaranteed to reject all outliers from the data sequence.

Figure 1.12 provides a second example of the GSA framework, illustrating its use in comparing the following three scale estimators:

- the standard deviation (SD),

- the normalized IQD,

- the normalized MAD scale estimator.

The scenarios and sampling scheme are exactly the same as in Figure 1.11. As in the case of the trimmed mean comparison, differences are apparent when these three scale estimators are applied to Sequence 0, but these estimates are generally in agreement with the correct standard deviation $\sigma = \sqrt{1.1/3} \simeq 0.606$ for this sequence. These results illustrate that the three methods do yield roughly comparable results when applied to well-behaved data sequences that are free of outliers or other data anomalies. Also as in the previous example, dramatic differences are seen in these scale estimates when they are applied to the highly heterogeneous Sequence 1: both the standard deviation and the interquartile range exhibit narrow ranges of variation, whereas the MAD scale estimate spans an enormous range of about an order of magnitude. The MAD scale estimate also exhibits an unusually wide range of variation for Sequence 2, reflecting the significant influence that repeated data values can have on median-based data characterizations. This point is important and is discussed further in Chapter 3. Interestingly, note that whereas the IQD scale estimate is more consistent than the standard deviation for Sequence 1, it is less consistent for Sequence 2. Finally, the results shown for Sequence 3 reflect the extreme outlier-sensitivity of the standard deviation and the outlier-resistance of both the IQD and the MAD scale estimates. Also, note that these three results are all in substantial agreement for the single data subsequence for which both outliers have been removed: this value appears as an extreme outlier in the standard deviation results and it illustrates the fundamental idea underlying effective deletion diagnostics. Specifically, deletion of outlying observations can profoundly influence the results of standard, outlier-sensitive analysis procedures. Also, note the narrow range of standard deviation values observed for the 105 samples containing both outliers (i.e., the values clustered around 0.68) and the cluster of 30 values at $\hat{\sigma} \sim 0.5$ obtained when only one of the pair of outlying values from Sequence 3 is included.

Overall, both of these examples illustrate the two primary applications of the GSA approach: first, the comparison of different analysis methods, and, second, the detection of significant differences between datasets. Although the primary emphasis of this book is on this second application, it is important to note that these two problems cannot be cleanly decoupled. As a specific example, note that both the sample median and the median-based MAD scale estimator exhibit extremely good outlier-resistance but behave badly for heterogeneous examples such as Sequence 1. Given this knowledge and results like those shown in Figures 1.11 and 1.12, we are led to suspect that Sequence 3 contains outliers and Sequence 1 exhibits pronounced heterogeneity. Without such insight, we can only say that there appear to be pronounced differences *of some kind* between Sequences 1 and 3.

Finally, it is important to say something about the sampling scheme considered here, which corresponds to a *leave-k-out deletion strategy* for $k = 2$. This general strategy is discussed at length in Chapter 7, where it is noted that it rapidly becomes impractical with increasing k. As a specific example, Table 1.1 lists the number of possible subsequences of length $N - k$ for $k = 1$ through 8 when $N = 17$. The largest number of possible subsequences is obtained for $k = 8$ and is equal to 24,310; since there is the same number of ways of deleting k points as of retaining k points, we obtain the same number of subsequences when we delete k points as when we delete $N - k$ points, so we obtain the same result for $k = 9$ as for $k = 8$, and the number of possible subsequences decreases for $k > 9$. The key point here is that even in short data sequences like those considered in this example, the number of possible subsequences grows so rapidly that exhaustive comparison of all

Number of deleted points, k	Number of subsequences
1	17
2	136
3	680
4	2,380
5	6,188
6	12,376
7	19,448
8	24,310

Table 1.1. *Number of subsequences of length $N - k$ versus k for $N = 17$.*

possible subsequences of size k is almost never feasible. It is for this reason that an entire chapter is devoted to the subset selection problem.

1.6   Organization of this book

The preceding sections of this chapter represent an extended overview of the material that appears in subsequent chapters. Hence, it seems useful to conclude with a brief discussion of how these chapters are organized. Chapter 2 is devoted to a detailed discussion of the problem of data anomalies, focusing on the different types of anomalies we are likely to encounter in practice, the consequences of these anomalies, and some of their sources. Next, Chapter 3 considers the problem of univariate outlier detection, introducing several simple mathematical outlier models and examining the influence of both outlier type and contamination level on three different univariate outlier detection strategies. Attention is restricted to the univariate case because univariate outlier detection is an extremely important issue in practice, in part because it provides very useful background for other, more difficult, outlier detection problems, and in part because the GSA formulation often converts other types of data anomalies to univariate outliers. Chapter 4 is devoted to data pretreatment, addressing more general outlier detection problems, missing data handling questions, the detection of noninformative variables that should be removed from a dataset before detailed analysis, and the use of auxiliary data and prior knowledge in detecting data anomalies.

Chapter 5 takes a somewhat broader look at the data characterization problem, posing the provocative question, "What is a good data characterization?" While no pretense is made that a complete answer is given, the problem is analyzed from several different points of view, including general characterizations such as *location-* and *scale-invariance* that have strong connections with *functional equations*. In addition, a number of important inequalities are discussed that are useful in interpreting analysis results, quantifying relationships between different data characterizations, computing approximate solutions, and formulating new analysis approaches. Ultimately, however, the chapter concludes that, analogous to the results of the Princeton Robustness Study (Andrews et al., 1972) for location estimators, rarely will we be able to declare a single analysis method "best" under realistic circumstances. This conclusion provides a strong motivation for comparing analysis results across different methods. To facilitate the construction of systematic comparisons of methods that may be complicated or even incompletely understood, Chapter 6 presents a detailed account of GSA that is much more specific and complete than the introduction to the basic idea presented in Sec. 1.5. In particular, the formal definition of exchangeability proposed by Draper et al. (1993) is described, followed by a much more complete description of the components of the GSA framework. The chapter includes a brief simulation-based dynamic modelling case study that illustrates both the detailed mechanics of GSA and its range of applicability. An extremely important practical problem, in the limited context of GSA and in the broader context of analyzing large datasets, is that of extracting "representative," "interesting," or even "highly suspicious" subsets of a larger dataset. Chapter 7 is devoted to this topic, giving detailed discussions of random subset selection strategies, deletion strategies, partially systematic segmentation strategies, and a number of related ideas. This chapter also presents several GSA case studies to further illustrate the basic approach and to examine the influence of different choices of sampling scheme on the results.

Finally, Chapter 8 concludes the book with a brief summary of some pertinent observations by other authors on the practical problems of analyzing data and brief discussions of some important issues that appear to be unresolved at present.

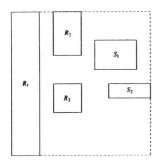

Chapter 2

Imperfect Datasets: Character, Consequences, and Causes

Although it was emphasized in Chapter 1 that data anomalies need not be "imperfections" in the usual sense of the term (e.g., gross measurement errors), such imperfections are certainly one of the most common sources of data anomalies. Further, the examples discussed in Chapter 1 also illustrated that the presence of unsuspected data imperfections can badly distort the results of an otherwise reasonable data analysis. Hence, this chapter presents a more detailed look at some of these data imperfections, their sources, and their consequences.

It may sound obvious enough once it is stated, but imperfect datasets occur frequently in practice because real-world data collection systems are not perfect. In fact, it is useful to briefly consider this point to clearly distinguish between the different types of data anomalies that can and do arise in practice. Figure 2.1 shows the components we need to consider in discussing imperfect datasets: the physical source of the data of interest is shown as the leftmost block in this figure, and this data source feeds two parallel paths. The upper one is the ideal path, leading from the data source, through an ideal data acquisition system, into an ideal (i.e., error-free) dataset $\mathcal{D}_I$. The lower path leads from this same data source through a real data acquisition system, generating the real dataset $\mathcal{D}_R$. Imperfections in the dataset correspond to differences between $\mathcal{D}_I$ and $\mathcal{D}_R$, and they can be of several different kinds. To describe these different data imperfections, suppose x is an ideal data record in $\mathcal{D}_I$ and define $\mathcal{R}x$ to be its counterpart, if any, in $\mathcal{D}_R$. Also, suppose $\rho(x, y)$ is a given scalar-valued distance function defined on $\mathcal{D}_I \times \mathcal{D}_R$. We can usefully distinguish the following five types of data imperfections:

1. *noise* or *observation error:* $x \in \mathcal{D}_I$, $\mathcal{R}x \in \mathcal{D}_R$, $\rho(x, \mathcal{R}x) \lesssim \epsilon$;

2. *gross errors:* $x \in \mathcal{D}_I$, $\mathcal{R}x \in \mathcal{D}_R$, $\rho(x, \mathcal{R}x) >> \epsilon$;

3. *simple missing data:* $x \in \mathcal{D}_I$, $\mathcal{R}x \notin \mathcal{D}_R$;

4. *coded missing data:* $x \in \mathcal{D}_I$, $\mathcal{R}x = m^* \in \mathcal{D}_R$, $m^* = $ special;

5. *disguised missing data:* $x \in \mathcal{D}_I$, $\mathcal{R}x = y \in \mathcal{D}_R$, $y = $ arbitrary.

In these descriptions, ϵ is a "small" value used to distinguish between noise and gross errors. In practice, this distinction is extremely important because almost all standard data

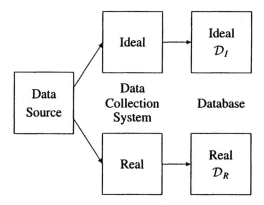

Figure 2.1. *Real versus ideal data collection systems.*

analysis procedures are designed to tolerate noise, which is almost always present. In marked contrast, many standard data analysis procedures suffer badly in the face of gross errors, even if they are only present in small concentration. Note here that the class of gross errors includes both large measurement system errors that result in outlying data values in the database and (possibly "small") software errors that result in misalignments like those discussed in Chapter 1. It was also noted in Chapter 1 that missing data arise quite frequently in practice, but this problem can manifest itself in at least three different ways: the desired record x can simply be missing from the dataset (Case 3); it can be *coded* as a special "missing" data value like NA, NaN, or ? (Case 4); or it can be *disguised* as a *valid* data value with no indication that the correct value of x is either unknown or undefinable (Case 5). This last case is particularly insidious because it can convert missing data values into multivariate outliers that may be difficult to detect.

2.1   Outliers

As discussed in Chapter 1, a useful working definition of an outlier is a data point that appears to be inconsistent with the nominal behavior exhibited by most of the other data points in a specified collection. Within this broad general definition is a lot of room for interpretation and, to make it specific enough to serve as a basis for quantitative outlier detection procedures, it is necessary to provide mathematical characterizations of what we mean by "nominal behavior" and "inconsistency." The following discussions emphasize the practical differences among three important outlier classes, each based on a different model for nominal behavior: univariate outliers, multivariate outliers, and time-series outliers. Consideration of other nominal behavior models leads to other, generally more complex and subtle outlier classes that are not discussed here; discussions of some of these other outlier classes are given by Barnett and Lewis (1994).

2.1.1   Univariate outliers

Although it was noted in Chapter 1, it bears repeating here that the simplest type of data anomaly is the univariate outlier, based on the notion that "most" of the data should exhibit

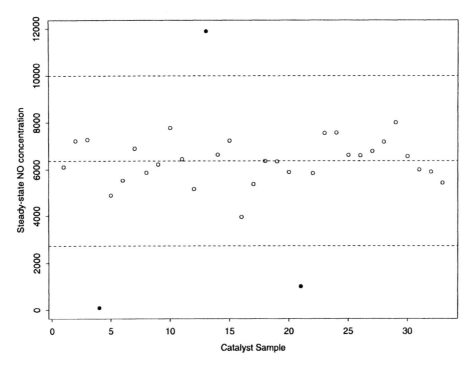

Figure 2.2. *Steady-state NO concentration, fuel-rich phase, $T = 300$. Outliers detected with the Hampel identifier are catalyst samples 4, 13, and 21 and are marked with solid circles. The median value and upper and lower Hampel identifier detection limits are shown as dashed lines.*

approximately the same value, c. Under this model, the observed sequence $\{x_k\}$ of data values may be modelled as

$$x_k = c + e_k, \qquad (2.1)$$

where $\{e_k\}$ is a sequence of deviations about the nominal value c. Univariate outliers correspond to data points x_k for which e_k is "unusually large." A typical example is that shown in Figure 2.2, which plots the steady-state concentrations of nitrous oxide (NO) measured in 33 automotive catalyst characterization experiments (Hendershot et al., 2003). Most of these points (30 of the 33) fall within the range of 4000 to 8000 parts per million (ppm), but 3 of them fall well outside this range. The dashed horizontal lines in this plot correspond to the outlier detection limits obtained for this data sequence using the Hampel identifier discussed in Chapter 3. Points falling between these dashed lines are consistent with the nominal data model on which this outlier detection procedure is based. These points are marked with open circles, while the three points falling outside these limits and thus identified as outliers by this detection procedure are marked with solid circles.

Although a detailed discussion of the Hampel identifier is deferred until Chapter 3, it is important to note that this outlier detection procedure assumes a *symmetric* nominal data distribution. Consequently, if a large positive deviation $e_k > 0$ from the nominal data value c in (2.1) determines an outlier, then any negative deviation that is equally extreme or more

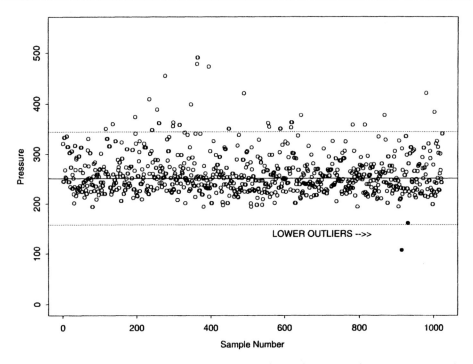

Figure 2.3. *Asymmetrically distributed industrial pressure data sequence exhibiting clear lower outliers but no unambiguous upper outliers.*

extreme (i.e., e_j such that $e_j \leq -e_k < 0$) necessarily also determines an outlier. In cases where this symmetry assumption is not met, a less restrictive alternative is *unimodality*, which implies that even if the distribution of values is asymmetric, it is still characterized by a single connected interval of most probable values. Outside of this interval, the probability of observing a data value decays monotonically to zero as we move farther away. In this case, we must distinguish between *lower outliers*, which are anomalously smaller than these nominal values, and *upper outliers*, which are anomalously larger than these nominal values.

   This point is illustrated in Figure 2.3, which shows a plot of 1024 pressure measurements from an industrial chemical reactor. The solid horizontal reference line in this plot is the median reactor pressure and it is clear that, with the exception of two data points, these data values are much more likely to lie significantly above the median than they are to lie significantly below the median. This point is emphasized by the two dashed horizontal lines, lying at the upper and lower outlier detection limits defined by the Hampel outlier detection procedure discussed in Chapter 3: the one point lying clearly below the lower outlier detection limit and the second point lying essentially on this lower dashed line are clear candidates for lower outliers, falling well below the range of variation seen in the rest of the data. In contrast, the points lying above the upper detection limit are not obviously inconsistent with the rest of the data values above the median. Hence, we are not in a position to declare any of these points as unambiguous upper outliers. The clear asymmetry of this example is problematic because many of the methods developed for dealing with outliers are strongly tied to distributional symmetry assumptions and may fail in the face

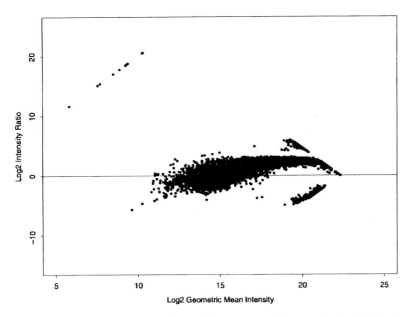

Figure 2.4. *An uncorrected MA plot, generated from a single cDNA microarray.*

of pronounced asymmetry like that seen in Figure 2.3. This important point is revisited in Chapter 8.

2.1.2 Multivariate outliers

The basic idea of multivariate outliers was introduced in Chapter 1 and illustrated with some simple examples. It is worth repeating that, essentially, a multivariable outlier is a vector x_j in a sequence $\{x_k\}$ of vectors that is anomalous with respect to the intercomponent relationships typically seen in the data sequence. In particular, it was shown in Chapter 1 that—in marked contrast to the case of univariate outliers just discussed—multivariate outliers need not be extreme with respect to any of their individual component values. As a consequence, multivariate outliers tend to be both harder to detect and more varied in character than univariate outliers.

The simplest multivariate outliers are *bivariate outliers*, where each vector has only two components. An advantage of considering this special case is that bivariate quantities may be examined visually with scatterplots, and bivariate outliers usually appear as visual anomalies in these plots. This point is illustrated in Figure 2.4, which shows an *MA plot*, commonly used in analyzing cDNA microarray data. Recall from the discussion in Chapter 1 that microarrays measure differences in gene expression between two biologically distinct samples, each labelled with a different fluorescent dye. Optical intensity measurements are made for each dye and differences in the gene expression level are inferred from the differences in these optical intensities. Figure 2.4 plots the difference in $\log_2$ intensities for the two channels, corresponding to the log of the ratio of these two intensities, against the average of these $\log_2$ intensity values, corresponding to the log of the geometric mean of these two intensities. In practice, a great deal is done before forming these plots to correct for artifacts and systematic method effects, but the plots shown in Figure 2.4 are based on the uncorrected data values, with only one minor compensation. Specifically, although intensity values should be strictly positive, zero intensity values are sometimes observed. Since $\log_2 0 = -\infty$, it is useful to construct *MA* plots using $\log_2(1 + I)$ rather than $\log_2 I$, where I represents the uncorrected intensity values. That is, the horizontal axis in the plot shown in Figure 2.4 corresponds to $M = \log_2[(1 + I_2)/(1 + I_1)]$ and the vertical axis corresponds to $A = [\log_2(1 + I_1) + \log_2(1 + I_2)]/2$, where I_1 and I_2 represent the two individual optical intensity values.

The main cluster of points in this plot lies along the horizontal line at zero log intensity ratio, corresponding to the line $I_2 = I_1$, but there are at least three other clusters of points that are clearly discordant with this main group. Most obvious is the cluster in the upper left corner of the plot, lying along a line and well away from the rest of the data values. These points would be easily detected as univariate outliers with respect to the vertical M variable and most of them would also be detected as univariate outliers with respect to the horizontal A variable. Conversely, the other two discordant clusters in this data plot are those lying approximately along lines above and below the main cluster of points at the right end of the plot. The upper cluster *might* be detectable as a univariate outlier with respect to the M variable ($\log_2$ intensity ratio), but it is clearly not anomalous with respect to the A variable ($\log_2$ geometric mean intensity). The lower cluster is more clearly discordant *visually* than the upper cluster, but it lies well within the range of acceptable A values and lies mostly within the range of acceptable M values. Hence, these two clusters are unlikely to be detected as univariate outliers with respect to either variable individually, but they are clearly discordant with the relationship seen between these variables and therefore represent clear bivariate outliers.

Before leaving this example, it is reasonable to say something about the source of these multivariate outlier clusters. If we define $x = \log_2(1 + I_2)$ and $y = \log_2(1 + I_1)$, the *MA* plot shown in Figure 2.4 corresponds to a plot of $x - y$ versus $(x + y)/2$. Note that for those data pairs where $I_1 = 0$, it follows that $y = 0$ and this relationship reduces to a plot of x versus $x/2$. Figure 2.5 shows the same *MA* plot as in Figure 2.4, but plotted with slightly different scaling and with the addition of four dashed reference lines. The dashed line with positive slope in the upper left portion of the plot corresponds to $M = 2A$, equivalent to the condition $I_2 = 0$, and it passes exactly through the upper left cluster of outlying points seen in Figure 2.4. In more physical terms, this line corresponds to the locus of points obtained when the second channel saturates at its lower limit ($I_2 = 0$). The dashed line with negative slope in the upper right portion of Figure 2.5 corresponds to the upper saturation limit for this channel ($I_2 \simeq 5.16 \times 10^6$), and the dashed line with positive slope in the lower right portion of the plot corresponds to the upper saturation limit for the other channel ($I_1 \simeq 5.16 \times 10^6$). Note that these lines pass through the two outlying clusters lying above and below the main cluster of points in Figure 2.4, offering a physical interpretation for these multivariate outliers. In fact, these points correspond to "spotlights," which are artificially doped spots on the microarray that are included precisely because they give a very intense (nonbiological) response. Hence, they are used for calibration, adjusting the optical imaging system to cause the spotlights to saturate without causing any of the biological gene responses to saturate. Finally, the dashed line with negative slope shown in the lower left portion of the plot corresponds to the lower saturation limit for the first

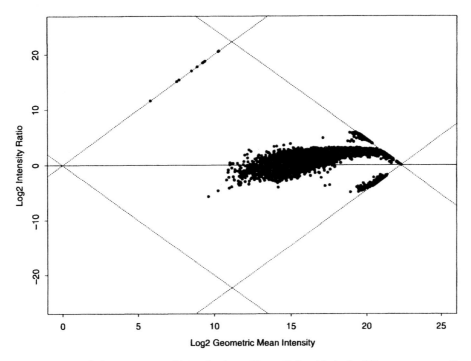

Figure 2.5. *Uncorrected MA plot from Figure 2.4, with dashed lines corresponding to intensity saturation limits.*

channel ($I_1 = 0$), and the fact that no data points lie along this line implies that none of the first channel intensities exhibited this lower saturation value, a conclusion that may be confirmed by examining the individual intensity values in this dataset.

In the case of asymmetrically distributed data sequences, it was noted in Sec. 2.1.1 that outliers exhibit directionality, with upper and lower outliers having distinct characteristics. In the case of multivariate outliers, this directionality becomes more general even when the nominal data model is taken as Gaussian. This point is illustrated in Figure 2.6, which shows scatterplots of four bivariate data sequences. The upper left plot (Dataset A) shows 100 samples from an uncontaminated bivariate Gaussian distribution; here, the mean of each component is 0, the standard deviation of each component is 1, and the correlation coefficient (see Sec. 2.2.3 for a discussion) is $\rho = +0.8$. This relatively large positive correlation coefficient means that the two components of these random vectors exhibit a pronounced linear relationship. This relationship explains the shape of the plot and its orientation along the line $y = x$ in the (x, y) plane. The other three datasets each contain a single outlier that has the same probability relative to the Gaussian distribution used to generate the elliptical cloud of points in each case. More specifically, in all three of these cases (Datasets B, C, and D), a single point from the original dataset (Dataset A) has been replaced with an outlier lying the same *Mahalanobis distance* from the origin (i.e., the true mean of the uncontaminated dataset), but differing in *orientation*. Since the Mahalanobis distance is intimately related to the correlation coefficient, a detailed discussion of this distance is deferred to Sec. 2.2.3. There are two key points here. First, data values lying at

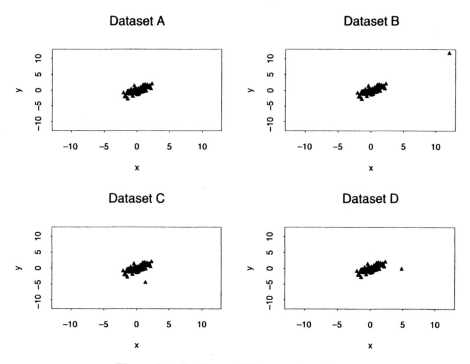

Figure 2.6. *Outliers at different orientations.*

the same Mahalanobis distance from the center of these clusters have the same probabilities. Second, both the distance and orientation must be specified to characterize multivariate outliers. Further, these two outlier characteristics can have different influences on different analysis procedures, a point discussed further in Sec. 2.2.3.

2.1.3 Time-series outliers

Figure 2.7 shows a sequence of 400 physical property measurements, taken uniformly in time, plotted against the time index k. All of these data values fall between 225 and 235, with no points falling sufficiently far from the others to be declared univariate outliers. Conversely, there are isolated data points at $k \sim 170$, $k \sim 260$, and $k \sim 325$ that lie sufficiently far from their immediate neighbors to qualify as *time-series outliers*. In particular, a *time-series outlier* need not be extreme with respect to the total range of data variation, but it is extreme relative to the variation seen *locally*. More specifically, time-series outliers may be defined as data points that violate the general pattern of smooth or otherwise regular (e.g., discontinuous but periodic) variation seen in the data sequence. The significance of these outliers is that they can profoundly distort various dynamic data characterizations, including correlation estimates, estimated power spectra, and linear or nonlinear dynamic models fit to collections of data sequences. For the most part, the topic of dynamic data characterization is beyond the scope of this book, although this example is revisited in Chapters 4 and 6.

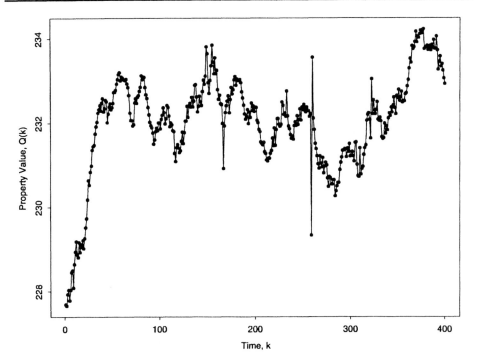

Figure 2.7. *A sequence of product property measurements illustrating the phenomenon of time-series outliers.*

2.2 Consequences of outliers

One reason that outliers are extremely important in practice is that, even if only a few of them are present in a large dataset, their influence can be profound. This point was made in Chapter 1 but it is important enough that it bears repeating, so the following sections describe some simple examples that further illustrate the nature and severity of these consequences.

2.2.1 Moments versus order statistics

The brief kurtosis case study presented in Chapter 1 gives some insight into the extreme sensitivity of moment characterizations. The following discussion attempts to put these results into clearer perspective by examining the rate at which outlier-sensitivity grows with the order of the moments involved in moment characterizations. In particular, the examples considered here examine the sensitivity of the first three moments to univariate outliers. One reason for presenting these results is that we then compare the corresponding results obtained using analogous data characterizations based on *order statistics*. As the following results demonstrate, order statistics exhibit much better outlier-resistance than moments do, providing one practical route to a variety of outlier-resistant data analysis procedures. The situation is somewhat complicated, however, by the fact that standard estimators such as skewness and kurtosis that are based on higher moments normalize them using second

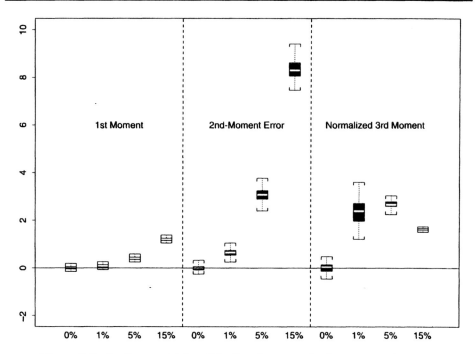

Figure 2.8. *Outlier-sensitivity of the first three standard moment estimators.*

moments, leading to a nonmonotonic dependence on contamination, as seen in the kurtosis example discussed in Chapter 1.

Figure 2.8 presents boxplot summaries of $m = 200$ results obtained using the first three moments under four different contamination scenarios. In all cases, the nominal data sequence (marked "0%" in Figure 2.8) corresponds to a zero-mean, unit-variance Gaussian sequence of length $N = 100$. Contaminated sequences are then obtained by adding 1%, 5%, or 15% outliers, all of magnitude $+8\sigma$. The three moment characterizations compared in Figure 2.8 are the sample mean $\bar{x}$, the variance estimation error $\hat{\sigma}^2 - 1$, and the estimated skewness, given by

$$\gamma = \frac{\sum_{k=1}^{N}(x_k - \bar{x})^3}{\left[\sum_{k=1}^{N}(x_k - \bar{x})^2\right]^{3/2}}. \tag{2.2}$$

The correct value for all of these moment-based characterizations is zero since the uncontaminated data sequence has a zero-mean, unit-variance Gaussian distribution, implying zero skewness. In all cases, the results computed from the uncontaminated data sequence are consistent with these expectations, exhibiting approximately zero median values and ranges of variation that increase with increasing moment order.

The first moment results show an increasing bias with increasing contamination level: the median value of the computed sample means increases monotonically as the fraction of outliers in the dataset increases. This change is expected since the outliers lie eight standard deviations above the mean, causing a shift of the sample mean toward this common value, increasingly as the contamination level increases. Note, however, that the variability of this result is not significantly affected: the range of variation seen in the four first-moment boxplots in Figure 2.8 is about the same. In contrast, the results obtained for the second-moment characterization $\hat{\sigma}^2 - 1$ exhibit a much more dramatic outlier-dependence. In particular, note that the variance inflation—the overestimation of the variance caused by the outliers in the data sequence—increases much faster than the mean shift just described. For example, when the contamination level reaches 15%, the variance is overestimated by about an order of magnitude. In addition, the variability of the estimated variance also increases significantly with increasing contamination levels.

As in the kurtosis example discussed in Chapter 1, the dependence of the skewness γ on increasing contamination levels is nonmonotonic, with respect to both the median value and the spread of values around the median. For example, note that at a 1% contamination level, both the bias (i.e., the difference of the median estimate from the true value of zero) and the variability (either the width of the central box or the total range of observed values) are substantially worse for the skewness than for either the mean or the variance. This difference reflects the fact that the estimated third moment on which the skewness is based (i.e., the numerator in (2.2)) is more sensitive to contamination than the first and second moments on which the mean and variance estimators are based. Conversely, the skewness results are slightly *better* in the face of 5% contamination and *dramatically better* in the face of 15% contamination. This result reflects the fact that two things are happening as the contamination level becomes large: First, the variance inflation seen clearly in the second-moment results means that the denominator in (2.2) is becoming larger. Second, as the contamination level approaches 50%, the true distribution of the contaminated sample becomes bimodal and approximately symmetric: 50% of the observed data values are distributed around 0 with a standard deviation of 1, and 50% of the data values are distributed around +8 with the same standard deviation. This limiting distribution is approximately the same as a binary distribution in which 50% of the values are 0 and 50% of the values are 8, which is symmetric around the mean value of 4. Since skewness is a measure of distributional asymmetry (i.e., all symmetric distributions have zero skewness), the numerator in (2.2) becomes small as the contamination level approaches 50% and the estimated skewness γ tends to zero. Recall that similar behavior occurs for related reasons in the kurtosis example discussed in Chapter 1.

For comparison, Figure 2.9 shows results analogous to those shown in Figure 2.8, but based on estimates derived from order statistics rather than moments. Specifically, the first four boxplots show the sample medians $x^\dagger$ computed under each of the four contamination levels considered previously: 0%, 1%, 5%, and 15%. As before, all samples are of size $N = 100$; the nominal data sequences are zero-mean, unit-variance Gaussian sequences; and all outliers have the common value +8. Also, each boxplot summarizes $m = 200$ results, just as in Figure 2.8. The middle group of results is obtained for $S_Q^2 - 1$, where S_Q is the alternative to the standard deviation estimate derived from the interquartile range:

$$S_Q = \frac{x_U - x_L}{1.35}. \tag{2.3}$$

Here, x_U denotes the upper quartile computed from the data, x_L denotes the lower quartile, and the constant 1.35 appearing in the denominator of the expression is the reciprocal of the interquartile range for the standard Gaussian distribution, making S_Q an unbiased estimator

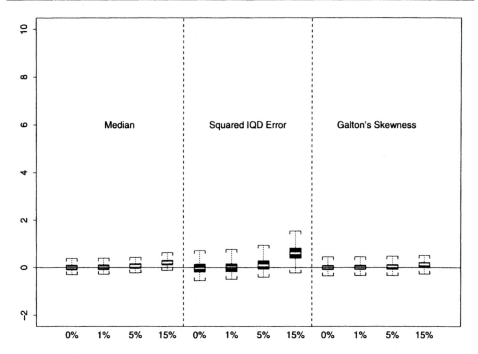

Figure 2.9. *Outlier-sensitivity of three order–statistic-based estimators.*

of the standard deviation for Gaussian data. Finally, the rightmost four boxplots shown in Figure 2.9 summarize the computed values for *Galton's skewness measure* (Johnson, Kotz, and Balakrishnan, 1994, p. 3), defined as

$$\gamma_G = \frac{x_U + x_L - 2x^{\dagger}}{x_U - x_L}. \tag{2.4}$$

Note that for a symmetric distribution, the median $x^{\dagger}$ lies midway between the lower quartile x_L and the upper quartile x_U, implying $\gamma_G = 0$.

Comparing the results shown in Figure 2.9 for these order–statistic-based estimators with those shown in Figure 2.8 for their moment-based counterparts reveals the dramatically reduced outlier-sensitivity of the order–statistic-based estimators. In particular, since the scale is the same for these two plots, it is clear that the worst degradation caused by outliers for any of the order–statistic-based estimators occurs for the same case that caused the worst degradation for the moment-based estimators, but the effect is roughly an order of magnitude smaller. Specifically, the poorest result seen here is that for 15% contamination with the squared IQD, but this result is roughly comparable with that obtained for 1% contamination with the corresponding moment-based estimator. One price we pay for this improved outlier-resistance is a somewhat larger variability, as may be seen by comparing the uncontaminated results from Figures 2.8 and 2.9. Still, the improvement in outlier-resistance is sufficiently impressive that this price is generally worth paying if outliers are likely to be present in the dataset we wish to characterize.

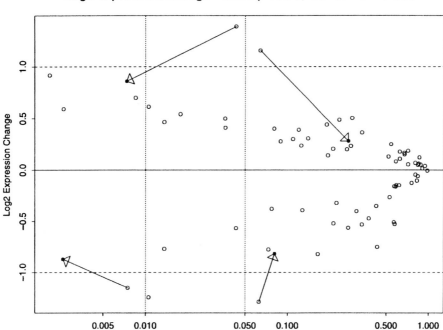

Figure 2.10. *Standard volcano plot with outliers.*

2.2.2 The effect of outliers on volcano plots

The following example is based on the same microarray dataset used to illustrate the concept of a univariate outlier in Chapter 1. As noted previously, these experiments attempt to measure the changes in gene expression levels in the brainstem of rats exposed to ethanol, so an important practical question is which genes show evidence of significant ethanol response given the substantial natural variability of the data even in the absence of ethanol exposure. A classical approach to this question is the *t*-test, which tests the hypothesis that there is no difference between the results obtained for the control animals and for the ethanol-treated animals. This test is based on the assumption that individual measurements made under each condition correspond to statistically independent, Gaussian random variables with a constant variance. Under this assumption, if there is no treatment effect (the null hypothesis), both the control and treatment results will have the same mean, but if there is a systematic treatment effect, it will appear as a difference in the means of the two samples.

One way of summarizing the results of microarray data analysis is through the use of a *volcano plot* like that shown in Figure 2.10. This plot shows the difference between the means of the ethanol-treated and control samples plotted against the probability value computed from the *t*-test just described. If every gene exhibited the same variance and this value could be computed without error from the available data, these two numbers would

Log2 expression change versus p-value, Genes 201 to 300

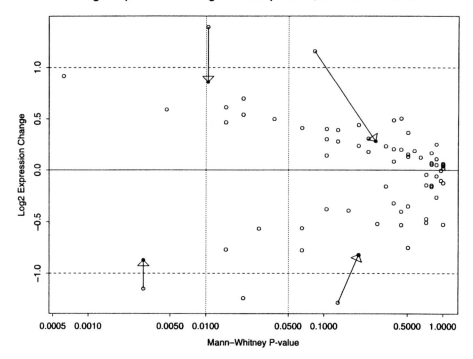

Figure 2.11. *Rank-based volcano plot with outliers.*

be in one-to-one correspondence and the points would all lie along a smooth curve. In the presence of low-level random variations, we would expect to see an increase in the scatter due to sampling effects, but some of the points shown in Figure 2.10 lie far enough from their neighbors to raise suspicion. In particular, the four points from which arrows are drawn correspond to results computed from outlier-contaminated data sequences like the one discussed in Chapter 1. Replacing the outlying values in these data sequences with the median of the corresponding eight samples and recomputing the *t*-test probabilities yields the points shown as solid circles at the ends of the arrows in Figure 2.10. Note that these results are generally in better agreement with the overall pattern seen in the volcano plot than the original results are.

An extremely important practical observation is that outlier-sensitivity is a strong function of analysis method. Figure 2.11 provides a nice illustration of this point, showing the volcano plot obtained using the Mann–Whitney test for significant treatment effects instead of the classical *t*-test. The Mann–Whitney test is based on data ranks rather than the data values themselves, so, because data ranks are only weakly influenced by outliers, the results of the Mann–Whitney test are much less influenced by outliers than are the *t*-test results. As in Figure 2.10, the results obtained for the four genes containing outlying measurements are indicated by open circles attached to arrows, and the results obtained when the outliers are replaced with the appropriate medians are indicated by solid circles at the ends of these arrows. Comparing Figures 2.10 and 2.11 shows that there are significant

Dataset	$\hat{\rho}_{xy},$ $d = 8$	$\hat{\rho}_{xy},$ $d = 128$
A	0.738	0.738
B	0.898	0.990
C	0.600	0.311
D	0.657	0.327

Table 2.1. *Product-moment correlations for the outliers shown in Figure 2.6.*

differences between the probability values obtained from the Mann–Whitney test and those obtained from the t-test, but if we compare the arrows in the two figures, it is clear that the Mann–Whitney probability values are much less influenced by the treatment of the outliers than the t-test values are. In particular, note that two of these cases with the smallest probability values (i.e., the two most significant anomalous cases) exhibit no change at all in probability, although the reduction in the mean shift is the same as in Figure 2.10.

2.2.3 Product-moment correlations

Without question, the best-known approach to assessing the relationship between two data sequences, $\{x_k\}$ and $\{y_k\}$, each of the same length N, is the *product-moment correlation coefficient,* advocated by Karl Pearson at the end of the 19th century. This association measure, denoted $\hat{\rho}_{xy}$, is given by

$$\hat{\rho}_{xy} = \frac{1}{(N-1)\hat{\sigma}_x\hat{\sigma}_y} \sum_{k=1}^{N} (x_k - \bar{x})(y_k - \bar{y}), \tag{2.5}$$

where $\bar{x}$ and $\bar{y}$ denote the usual arithmetic means of the data sequences and $\hat{\sigma}_x$ and $\hat{\sigma}_y$ represent the usual standard deviation estimates. Not surprisingly, since this association measure is moment-based, it exhibits comparable outlier-sensitivity to the moment-based univariate data characterizations discussed in Sec. 2.2.1. This point is illustrated in Table 2.1, which gives the product-moment correlation values computed from the four bivariate Gaussian data sequences shown in Figure 2.6. Specifically, the leftmost column lists the scenarios compared (uncontaminated Scenario A and the three contaminated Scenarios B, C, and D) and the middle column gives the computed product-moment correlations computed from these data sequences. Recall that the exact correlation value for these examples is $\rho = 0.8$, which is in reasonable agreement with the outlier-free result (Scenario A, $\hat{\rho} = 0.738$). In marked contrast, the correlation estimate is substantially larger for Scenario B and substantially smaller for Scenarios C and D.

The three contaminated data sequences considered in this example have orientations specified by the three outlier scenarios (B, C, and D), and a Mahalanobis distance d from the mean $(\bar{x}, \bar{y})$ of $d = 8$, corresponding roughly to a univariate outlier eight standard deviations from the mean. More specifically, the Mahalanobis distance may be defined in two different but closely related ways. The first is as a data characterization (i.e., a sample statistic) defined as follows. First, define the mean $\bar{\mathbf{x}}$ of a set of N multivariate random vectors $\{\mathbf{x}_k\}$ as

$$\bar{\mathbf{x}} = \frac{1}{N} \sum_{k=1}^{N} \mathbf{x}_k \Rightarrow \bar{\mathbf{x}}^i = \frac{1}{N} \sum_{k=1}^{N} \mathbf{x}_k^i, \tag{2.6}$$

where x^i denotes the ith component of the vector x. Next, define the sample covariance matrix $\hat{\Sigma}$ of the set $\{x_k\}$ as the $p \times p$ matrix whose i, j element is

$$\hat{\Sigma}_{ij} = \frac{1}{N-1} \sum_{k=1}^{N} (x_k^i - \bar{x}^i)(x_k^j - \bar{x}^j). \tag{2.7}$$

The Mahalanobis distance of the vector x_k from the mean vector $\bar{x}$ is defined as

$$d(x_k, \bar{x}) = (x_k - \bar{x})^T \hat{\Sigma}^{-1}(x_k - \bar{x}). \tag{2.8}$$

Intuitively, the Mahalanobis distance represents a multivariate extension of the z-score, $z_k = (x_k - \bar{x})/\hat{\sigma}$, for a univariate data sample, providing a useful measure of "extremeness" for multivariate data. The second definition of Mahalanobis distance is the corresponding population statistic for a random vector x with mean μ and covariance matrix Σ, that is, the population version of the Mahalanobis distance d for each observation x_k is the value defined by (2.8) with the sample mean $\bar{x}$ replaced with the population mean μ and the sample covariance matrix $\hat{\Sigma}$ replaced with the population covariance matrix Σ. The Mahalanobis distances listed in Table 2.1 correspond to the population distances used to generate the simulated Gaussian datasets on which subsequent product-moment correlation estimates were based. The rightmost column in Table 2.1 shows the estimated correlations obtained when the outliers have the same orientations as in Figure 2.6, but have the much more extreme Mahalanobis distance $d = 128$. Relative to the less severe case considered before ($d = 8$), the general trend is the same (i.e., estimated correlations are increased in Scenario B, decreased in Scenario C, and decreased somewhat less in Scenario D), but the magnitude of the effect is greater.

A different characterization of the outlier-sensitivity of the product-moment correlation coefficient is given in Figure 2.12. There, boxplot summaries are given for 100 simulation experiments, each conducted as follows. First, 100 statistically independent sequences, each of $N = 100$ bivariate normal random samples, are generated with 1 of 9 specified correlation values: $\rho = -0.90, -0.75, -0.50, -0.25, 0, 0.25, 0.50, 0.75$, or 0.90. Then, each sequence is contaminated by replacing a single data point with the outlying value $x_k^* = +8\sigma$, $y_k^* = +8\sigma$. The boxplots shown in Figure 2.12 summarize the range of product-moment correlations computed from each of these simulated data sequences. The solid circles in this figure represent the correct value ρ that would be obtained in the absence of sampling errors and contamination effects. It is clear from these results that the presence of these outliers is responsible for a positive bias in all of the estimated correlations. More significantly, this bias becomes *much* more severe as the true correlation decreases, reflecting the fact that two components are present in the dataset: the outlier, which effectively has a correlation coefficient of $+1$, and the nominal data sequence, which exhibits a smaller correlation coefficient. Note that for true correlations less than 0.50, this correct value lies completely outside the range of variation of the 100 estimated correlations.

The situation becomes rapidly worse with increasing contamination level. This point is illustrated in Figure 2.13, which shows the consequences of increasing the contamination level from 1% to 4%, still well within the range of contamination levels we should expect to encounter routinely in practice. Here, the format of the plot is the same as in Figure 2.12, but the positive bias is much worse. In particular, note that the true correlation value *never* lies within the range of the 100 correlation estimates shown here and the estimate never even gets the sign of the correlations correct for negative correlations.

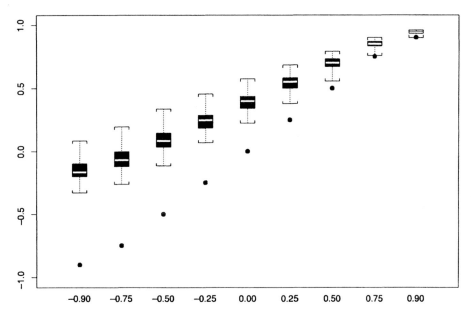

Figure 2.12. *1% contamination results: boxplot summaries of* 100 *product-moment correlation estimates* $\hat{\rho}_{xy}$ *plotted against the population correlation* ρ.

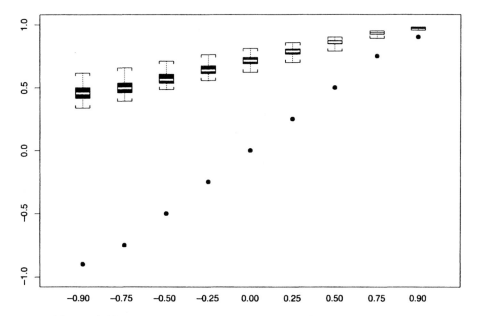

Figure 2.13. *4% contamination results: boxplot summaries of* 100 *product-moment correlation estimates* $\hat{\rho}_{xy}$ *plotted against the population correlation* ρ.

Dataset	ρ_S, $d = 8$	$\hat{\rho}_{xy}$, $d = 8$	ρ_S, $d = 128$	$\hat{\rho}_{xy}$, $d = 128$
A	0.721	0.738	0.721	0.738
B	0.724	0.898	0.724	0.990
C	0.678	0.600	0.664	0.311
D	0.707	0.657	0.707	0.327

Table 2.2. *Rank correlations versus product-moment correlations for the four contaminated data sequences shown in Figure 2.6.*

2.2.4 Spearman rank correlations

One of the key points of Sec. 2.2.1 was that order statistics are far less sensitive to outliers than moments are. This observation is the basic idea behind the *Spearman rank correlation coefficient*, which measures the extent to which "large" values in one variable, x, are associated with "large" values in a second variable y. To accomplish this measurement, Spearman (1904) proposed to replace the data values with their *ranks* in computing the correlations defined in (2.5). That is, the data values $\{x_k\}$ and $\{y_k\}$ are first rank-ordered to yield the corresponding sequences $\{x_{(i)}\}$ and $\{y_{(i)}\}$, from which the product-moment correlations are computed as defined in (2.5). The result is the Spearman rank correlation coefficient ρ_S. In the absence of ties—which can only occur if the data values have a discrete distribution—the mean of the ranks for N observations x_k is $(N + 1)/2$, and the variance σ_r^2 of the ranks is given by (Hajek, Sidak, and Sen, 1999, p. 89)

$$\sigma_r^2 = \frac{N(N^2 - 1)}{12}. \tag{2.9}$$

It is worth emphasizing that these results hold *independent of the data values* $\{x_k\}$, so the Spearman rank correlations may be computed as

$$\rho_S = \frac{12}{N(N^2 - 1)} \sum_{k=1}^{N} \left(R_x(k) - \frac{N+1}{2}\right)\left(R_y(k) - \frac{N+1}{2}\right), \tag{2.10}$$

where $R_x(k)$ is the rank of the kth data value x_k in the rank-ordered list $\{x_{(i)}\}$ (i.e., $R_x(k) = j$ if $x_k = x_{(j)}$). Because the data ranks $R_x(k)$ are much less sensitive to outliers than the data values themselves are, rank correlations are correspondingly less outlier-sensitive than product-moment correlations.

Table 2.2 extends the summary given in Table 2.1 for the product-moment correlations computed from the four data sequences shown in Figure 2.6. In particular, this table lists the four scenarios considered, the product-moment and rank correlations computed when the outlier lies at Mahalanobis distance $d = +8$, and the corresponding results when the outlier lies at Mahalanobis distance $d = +128$. Recall that the true correlation coefficient for the nominal data sequence is $\rho = 0.8$ and that Dataset A is an uncontaminated set of $N = 100$ samples. The results given for this dataset in Table 2.2 show that both the

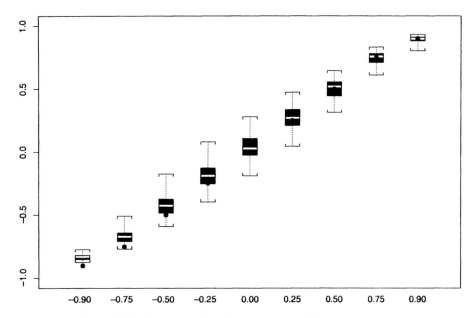

Figure 2.14. *Boxplots of rank correlations, 1% contamination.*

product-moment correlation coefficient and the Spearman rank correlation coefficient give reasonable results for this dataset, and they suggest—correctly—that the product-moment correlation coefficient provides a better estimate of ρ for this case. Conversely, these results also show that the Spearman rank correlation coefficient is far less influenced by the outliers present in Datasets B, C, and D than the product-moment correlation coefficient is. This difference is especially pronounced for the extreme cases where the outliers lie at Mahalanobis distance $d = 128$ from the mean. In particular, note that there is no difference between the Spearman rank correlations for $d = 8$ and those for $d = 128$ for datasets B and D, while the corresponding product-moment correlations are *much* worse for $d = 128$ than for $d = 8$.

Figures 2.14 and 2.15 provide further illustrations of the outlier-resistance of the Spearman rank correlation coefficient. Figure 2.14 shows the estimated and exact correlations for the nine scenarios shown in Figure 2.12, in the same format as before. In contrast to the product-moment correlation results, here the true correlation coefficient lies well within the range of the 100 estimated correlations, except for the most negative correlation values. Even there, however, the errors are comparable with the *smallest* errors seen in the product-moment correlation estimates. Conversely, a price we pay for this improved outlier-resistance is the fact that the ranges of variation seen in Figure 2.14 are somewhat larger than those seen in Figure 2.12. Not surprisingly, the Spearman rank correlation results do degrade somewhat as the contamination level increases. This point may be seen clearly by comparing Figures 2.14 and 2.15: although the same variability is seen in both results, the bias is worse, particularly for negative true correlations, where the true correlation values generally fall outside the range of estimated values. It is worth emphasizing, however, the dramatic improvement of these results relative to those seen in Figure 2.13 for the product-moment correlations.

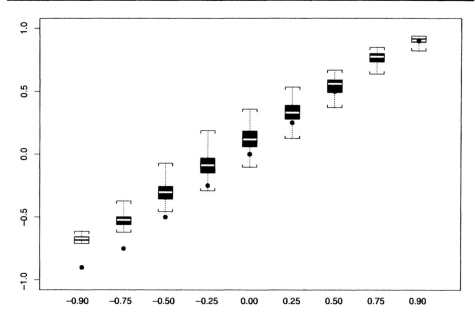

Figure 2.15. *Boxplots of rank correlations,* 4% *contamination.*

2.3   Sources of data anomalies

An extremely important practical question with regard to any type of apparent data anomaly is, "Where did it come from?" Unfortunately, this question is not a mathematical one, so it cannot be answered on the basis of mathematical analyses alone. Hence, it is useful to briefly consider some outlier sources to aid in the interpretation of whatever unusual features our mathematical analysis may reveal.

2.3.1   Gross measurement errors and outliers

Although, as emphasized in Chapter 1, gross measurement errors are *not* the only source of outliers, they are a particularly important source, so it is useful to briefly consider their origin. Survey data analysis distinguishes between *sampling errors*—the expected random variation of individual responses—and *nonsampling errors,* with at least three possible sources (Govindarajulu, 1999, p. 263):

1. *errors of reporting*, corresponding to gross measurement errors;

2. *nonresponse errors*, corresponding to missing data, discussed in Sec. 2.4;

3. *errors in sample selection*, closely related to the problem of nonignorable missing data, also discussed in Sec. 2.4.

In the context of survey responses, errors in reporting can arise from dishonesty (e.g., annual income reported to tax authorities may be significantly smaller than that listed on a mortgage or credit card application) or from imprecise knowledge on the part of the respondent (e.g.,

"What fraction of your monthly income do you spend on take-out pizza?"). A third source of reporting errors in survey data is misunderstanding. A specific example is that described by Marden (1995), who analyzed the results of a survey by Goldberg (1976) of Technion graduates, ranking the perceived prestige of 10 occupations. Three of the 143 responses were sufficiently discordant with the others that it was ultimately concluded that these respondents had inverted the ratings, ranking the most prestigious occupation 10 rather than 1. Under this assumption, these three responses fell into general agreement with the others. Additional sources of errors in survey data are discussed by Tanur (1992, p. 63). Finally, another important source of human error in the analysis of survey data is the manual processing involved. Indeed, Dasu and Johnson (2003, p. 187) note that, even in connection with the analysis of quantitative business data,

> *A major source of data quality errors is manual entry and manual intervention.*

Since even the most highly automated data collection systems are designed and implemented by humans, all of the sources of gross measurement errors just described have their counterparts in datasets that are collected with little or no direct human intervention. That is, through misunderstanding of design objectives, implementation errors, or various other human failings, the contents of a dataset may not be exactly what the data analyst assumes they are. Since the special case of software errors in data collection and conversion systems represents an extremely important source of data anomalies, these errors are discussed in some detail in Sec. 2.3.2. Another related source of gross measurement errors is disguised missing data values, discussed further in Sec. 2.4.

In addition to design and implementation errors, automated data collection systems are also prone to a wide variety of mechanical and electrical failure mechanisms. As a specific example, Thomson (1995) notes that temperature records date back to 1659 in central England, but some early measurements in the north give *average* winter temperatures of $-40°$ because mercury thermometers froze. Frequent sources of gross measurement errors in contemporary systems include electrical power failures; partial failures caused by temperature, age, or extreme conditions of use; and incorrect recalibration of measurement systems following the repair or upgrade of one or more system components.

Often, it is assumed that gross measurement errors, whatever their source, occur at random times and independently in different variables, but this assumption is not always reasonable. In particular, the data sequences shown in Figure 2.16 demonstrate the important concept of *common-mode outliers*, which occur simultaneously in several different variables. Specifically, the left-hand pair of plots in Figure 2.16 show sequences of 100 hourly physical property measurements, made at the inlet and outlet of an intermediate product storage tank in an industrial manufacturing process. Both of these measurements were obtained from a computer-based data collection system that failed briefly at hour 41. The missing results were written as "blanks" to an intermediate data file, which was then read by a FORTRAN program that interprets blanks as zeros, giving the sequence of numbers shown in the left-hand pair of plots in Figure 2.16. Applying the simple median replacement strategy discussed in Chapter 4 yields the two cleaned data sequences shown in the right-hand pair of plots. The key point here is that common-mode failure mechanisms can lead to simultaneous outliers in several variables. In cases where possible relationships between these variables are of interest, this potentially confounding relationship between outliers can be extremely damaging. This point is illustrated in Chapter 7, where this example is revisited.

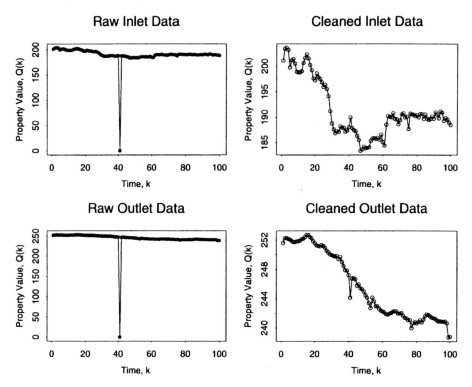

Figure 2.16. *Raw and cleaned product property measurement sequences from the inlet and outlet of an industrial product storage tank.*

2.3.2 Misalignments and software errors

The CAMDA'02 normal mouse dataset discussed in Chapter 1 illustrates that data misalignments or mislabellings can and do arise in real datasets, and the simple simulation-based examples discussed in Chapter 1 illustrate the potentially severe consequences of such misalignments on the results of subsequent analysis. Two common sources of misalignments are mismatches between data file formats and the programs intended to read them, and software errors in "utility" data-handling programs that reformat, combine, or extract records from one or more original data files to create one or more new files, matched to the needs of subsequent analysis routines. The following paragraphs discuss both of these problems.

The first of these difficulties is illustrated in Figure 2.17, which shows four subsets of data records read from a data file with unexpected blank records. Specifically, the original data file contained 33 numerical and character summary variables for each of 18,240 spots from a single cDNA microarray, stored in the form of an Excel™ spreadsheet. From this spreadsheet, a tab-delimited text file was created and subsequently read into a data matrix in an S-PLUS® (Insightful, 2001) analysis environment. Unfortunately, several records in this data file were incomplete: the first occurrence of this problem in the data file occurs at record number 2,874, for which 27 of the 33 summary variables were not available and appear as blank cells in the original spreadsheet. These blank cells cause the S-PLUS

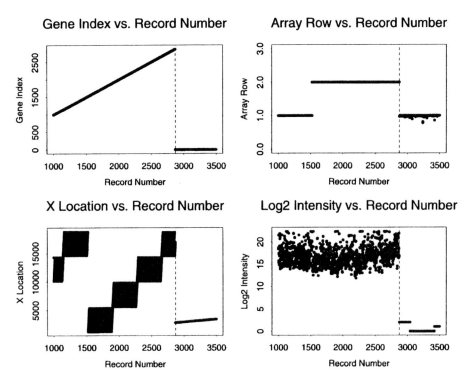

Figure 2.17. *Four examples of misalignment errors caused by unexpected blank records in a microarray data file.*

data-reading procedure to skip to the next nonblank value, resulting in a mislabelling of all data values corresponding to records later than 2,873 in the S-PLUS data object. The plots in Figure 2.17 show 4 of the 33 variables as they appear in the S-PLUS data object, from record number 1,000 to record number 3,500, with the location of the misalignment at record 2,873 shown as a dashed vertical line. The upper left plot shows the gene index (i.e., the spot number on the microarray), which should be equal to the record number for all records. The discontinuity in this plot shows the misalignment error clearly. Note that this particular misalignment error is easily detected, either by noting the discontinuous change in the linear pattern seen before the misalignment or by noting that valid gene index values should be positive integers, but the values appearing after the misalignment error are positive real numbers smaller than 1. Detection of the misalignment error in the array row data shown in the upper right plot is potentially more difficult, since the valid data values appearing before the misalignment error exhibit discontinuous, piecewise-constant behavior, and neither the behavior nor the recorded data values are obviously inconsistent following the misalignment error aside from what appear to be a few outliers, but even these outliers appear somewhat mild. The plot in the lower left shows the x position values for spots on the array, which should exhibit the "checkerboard" character shown in the data values before the misalignment error. After the misalignment error, the range of values seen in the corrupted data record is consistent with the range of the valid data values, but the pattern of variation is inconsistent. Although this problem is visually obvious in the plot of data values shown here, note that the misaligned data values do not appear as univariate outliers in the data sequence. Hence, automated detection of the misalignment error from this data sequence alone would require detection of the violation seen in the *pattern* of the data, as in the problem of detecting time-series outliers discussed in Sec. 2.1.3. Finally, the lower right plot shows the effect of the misalignment at record 2,873 on the $\log_2$ channel 1 optical intensity values recorded for the microarray. The misalignment creates very obvious outliers here, although the source of these outliers as a misalignment error might not be obvious without careful examination since very low intensity outliers do arise from other sources as well.

Fortunately, when S-PLUS reads the data records in this example, it generates error messages that at least provide some indication that a problem has occurred. In the particular procedure used here, these warning messages are saved and not automatically displayed, so it is possible to create a data object that resides within the S-PLUS analysis environment without knowing that a serious data-reading error has occurred. However, many subsequent operations will fail in this case because the original data file contains both character and numeric values. In particular, the misalignment causes some numeric variables to be assigned character values, causing fatal execution errors when numerical operations are attempted. Had the original data file contained only numeric values, these errors might not have occurred, and it is possible that the misalignment error could have gone completely undetected.

The second major source of misalignment errors is sofware errors in the programs frequently used to convert data formats (e.g., from that of the data acquisition program or database to that of the analysis program), to combine data files from different sources, or to extract subsets of data files for detailed analysis. In fact, it is worth repeating the comments of Stivers et al. (2003) quoted in Chapter 1 regarding the source of the misalignment error in the CAMDA normal mouse dataset discussed there:

> *The data used here was assembled into packages, probably manually using an ad hoc database, spreadsheet, or perl script. Under these conditions, it is remarkably easy for the row order to be changed accidentally; for example, by sorting the rows based on the values in an arbitrarily chosen column.*

Since it is so well suited to the necessary data management tasks in large-scale data analysis efforts, it is useful to make a few observations about Perl in particular. Because it is available at no cost, highly portable, and extremely flexible, Perl is especially well suited to problems of merging or splitting files, extracting subsets, and performing a variety of "simple" data format conversions (e.g., character strings to real numbers). Conversely, as Wall, Christiansen, and Orwant (2000, p. xvi) note, it is a standing joke in the Perl community that the next big stock market crash will probably be triggered by a bug in someone's Perl script. These authors include a section on "Common Goofs for Novices," in which they note that the two most common sources of difficulty are, first, failure to use the *warnings pragma*, which causes the generation of error messages in response to a wide variety of program errors, and, second, failure to use the *strict pragma*, which requires variables to be declared before they can be used, among other things.

In addition, these authors list a number of "Universal Blunders," including that of forgetting that all Perl arrays begin at an initial index of zero, not one. Note that this error can cause record misalignments like those shown in Figure 2.17, and recall from the brief discussion given in Chapter 1 that these errors can be extremely damaging, completely obscuring important relationships between variables that our analysis efforts are aimed at uncovering. Another "Universal Blunder" is the confusion of numeric comparison operations with their character string counterparts. As a specific example, note the difference between the following logical comparisons:

- numerical comparison: $123 == 123.0$ is TRUE;

- string comparison: 123 eq 123.0 is FALSE.

Like gross measurement errors, software errors should not arise, but in practice they do. Further, note that in practical terms, software performance is not "continuous" with respect to code changes: "small" changes in a single executable statement can have "large" consequences. The Perl array subscript error discussed in the previous paragraph provides an important illustration of this point. Kaner, Falk, and Nguyen (1999, p. 23) cite a survey by Beizer (1990) on software-testing techniques that estimates the typical frequency of software errors at between 1 and 3 for every 100 executable statements, *after the program has been debugged.* In addition, Kaner, Falk, and Nguyen (1999, p. 13) note:

> *About one in three attempts to fix a program doesn't work or causes a new problem.*

These authors also cite a study by Martin and McClure (1983), who estimate the following probabilities of correctly changing a computer program on the first attempt:

- 50% if the change involves 10 or fewer source statements;

- 20% if the change involves approximately 50 statements.

Finally, Kaner, Falk, and Nguyen (1999) also note that attempts to correct a program bug can have the undesirable side effect of creating new program bugs, or that the presence of certain errors can mask the presence of other errors. For all of these reasons, these authors and many others advocate the development of detailed, systematic software-testing procedures that involve their own design, development, verification, and debugging cycle. The key point here is that many "one-time" data management procedures (e.g., Perl scripts developed to extract records from five different files obtained from three different sources and write them out to a new file, correctly formatted for a custom-built data analysis procedure) are developed in a "quick and dirty" fashion and are typically *not* subjected to the extensive testing regimes advocated by Kaner, Falk, and Nguyen (1999). As a consequence, these programs often represent weak links in the data analysis chain and can be expected to be the source of a number of potentially damaging data anomalies.

In principle and to some extent in practice, many of the difficulties just described may be circumvented through the use of *relational databases*. Although this description is somewhat oversimplified, the basic idea is that relational databases essentially correspond to systems that perform a number of useful algebraic operations on data tables. (For a detailed introduction to the notion of a relational database and its underlying algebraic structure, refer to the book by Date (2000), particularly Chapter 6, where relational algebra is discussed.) Ideally, once (error-free) data tables have been created, relational database software facilitates many of the necessary data management operations discussed in the preceding paragraphs: merging parts of two or more original data tables into a new data table, extracting subsets of larger data tables, and performing various simple data conversions (e.g., unit conversions). Unfortunately, one of the main points that Date (2000) makes in his discussion of real relational database software is that it is almost without exception based on the Structured Query Language (SQL) standard, which does not force conformance with the strict relational model. For example, data tables in the strict relational model cannot have duplicate rows, but the results of SQL queries can (Date, 2000, p. 220). As a consequence, theorems that can be proved on the basis of the relational model may fail to hold in SQL-based implementations (i.e., approximations) of the relational model. The "SELECT *" construct in SQL, discussed by Date (2000, p. 220) and highly relevant to the misalignment problem considered here, permits selection of columns from a data table without specifying their column names explicitly. Date notes that this operation is inherently dangerous in embedded SQL procedures because the interpretation of the column specification "*" can change if a data column is dropped from or added to a table. The key point here is that constructs like "SELECT *" permit the replacement of variable selection by name with the much riskier variable selection by position, which can lead to misalignment errors.

2.3.3   Constraints and hidden symmetries

The problem of collinearity—the existence of an approximate linear relationship between candidate explanatory variables—was discussed in Chapter 1 in connection with the estimation of parameters in a linear regression model. More generally, the following example shows how the inclusion of several closely related explanatory variables in a data prediction model can cause analytical difficulties. That is, suppose we wish to predict the values of a sequence $\{y_k\}$ of response variables from a set $S = \{\mathbf{x}_k\}$ of candidate explanatory vectors. While not all data analysis problems can be cast in this form, many important examples can, including the linear regression problem that arises in one form or another in almost all data analysis application areas. Next, suppose the set S of p component explanatory vectors can be partitioned into three mutually exclusive subsets as follows: $S_A = \{\mathbf{x}_k^A\}$ contains p_A of the p components of $\mathbf{x}_k$, $S_B = \{\mathbf{x}_k^B\}$ contains another p_B components of $\mathbf{x}_k$, and $S_C = \{\mathbf{x}_k^C\}$ contains the remaining p_C components of $\mathbf{x}_k$, where $p = p_A + p_B + p_C$. Further, suppose

$$y_k = f(\mathbf{x}_k^A, \mathbf{x}_k^B) + e_k, \tag{2.11}$$

where $\{e_k\}$ is a sequence of prediction errors that is sufficiently "small" and "well-behaved" for (2.11) to be regarded as an adequate prediction model for the response sequence $\{y_k\}$. Finally, suppose the explanatory vectors $\{\mathbf{x}_k^C\}$ provide the basis for a *perfect* prediction of the explanatory vector $\{\mathbf{x}_k^B\}$. In other words, assume that there exists a vector mapping $\mathbf{G} : R^{p_C} \to R^{p_B}$ such that

$$\mathbf{x}_k^B = \mathbf{G}(\mathbf{x}_k^C). \tag{2.12}$$

It is a trivial consequence of this result that

$$\mathbf{x}_k^B = \mathbf{M}\mathbf{G}(\mathbf{x}_k^C) + (\mathbf{I} - \mathbf{M})\mathbf{x}_k^B \tag{2.13}$$

for *any* $p_B \times p_B$ matrix $\mathbf{M}$. Substituting this result into (2.11) then gives the following fully equivalent family of prediction models:

$$
\begin{aligned}
y_k &= f(\mathbf{x}_k^A, \mathbf{MG}(\mathbf{x}_k^C) + (\mathbf{I} - \mathbf{M})\mathbf{x}_k^B) + e_k \\
&\equiv h(\mathbf{x}_k^A, \mathbf{x}_k^B, \mathbf{x}_k^C; \mathbf{M}) + e_k.
\end{aligned}
\tag{2.14}
$$

Since all of the prediction models in this family, indexed by the arbitrary matrix $\mathbf{M}$, give exactly the same prediction errors, they cannot be distinguished on the basis of goodness-of-fit criteria derived solely from these prediction errors. In the common case where the mappings $f(\cdot)$ and $\mathbf{G}(\cdot)$ are linear, so is the composite map $h(\cdot)$, and the situation just described corresponds to the collinearity problem well known in regression analysis (Belsley, Kuh, and Welsch, 1980; Jobson, 1991).

A closely related point of great practical importance is that even if (2.12) does not hold *exactly* but is merely a good approximation (i.e., if $\mathbf{x}_k^B \simeq \mathbf{G}(\mathbf{x}_k^C)$), then the family of models defined by (2.14) will no longer be exactly equivalent, but they will remain *nearly equivalent*. This situation is also bad because now, even if there is a unique best-fit model with respect to some measure $J(\cdot)$ of the prediction error sequence, very different models— corresponding to very different choices of $\mathbf{M}$ in (2.14)—will be "almost as good" with respect to $J(\cdot)$. Hence, small changes in the original dataset can cause one of these "nearly best fit" models to become the new best-fit model, meaning that these small changes in the dataset can cause large changes in the best-fit model. This point was illustrated in Chapter 1 in connection with the extreme sensitivity of linear regression model coefficients caused by the inclusion of highly correlated explanatory variables in the model.

Ellis (2002) considers a general class of data-fitting problems that includes OLS, least absolute deviations (LAD) (Bloomfield and Steiger, 1983), and PCA (Basilevsky, 1994). He notes that all problems in this class exhibit extreme sensitivity like that just described for datasets that lie too near certain singular configurations. An important consequence is that all of these analysis methods exhibit characteristic families of "bad datasets" such that if the dataset to be analyzed lies too near some member of this family, extreme sensitivity problems will result. Ellis (2002) gives an excellent description of this singularity problem, but he also argues that the "bad datasets" he describes are unlikely to be exactly encountered in practice since they are highly structured and completely characterized by low-order parametric models. Unfortunately, this argument overlooks the possibility that unrecognized constraints may impose considerable structure on real datasets, as in the compositional data analysis problems discussed by Aitchison (1994) and the mixture data problems considered by Cornell (2002). Both cases involve constraints of the general form

$$
\sum_{i=1}^{n} c_i = 1 \quad \Rightarrow \quad c_n = 1 - \sum_{i=1}^{n-1} c_i,
\tag{2.15}
$$

where the variables c_i must satisfy $0 \leq c_i \leq 1$ for all i. Aitchison (1994) notes that constraints of this form arise in many different applications, including problems of materials characterization, economic analysis of budget share patterns, certain medical data analysis problems, and psychological analysis of activity patterns in experimental subjects. The practical importance of this observation lies in the word "unrecognized": important constraints may be unknown to the data analyst, particularly if they involve more than two variables, making them difficult or impossible to see in simple visual examinations of the data. This problem is discussed further in Chapter 4 in connection with data pretreatment.

2.4   Missing data

As discussed in Chapter 1, missing data represent another particularly important type of data anomaly: values that should have been recorded are not included in the available data for one reason or another. Govindarajulu (1999, pp. 347–348) describes the following four approaches to dealing with missing data:

1. Omit all incomplete records from the data analysis.

2. Treat the unknown values as a special category.

3. Reweight the complete records in the analysis to account for the presence of incomplete records.

4. *Impute* the missing data values—replace them with reasonable estimates based on other available data values.

In the autocorrelation example discussed in Chapter 1 (Sec. 1.1.3), it was shown that the first of these options—omitting incomplete records—can be useful in the case of ignorable missing data but not in the case of nonignorable missing data. Since the nonignorable missing data problem is closely related to the problem of sampling bias, these topics are discussed briefly in Sec. 2.4.1. The second option—treatment of missing values as a special category—is closely related to the general question of how missing values are (or should be) represented in a dataset, a topic discussed in Sec. 2.4.2. A particularly insidious aspect of missing data representation is the problem of *disguised missing data*, frequently caused by *idempotent data transformations,* discussed in Sec. 2.4.3. The third option listed above—reweighting the complete data records in the analysis—is necessarily method-specific and is not discussed here; Govindarajulu (1999) regards this option as a variation of the first option and one that he does not recommend. Finally, the fourth option—imputing missing data values—is discussed at length in Chapter 4.

2.4.1   Nonignorable missing data and sampling bias

Recall from the discussion in Chapter 1 that *ignorable* missing data consist of *representative* data values missing from a dataset and that simply omitting these data samples from our analysis generally results in an undesirable but often not unacceptable increase in variability. In contrast, the presence of *nonignorable* missing data either prevents us from obtaining any result at all, as in the autocorrelation example discussed in Chapter 1, or causes large biases in whatever results we do obtain. A characteristic feature of nonignorable missing data is that certain types of data samples are *systematically* omitted from the dataset. This problem is closely related to the biases caused by poorly designed sampling schemes in survey sampling.

One of the most famous examples of this kind of sampling bias is the *Literary Digest* prediction that Landon would defeat Roosevelt in the 1936 U.S. Presidential election, 370 electoral votes to 161 (Huff, 1954, p. 20). This embarrassingly erroneous prediction followed the successful predictions of a number of previous presidential election outcomes, and it was based on the analysis of 2.4 million survey responses. These responses were obtained on the basis of surveys sent by *Literary Digest* to respondents selected randomly from "every telephone book in the United States, from the rosters of clubs and associations, from city directories, from lists of registered voters, classified mail order and occupational data" (Tanur, 1992, p. 57). Unfortunately, this sampling scheme did not adequately represent less affluent voters who, in the midst of the Great Depression, overwhelmingly supported Roosevelt in the 1936 presidential election, enough to elect him by a wide margin.

Sampling bias of the type just described may be viewed as a case of "unrecognized missing data": data values that were not collected corresponded to nonignorable missing data. Frequently, as in the example just described, this difficulty is not detected until after the analysis is complete; indeed, such nonrepresentative sampling problems can be difficult to detect beforehand. In the case of missing data, however, we have the advantage of knowing *something* about the data values that are not available. That is, even if a data record R_k is completely missing, we know at least its record identifier k and we can look for patterns in these values that may suggest systematic omission. More generally, we often have auxiliary data available regarding these missing records, which we can compare with the corresponding data for the nonmissing records to see whether there is any evidence for systematic differences. If the record R_k is incomplete rather than missing entirely, we have greater flexibility in looking for systematic patterns of omission.

Finally, another closely related idea for treating nonignorable missing data—and for determining whether it is ignorable or not—is the use of multiple imputation strategies, discussed in Chapter 4. There, the basic idea is to compare the results we obtain under both "typical" and "nontypical but realistic" replacement values for missing data to see how much they change the analytical outcome.

2.4.2   Special codes, nulls, and disguises

A conceptually trivial but practically important issue is how missing data values should be represented. For example, recall that in the common-mode outlier example discussed in Sec. 2.3.1, missing data values were initially recorded as blanks, which were then converted to zeros by a FORTRAN program. Similarly, the misalignments in the cDNA microarray dataset discussed in Sec. 2.3.2 resulted from blank records in an Excel spreadsheet that were ignored when the spreadsheet data was read into an S-PLUS computing environment. The key point of both of these examples is that "obvious," "standard," or "default" encodings of missing data values in one computational environment may not be recognized as such in another computational environment. This discrepancy can have serious consequences when data records must be shared between different data collection and analysis procedures, as is typically the case in large-scale data analysis tasks.

One way of representing unknown values is with a special code such as "?" or "UNK," but this idea often leads to computational difficulties. For example, simple data transformations such as $y_k = \ln x_k$ or $y_k = \sqrt{x_k}$ that may be very appropriate as a preprocessing step for a sequence of positive numbers will generally fail if x_k assumes a value like ? or UNK. Although this problem can be corrected, it complicates the development of the preprocessing software. An alternative approach that overcomes this difficulty is to encode missing values with a special *numerical* value that effectively converts missing data values into outliers. This approach has the serious disadvantage, however, that it may generate *disguised missing data* that are not clearly distinguishable from nominal (i.e., nonmissing) data values, particularly if a great deal of preprocessing is involved. One of the most common sources of disguised missing data is the presence of idempotent transformations in the data collection and preprocessing system, a topic discussed in detail in Sec. 2.4.3. It is important to note, however, that well-intentioned missing data encoding can also generate disguised missing data values, which can be very difficult to detect.

Missing data values are a particular problem in the context of relational databases, where queries like "Find all records R_k for which field x_k is greater than 100" are common. In this query, the condition $x_k > 100$ is a logical construct that should evaluate to either "TRUE" or "FALSE." If the value of x_k is unknown, however, this condition cannot be evaluated directly. One approach to this problem is to introduce *three-valued logic*, in which logical statements can take the value "TRUE," "FALSE," or "UNKNOWN" if any of the data values involved are NULL, the value assigned to missing data elements. Date (2000) argues strongly against this approach, although it is supported in the SQL standard on which essentially all commercial database software is based. The source of Date's objection is that certain logical expressions can be evaluated even when some data values are unknown, and these expressions yield different results in three-valued logic. As a specific example, consider the query, "Find all records R_k for which $x_k > 100$ and $y_k < 3$." If R_k contains the field $y_k = 5$ and x_k is missing, record R_k should not be retrieved since at least one of the selection conditions is not satisfied. That is, the correct value for "$(x_k > 100)$ AND $(y_k < 3)$" is "FALSE," regardless of the unknown value of x_k. In the three-valued logic described by Date (2000), however, "$x_k > 100$" evaluates to "UNKNOWN," "$y_k < 3$" evaluates to "FALSE," and the final result "UNKNOWN AND FALSE" evaluates to "UNKNOWN" rather than "FALSE." Similarly, in his discussion of the SQL3 language standard, Date (2000, p. 915) notes that if V is a structured data type containing one or more NULL components, the logical expression "$V = V$" evaluates to "UNKNOWN," and the expression "V IS NULL" evaluates to "FALSE." Detection of records with missing (i.e., NULL) components requires evaluation of nonintuitive expressions like

$$E = ((V = V) \text{ IS NOT TRUE}) \text{ IS TRUE}.$$

If E evaluates to "TRUE," then multicomponent data object V either is NULL (i.e., completely missing) or contains NULL components (i.e., incomplete). In the context of developing SQL procedures as part of a data analysis pipeline, note that the need for such constructions only exacerbates the software development difficulties described in Sec. 2.3.2. In particular, note that the logical expression E given above is *not* equivalent to the expression

$$F = ((V = V) \text{ IS FALSE}) \text{ IS TRUE}.$$

Specifically, in three-valued logic, NOT TRUE can be either FALSE or UNKNOWN. Since the logical statement $V = V$ can be either TRUE, when V contains no NULL elements or UNKNOWN, when V does contain NULL elements, the logical statement "$V = V$ IS FALSE" is always FALSE, meaning that the logical variable F defined above always has the value "FALSE."

In summary, the question of how to handle missing data values in practice is a complicated one, with no clear "right answer." Ideally, missing data values should be marked unambiguously as such, but this is usually only possible within a given computational environment. Since large-scale data analysis usually involves transfer of data between environments, the missing data problem is a potential source of many different data anomalies, as the examples discussed in Secs. 2.3.1 and 2.3.2 have demonstrated.

2.4.3 Idempotent data transformations

As noted earlier, *idempotent data transformations* can be responsible for the generation of disguised missing data, motivating the following brief discussion of these transformations. In general, a data transformation $\mathcal{T}$ corresponds to a mapping from one dataset $\mathcal{D}$ into another, say $\mathcal{E}$. Although the most popular data transformations are probably scalar transformations such as logarithms and powers that take one real-valued sequence $\mathcal{D} = \{x_k\}$ into another real-valued sequence $\mathcal{E} = \{y_k\}$, more general transformations like the fast Fourier transform (FFT) are also quite important in practice. Most of these transformations are *invertible*, meaning that an inverse transform $\mathcal{T}^{-1}$ exists and is given by

$$\mathcal{T}^{-1}\mathcal{T}\{x_k\} = \mathcal{T}\mathcal{T}^{-1}\{x_k\} = \{x_k\} \qquad (2.16)$$

for all real-valued sequences $\{x_k\}$ in some specified domain $\mathcal{D}$. An important consequence of invertibility is that no information is lost, since the original data sequence $\{x_k\}$ can be recovered exactly from the transformed data sequence $\{y_k\} = \mathcal{T}\{x_k\}$ via the inverse transformation $\{x_k\} = \mathcal{T}^{-1}\{y_k\}$.

Another important class of data transformations are the *idempotent transformations*, defined by the characteristic

$$\mathcal{T}^2\{x_k\} = \mathcal{T}\{x_k\}, \qquad (2.17)$$

where $\mathcal{T}^2\{x_k\} = \mathcal{T}[\mathcal{T}\{x_k\}]$. That is, the effect of applying an idempotent transformation $\mathcal{T}$ *iteratively* (i.e., twice in succession) to a data sequence is the same as applying it once. More generally, it follows that for any idempotent transformation $\mathcal{T}$, $\mathcal{T}^n\{x_k\} = \mathcal{T}\{x_k\}$ for all integers $n \geq 1$. Probably the best-known example of an idempotent transformation is the *projection* **P** from an n-dimensional vector space into some lower-dimensional vector space. More generally, note that an idempotent transformation $\mathcal{T}$ is invertible if and only if it is the identity transformation, $\mathcal{T}\{x_k\} = \{x_k\}$ for all $\{x_k\}$, since, for any $\{x_k\}$,

$$\mathcal{T}\{x_k\} = [\mathcal{T}^{-1}\mathcal{T}]\mathcal{T}\{x_k\} = \mathcal{T}^{-1}[\mathcal{T}^2\{x_k\}] = \mathcal{T}^{-1}[\mathcal{T}\{x_k\}] = \{x_k\}. \qquad (2.18)$$

Hence, it follows that any nontrivial idempotent mapping causes information loss, since the original data sequence cannot be recovered from the results of the idempotent transformation. The practical importance of this observation is that idempotent transformations of various types arise frequently in both the hardware and the software components of computer-based data acquisition systems, as well as in manual data collection systems.

The relevance of these results to data anomalies is that the range space of an idempotent data transformation can be much "smaller" than the domain. As a consequence, there may be points in the domain that lie far from their transformed values, so if we must take the transformed data values as a representation of the original data values, we may have no way of telling that certain recorded values lie far from these original values.

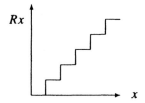

Figure 2.18. *Ideal quantizer.*

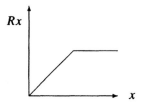

Figure 2.19. *Hard saturation nonlinearity.*

A simple example of a real-valued idempotent data transformation is the ideal quantizer, shown in Figure 2.18. Mathematically, this data transformation is described by the nonlinear input/output relationship

$$
T[x] = \begin{cases}
v_0, & x \le v_0, \\
v_1, & v_0 < x \le v_1, \\
\vdots & \vdots \\
v_{Q-1}, & v_{Q-2} < x \le v_{Q-1}, \\
v_Q, & x > v_{Q-1}.
\end{cases}
\tag{2.19}
$$

Here, $\{v_j\}$ consists of a sequence of $Q+1$ monotonically increasing values from v_0 to v_Q, where Q is a positive integer. The idempotence of this data transformation follows from the observation that $T[v_j] = v_j$ for $j = 0, 1, \ldots, Q$. The importance of this transformation is that it describes the behavior of an ideal analog-to-digital converter; specifically, the ideal behavior of an n-bit analog-to-digital converter is described by (2.19) with $Q = 2^n - 1$.

Another example of an idempotent data transformation is the *hard saturation nonlinearity* shown in Figure 2.19. This scalar idempotent transformation is defined by the function

$$
T[x] = \begin{cases}
v_-, & x \le v_-, \\
x, & v_- < x < v_+, \\
v_+, & x \ge v_+.
\end{cases}
\tag{2.20}
$$

This function represents the simplest model of a data collection system exhibiting a finite range: input values between v_- and v_+ are preserved perfectly, but values outside this range are recorded as the nearest limit of this finite measurement range. Since the actual value of x can be arbitrarily far from this recorded value, it is clear that the recorded value can be grossly in error.

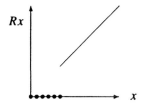

Figure 2.20. *Deadzone nonlinearity.*

Finally, a third example of an idempotent scalar nonlinearity is the *deadzone nonlinearity* shown in Figure 2.20. This transformation may be regarded as dual to the saturation nonlinearity: sufficiently small values of x cause no measurable response, but once x exceeds a specified threshold, the correct value is recorded. Mathematically, the specific deadzone nonlinearity shown in Figure 2.20 is described by the expression

$$T[x] = \begin{cases} 0, & 0 \le x < \theta, \\ x, & x \ge \theta. \end{cases} \tag{2.21}$$

In mechanical systems, stick-slip (i.e., "stiction") phenomena can cause responses to external stimuli that are reasonably well approximated by deadzone nonlinearities. "Stampede phenomena" in socioeconomic systems can cause similar behavior, as in the case of little-known vacation resorts that attract almost no visitors until they are "discovered" by the masses and quickly overrun.

An important software source of idempotent data transformations is *form-based data entry systems.* Ironically, although the motivation for these systems is often the improvement of data quality, they can virtually guarantee the presence of disguised missing data in a large dataset. As a simple but important example, note that many business databases include phone numbers and addresses as part of their customer or client data records. Also, presumably to reduce the probability of errors on the part of data entry personnel, these systems are often form-based with rigid data validation procedures. Specifically, in the case of phone numbers, 10 spaces are typically provided for the 10 digits of a U.S. telephone number, including the area code. Further, because this is important information, it may not be possible to complete the creation of a new customer data record without entering 10 digits into this field. If, however, the customer resides outside the U.S., he or she may not have a 10-digit telephone number. In cases where the form must be completed as part of the transaction, the customer has two options: cancel the transaction or provide a *formally valid* (i.e., 10-digit) telephone number, *despite the fact that this phone number is not the information sought.* In the most favorable cases, a formally valid but obviously nonsensical value would be entered (e.g., the phone number 000 000 0000), but in less favorable cases, a number could be entered that aroused no suspicion at all (e.g., the phone number of the car rental agency or a local pizza shop). Also, note that even in cases where an obviously incorrect but formally valid entry is used to code what is effectively missing data (e.g., the all-zero phone number), subsequent interpretation may be extremely misleading. In particular, note that this information *could* correspond to a person too poor to afford a telephone, to a highly paid corporate executive living outside the U.S., or to someone who refuses to give their phone number. Further,

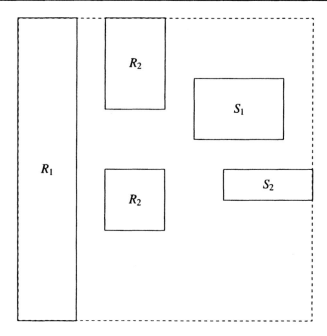

Figure 2.21. *An incomplete composite dataset example.*

note that if the use of "special" missing data codes is likely to cause unpleasantness for data entry personnel, the use of "nonsuspicious" replacement data can be expected to occur frequently.

2.4.4   Missing data from file merging

One practically important source of highly structured missing data is the merging of data files originally collected for different purposes. As a specific example, Kooiman, Kroze, and Ressen (2000) describe a dataset obtained by combining a complete dataset R_1 containing age, gender, and other demographic information for a group of individuals; a second incomplete dataset R_2 containing salary information for a subset of these individuals; a labor survey S_1 containing information on the profession and education for some of these individuals; and a health survey S_2 with education information that overlaps S_1 and that also contains health information for these individuals. If we combine these individual collections into a single large dataset, the result contains significant missing data, which appears in blocks rather than being randomly distributed throughout the dataset.

This point is illustrated in Figure 2.21, which is based on Figure 1 of Kooiman, Kroze, and Ressen (2000). Here, the boxes with solid borders represent the data contained in sets R_1, R_2, S_1, and S_2, while the dashed line represents the *complete* dataset containing all of the variables from these datasets for all individuals. The available data correspond to the union $R_1 \cup R_2 \cup S_1 \cup S_2$ of the individual datasets, while the spaces between the boxes in Figure 2.21 represent the missing data in the combined dataset. This missing portion can be seen to be both substantial and highly structured.

Kooiman, Kroze, and Ressen (2000) describe eight subsets that can be extracted from this combined dataset for analysis, illustrating that they vary enormously in size. For example, the available subset of age, gender, and salary data corresponds to $R_1 \cap R_2$, including approximately 50% of the individuals in the complete dataset, while the available subset of age, gender, education, and health data corresponds to $R_1 \cap S_2$, which includes only about 10% of these individuals. The loss of data in cases like this, arising from the inclusion of several incomplete variables in an analysis, is an extremely important practical problem, discussed further in Chapter 4.

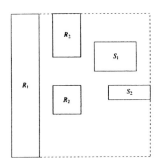

Chapter 3

Univariate Outlier Detection

Two things were emphasized in Chapters 1 and 2. First, outliers are an important practical complication in data analysis. Second, they come in several different varieties. This chapter is devoted to the problem of detecting one of these outlier classes—univariate outliers—for two main reasons. First, univariate outliers are the easiest to detect in a dataset even though, as the examples presented here illustrate, their detection is a nontrivial task. An important advantage of considering the univariate case first is that the results lay the foundation for consideration of the more complicated outlier detection problems discussed in Chapter 4. Second, the GSA framework converts the search for various types of data anomalies into a univariate outlier detection problem, a point discussed further in Chapter 6.

Many different univariate outlier detection procedures have been proposed, but the main three considered here are of the following general form. First, a reference value x_0 and a measure of variation ζ are computed from the data sequence $\{x_k\}$. Then, a threshold parameter t is chosen. Finally, every data value in the sequence $\{x_k\}$ is tested to determine whether it is an outlier according to the rule

$$|x_k - x_0| > t\zeta \implies x_k \text{ is an outlier.} \tag{3.1}$$

To convert this rule into a practical outlier detection procedure, it is necessary to answer the following three questions, and the main purpose of this chapter is to provide some practical guidance in answering them:

1. How do we define the nominal data reference value x_0?

2. How do we define the scale of natural variation ζ?

3. How do we choose the threshold parameter t?

Intuitively, (3.1) says that if observation x_k lies too far from the reference value x_0, it is declared an outlier. The variation measure ζ characterizes the "natural spread" of the data values, giving us a useful basis for calibrating distances from x_0, and the threshold parameter t determines the aggressiveness of the detection procedures. In particular, setting $t = 0$ declares any value different from x_0 an outlier, no matter how small the difference between x_k and x_0, and taking t large enough usually guarantees that no outliers will ever be detected.

Before addressing these questions, three points should be noted. First, not all univariate outlier detection procedures belong to the class defined by (3.1). Motivation for restricting consideration to this class comes from the fact that (3.1) provides a simple, intuitive description of univariate outliers and that this class includes probably the three most common outlier detection procedures seen in practice: the 3σ edit rule, the Hampel identifier, and the standard boxplot outlier detection rule. All three of these procedures are examined in detail in this chapter; for a discussion of other outlier detection procedures, refer to Barnett and Lewis (1994). The second point to note here is that (3.1) assumes that the nominal data values are at least approximately symmetric in their distribution about the central value x_0. It was noted in Chapter 2 in connection with the industrial pressure data example that this working assumption does not always hold, but it was also noted that the question of how to handle outliers in asymmetrically distributed nominal data sequences is not fully resolved. This problem is discussed further in Secs. 3.2.3 and 3.4.3 and revisited in Chapter 8. Finally, the third point is that even univariate outliers come in different varieties, and these different univariate outlier classes can affect the performance of univariate outlier detection procedures in different ways. For this reason, Sec. 3.1 introduces several different mathematical outlier models before Sec. 3.2 describes the three univariate outlier detection procedures considered here. Next, Sec. 3.3 presents a simulation-based GSA case study that compares the performance of these outlier detection procedures in the face of several of the univariate outlier classes introduced in Sec. 3.1. Sec. 3.4 then compares the results obtained using these outlier detection procedures with three real datasets.

3.1   Univariate outlier models

A number of simple mathematical models for univariate outliers have been proposed in the statistics literature, each having somewhat different characteristics. Perhaps the simplest is the *additive outlier model,* which represents a sequence $\{z_k\}$ of observed data values as

$$z_k = x_k + o_k. \tag{3.2}$$

Here, $\{x_k\}$ represents the unobserved nominal data sequence we would like to characterize and $\{o_k\}$ represents a sequence of contaminating data perturbations, equal to zero for most k. Whenever o_k is nonzero, its value is large enough in magnitude relative to the range of variation of the nominal x_k values that z_k is anomalous. This outlier model is popular in the time-series modelling literature (Fox, 1972) because it provides a useful basis for quantifying the influence of outliers on a variety of important dynamic characterizations, including power spectral density estimates (Martin and Thomson, 1982) and estimated time-series model parameters (Denby and Martin, 1979). The nonzero values of the outliers o_k can be either deterministic or random, but if they are random they are usually assumed to be statistically independent of the nominal data sequence $\{x_k\}$. Note that this outlier model was used in the GSA characterizations of moment-based and order–statistic-based estimators presented in Chapter 2. Specifically, the additive outliers o_k were assumed to take the constant value $o_k = +8\sigma$ whenever they were nonzero, where σ was the known standard deviation of the nominal Gaussian data sequence $\{x_k\}$.

Another simple univariate outlier model is the *replacement model,* which describes the observed data sequence $\{z_k\}$ as

$$z_k = \begin{cases} x_k & \text{with probability } 1 - p, \\ o_k & \text{with probability } p. \end{cases} \tag{3.3}$$

As in the additive outlier model, $\{x_k\}$ represents the sequence of nominal values we wish to characterize, but now $\{o_k\}$ represents a sequence of anomalous replacement observations rather than anomalous perturbations of nominal values. This model has also been used in the time-series analysis literature (Martin and Yohai, 1986), where it is written as

$$z_k = (1 - \xi_k)x_k + \xi_k o_k. \tag{3.4}$$

The sequence $\{\xi_k\}$ consists of binary random variables that assume the value $\xi_k = 1$ with probability p and $\xi_k = 0$ with probability $1 - p$. The advantage of representing (3.3) as (3.4) in the context of time-series analysis is that we can describe different *patterns* of outliers by assuming different dependence structures for $\{\xi_k\}$ (i.e., different correlation patterns between ξ_k and ξ_ℓ for $k \neq \ell$). These different patterns can be extremely important in the case of time-series outliers, a point discussed further in Chapter 4.

As in the additive outlier model, the sequence $\{o_k\}$ of anomalous replacement values in the replacement model may be either deterministic or random. An important deterministic example is the *point contamination model,* corresponding to $o_k = \lambda$ for all k. This outlier model is appropriate when intermittent measurement system failures always cause the same value to be recorded, or in the case of numerically coded missing data values, where λ is the special value assigned to missing data observations. Similarly, disguised missing data values originating from any of the mechanisms discussed in Chapter 2 can give rise to point contamination outliers. This model also clearly illustrates the differences between the additive and replacement outlier models. Specifically, taking $o_k = \lambda$ for all k in the replacement model always yields the same anomalous observation, while taking $o_{k'} = \lambda$ whenever it is nonzero in the additive outlier model yields the anomalous subsequence $z_{k'} = x_{k'} + \lambda$, which inherits the variability of the nominal data.

If $\{x_k\}$ is modelled as a random data sequence with density $\phi_n(x)$ and $\{o_k\}$ is modelled as a second, independent, random variable sequence with density $\phi_o(x)$, the replacement model defined in (3.3) may also be represented as a *discrete mixture model* (McLachlan and Bashford, 1988). There, the contaminated sequence $\{z_k\}$ represents a random variable sequence with density $\psi(z)$ given by

$$\psi(z) = (1 - p)\phi_n(z) + p\phi_o(z). \tag{3.5}$$

This representation is extremely useful because it permits a wide range of specific characterizations of the contaminated sequence $\{z_k\}$ in terms of the nominal data distribution, the outlier distribution, and the contaminating fraction p. For example, the population mean of the contaminated data is

$$E\{z\} = (1 - p)E\{x\} + pE\{o\} \equiv (1 - p)\mu_x + p\mu_o, \tag{3.6}$$

where $E\{x\}$ is the population mean of the nominal data and $E\{o\}$ is the population mean of the outliers. This result is a special case of the general moment result

$$E\{z^n\} = (1 - p)E\{x^n\} + pE\{o^n\}. \tag{3.7}$$

Taking $n = 2$ gives the basis for the variance result

$$\text{var } \{z\} = \sigma_z^2 = E\{z^2\} - [E\{z\}]^2$$
$$= (1 - p)\sigma_x^2 + p\sigma_o^2 + p(1 - p)(\mu_x - \mu_o)^2. \tag{3.8}$$

Again, it is instructive to compare the point contamination model with the constant perturbation additive outlier model, both of which may be recast in terms of this two-component mixture model. In the case of point contamination, the outlier distribution $\phi_o(z)$ is degenerate, with variance $\sigma_o^2 = 0$ and mean $\mu_o = \lambda$, the value of the point contamination. Hence, (3.6) predicts a mean shift from the uncontaminated value μ_x to the perturbed value $\mu_x + p(\lambda - \mu_x)$ that depends on both the contamination fraction p and the distance of the point contamination value λ from the uncontaminated mean μ_x. Similarly, point contamination changes the variance from the nominal value σ_x^2 to the contaminated value

$$\sigma_z^2 = (1 - p)\sigma_x^2 + p(1 - p)(\lambda - \mu_x)^2. \tag{3.9}$$

It is interesting to note that point contamination can cause either an increase or a decrease in the variance relative to σ_x^2. In particular, we have

$$\sigma_z^2 > \sigma_x^2 \Leftrightarrow (1 - p)(\lambda - \mu_x)^2 > \sigma_x^2. \tag{3.10}$$

Intuitively, this result means that point contamination near the uncontaminated mean ($\lambda \simeq \mu_x$) can decrease the variance, while point contamination sufficiently far from the mean ($|\lambda| >> |\mu_x|$) can cause arbitrarily severe variance inflation.

For the constant perturbation additive outlier model, $\phi_o(z) = \phi_n(z + \lambda)$, meaning that $\mu_o = \mu_x + \lambda$ and $\sigma_o = \sigma_x$. Substituting these results into (3.6) shows that here the mean shifts from μ_x to $\mu_x + p\lambda$, compared with $\mu_x + p(\lambda - \mu_x)$ for the point contamination model. In the case of the additive outlier model, the effect on the variance is always inflationary, increasing σ_z^2 from the nominal value σ_x^2 to the larger value

$$\sigma_z^2 = \sigma_x^2 + p(1 - p)\lambda^2. \tag{3.11}$$

A particularly important special case of the two-component mixture density model for outliers defined by (3.5) is the *contaminated normal model* (Huber, 1981). In this model, the nominal data sequence is assumed normally distributed with mean μ and variance σ^2, while the outliers are assumed to exhibit a different distribution. In the simplest and most popular special case, this contaminating distribution is also assumed to be Gaussian, with a possibly distinct mean v and a possibly distinct variance τ^2. This normally contaminated Gaussian model is often denoted $CN(\mu, \sigma^2, v, \tau^2, p)$, where p is the contamination percentage. A particularly common special case is the contaminated noise model advocated by Huber (1981, p. 3), where $\tau = 3\sigma$, $v = \mu$, with $p = \epsilon$ typically assumed to lie between 1% and 10%. This outlier model represents a special case of what Lehmann (1983, p. 357) calls the Tukey model, although he notes that it was discussed by Newcomb at the end of the 19th century. In this model, it is assumed that $\phi_n(z)$ and $\phi_o(z)$ are both Gaussian with the same mean, differing only in that $\phi_o(z)$ has a standard deviation larger than that of $\phi_n(z)$ by a factor of $\gamma > 1$. Note that under this outlier model, there is no mean shift, but the variance is inflated from σ_x^2 to $[1 + (\gamma^2 - 1)p]\sigma_x^2$. For Huber's model, this means that a 10% contamination level causes an 80% variance inflation. Alternatively, similar effects—variance inflation without a mean shift for a Gaussian nominal model—are sometimes modelled with a heavy-tailed non-Gaussian contaminating distribution $\phi_o(z)$ that is symmetric around the uncontaminated mean μ_x (Andrews et al., 1972).

Finally, another important special case of the two-component mixture model for contaminated data is the class of *slippage models* discussed by Barnett and Lewis (1994). In these models, $\phi_o(z)$ has the same form as $\phi_n(z)$, but now differs arbitrarily in mean and has a variance σ_o^2 that is generally as large as or larger than the nominal variance σ_x^2. Note that the additive outlier model with constant perturbation magnitude λ corresponds to the general slippage model with $\sigma_o^2 = \sigma_x^2$. That is, the form of $\phi_n(z)$ is not specified, but $\phi_o(z) = \phi_n(z + \lambda)$.

3.2 Three outlier detection procedures

Under the assumption of distributional symmetry for the nominal data values made at the beginning of this chapter, the two most obvious choices for the nominal reference value x_0 in (3.1) are the sample mean $\bar{x}$ and the sample median $x^\dagger$. That is, for a symmetric data distribution, the *population mean* (i.e., the expected value of the distribution) and the *population median* (i.e., the 50th percentile of the distribution) are equal, so the corresponding sample values represent reasonable estimators for this common value. Other choices are certainly possible, including any one of the 66 other location estimators considered in the Princeton Robustness Study (Andrews et al., 1972), but these two are both the best-known and among the simplest choices for x_0. Similarly, there exist a variety of possible choices for the scale estimate ζ in (3.1) (Rousseeuw and Croux, 1993), but the following three are perhaps the most obvious choices: the standard deviation $\hat{\sigma}$, the MAD scale estimator S introduced in Chapter 1, and the IQD Q, also introduced in Chapter 1. These choices lead to the following three outlier detection procedures, each examined in detail throughout the rest of this chapter:

1. the 3σ edit rule: $x_0 = \bar{x}, \zeta = \hat{\sigma}$;

2. the Hampel identifier: $x_0 = x^\dagger, \zeta = S$;

3. the standard boxplot outlier rule: $x_0 = x^\dagger, \zeta = Q$.

Before discussing these outlier detection rules in detail, it is worth noting the following points. First, a location estimator $x_0 = T\{x_k\}$ is said to be *equivariant* if

$$T\{ax_k + b\} = aT\{x_k\} + b \qquad (3.12)$$

for all real numbers a and b. Similarly, a scale estimator $\zeta = S\{x_k\}$ is said to be equivariant if

$$S\{ax_k + b\} = |a|S\{x_k\}, \qquad (3.13)$$

again for all real a and b. These notions and their consequences are discussed further in Chapter 5, but here it is enough to note the following. Suppose $z_k = ax_k + b$ for some real $a \neq 0$ and any real b. Further, suppose $x_0 = T\{x_k\}$ is an equivariant location estimate and $\zeta = S\{x_k\}$ is an equivariant scale estimate. Next, suppose x_j is declared an outlier in the sequence $\{x_k\}$ by the detection rule (3.1) based on these location and scale estimates. Defining $z_0 = T\{z_k\}$ and $\zeta_z = S\{z_k\}$ as the corresponding location and scale estimates for the sequence $\{z_k\}$, it follows that

$$
\begin{aligned}
|z_j - z_0| &= |ax_j + b - ax_0 - b| \\
&= |a| \cdot |x_j - x_0| \\
&> |a|\zeta = \zeta_z.
\end{aligned}
\tag{3.14}
$$

In other words, outlier detection procedures based on equivariant location and scale estimates are insensitive to (nonsingular) affine transformations. This observation has two important consequences. First, it simplifies certain analytical characterizations, a point illustrated in Sec. 3.2.1. Second, the points declared as outliers in a data sequence are invariant under arbitrary rescalings of measurement units: outliers detected in a sequence of temperatures in degrees Celsius correspond to those in the same sequence reexpressed in degrees Fahrenheit or degrees Kelvin. All of the outlier detection procedures considered in this book satisfy these equivariance conditions.

3.2.1 The 3σ edit rule

Without question, one of the most popular approaches to outlier detection is the 3σ edit rule, dating back at least to the end of the 19th century (Wright, 1884). The basic idea is that, if a data sequence $\{x_k\}$ is well approximated by an i.i.d. sequence of Gaussian random variables with mean μ and standard deviation σ, the probability of observing a value x_k farther than three standard deviations from the mean is only about 0.3%. The historical and continuing popularity of the Gaussian working assumption for nominal data sequences provides the basis for the following answers to the three questions posed at the beginning of this chapter:

1. Choose the mean $\bar{x}$ as the nominal reference value x_0.

2. Choose the estimated standard devation $\hat{\sigma}$ as the scale parameter ζ.

3. Choose $t = 3$ based on the above reasoning.

Because of its connection with the Student's t-test, this outlier detection procedure has also been called the *extreme studentized deviation (ESD) identifier* (Davies and Gather, 1993). Unfortunately, despite its historical importance and intuitive appeal, this outlier detection procedure tends to be ineffective in practice. The basic difficulty is that the presence of outliers in the dataset can cause substantial errors in both the estimated mean and the estimated standard deviation on which the procedure is based. As a consequence, the deviations $x_k - x_0$ tend to be too small in magnitude and the scale estimate ζ tends to be much too large, making outliers harder to detect than they should be.

This phenomenon is called *masking* (Barnett and Lewis, 1994; Davies and Gather, 1993; Rousseeuw and Leroy, 1987), and it is illustrated further in the following simple analytical result. Suppose an observed sequence $\{z_k\}$ consists of $N + P$ real values, the first N of which have mean $\bar{x}_N = 0$ and standard deviation $\hat{\sigma}_x = 1$. Note that there is no loss of generality in this assumption since, given any nominal data sequence $\{v_k\}$ with arbitrary mean $\bar{v}$ and nonzero standard deviation $\hat{\sigma}_v$, we can always apply the affine transformation

$x_k = (v_k - \bar{v})/\hat{\sigma}_v$ to obtain a sequence $\{x_k\}$ with the desired characteristics. Since the 3σ edit rule is an equivariant outlier detection procedure, this renormalization of the data does not influence its performance. Next, suppose the last P points in the sequence $\{z_k\}$ are point contamination outliers with the common value $z_k = \lambda$. The mean of the composite sequence $\{z_k\}$ is then given by

$$\bar{z} = \frac{1}{N+P} \sum_{k=1}^{N+P} z_k = \frac{1}{N+P}[N\bar{x}_N + P\lambda] = \left(\frac{P}{N+P}\right)\lambda \equiv p\lambda, \qquad (3.15)$$

where p represents the contamination fraction, assumed here to satisfy $0 < p < 1/2$. Similarly, the estimated variance of the observed sequence $\{z_k\}$ is

$$\hat{\sigma}_z^2 = \frac{1}{N+P-1} \sum_{k=1}^{N+P} (z_k - \bar{z})^2$$

$$= \frac{1}{N+P-1} \left\{ \sum_{k=1}^{N} (x_k - p\lambda)^2 + \sum_{k=N+1}^{N+P} (\lambda - p\lambda)^2 \right\}. \qquad (3.16)$$

Simple algebraic manipulation reduces this expression to the final result

$$\hat{\sigma}_z^2 = \left[\frac{N+P}{N+P-1}\right](1-p)(1+p\lambda^2). \qquad (3.17)$$

The ESD outlier detection condition may be rewritten as

$$|z_k - \bar{z}| > t\hat{\sigma}_z \quad \Leftrightarrow \quad (z_k - \bar{z})^2 > t^2\hat{\sigma}_z^2. \qquad (3.18)$$

Expressing this condition in terms of the above results for $\bar{z}$ and $\hat{\sigma}_z^2$ gives the general detection condition

$$(z_k - p\lambda)^2 > \left[\frac{N+P}{N+P-1}\right](1-p)(1+p\lambda^2)t^2. \qquad (3.19)$$

Now, suppose z_k is one of the outliers in this data sequence, implying $z_k = \lambda$. This point will be correctly identified as an outlier if

$$(1-p)^2\lambda^2 > \left[\frac{N+p}{N+p-1}\right](1-p)(1+p\lambda^2)t^2$$

$$\Rightarrow (1-p)\lambda^2 > \left[\frac{N+p}{N+p-1}\right](1+p\lambda^2)t^2 > p\lambda^2 t^2$$

$$\Rightarrow 1 - p > pt^2. \qquad (3.20)$$

Note that, although this last inequality is not tight, it does represent a necessary condition for z_k to be declared an outlier. Further, this condition may be rewritten in the more easily interpretable form

$$p < \frac{1}{1+t^2}. \qquad (3.21)$$

Taking $t = 3$, it follows that the usual 3σ edit rule fails completely (i.e., cannot detect any outliers in the dataset) at point contamination levels greater than 10%. Conversely, this observation means that the 3σ edit rule cannot detect a single isolated outlier in a sequence of fewer than $N = 10$ observations, no matter how aberrant. This behavior may be seen in the microarray data example discussed at the beginning of Chapter 1 (Figure 1.1), where the visually obvious outlier in a sequence of eight measurements is not detected by the 3σ edit rule.

In the robust statistics literature, a data characterization is said to *break down* if its performance can be made arbitrarily poor by the presence of enough anomalous data points. Rousseeuw and Leroy (1987, p. 9) present a brief historical discussion of this idea in the context of an estimator T that acts on a data sequence $\{x_k\}$ of N data values to give a parameter estimate $\hat{\theta}$. The definition they adopt is that proposed by Donoho and Huber (1983) for the *finite sample breakdown point* of the estimator T, which can be any vector-valued estimator computed from any real-valued or multivariate data sequence $\{x_k\}$. Let $\{z_k\}$ denote a data sequence obtained by replacing any m of the original data values x_k with arbitrary vectors of the same dimension, and define $\beta(m; T, \{x_k\})$ as the worst-case bias that can be caused by any such contamination, i.e.,

$$\beta(m; T, \{x_k\}) = \sup_{z_k} \; \|T(\{z_k\}) - T(\{x_k\})\|, \qquad (3.22)$$

where the supremum is taken over all possible replacements of m original data values. If, as often happens, this worst-case bias is infinite, the estimator T is said to have broken down and the finite sample breakdown point of T is defined as the smallest contamination fraction m/N that can cause an infinite worst-case bias. It is well-known that both the sample mean and the usual standard deviation estimator have finite sample breakdown points of $1/N$. That is, a single anomalous data point can completely dominate either of these estimates in any dataset, no matter how large. Since this contamination fraction approaches zero in the limit of large N, estimators exhibiting this behavior are typically said to exhibit a 0% breakdown point. In the context of outlier detection procedures, Davies and Gather (1993) define the *masking breakdown point* of any such procedure as the minimum number of anomalous data observations k that, when added to a nominal data sequence of length N, can cause the estimator to break down. In this context, they define breakdown as failure to identify an arbitrarily large outlier as such and they show that the ESD identifier exhibits a masking breakdown point of 0%.

3.2.2   The Hampel identifier

Since, as noted in the preceding discussion, the masking sensitivity of the 3σ edit rule is a consequence of the outlier-sensitivity of the estimated mean μ and the standard deviation $\hat{\sigma}$, it is logical to seek outlier-resistant alternatives. The obvious alternative to the mean is the median $x^\dagger$, and one attractive alternative to the standard deviation is the MAD scale estimate S introduced in Chapter 1. Taking $x_0 = x^\dagger$ and $\zeta = S$ in the general outlier detection rule of (3.1) leads to the *Hampel identifier* (Davies and Gather, 1993), named in honor of F.R. Hampel, who described the useful properties of the MAD scale estimator S (Hampel, 1985).

Because the median and MAD scale estimator both have much lower outlier-sensitivities than the mean and standard deviation, the Hampel identifier is generally much more effective than the 3σ edit rule, a point further illustrated by the examples discussed in Secs. 3.3 and 3.4. Davies and Gather (1993) show that any outlier detection rule based on equivariant location and scale estimates exhibits a masking breakdown point of at most 50%, and they show that the Hampel identifier achieves this best possible performance with respect to masking. Unfortunately, the MAD scale estimator does exhibit a form of undesirable behavior that can cause the Hampel identifier to perform badly for some datasets. Specifically, note that the MAD scale estimate is identically zero if more than 50% of the data observations x_k have the same value. In contrast, since it is a scaled sum of squared deviations from the mean, the usual standard deviation estimate $\hat{\sigma}$ can only be zero if *all* of the x_k observations have the same value. Under the common working assumption that the data sample $\{x_k\}$ is drawn from a continuous probability distribution, all x_k values are necessarily distinct (i.e., the probability that $x_k = x_\ell$ for any $k \neq \ell$ is zero). In practice, however, saturation effects, quantization effects (e.g., recording temperatures with only 0.1-degree resolution), and other phenomena can give rise to identical data values. In cases where these effects are severe enough to cause the MAD scale estimate to *implode* (i.e., to give the estimate $S = 0$), the Hampel identifier will declare *any* value distinct from the median to be an outlier, regardless of its distance from the median.

This difficulty is closely related to the phenomenon of *swamping* (Davies and Gather, 1993), a complementary problem to the masking phenomenon discussed in Sec. 3.2.1. More specifically, swamping refers to the problem of declaring normal data observations to be outliers. Davies and Gather (1993) define the *swamping breakdown point* of an outlier detection procedure as the minimum number of anomalous observations that must be added to a dataset to cause a nominal data observation to be declared an arbitrarily large outlier. The authors note that the swamping breakdown point can be anywhere between 0% for outlier detection procedures that are severely susceptible to swamping and 100% for procedures that are completely immune to swamping. Further, they show that there is an inherent trade-off between masking and swamping: an outlier detection procedure that exhibits the best possible masking breakdown point of 50% can at most exhibit a swamping breakdown point of 50%. Finally, Davies and Gather (1993) show that the Hampel identifier achieves this best possible compromise behavior, while the ESD identifier is completely immune to swamping (i.e., exhibits a swamping breakdown point of 100%). Unfortunately, the authors also show that the most pessimistic possible performance is also achievable, describing an outlier detection rule that exhibits both 0% masking and 0% swamping breakdown points.

3.2.3   Quartile-based detection and boxplots

Another possible outlier-resistant scale estimator is the IQD Q introduced in Chapter 1. Recall that x_L denotes the lower quartile, $x_{(0.25)}$, and x_U denotes the upper quartile, $x_{(0.75)}$. The IQD is given by $Q = x_U - x_L$, and for a symmetric data distribution, the median lies midway between x_L and x_U. Hence, for a symmetric distribution,

$$\begin{array}{l} Q = x_U - x_L \\ x^\dagger = (x_U + x_L)/2 \end{array} \quad \Rightarrow \quad \begin{array}{l} x_U = x^\dagger + Q/2 \\ x_L = x^\dagger - Q/2. \end{array} \tag{3.23}$$

These observations suggest taking $x_0 = x^\dagger$ and $\zeta = Q$ in the general outlier detection rule given in (3.1).

A practical disadvantage of this outlier detection strategy relative to the Hampel identifier is that Q is not as outlier-resistant as the MAD scale estimate S. In particular, while S can tolerate anything less than 50% contamination, Q breaks down at contamination levels greater than 25%. Still, Q has much better outlier-resistance than $\hat{\sigma}$, which can be made arbitrarily large by a single aberrant data observation. Like the MAD scale estimate, the IQD Q also yields a zero value if more than 50% of the x_k observations have the same value, regardless of the other data values. Consequently, the outlier detection procedure based on $x^\dagger$ and Q is also prone to swamping, like the Hampel identifier.

A practical advantage of the outlier detection procedure just described is that, unlike either the 3σ edit rule or the Hampel identifier, it has a simple extension to asymmetric data distributions. Specifically, the default outlier detection procedure used in the boxplots generated by the S-PLUS statistics package (Insightful, 2001) is to declare x_k an outlier under either of the two conditions

$$x_k > x_U + 1.5Q \;=\; 2.5x_U - 1.5x_L,$$
$$x_k < x_L - 1.5Q \;=\; 2.5x_L - 1.5x_U. \tag{3.24}$$

Note that for an asymmetric distribution, the median $x^\dagger$ can lie anywhere between x_L and x_U, raising the possibility of cutoff limits for upper and lower outliers that are not symmetric about the median. This idea is examined further in Sec. 3.4 and revisited in Chapter 8.

Finally, note that for the symmetric case, the boxplot outlier detection procedure defined in (3.24) may be rewritten as

$$|x_k - x^\dagger| > 2Q. \tag{3.25}$$

Since Q must be divided by 1.35 to obtain an unbiased estimate of the standard deviation for Gaussian data, these $\pm 2Q$ outlier detection limits correspond to approximately $\pm 2.7\sigma$, reasonably consistent with the popular 3σ edit rule discussed in Sec. 3.2.1. More generally, since it is an appropriate outlier detection procedure for symmetrically distributed data, the following outlier detection procedure will be referred to as the *symmetric boxplot rule:*

$$|x_k - x^\dagger| > tQ \;\Rightarrow\; x_k \text{ is an outlier.} \tag{3.26}$$

The general case, appropriate to asymmetric distributions, will be referred to as the *asymmetric boxplot rule:*

$$x_k > x_U + tQ \Rightarrow x_k \text{ is an upper outlier;}$$
$$x_k < x_L - tQ \Rightarrow x_k \text{ is a lower outlier.} \tag{3.27}$$

3.3   Performance comparison

The following sections compare the performance of the three outlier detection procedures described in Sec. 3.2 for several of the univariate outlier models introduced in Sec. 3.1. The overall formulation of the case study is described in Sec. 3.3.1 and detailed results are presented in Secs. 3.3.2 through 3.3.5 for increasing contamination levels.

3.3.1 Formulation of the case study

The main scenarios compared in this case study correspond to the standard forms of the three outlier detection rules presented in Sec. 3.2, along with a slight modification of the standard boxplot rule. Specifically, results are compared for the following detection procedures:

A. the 3σ edit rule: $x_0 = \bar{x}$, $\zeta = \hat{\sigma}$, $t = 3$;

B. the corresponding Hampel identifier: $x_0 = x^\dagger$, $\zeta = S$, $t = 3$;

C. the standard symmetric boxplot rule: $x_0 = x^\dagger$, $\zeta = Q$, $t = 2$;

C'. rule C with threshold $t' = 3/1.35 \simeq 2.22$, corresponding to the replacement $\hat{\sigma} \rightarrow Q/1.35$ in the 3σ edit rule.

Associated with each scenario is a matched set of subscenarios, each corresponding to a different univariate outlier model. In fact, each of these subscenarios corresponds to a different special case of the contaminated Gaussian mixture model introduced in Sec. 3.1. Specifically, these subscenarios are

0. the uncontaminated reference case, $CN(0, 1, 0, 1, p)$;

1. Huber's measurement noise model, $CN(0, 1, 0, 9, p)$;

2. the slippage model, $CN(0, 1, 4, 9, p)$;

3. the additive outlier model with $\lambda = 4$, $CN(0, 1, 4, 1, p)$;

4. the additive outlier model with $\lambda = 8$, $CN(0, 1, 8, 1, p)$;

5. the point contamination model with $\lambda = 8$, $CN(0, 1, 8, 0, p)$.

Here, p represents the contamination level, which will be taken as 1% ($p = 0.01$), 5% ($p = 0.05$), or 15% ($p = 0.15$) in all cases except the uncontaminated reference case, which does not depend on p. Scenario/subscenario pairs will be denoted by number and letter combinations (e.g., Scenario A1 corresponds to the 3σ edit rule applied to Huber's measurement noise model).

The sampling scheme for each scenario generates $m = 100$ statistically independent datasets, each of length $N = 100$, with the distribution specified by the subscenario designation. The descriptor $d(\cdot)$ used to compare performance within and across scenarios is the absolute number of outliers detected, $\hat{N}_{out}$. Ideally, we expect $\hat{N}_{out} = pN$, and deviations from this value indicate performance degradation of the outlier detection procedure under consideration. Because the results obtained here are integers, typically varying over a fairly restricted range, the boxplots normally used in presenting GSA results will be replaced with tables of values, which are more informative in this case.

3.3.2 The uncontaminated reference case

Although it is important for an outlier detection procedure to find the outliers present in a dataset, it is also important that this procedure *not* detect too many outliers in an uncontaminated dataset. Table 3.1 summarizes the number $\hat{N}_{out}$ of outliers detected by each of the

$\hat{N}_{out}$	Rule A	Rule B	Rule C	Rule C'
0	83	72	46	71
1	16	14	23	18
2	1	11	18	7
3	0	2	7	3
4	0	1	4	1
5	0	0	0	0
6	0	0	2	0

Table 3.1. *Number of outliers detected, $\hat{N}_{out}$, by each of the four detection rules considered here in* 100 *uncontaminated datasets, each of length* $N = 100$.

four procedures considered here for Subscenario 0. Rule A exhibits the best performance for this case, corresponding to the fact that the 3σ edit rule exhibits the best swamping behavior of the four procedures considered here. It gives the correct result, $\hat{N}_{out} = 0$, in 83% of the cases considered here. Only once does it detect more than a single outlier, and it never detects more than two outliers. In contrast, the Hampel identifier only gives the correct result 72% of the time, it detects more than one outlier in fourteen cases, and it finds as many as four outliers in this example. The standard boxplot identifier Rule C is much worse in this case, only obtaining the correct result 46% of the time and detecting as many as six outliers in two cases. For comparison, Rule C' does much better, giving results that are quite close to those of the Hampel identifier and suggesting the use of a more conservative (i.e., larger) threshold value than the standard boxplot rule. For this reason, subsequent comparisons consider only Rules A, B, and C'.

3.3.3   Results for 1% contamination

For datasets of size $N = 100$, 1% contamination corresponds to the presence of a single outlier, a special case of considerable historical importance (Barnett and Lewis, 1994). The following discussion compares the performance of the three outlier detection rules considered here in each of the five contamination subscenarios defined in Sec. 3.3.1.

Table 3.2 summarizes the results obtained with Rule A, the 3σ edit rule, for each of these five scenarios. The correct result $\hat{N}_{out} = 1$ for this case is marked with the symbol "⤳" and it is clear from the results presented in Table 3.2 that the performance of the 3σ edit rule is a strong function of the outlier scenario considered. In particular, note that the performance of this procedure is perfect in Scenario 5, corresponding to a single point contaminant of magnitude $+8\sigma$ in a standard Gaussian dataset of size $N = 100$. Similarly, the performance of this procedure is nearly perfect for Scenario 4, corresponding to an additive outlier of the same magnitude. In fact, these two cases correspond to the most glaring of the outlier scenarios considered here and are therefore the easiest to handle: it will be seen that although the overall performance varies significantly among the three outlier detection rules considered here, these two cases uniformly give the best results for all three rules. Scenario 3 corresponds to a weaker version of Scenario 4, having the same basic mechanism (i.e., the additive outlier model), but with a smaller-amplitude outlier. Not surprisingly, the 3σ edit rule fails to find any outliers under this scenario in 17 of 100 cases. Scenario 2 corresponds to a slippage model that may be regarded as a "noisy" version of Scenario 3 since the contamination is more variable in Scenario 2 (standard deviation 3)

$\hat{N}_{out}$	Scenario 1	Scenario 2	Scenario 3	Scenario 4	Scenario 5
0	53	30	17	0	0
⤳ 1	45	69	79	99	100
2	2	1	2	1	0

Table 3.2. *Performance of the 3σ edit rule for the five scenarios considered here, at the 1% contamination level.*

$\hat{N}_{out}$	Scenario 1	Scenario 2	Scenario 3	Scenario 4	Scenario 5
0	49	28	17	0	0
⤳ 1	31	53	61	73	69
2	18	15	17	21	19
3	2	3	4	5	9
4	0	1	1	1	1
5	0	0	0	0	2

Table 3.3. *Performance of the Hampel identifier for the five scenarios considered here, at the 1% contamination level.*

than in Scenario 3 (standard deviation 1). Comparing the results for Scenarios 2 and 3, it is clear that the noisier slippage model (Scenario 2) is more difficult to handle, as the fraction of undetected outliers increases from 17% for Scenario 3 to 30% for Scenario 2. Scenario 1 corresponds to the popular heavy-tailed measurement noise model advocated by Huber (1981), which may be regarded as a less extreme version of the slippage model since there is now no difference in means and the outliers are characterized only by a larger standard deviation than the nominal observations. Not surprisingly, this case is the most difficult for the 3σ edit rule, which fails to detect any outliers in a majority of the cases (53%). Finally, note that the 3σ edit rule very seldom detects more outliers than are present in the data sample, consistent with the results presented earlier concerning its favorable swamping behavior.

Table 3.3 presents the corresponding results obtained using the Hampel identifier for the same five scenarios at the 1% contamination level. Three conclusions are apparent from a comparison of these results with those just presented for the 3σ edit rule. First, a comparable degree of dependence on scenario is seen for both procedures: Scenarios 4 and 5 give the best results, Scenario 1 gives the worst results, and Scenarios 2 and 3 are intermediate, with Scenario 3 giving somewhat better results than Scenario 2. Second, the 3σ edit rule gives uniformly better results than the Hampel identifier at this contamination level, although it is important to emphasize that this contamination level corresponds to the case of a *single* outlier in the dataset, so there is no possibility of masking effects. This point is important since it is these masking effects that ultimately render the 3σ edit rule useless. Third, the swamping behavior is clearly much worse for the Hampel identifier than for the 3σ edit rule: in the five scenarios considered here, the tendency for the Hampel identifier to detect too many outliers is always worse than that of the 3σ edit rule.

Finally, Table 3.4 summarizes the corresponding results obtained with Rule C', the modified boxplot identification procedure. As with the other two outlier detection procedures considered here, a strong dependence on outlier scenario is observed, with the same general ordering: Scenarios 4 and 5 give the best results, Scenario 1 gives the poorest results, and

$\hat{N}_{out}$	Scenario 1	Scenario 2	Scenario 3	Scenario 4	Scenario 5
0	76	52	52	1	0
⤳ 1	24	48	48	99	97
2	0	0	0	0	3

Table 3.4. *Performance of the modified boxplot identifier for the five scenarios considered here, at the 1% contamination level.*

$\hat{N}_{out}$	Scenario 1	Scenario 2	Scenario 3	Scenario 4	Scenario 5
0	11	1	2	0	0
1	53	20	21	0	0
2	31	43	37	0	0
3	5	29	35	1	0
4	0	7	5	33	0
⤳ 5	0	0	0	66	100

Table 3.5. *Performance of the 3σ edit rule for the five scenarios considered here, at the 5% contamination level.*

Scenarios 2 and 3 are intermediate in difficulty. Interestingly, the results obtained with the modified boxplot rule are essentially as good as those obtained for the 3σ edit rule for Scenarios 4 and 5, and much better than those obtained with the Hampel identifier for these cases. Conversely, the results are generally poorer for the other three scenarios than those obtained with the Hampel identifier. In fact, the results obtained by the modified boxplot rule are arguably the worst of the three for Scenario 1. Finally, it is interesting to note that essentially no swamping is evident in these results: only for Scenario 5 does the modified boxplot rule ever detect more than the 1 outlier that is present in these datasets, and this occurs in only 3 of 100 cases.

3.3.4   Results for 5% contamination

Increasing the contamination level from 1% to 5% gives the results summarized in Tables 3.5 through 3.7. An important difference between these two cases is that, with 5% contamination, multiple outliers are now present in the dataset, so that classical masking phenomena (i.e., the presence of one or more outliers hiding the presence of others in the dataset) are now possible, in contrast to the 1% contamination case just considered.

The results obtained using the 3σ edit rule are summarized in Table 3.5, and a number of significant conclusions are immediately apparent. First, the pronounced dependence on scenario seen in the 1% contamination results is even more pronounced here. In particular, the performance of this outlier identifier is *perfect* in Scenario 5: the correct number of outliers is obtained in every case. Performance remains good for Scenario 4, but not nearly as good: one third of the time, only four outliers are detected instead of five, suggesting that the masking effect discussed previously can depend significantly on the outlier scenario considered. Indeed, masking effects become quite pronounced in Scenarios 1, 2, and 3, where the 3σ edit rule *never* identifies the correct number of outliers. Instead, the 3σ edit rule consistently declares too few outliers, consistent with both its sensitivity to masking effects and its insensitivity to swamping effects. Also, the sensitivity of this outlier detection

$\hat{N}_{out}$	Scenario 1	Scenario 2	Scenario 3	Scenario 4	Scenario 5
0	9	1	1	0	0
1	36	7	1	0	0
2	31	19	6	0	0
3	9	26	30	0	0
4	9	28	29	0	0
⤳ 5	5	16	24	85	83
6	1	1	6	9	12
7	0	2	3	6	3
8	0	0	0	0	1
9	0	0	0	0	1

Table 3.6. *Performance of the Hampel identifier for the five scenarios considered here, at the 5% contamination level.*

$\hat{N}_{out}$	Scenario 1	Scenario 2	Scenario 3	Scenario 4	Scenario 5
0	29	4	12	0	0
1	45	21	31	0	0
2	21	31	23	0	0
3	5	28	18	0	0
4	0	12	11	1	0
⤳ 5	0	4	5	99	99
6	0	0	0	0	1

Table 3.7. *Performance of the modified boxplot identifier for the five scenarios considered here, at the 5% contamination level.*

procedure to masking effects is clear from a comparison of the results for 5% contamination shown here with those for 1% contamination presented in Sec. 3.3.3. In particular, with the exception of Scenario 5, where the results are perfect in both cases, the results obtained at 5% contamination are uniformly poorer than those obtained at 1% contamination.

Table 3.6 shows the results obtained with the Hampel identifier for the five scenarios considered here, at the 5% contamination level. As in all of the other results presented here, these again illustrate the significant difference in difficulty of outlier detection in these five scenarios. Although the Hampel identifier does not achieve the perfect performance of the 3σ edit rule in Scenario 5, the results it does achieve are uniformly better than those for the 3σ edit rule in all of the other four scenarios. Having said this, it is again worth noting that the performance of the Hampel identifier is rather poor for Scenarios 1, 2, and 3, where the wrong number of outliers is identified a majority of the time. In fact, a useful comparative performance measure here is the fraction of the cases where 5 ± 1 outliers are identified. Under Scenario 3, this number is 59% for the Hampel identifier versus 5% for the 3σ edit rule, while under Scenario 2, this number is 45% for the Hampel identifier versus 7% for the 3σ edit rule. The extreme difficulty of Scenario 1 is also evident from this comparison: the Hampel identifier only achieves this result 15% of the time, while the 3σ edit rule never does this well.

Finally, Table 3.7 summarizes the results obtained using the modified boxplot rule. As in the case of 1% contamination, this procedure achieves nearly perfect results under Scenarios 4 and 5, and substantially poorer results for Scenarios 1, 2, and 3. Using the

$\hat{N}_{out}$	Scenario 1	Scenario 2	Scenario 3	Scenario 4	Scenario 5
0	2	2	56	86	100
1	18	6	40	13	0
2	41	39	4	1	0
3	29	41	0	0	0
4	9	12	0	0	0
5	1	0	0	0	0

Table 3.8. *Performance of the 3σ edit rule for the five scenarios considered here, at the* 15% *contamination level.*

same evaluation criterion just considered for the Hampel identifier, the modified boxplot procedure identifies 5 ± 1 outliers in 100% of the cases in Scenarios 4 and 5, in only 16% of the cases in Scenarios 2 and 3, and never in Scenario 1. Also, like the 3σ edit rule, the modified boxplot rule appears largely immune to swamping effects in these examples, since it almost never identifies more outliers than are actually present (i.e., in 1 case out of 500 considered).

3.3.5 Results for 15% contamination

Although some may regard 15% contamination as excessive, real datasets do regularly exhibit contamination levels this high or higher. As a specific example, the industrial flow rate dataset considered in Sec. 3.4.2 exhibits a contamination level of approximately 20%. Further, developments in the general area of high-breakdown estimators, discussed further in Chapter 4, aim at achieving the highest possible breakdown point (50%) to permit consideration of contamination levels approaching this limit. Here, 15% contamination is considered as a compromise between the high-breakdown limit and the single outlier scenarios considered in Sec. 3.3.3. Outlier detection results for the five contamination scenarios considered here with $p = 0.15$ are summarized in Tables 3.8 through 3.10.

Table 3.8 summarizes the results obtained with the 3σ edit rule for this highly contaminated situation, comparing the same five scenarios as before. There are two striking results from this table. First, the 3σ edit rule never even comes close to identifying the correct number of outliers: the most outliers ever detected is $\hat{N}_{out} = 5$, occurring only for a single case out of 500, with most results falling between $\hat{N}_{out} = 0$ and $\hat{N}_{out} = 3$. Second, the role of the "easy" and "hard" scenarios appears dramatically reversed here: no outliers are ever detected in Scenario 5, and outliers are only detected 14% of the time in Scenario 4. It could be argued that Scenario 3 is somewhat better than Scenario 4, with Scenario 2 best and Scenario 1 second-best, although this would be stretching the point in view of the extremely poor performance observed overall. Note that the observed result for Scenario 5 is a consequence of the mathematical result presented in Sec. 3.2.1 establishing the complete breakdown of the 3σ edit rule for point contamination levels in excess of 10%.

The results obtained with the Hampel identifier are shown in Table 3.9, and it is clear that these results are dramatically different from those obtained with the 3σ edit rule for this case. In particular, note that for Scenarios 4 and 5, the Hampel identifier obtains the range of results $\hat{N}_{out} = 15 \pm 1$ in 99% of the cases, whereas the 3σ edit rule never identified any

$\hat{N}_{out}$	Scenario 1	Scenario 2	Scenario 3	Scenario 4	Scenario 5
0	1	0	0	0	0
1	2	0	0	0	0
2	13	0	2	0	0
3	20	1	2	0	0
4	21	0	8	0	0
5	17	5	10	0	0
6	14	14	7	0	0
7	7	18	8	0	0
8	3	23	18	0	0
9	1	10	11	0	0
10	0	12	11	0	0
11	1	12	10	0	0
12	0	4	6	0	0
13	0	0	5	0	0
14	0	1	1	1	0
⇝ 15	0	0	1	97	95
16	0	0	0	1	4
17	0	0	0	1	1

Table 3.9. *Performance of the Hampel identifier for the five scenarios considered here, at the* 15% *contamination level.*

$\hat{N}_{out}$	Scenario 1	Scenario 2	Scenario 3	Scenario 4	Scenario 5
0	8	0	26	0	0
1	23	0	29	0	0
2	29	3	10	0	0
3	20	12	19	0	0
4	12	14	8	0	0
5	4	21	2	0	0
6	4	16	4	0	0
7	0	20	1	0	0
8	0	9	1	0	0
9	0	2	0	0	0
10	0	1	0	0	0
11	0	2	0	0	0
12	0	0	0	0	0
13	0	0	0	3	0
14	0	0	0	11	0
⇝ 15	0	0	0	86	100

Table 3.10. *Performance of the modified boxplot rule for the five scenarios considered here, at the* 15% *contamination level.*

outliers for Scenario 5 and only once identified more than a single outlier for Scenario 4. As in all of the other cases considered here except for the 3σ edit rule with 15% contamination, Scenario 1 is the most troublesome, with Scenarios 2 and 3 intermediate but still giving rather poor results. For example, $\hat{N}_{out}$ assumes values 15 ± 5 for 34 cases under Scenario 3, for 29 cases under Scenario 2, but only for 1 case under Scenario 1.

To conclude this example, Table 3.10 summarizes the results obtained with the modified boxplot rule. As with the Hampel identifier, the results obtained under Scenarios 4 and 5 are extremely good; in fact, they are perfect for Scenario 5 and extremely close (i.e., $\hat{N}_{out} = 15 \pm 1$) 97% of the time for Scenario 4. Again, results obtained under Scenarios 1, 2, and 3 are really rather poor, but interestingly in this case the worst results appear to be obtained under Scenario 3 rather than Scenario 1. Also, it is interesting to note that, while the Hampel identifier occasionally identifies too many outliers in the dataset, the modified boxplot estimator considered here never does. Indeed, this behavior appears to be characteristic of this procedure: in the 1500 cases summarized here (3 contamination levels $\times$ 5 outlier scenarios $\times$ 100 simulations per scenario), the modified boxplot rule only detected more outliers than were present 4 times. In contrast, the Hampel identifier detected more outliers than were present in the dataset 171 times out of 1500 simulations.

3.3.6   Brief summary of the results

The results just presented emphasize a number of important features of the outlier detection problem. First and foremost, none of the three procedures compared here—the 3σ edit rule, the Hampel identifier, and the modified boxplot rule—emerged as universally superior. In particular, the relative performance of these procedures was seen to depend strongly on both the contamination level and the character of the outliers in the dataset. The classical 3σ edit rule emerges as the method of choice in the absence of outliers or in the presence of very few outliers (e.g., the historically popular single outlier assumption). As shown in Sec. 3.2.1, however, this procedure breaks down badly at moderate to high contamination levels. In fact, the interaction between contamination level and outlier scenario is extremely strong: high-concentration point contamination was detected perfectly or almost perfectly by the modified boxplot and Hampel identification procedures, while the 3σ edit rule broke down completely, detecting no outliers at all in the dataset. Finally, although the results presented here did not demonstrate this fact, the relative performance of these procedures also depends on the character of the nominal data sequence $\{x_k\}$.

Perhaps the most disconcerting conclusion of this comparison is that the contaminated error model favored by Huber (1981) was always the most difficult to deal with using any of the three outlier detection procedures considered here, aside from the total breakdown of the 3σ edit rule at high point contamination levels. In retrospect, this result is not surprising since some of the samples generated by the contaminating distribution in this mixture model will be perfectly consistent with the nominal data subsequence. In fact, under this model, *contaminants* (i.e., samples drawn from the $N(0, 3\sigma)$ distribution) can only be expected to exceed the 3σ limits about 68% of the time. Scaling the number of *potentially detectable* outliers by this factor generally improves the level of agreement for Scenario 1, but even after this attempted correction of the results, agreement is still poor. The key point is that the outlier detection procedures described here exhibit performance that is strongly scenario-dependent, posing the question of what constitutes a reasonable contamination scenario. This vitally important question is revisited in Chapter 8.

3.4   Application to real datasets

The results presented in Sec. 3.3 give useful insight into the comparative performance of the three outlier detection procedures described in Sec. 3.2 under a variety of circumstances. The

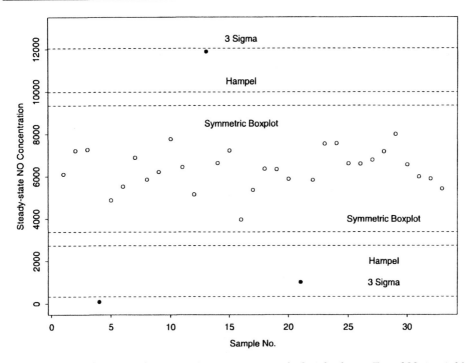

Figure 3.1. *Steady-state NO concentration, fuel-rich phase, $T = 300$ (variable 47). Outliers detected with the Hampel identifier are catalyst samples 4, 13, and 21 and are marked with solid circles. The dashed horizontal lines indicate the upper and lower outlier detection limits for the 3σ edit rule, the Hampel identifier, and the standard symmetric boxplot rule.*

following subsections examine the results obtained with these outlier detection procedures for three real datasets.

3.4.1   The catalyst dataset

This first example compares the results obtained with the 3σ edit rule, the Hampel identifier, and the modified boxplot rule for the catalyst dataset examined in Chapter 2. The primary motivation for considering this small dataset (33 data points) is that it provides a realistic comparison of the results obtained with these outlier detection rules in a setting where detailed follow-up examination of the results is relatively easy. Also, large datasets are often composed of many similar but not identical replications of datasets like this one, as in the microarray example considered in Chapter 1, which may be usefully viewed as 9,120 different 16-observation datasets to be jointly characterized. In such cases, characterization at the level of detail considered in the present example is not feasible, but it is critically important to base the characterization of such datasets, necessarily mostly automated, on reasonable outlier detection procedures.

Figure 3.1 shows the 33-point catalyst dataset considered in Chapter 2, with horizontal lines indicating the upper and lower detection limits computed from this dataset for the following three outlier detection procedures:

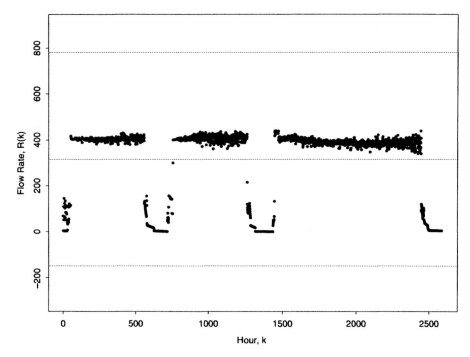

Figure 3.2. *Hourly average flow rate measurements from an industrial manufacturing process, with 3σ edit rule outlier limits shown as dashed lines.*

1. the 3σ edit rule: $x_0 = \bar{x}$, $\zeta = \hat{\sigma}$, $t = 3$;

2. the Hampel identifier: $x_0 = x^\dagger$, $\zeta = S$, $t = 3$;

3. the standard symmetric boxplot rule: $x_0 = x^\dagger$, $\zeta = Q$, $t = 2$.

As in the examples considered previously, the 3σ edit rule is the least aggressive, declaring only the smallest value (sample $k = 4$) to be an outlier. The Hampel identifier and the symmetric boxplot rule both find the same three outliers (samples $k = 4$, 13, and 21), all of which are visually well separated from the other 30 data values. Note that the symmetric boxplot limits are somewhat more conservative than those for the Hampel identifier, but this difference partially reflects the fact that $\pm 2Q \sim \pm 2.7\sigma$, whereas $\pm 3S \sim \pm 3\sigma$. In particular, the scaled IQD estimate of the standard deviation for this dataset is $Q/1.35 \simeq 996$, while $S \simeq 1{,}208$, about 20% larger. For comparison, the usual standard deviation estimate gives $\hat{\sigma} \simeq 1{,}951$, almost twice the scaled IQD.

3.4.2 The flow rate dataset

Figure 3.2 shows a plot of 2,589 hourly average flow rate measurements from an industrial manufacturing process. One of the reasons for considering this example is that it is highly contaminated, with approximately 20% outliers. Here, the classification is unambiguous because the source of the visually obvious anomaly in this dataset is known, so we can say

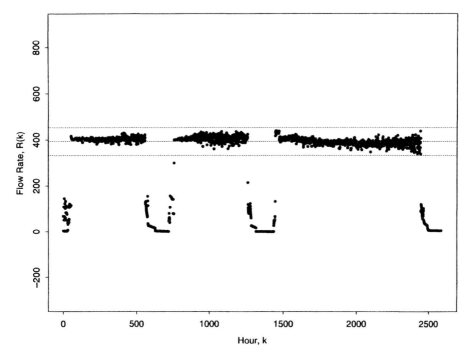

Figure 3.3. *Hourly average flow rate measurements from an industrial manufacturing process, with the Hampel identifier outlier limits shown as dashed lines.*

with certainty which data points are outliers and which ones correspond to normal process operation. Specifically, in normal process operation, flow rates fluctuate around $R(k) \sim 400$, but this data record is long enough to encompass both periods of normal operation and several process shutdowns (note that 2,589 hours is approximately three months). In particular, periods during which $R(k) \simeq 0$ correspond to times when the process is not operating, so the flow rate is zero. Further, since the manufacturing process is a large one, the shutdown and start-up procedures take several hours, explaining the intermediate flow rates before and after each of the episodes when $R(k) \simeq 0$.

Figure 3.2 shows the results obtained when the 3σ edit rule is applied to this dataset. Here, masking effects are pronounced enough that no outliers are detected at all, consistent with the results derived at the end of Sec. 3.2.1: since this dataset contains more than 10% outliers, the 3σ edit rule fails completely. Conversely, the fact that the lower cutoff limit corresponds to a *negative* flow rate should be grounds for suspicion here since negative flow rates correspond to reversals of flow direction, which are physically impossible in the situation considered here.

In contrast, the Hampel identifier achieves a perfect separation of the nominal operating data from the shutdown episodes in this example. This point is illustrated in Figure 3.3, which shows the median and the Hampel identifier cutoff limits. This figure is plotted on the same scale as Figure 3.2 to emphasize the dramatic difference in performance of these two outlier detection procedures. The symmetric boxplot rule (not shown) gives results that are virtually identical to those obtained with the Hampel identifier. Again,

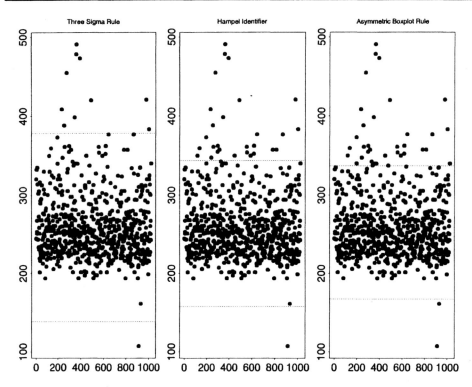

Figure 3.4. *Three plots of the industrial pressure dataset, each with a different pair of outlier detection limits: one for the 3σ edit rule, one for the Hampel identifier, and one with the asymmetric boxplot identification rule.*

a significant part of the difference between these outlier detection procedures may be seen in the three standard deviation estimates on which they are based: $\hat{\sigma} \simeq 155$, $S \simeq 20$, and $Q/1.35 \simeq 25$.

3.4.3 The industrial pressure dataset

Figure 3.4 shows three plots of the industrial pressure dataset considered in Chapter 2 to illustrate the problem of outliers in asymmetrically distributed data. The leftmost plot shows the upper and lower 3σ edit rule outlier detection limits as dashed horizontal lines. This procedure declares 10 points above the mean as outliers, along with the single smallest point. As noted in the discussion of this dataset in Chapter 2, however, this dataset appears quite asymmetric in its distribution, and the points declared as upper outliers by the 3σ edit rule actually appear much more consistent with the overall dataset than the two smallest values do.

The central plot in Figure 3.4 shows the upper and lower cutoff limits for the Hampel identifier as horizontal dashed lines. Here, the lower threshold almost declares the second-smallest data value as a lower outlier, but not quite. Unfortunately, the upper outlier detection threshold for the Hampel identifier is smaller than that for the 3σ edit rule, so even more points are declared upper outliers. Overall, these results are arguably worse than those obtained with the 3σ edit rule for this example.

Finally, the rightmost plot in Figure 3.4 shows the upper and lower cutoff limits obtained with the *asymmetric* boxplot rule for $t = 3/1.35 \simeq 2.22$, chosen so that all three outlier detection procedures ideally correspond to $\pm 3\sigma$ detection limits. Here, both of the visually suspicious points in the lower tail of the data distribution are declared lower outliers, but the upper outlier detection limit also becomes slightly more conservative relative to the Hampel identifier, so even more points are declared as upper outliers by this procedure. Careful comparison of the cutoff limits for the Hampel identifier and the asymmetric boxplot rule reveal that the difference between the lower limits is somewhat larger than the difference between the upper limits. This observation confirms the asymmetry of the asymmetric boxplot rule, but the effect is quite modest for this dataset. Overall, this example serves to further illustrate the difficulties of outlier detection in asymmetrically distributed data sequences, previously noted in Chapter 2 and discussed further in Chapter 8.

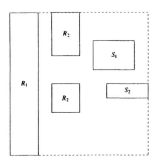

Chapter 4

Data Pretreatment

The term *data pretreatment* refers to a range of preliminary data characterization and processing steps that precede detailed analysis using standard methods. The three main pretreatment tasks considered here are the elimination of *noninformative variables*, the treatment of missing data values, and the detection and treatment of outliers. The problem of univariate outlier detection was treated in detail in Chapter 3, but the question of how to treat these outliers once we have detected them was not considered. The approach adopted here is to view univariate outliers as missing valid data values once they have been detected, permitting us to adopt any of the missing data treatment strategies described in this chapter. Also, since Chapter 3 did not consider more complicated outlier classes such as multivariate or time-series outliers, they are discussed here. Finally, a fourth data pretreatment approach that is sometimes very useful is to perform one or more detailed preliminary analyses whose expected outcome is known, and this strategy is also briefly discussed here.

These discussions are organized as follows. Sec. 4.1 considers the problem of noninformative variables, defining different classes, illustrating the undesirable consequences of retaining them in an analysis, and making connections with the closely related problem of collinearity. Next, Sec. 4.2 considers a range of strategies for treating missing data, including simple omission, single imputation, and multiple imputation. Sec. 4.3 considers the problem of time-series outliers, building on the results presented in Chapter 3 and emphasizing imputation strategies that come from the nonlinear digital filtering literature. Sec. 4.4 considers the multivariable outlier detection problem, for which a variety of approaches have been proposed in the robust statistics literature. Finally, Sec. 4.5 briefly considers the use of more detailed preliminary analysis as a pretreatment strategy, emphasizing the roles of auxiliary variables and prior knowledge.

4.1 Noninformative variables

In real datasets, it often happens that some of the variables included are of little or no use in the analysis we wish to perform. This situation can arise for a number of different reasons, leading to the different classes of noninformative variables discussed and illustrated in Secs. 4.1.1, 4.1.2, and 4.1.3. As the examples discussed in Sec. 4.1.3 demonstrate, it is

usually best to omit variables that are clearly noninformative before detailed analysis of a
dataset, but problems can arise if we are overzealous in eliminating as "noninformative"
certain variables that actually belong in the analysis. Since a number of specific results are
available for the OLS regression problem concerning the consequences of either retaining
noninformative variables in our analysis or omitting informative ones, Sec. 4.1.4 presents a
brief summary of these results. Although the detailed results are OLS-specific, some of the
general conclusions are not and they provide us with some useful insight into how to deal
with these problems in practice.

4.1.1   Classes of noninformative variables

In searching for noninformative variables to be omitted from a particular data analysis effort,
it is useful to distinguish three different classes of noninformative variables. An *externally
noninformative variable* is one that is known to be irrelevant based on detailed subject
matter knowledge. *As the following example illustrates, this classification is an inherently
dangerous one, since even the most astute subject matter expert can be wrong.* A colleague
(McClure, 1985), analyzing a collection of operating data for an industrial manufacturing
process, was attempting to explain significant quality variations between different manufacturing batches of the same product. Unable to find a satisfactory explanation in terms of
the physical variables that were believed to be most relevant, he color-coded the results by
the identity of the operator running the process. From this display, it was immediately clear
that operator identity was the key explanatory variable: the product batches produced by
one operator were consistently superior to the rest. This discovery was the source of some
consternation to the management of the manufacturing plant, who were considering disci-
plinary actions against this operator for poor performance. In the end, it was determined
that this operator was consistently deviating from the standard operating procedure for the
process, leaving it in one condition significantly longer than specified in order to give himself a longer break. Subsequent revision of the standard operating procedure to leave the
process longer in this condition resulted in a uniform quality improvement. The fate of the
operator who was ultimately responsible for this quality improvement is lost in history.

A second class is the *inherently noninformative variable*, defined as one that cannot
influence our analysis results in any useful way, regardless of the nature of that analysis.
Three important subsets of this class are

1. completely missing variables;

2. constant variables: $x_k = c$ for all k;

3. duplicated variables: $y_k = x_k$ for all k.

It should be clear that, in the absence of auxiliary information (e.g., some basis for distinguishing between ignorable and nonignorable missing data), a variable that is completely
missing (Case 1) is of no use in analyzing a dataset, although it is important to bear in mind
that missing values can be disguised in a dataset, most obviously by encoding them as some
constant numerical value. It should also be clear that Case 2 ($x_k = c$ for all k) is inherently
noninformative since this variable cannot be used to explain observed differences in any
other variables in the dataset. Hence, again, unless some external interpretation of the constant value of this variable is available (e.g., "c seems like an unusually large value for x"),

it can have no influence on our analysis results. Case 3 (exact duplication) may be viewed as the extreme limiting case of the collinearity problem introduced in Chapter 1 and discussed further in Sec. 4.1.4. Conversely, it is important to note that duplication is not equivalent to transformation, in general, since the variables x_k and $y_k = f(x_k)$ for some nonlinear function $f(\cdot)$ can both be useful in analyzing a dataset, *provided this relationship is recognized at the outset.* In fact, an important special case of this situation is polynomial regression, which includes several distinct powers of a single variable x_k in the same data model.

As a practical matter, we will generally classify a variable as inherently noninformative if it satisfies the above criteria for *almost* all observations in a dataset. As a specific example, Pearson (2001a) considers the analysis of a small physical property dataset, consisting of 21 observations of each of 6 variables. One of these 6 variables is "ionicity," which has the value 0 for 17 of the 21 observations, with values 0.04, 0.25, 0.25, and 0.50 for the other 4 observations. Hence, it seems reasonable to regard ionicity as a noninformative variable in this case, since only 3 of 21 observations seem to exhibit "significant" ionicity values.

An *application-specific noninformative variable* or, equivalently, an *application-irrelevant variable* is one that may be informative in other contexts but contains no information relevant to the application at hand. This situation arises most commonly when a large dataset is partitioned into subsets for subsequent analysis. In this case, it may happen that one or more variables from the original dataset become inherently noninformative when restricted to these subsets. As a specific example, if a variable x serves as a basis for partitioning the dataset into classes for subsequent analysis (e.g., "anomalous" versus "nonanomalous" or some other multilevel partitioning), this variable will typically be constant across each of the subsets generated. Again referring to the small dataset discussed in the previous paragraph (Pearson, 2001a), in the subset of 17 nonionic cases for which ionicity is 0, this variable becomes fully noninformative. Similarly, another partitioning of this dataset considered by Pearson (2001a) generated a subset of size 10 in which another of the 6 physical property variables (specifically, density) is constant, becoming noninformative for any analysis of this subset. Finally, note that the concept of an application-irrelevant variable defined here is closely related to the first step of the procedure described by Dasu and Johnson (2003) for prescreening candidate key fields in corrupted relational databases. There, a fundamental requirement is that each record in the database have a unique key, but an exhaustive search for candidate keys in a large database can be undesirably expensive in processing time. Hence, Dasu and Johnson (2003, p. 174) recommend a four-step search procedure that begins with the following preprocessing step:

> *Eliminate all fields which are obviously bad candidates, for instance, because there are few unique values, because they are mostly null, because they have (an unacceptable) data type such as floating point, and so forth.*

4.1.2 A microarray dataset

To place the notions just described in a realistic framework, consider the following example of a real microarray dataset, which illustrates most of the noninformative variable types defined in Sec. 4.1.1. This dataset contains 18,240 observations for each of 33 variables, corresponding to 601,920 numbers. As noted in previous discussions, only 2 of these 33 variables are usually of primary interest, but analysis of auxiliary variables is sometimes extremely informative, a point discussed further in Sec. 4.5. Of the 31 auxiliary variables in this dataset, the first is a spot identifier, ranging from 1 to 18,240 and corresponding to the data value index k. Another is a character variable that identifies the material spotted on each location on the microarray and, although this variable is quite useful, it is not easy to incorporate directly into standard analysis because it is nonnumeric and it assumes a large number of distinct values (approximately 9,000, corresponding to the unique identifier of each gene spotted on the array, together with identifiers of "BLANK" spots that contain no DNA, and various other "control" spots that have been included).

Four of the remaining 29 auxiliary variables are integers that define each spot on the array according to its position in 1 of 48 subarrays and its position as 1 of 380 spots within each subarray. These values are highly correlated with the x and y position variables that more precisely define the actual locations of the spots on the microarray. Hence, these position variables may be regarded as "near duplicates" of the integer (ideal) location variables and these two sets of variables should probably not be included in our analysis together unless we are attempting to characterize either systematic differences between real and ideal spot locations on the slide or differences between slides. Then, explicit measures of "nonideality" computed from both of these sets of variables might be extremely useful.

The "ignore filter" variable illustrates the notion of an application-irrelevant selection variable noted in Sec. 4.1.1. Specifically, this variable is used to manually flag individual spots on the microarray that appear anomalous on the basis of a visual inspection. This is a binary variable that takes the value 0 whenever the spot is deemed anomalous and 1 otherwise. In the specific microarray dataset considered here, this variable is equal to 0 for 95 of 18,240 spots and 1 for the remaining 18,145 spots. Hence, aside from its possible use in flagging 95 anomalous data values, this variable may be classed as noninformative. In particular, note that if we remove these anomalous records from the dataset, this variable becomes constant and thus inherently noninformative.

The remaining 22 auxiliary variables consist of 11 pairs of variables characterizing the 2 different optical responses measured from each spot on the microarray, including such characterizations as the diameter and area of each spot. For reasons that are not clear, the recorded areas are constant for all spots and both channels in the dataset considered here, making this variable inherently noninformative. Similarly, the variable designated "confidence" for each channel and every spot also assumes a constant value in this dataset, making it inherently noninformative.

4.1.3 Noise variables

Another class of *potentially* noninformative variables is the class of i.i.d. random noise sequences $\{x_k\}$. In practice, this model is an idealization, but it is often a useful one, describing variables that exhibit no information-bearing pattern of regular variation. In cases where these variables are unrelated to other variables in the dataset, they cannot be informative and are a reasonable candidate for elimination in preprocessing. Unfortunately, noninformative variables of this type may be difficult to detect since detection requires an assessment of their relationship to other variables. In particular, the key factor that determines whether these noise variables are informative or not is whether they are associated with response variables or other informative variables that will be included in the analysis. That is, if these variables represent random variations in an uncontrolled but highly influential

variable (e.g., ambient temperature or humidity), they may be important in explaining irregular variations in response variables and are therefore *not* noninformative in the sense
considered here. Similarly, if these variables are strongly associated with other candidate
explanatory variables, the possibility of collinearity arises, a problem discussed further in
Sec. 4.1.4.

While it should be fairly clear that the inclusion of noninformative noise variables
cannot improve data analysis results, the fact that this inclusion can significantly degrade
our results is not as obvious. Indeed, there is a school of thought that argues in favor
of leaving all variables in a dataset, trusting the analysis method to separate the useful
ones from the irrelevant ones. This point is noted by Gordon (1999), who observes that
it is often motivated by a desire not to omit anything important. Unfortunately, he also
presents a clustering example that shows that inclusion of extraneous variables can have
decidedly undesirable consequences. Specifically, he considers a problem in which 42
objects are each characterized by attribute vectors of dimension 8. The first two components
of these attribute vectors clearly partition the objects into three equal-sized, well-separated
classes, as may be seen from a scatterplot of the first component against the second (Gordon,
1999, Figure 2.1). This scatterplot also shows the classifications obtained by applying
the same clustering procedure to the full eight-dimensional attribute vector set, where the
remaining six components of these attribute vectors are independent random variables,
clearly irrelevant to the classification problem of interest. The consequence of including
these extraneous variables is to mix the classifications, assigning objects from each group
erroneously to one of the other two groups.

A very similar example is summarized in Table 4.1, which compares a set of *silhouette
coefficients*, a useful cluster quality measure discussed further in Chapter 6. The key point
here is that larger values indicate stronger evidence in support of a putative clustering result.
In Table 4.1, these values are shown for a clustering obtained by applying the same method
to eight datasets, differing in the number of extraneous noise components included in the
attribute vector for each object. The clustering method used in all cases was the partitioning
around medoids (PAM) procedure of Kaufman and Rousseeuw (1990), discussed further
in Chapter 7, based on Euclidean dissimilarities. As in the example considered by Gordon
(1999), each dataset exhibits a clear inherent cluster structure: the first 3 components of
the attribute vector partition the 75-object dataset into 4 well-separated clusters. The difference between the eight datasets lies in the inclusion of noninformative noise components:
none are included in the first dataset, and subsequent datasets include an increasing number
of random noise components, from one through seven.

The results presented in Table 4.1 compare the average silhouette coefficient values
$\bar{s}$ computed for two different clusterings: the correct result, $k = 4$, and the second-best
result, $k = 2$. In the absence of spurious noise components in the attribute vector, the
correct clustering is clearly favored by the silhouette coefficient over the alternative $k = 2$.
As we include more noise components, however, this difference diminishes until, with
seven noise components, it is only about 1%. In addition, note that the average silhouette
coefficients for both $k = 2$ and $k = 4$ decrease monotonically as more noise variables
are included in the attribute vector describing the objects, suggesting a general decline in
the overall quality of the clustering results. Taken together, this example and that of Gordon
(1999) demonstrate that the inclusion of extraneous variables in a data analysis can cause a
significant degradation of the results.

Noise Components	$\bar{s}$, $k = 2$	$\bar{s}$, $k = 4$
0	0.636	0.750
1	0.619	0.709
2	0.604	0.675
3	0.587	0.638
4	0.579	0.619
5	0.568	0.595
6	0.557	0.573
7	0.548	0.555

Table 4.1. *The influence of extraneous noise components on clustering results.*

4.1.4   Occam's hatchet and omission bias

The clustering examples presented in Sec. 4.1.3 illustrate the advantages of omitting non-informative variables from our data analysis, but the industrial process modelling example discussed in Sec. 4.1.1 demonstrates the difficulty of deciding whether a variable is noninformative or not. It turns out that this problem is closely related to the problems of collinearity discussed in Chapters 1 and 2. In particular, certain popular statistically based methods for deciding which explanatory variables to retain in a regression model tend to give the wrong answer (i.e., suggest omission of variables that should be retained) in the presence of severe collinearity. In addition, since collinearity arises due to strong associations between explanatory variables, it is frequently argued that a subset of these variables should be omitted from the analysis to overcome the collinearity problem. Belsley (1991, p. 301) argues strongly against this strategy, dubbing it "Occam's hatchet," an overzealous abuse of the 14th-century philosopher William of Occam's advice that, given a choice between otherwise equal alternatives, we should prefer the simpler (Occam's razor). As an alternative, Belsley advocates the use of prior information to constrain the solution of regression problems, leading to more reasonable results. Because explicit results are available for the OLS regression problem concerning the effects of both the omission of informative variables and the inclusion of noninformative variables, the following discussion focuses on the OLS regression problem. As noted above, this focus is less restrictive than it appears for two reasons. First, many historically important data analysis problems may be reduced to OLS regression problems. Second, although the detailed results presented here are OLS-specific, many of the general conclusions are not.

In the OLS regression problem, we have a sequence $\{y_k\}$ of response variables that we wish to predict for $k = 1, 2, \ldots, N$ from p explanatory variable sequences $\{x_{ki}\}$ for $i = 1, 2, \ldots, p$. These variables are assumed to be related by the data model

$$y_k = \sum_{i=1}^{p} \theta_i x_{ki} + e_k, \quad k = 1, 2, \ldots, N. \tag{4.1}$$

Here, $\{\theta_i\}$ represents a collection of p unknown parameter values that we wish to estimate from the available data and $\{e_k\}$ represents the sequence of model prediction errors that results when we choose a particular set of values for these parameters. It is convenient to rewrite this set of equations in vector form as

$$\mathbf{y} = \mathbf{X}\theta + \mathbf{e}, \tag{4.2}$$

where $\mathbf{y} \in R^N$ is the vector of observed responses, $\mathbf{X} \in R^{N \times p}$ is the matrix of explanatory variables $\{x_{ki}\}$, $\theta \in R^p$ is the vector of unknown parameters, and $\mathbf{e} \in R^N$ is the vector of model prediction errors e_k. The OLS solution is obtained by choosing $\hat{\theta}$ to minimize the sum of squared prediction errors

$$J(\theta) = \sum_{k=1}^{N} e_k^2 = \mathbf{e}^T \mathbf{e} = (\mathbf{y} - \mathbf{X}\theta)(\mathbf{y} - \mathbf{X}\theta). \tag{4.3}$$

Since this criterion is quadratic in the unknown parameter vector θ, the minimizer $\hat{\theta}$ is unique when it exists and is given by

$$\hat{\theta} = (\mathbf{X}^T \mathbf{X})^{-1} \mathbf{X}^T \mathbf{y}. \tag{4.4}$$

This solution exists whenever $\mathbf{X}^T \mathbf{X}$ is nonsingular, but the problem of collinearity arises when this matrix is nearly singular. Indeed, the term *collinearity* refers to the fact that for the $p \times p$ matrix $\mathbf{X}^T \mathbf{X}$ to be nonsingular, the $N \times p$ data matrix $\mathbf{X}$ must have rank p, meaning that its p columns must be linearly independent. This requirement means that no subset of the p explanatory variables $\{x_{ki}\}$ can be expressed as a linear combination of the others. Collinearity, then, refers to the existence of an approximate linear relationship between a subset of these variables, leading to near-singularity of $\mathbf{X}^T \mathbf{X}$.

In severe cases, this problem can have at least two closely related consequences: large variability of parameter estimates and the extreme sensitivity to small changes in data values discussed in Chapter 1. To see the first of these consequences, note that a standard assumption in regression modelling is that $\{e_k\}$ is a zero-mean sequence with covariance matrix

$$\Sigma = \mathrm{cov}\,\{\mathbf{e}\} = E\{\mathbf{e}\mathbf{e}^T\}. \tag{4.5}$$

Under this assumption, combining (4.2) and (4.4) gives

$$\begin{aligned}
\mathrm{cov}\,\{\hat{\theta}\} &= E\{(\hat{\theta} - \theta)(\hat{\theta} - \theta)^T\} \\
&= E\{(\mathbf{X}^T \mathbf{X})^{-1} \mathbf{X}^T \mathbf{e}\mathbf{e}^T \mathbf{X} (\mathbf{X}^T \mathbf{X})^{-1}\} \\
&= (\mathbf{X}^T \mathbf{X})^{-1} \mathbf{X}^T E\{\mathbf{e}\mathbf{e}^T\} \mathbf{X} (\mathbf{X}^T \mathbf{X})^{-1} \\
&= (\mathbf{X}^T \mathbf{X})^{-1} \mathbf{X}^T \Sigma \mathbf{X} (\mathbf{X}^T \mathbf{X})^{-1}.
\end{aligned} \tag{4.6}$$

It is usually assumed that $\{e_k\}$ is an i.i.d. sequence with finite variance σ^2, implying that $\Sigma = \sigma^2 \mathbf{I}$. Intuitively, this working assumption means that all explanatory variables $\{x_{ki}\}$ required to predict the responses $\{y_k\}$ have been included in the regression model so that the residuals $\{e_k\}$ correspond to a noninformative noise sequence. In this case, (4.6) simplifies to

$$\mathrm{cov}\,\{\hat{\theta}\} = \sigma^2 (\mathbf{X}^T \mathbf{X})^{-1}. \tag{4.7}$$

As noted, the problem of collinearity arises when $\mathbf{X}^T \mathbf{X}$ is nearly singular, meaning that $(\mathbf{X}^T \mathbf{X})^{-1}$ is "large." In particular, note that $\mathbf{X}^T \mathbf{X}$ is nonnegative definite and thus positive definite if it is nonsingular. If we denote the p eigenvalues of $\mathbf{X}^T \mathbf{X}$ by λ_i for $i = 1, 2, \ldots, p$, it follows that the eigenvalues of $(\mathbf{X}^T \mathbf{X})^{-1}$ are $1/\lambda_i$. Hence, the trace of $\mathrm{cov}\{\hat{\theta}\}$ will be given by

$$\mathrm{Tr}\,[\mathrm{cov}\,\{\hat{\theta}\}] = \sigma^2 \,\mathrm{Tr}\,[(\mathbf{X}^T \mathbf{X})^{-1}] = \sigma^2 \sum_{i=1}^{p} 1/\lambda_i. \tag{4.8}$$

Consequently, if one or more eigenvalues of $\mathbf{X}^T\mathbf{X}$ are small, the trace of the covariance matrix will be large. Since the diagonal elements of cov $\{\hat{\theta}\}$ correspond to the variances of the parameter estimates, a large value for this trace implies that one or more of these variances is large.

One important practical consequence of these large variances is the following. If the error sequence $\{e_k\}$ is assumed to be both i.i.d. and normally distributed, it is possible to formulate simple tests of the hypothesis that one or more of the parameters θ_i are equal to zero (Jobson, 1991, p. 229). Note that if we accept this hypothesis, we are effectively declaring variable x_{ki} noninformative and omitting it from the model. The basis for this hypothesis test is the quantity

$$t_i = \frac{\hat{\theta}_i}{\sqrt{s^2[(\mathbf{X}^T\mathbf{X})^{-1}]_{ii}}}, \tag{4.9}$$

which estimates the ratio of θ_i to the standard deviation of its estimation error and should therefore be large in magnitude if $\hat{\theta}_i \neq 0$. Here, s^2 is the variance estimate for the data prediction errors:

$$s^2 = \frac{1}{N-p-1} \sum_{k=1}^{N} \left(y_k - \sum_{i=1}^{p} \theta_i x_{ki} \right)^2. \tag{4.10}$$

Note that the denominator in (4.9) may be large when collinearity is present, making t_i small in magnitude, causing us to declare the parameter θ_i "not significant," and leading us to drop x_{ki} from the model. This effect of collinearity is well known (Belsley, 1991, p. 4).

To see the effects of omitting variables on OLS regression results, suppose the p variables appearing in the model are partitioned as follows: the first $p_1 < p$ are retained and the remaining $p - p_1$ are omitted. It is useful to partition both the data matrix $\mathbf{X}$ and the parameter vector θ into their corresponding parts:

$$\mathbf{y} = \mathbf{X}_1\theta_1 + \mathbf{X}_2\theta_2 + \mathbf{e}, \tag{4.11}$$

where the subscript 1 refers to the retained variables and their associated parameters and the subscript 2 refers to the omitted variables and their associated parameters. The least squares estimate $\hat{\theta}_1$ of θ_1 is obtained directly from (4.4) by simply replacing $\mathbf{X}$ with $\mathbf{X}_1$, and the estimate $\tilde{\mathbf{y}}$ of the data vector obtained using $\hat{\theta}_1$ and assuming (incorrectly) that $\theta_2 = 0$ is then given by

$$\begin{aligned}
\tilde{\mathbf{y}} = \mathbf{X}_1\hat{\theta}_1 &= \mathbf{X}_1(\mathbf{X}_1^T\mathbf{X}_1)^{-1}\mathbf{X}_1^T\mathbf{y} \\
&= \mathbf{X}_1(\mathbf{X}_1^T\mathbf{X}_1)^{-1}\mathbf{X}_1^T\mathbf{X}_1\theta_1 + \mathbf{X}_1(\mathbf{X}_1^T\mathbf{X}_1)^{-1}\mathbf{X}_1^T\mathbf{X}_2\theta_2 + \mathbf{X}_1(\mathbf{X}_1^T\mathbf{X}_1)^{-1}\mathbf{X}_1^T\mathbf{e} \\
&= \mathbf{X}_1\theta_1 + \mathbf{H}_1\mathbf{X}_2\theta_2 + \mathbf{H}_1\mathbf{e}, \tag{4.12}
\end{aligned}$$

where $\mathbf{H}_1 = \mathbf{X}_1(\mathbf{X}_1^T\mathbf{X}_1)^{-1}\mathbf{X}_1^T$. Note that if we drop the subscript, we obtain the so-called hat matrix (Belsley, Kuh, and Welsch, 1980) that "puts the hat on $\mathbf{y}$," i.e., $\hat{\mathbf{y}} = \mathbf{H}\mathbf{y}$.

Since the only random term in (4.12) is the error vector $\mathbf{e}$, it follows that the covariance matrix for $\tilde{\mathbf{y}}$ is given by

$$\text{cov}\{\tilde{\mathbf{y}}\} = \text{cov}\{\mathbf{H}_1\mathbf{e}\} = \mathbf{H}_1\Sigma\mathbf{H}_1. \tag{4.13}$$

Under the common independent error assumption ($\Sigma = \sigma^2 \mathbf{I}_p$), it follows from the idempotence of $\mathbf{H}_1$ (i.e., $\mathbf{H}_1 \mathbf{H}_1 = \mathbf{H}_1$) that

$$\text{cov} \{\bar{\mathbf{y}}\} = \sigma^2 \mathbf{H}_1. \tag{4.14}$$

Taking the trace of this covariance matrix as a measure of the variability of $\bar{\mathbf{y}}$, we have

$$\begin{aligned}
\text{Tr} \{\text{cov} \{\bar{\mathbf{y}}\}\} &= \sigma^2 \text{Tr} \{\mathbf{X}_1 (\mathbf{X}_1^T \mathbf{X}_1)^{-1} \mathbf{X}_1^T\} \\
&= \sigma^2 \text{Tr} \{(\mathbf{X}_1 \mathbf{X}_1^T)^{-1} \mathbf{X}_1^T \mathbf{X}_1\} = \sigma^2 \text{Tr} \{\mathbf{I}_{p_1}\} = p_1 \sigma^2,
\end{aligned} \tag{4.15}$$

where we have made use of the fact that $\text{Tr} \{\mathbf{AB}\} = \text{Tr} \{\mathbf{BA}\}$ for any two square matrices $\mathbf{A}$ and $\mathbf{B}$ of the same dimension n:

$$\text{Tr} \{\mathbf{AB}\} = \sum_{i=1}^{n} [\mathbf{AB}]_{ii} = \sum_{i=1}^{n} \sum_{j=1}^{n} A_{ij} B_{ji} = \sum_{j=1}^{n} \sum_{i=1}^{n} B_{ji} A_{ij} = \sum_{j=1}^{n} [\mathbf{BA}]_{jj} = \text{Tr} \{\mathbf{BA}\}.$$

$$\tag{4.16}$$

Note that if no variables are omitted from the analysis, the partition $\mathbf{X}_2$ is empty and we have $\theta_1 = \theta$, $\mathbf{X}_1 = \mathbf{X}$, and $\mathbf{H}_1 = \mathbf{H}$. Hence, it follows from this result that the trace of the covariance matrix of the full model prediction $\hat{\mathbf{y}}$ is $p\sigma^2$, which is strictly larger than $p_1 \sigma^2$. This result implies that the variability of the predictions from the reduced model is smaller than that of the predictions obtained from the full model. In fact, this result extends to the variance of predictions of any individual response y_i (Jobson, 1991, Sec. 4.1.5), a result that can be proved using the Cholesky factorizations of the $\mathbf{X}^T \mathbf{X}$ and $\mathbf{X}_1^T \mathbf{X}_1$ matrices (Miller, 1990, p. 6).

This last observation has two important practical corollaries. First, note that if we take this argument to its logical conclusion, it follows that the best model will be that involving no explanatory variables. Indeed, any constant prediction model will exhibit zero variance, although the resulting predictions will not generally be useful because the price we pay for this reduced variability is an increased bias. In particular, combining (4.11) and (4.12) leads to the useful result

$$\bar{\mathbf{y}} = \mathbf{y} + [\mathbf{I} - \mathbf{H}_1][\mathbf{X}_2 \theta_2 + \mathbf{e}]. \tag{4.17}$$

It follows on taking the expectation of this result that $\bar{\mathbf{y}}$ is a biased estimator of the observed data vector $\mathbf{y}$, with a bias given by

$$E\{\bar{\mathbf{y}} - \mathbf{y}\} = [\mathbf{I} - \mathbf{H}_1] \mathbf{X}_2 \theta_2 = [\mathbf{I} - \mathbf{X}_1 (\mathbf{X}_1^T \mathbf{X}_1)^{-1} \mathbf{X}_1^T] \mathbf{X}_2 \theta_2. \tag{4.18}$$

There is a corresponding bias in the parameter estimate $\hat{\theta}_1$, which is easily computed by analogous reasoning:

$$\begin{aligned}
E\{\hat{\theta}_1\} &= E\{(\mathbf{X}_1^T \mathbf{X}_1)^{-1} \mathbf{X}_1^T \mathbf{y}\} \\
&= \theta_1 + (\mathbf{X}_1^T \mathbf{X}_1)^{-1} \mathbf{X}_1^T \mathbf{X}_2 \theta_2.
\end{aligned} \tag{4.19}$$

These bias effects are called *omission bias* (Miller, 1990, p. 7) because they arise from the omission of the informative variables defining $\mathbf{X}_2$. Conversely, the second important practical point to note here is that if $\theta_2 = 0$, this omission bias vanishes. Since omission of these variables results in a reduction of variance, one can argue that they should be omitted in this case to improve prediction accuracy—that is, if $\theta_2 = 0$, the variables defining $\mathbf{X}_2$ are truly noninformative and should be omitted from the model.

4.2 Handling missing data

Whether they were missing from the original dataset or removed as "suspicious" points in a preliminary data-cleaning procedure, missing data values arise frequently in practice, as noted in Chapters 1 and 2. The following sections briefly discuss three ways of treating missing data: simple omission, single imputation strategies, and multiple imputation strategies. A fourth alternative—the iterative EM algorithm—is discussed briefly in Chapter 6 (Sec. 6.8.1). In addition, this section also briefly discusses the problem of unmeasured or unmeasurable variables that may be important in the analysis of a dataset.

4.2.1 Omission of missing values

One obvious approach to handling missing data values is to simply omit the corresponding data records from subsequent analysis. In some cases, this approach is quite reasonable and, because of its simplicity, it may be the best available alternative. There are, however, at least three situations where simple omission is *not* a reasonable alternative:

1. if the analysis cannot tolerate missing data values;

2. if the fraction of data records eliminated is excessively large;

3. if the missing data values are nonignorable.

The first situation typically arises when the analysis depends inherently on a regular pattern in the data that is disrupted by missing values. For example, classical spectral estimation procedures assume that data values are regularly sampled in time. Missing data values cause violations of this key working assumption, which can severely bias simple spectral estimates (Pearson et al., 2003). Although it is possible to modify many standard procedures to explicitly correct for these missing data effects, it may be simpler to impute the missing values and proceed with standard analysis methods, particularly if the fraction of missing data is small. Missing data also significantly complicate traditional analysis of variance (ANOVA) for two-way data tables, where similar imputation strategies have been advocated (Sahai and Ageel, 2000, p. 145).

The second situation—unreasonably large data losses—can occur for at least three reasons. The first is that one of the candidate model variables, say x_{ki}, is largely missing. In this case, it may be best to declare this variable noninformative and either omit it from our analysis or seek a surrogate, as in the campaign-spending example of Levitt and Snyder Jr. (1997) discussed in Sec. 4.2.4. The second possible source of large data losses is the combined effects of smaller missing data fractions occurring independently in several different variables that enter the analysis. In particular, suppose that n variables, say x_{k1} through x_{kn}, are to be included together in an analytical model (e.g., a regression model) and that each variable exhibits randomly missing data. Further, let p_i represent the probability that x_{ki} is missing for any given record index k and suppose that the missing value positions are statistically independent for each variable. Under these assumptions, the probability that *none* of the variables x_{k1} through x_{kn} is missing for sample k is

$$P = \prod_{i=1}^{n} (1 - p_i). \tag{4.20}$$

As a specific example, if we are considering a data model involving $n = 4$ variables, each with a missing data frequency of $p_i = 30\%$, the probability that the vector $\{x_{k1}, x_{k2}, x_{k3}, x_{k4}\}$ will be complete (i.e., will have no missing components) is approximately 24%. If we increase n to 8, this probability drops to approximately 6%. In any case, the effects of these compounded data losses render the utility of simple omission highly questionable. The third possible source of large data losses is asynchronous sampling, closely related to the previous example. In this case, the different variables required for a data model are not all acquired under the same conditions (e.g., at the same times or locations). Consequently, the synchronized dataset we desire for analysis is simply not available, mandating some form of interpolation or other imputation strategy.

The third case—nonignorable missing data—was discussed in Chapters 1 and 2. As noted in those discussions, simply omitting nonignorable missing data can either cause severe biases in our analysis results or cause our analysis efforts to fail altogether, as in the autocorrelation example discussed in Chapter 1. The multiple imputation strategies discussed in Sec. 4.2.3 can be helpful in two ways: first, in deciding whether we are possibly faced with a nonignorable missing data problem, and, second, in deciding how to proceed if this appears to be the case.

Finally, there is at least one other situation where simple omission yields unsatisfactory results. Rubin (1987, p. 9) notes that if means, variances, and correlations are estimated via simple omission from a set of variables with different missing entries, the covariance matrix constructed from these individual estimates can be indefinite. This can lead to negative variances in regression analysis or negative eigenvalues in PCA.

4.2.2 Single imputation strategies

Probably the most widely used approach to handling missing data in practice is *single imputation*, in which a missing observation x_{ki} is estimated from related data values that are available. A recent illustration is the microarray data cluster analysis described by Dudoit and Fridlyand (2002), who examined four cancer datasets, two that were complete, one with 3.3% missing data values, and one with 6.6% missing data values. To estimate these missing values, the authors first computed correlation-based dissimilarities for all pairs of genes (based on the nonmissing data), then identified the five nearest neighbors for each gene with a missing response, and finally estimated this missing response value as the average of the five nearest-neighbor responses.

This example illustrates one of the most popular general imputation strategies, that of *mean imputation*, in which missing values are replaced with the mean of an appropriately defined group of nonmissing values. The popularity of this procedure rests on both its simplicity and the fact that it *seems* like a reasonable strategy. There are, however, at least three potential limitations of this strategy, all of which can be important. First, the use of mean imputation generally decreases the variability inherent in the dataset, particularly if the same mean value is used as a replacement for several missing data values (Rubin, 1987, p. 13). The following simple example illustrates this point clearly. Suppose we are given a sequence $\{x_k\}$, nominally of length N, but with M values missing. Denote the average of the nonmissing values by $\bar{x}$, which we define as

$$\bar{x} = \frac{1}{N-M} \sum_{k \in \mathcal{O}} x_k, \tag{4.21}$$

where $\mathcal{O}$ is the set of indices k of the nonmissing data values x_k. Next, consider the simple mean imputation strategy given by

$$\hat{x}_k = \begin{cases} x_k & k \in \mathcal{O}, \\ \bar{x} & k \notin \mathcal{O}. \end{cases} \tag{4.22}$$

The mean of this imputed data sequence is

$$\tilde{x} = \frac{1}{N} \sum_{k=1}^{N} \hat{x}_k = \frac{1}{N} \left[\sum_{k \in \mathcal{O}} x_k + M\bar{x} \right]$$
$$= \frac{1}{N}[(N-M)\bar{x} + M\bar{x}] = \bar{x}. \tag{4.23}$$

Note that the variance estimated from the observed data values $k \in \mathcal{O}$ is given by

$$\hat{\sigma}^2 = \frac{1}{N-M-1} \sum_{k \in \mathcal{O}} (x_k - \bar{x})^2, \tag{4.24}$$

which should be approximately equal to the true variance of the observed data sequence under the following two assumptions: first, N is large enough for this variance estimate to be a good approximation, and, second, the missing x_k values exhibit the same distribution as the observed x_k values. This second assumption is extremely important, corresponding to one of ignorable missing data and representing a practical necessary condition for the use of the imputed mean $\bar{x}$ as a location estimate for the partially observed data sequence. If we estimate the variance of the data sequence from the sequence of imputed values using the standard estimator, we obtain

$$\tilde{\sigma}^2 = \frac{1}{N-1} \sum_{k=1}^{N} (\hat{x}_k - \bar{x})^2 = \frac{1}{N-1} \left[\sum_{k \in \mathcal{O}} (x_k - \bar{x})^2 + M \cdot 0 \right]$$
$$= \left(\frac{N-M-1}{N-1} \right) \hat{\sigma}^2 \simeq \left(1 - \frac{M}{N} \right) \hat{\sigma}^2, \tag{4.25}$$

where the final approximation is reasonable for even modest-sized datasets. Hence, $\tilde{\sigma}^2$ is smaller than $\hat{\sigma}^2$ by an amount that depends on the fraction of missing data.

The second important feature of mean imputation is that it can be implemented in different ways by averaging over different sets of candidate replacement values, and the reasonableness of the results can depend strongly on this choice. This point is illustrated by Bernaards (2000), who considers the problem of imputing missing responses in psychological questionnaire data. The results in this case take the integer values 1 through 5, and four imputation strategies were compared: imputation of missing items using the mean response for the same person (strategy PM), a variation of this strategy in which noise was added to correct for the variance reduction described above, imputation of missing items using the mean response for that item across all respondents (strategy IM), and the corresponding added-noise version of this strategy. Examining the bias in factor analysis results for simulated questionnaire data, the authors concluded that strategy PM and its variant gave significantly lower biases than strategy IM and its variant.

Finally, the third important feature of mean imputation is that, if outliers are present among the set of candidate replacement values, mean imputation can yield badly biased results. This problem can be overcome by replacing means with medians, the standard strategy adopted in nonlinear digital data-cleaning filters like those described in Sec. 4.3.

Many other single imputation strategies are possible besides mean imputation. One approach is *hot-deck imputation* (Rubin, 1987, p. 9), in which missing observations in a dataset are replaced with "nearby" data values from the same dataset. The term *nearby* may be interpreted in different ways, leading to a variety of different hot-deck imputation procedures. For example, Särndal, Swensson, and Wretman (1992, p. 592) describe hot-deck imputation procedures based on random selection from the available values for the variable with missing entries, random selection from a specified subset of these values, and replacement with nearest-neighbor data values, which may be defined using various distance measures. Alternatively, Särndal, Swensson, and Wretman (1992, p. 592) define *cold-deck imputation procedures* as analogous procedures based on other, related, datasets, distinct from the one being analyzed.

Another general approach to single imputation is *regression imputation* (Rubin, 1987; Särndal, Swensson, and Wretman, 1992), which uses regression models based on other variables to predict missing observations. Specifically, to impute missing values for a variable, say y, we first construct a regression model that predicts y from one or more predictor variables, say x^1 through x^n. Clearly, this approach requires the availability of other variables that are associated with the variable we wish to impute. In addition, it is necessary that the *complete* data subset containing both the predictors and the variable to be predicted be large enough to obtain reasonable regression models. Further, this basic idea can be generalized using more complex predictors than simple regression models. As a specific example, Conversano and Cappelli (2002) describe the use of *classification and regression tree (CART) models* (Breiman et al., 1984) to impute missing values. A characteristic of this approach is that it partitions the dataset into subsets and fits local regression models to these subsets. Here, the result may be viewed as a collection of simple models that can often describe the overall dataset better than a single regression model of greater complexity fit to the complete dataset. In the case of CART-based imputation, Conversano and Cappelli (2002) are also able to take advantage of the structure of the missing data, reordering rows and columns in the original dataset to make the incomplete portion of the dataset appear as a contiguous block. As noted at the end of Chapter 2, this structure can be significant, an issue that is practically important and is discussed further in the next section in connection with multiple imputation strategies.

4.2.3 Multiple imputation strategies

While they are intuitively appealing, relatively simple, and quite popular, the single imputation strategies discussed in Sec. 4.2.2 suffer from a number of problems. Perhaps the two most important of these problems are, first, their tendency to reduce the variability of the imputed dataset relative to the (unknown) complete dataset they are attempting to approximate, and, second, their inappropriateness for *nonignorable* missing data. The first of these problems was illustrated for the case of simple mean imputation in Sec. 4.2.2, and the second is discussed further here.

Rubin (1987) presents a very detailed discussion of multiple imputation for nonresponse in survey sampling using the machinery of Bayesian statistics. More recently, he has given a broader description of multiple imputation in a variety of other application areas, including discussions of available software to support these procedures and the limitations or lack of software support in some application areas (Rubin, 2000). In its simplest form, the basic idea is to generate $m > 1$ imputations for each missing data value, yielding a *collection* of imputed datasets, which may then be analyzed by standard methods. A single final result is then obtained by combining the characterizations of these imputed datasets. Rubin (1987) argues that this disadvantage, despite its added computational complexity, is strongly outweighed by the improved quality of the final result.

To illustrate the essential notion of multiple imputation, it is useful to consider the following example from Rubin (1987, p. 19). A simple bivariate dataset $\mathcal{D} = \{(x_k, y_k)\}$ consisting of $N = 10$ observations is considered. All of the x_k values are observed, but two of the y_k values, y_2 and y_4, are not. Two different imputation strategies are considered in analyzing this example, one corresponding to an ignorable missing data model and the other corresponding to a nonignorable missing data model. For the ignorable case, imputations are obtained by first identifying the two nearest neighbors of the missing observations y_k based on their associated x_k values. In this particular example, the nearest neighbors of y_2 are y_1 and y_3, since x_1 and x_3 are the closest x_k values to x_2. Based on the same reasoning, the nearest neighbors of the missing value y_4 are y_3 and y_5. Two complete $\{(x_k, y_k)\}$ datasets are then obtained by drawing y_2 and y_4 values randomly with replacement from the values (y_1, y_3) and (y_3, y_5), respectively.

As discussed in Chapter 1, the case of nonignorable missing data is characterized by the existence of *systematic* differences between the observed and unobserved data values. In the simple example of Rubin (1987), the nonignorable missing data model postulates that the unobserved y_k values are consistently 20% larger than the corresponding nonmissing y_k values. The same basic strategy is then followed as in the ignorable case, but with the nonignorable missing data model instead of the ignorable model. That is, the same nearest neighbors are defined as before and these values are randomly sampled with replacement as before, but now these sampled values are multiplied by 1.2 to obtain imputed values for the missing observations y_2 and y_4. Rubin notes that both the example and the specific imputation strategies considered are extremely simple, and he does not offer them as specific practical procedures, but rather to clearly illustrate the general ideas involved. There are two key points: First, multiple imputation provides a systematic procedure for generating a family of complete (i.e., imputed) datasets that can be analyzed by standard methods. Second, this scheme provides a mechanism for examining specific nonignorable missing data hypotheses.

The idea of multiple imputation is particularly well matched to the GSA framework introduced in Chapter 1 and discussed further in Chapter 6. In particular, suppose we are given a dataset $\mathcal{D}$ with Q missing entries. If we adopt any imputation strategy that can generate m distinct values for each of these missing entries, we can in principle generate m^Q distinct imputed datasets $\mathcal{D}_i$. In examples like the one just considered, not all of the

m imputed values are necessarily distinct for every missing entry, but it is still generally true that if the number Q of missing data entries is large, the number of imputed datasets we can generate using this approach is extremely large. This observation suggests using multiple imputation as a GSA sampling scheme. That is, given a dataset $\mathcal{D}$ and an imputation strategy—based on either an ignorable missing data model or a nonignorable one—we can often generate as large a collection $\mathcal{D}_i$ of imputed datasets as we like, characterize them with any relevant analysis method, and compare the results using any appropriate descriptor $d(\cdot)$. In cases of ignorable missing data and reasonable imputation strategies, the datasets $\mathcal{D}_i$ should be exchangeable and the GSA results should provide a useful measure of the sensitivity of our analysis results to the effects of missing data. Further, we can compare the results under one or more nonignorable missing data models by comparing different imputation strategies, as in the simple example of Rubin (1987) just described.

In the techniques developed for multiple imputation in survey data, the *structure* of the missing data plays an important role, as in the CART-based imputation strategy of Conversano and Cappelli (2002) discussed at the end of Sec. 4.2.2. In particular, Rubin (1987, p. 170) defines the concept of *monotone missingness* in a multivariable dataset. To describe this notion, we let $\text{obs}[j]$ represent the set of record indices $\{k\}$ for which x_{kj} is observed (i.e., not missing). The dataset $\mathcal{D}$ exhibits monotone missingness if

$$\text{obs}[p] \subseteq \text{obs}[p-1] \subseteq \cdots \subseteq \text{obs}[1], \tag{4.26}$$

where p is the number of variables in the dataset. Note that if the k values range from 1 to N and variable j exhibits no missing values, then $\text{obs}[j] = \{1, 2, \ldots, N\}$. Hence, it follows that a complete dataset with no missing data satisfies the monotone missingness condition. Also, note that any dataset in which all missing values occur in one variable, say $\{x_{kj}\}$, can be made to satisfy the monotone missingness condition by simply exchanging the variable labels j and p. More generally, it may be possible to reorder the columns in datasets with missing entries in several variables to satisfy condition (4.26), but it should be clear that this is not always possible.

The advantage of the monotone missingness condition is that it provides the basis for a simple nested strategy for multiple imputation considered in detail by Rubin (1987). In particular, suppose variables 1 through j are completely observed and condition (4.26) is satisfied. These j variables may then be used to impute the missing values in variable $j + 1$, generating a collection of imputed datasets in which variables 1 through $j + 1$ are complete. These variables may then be used to generate imputations for the missing values in variable $j + 2$, and so forth, repeating the process until a collection $\{\mathcal{D}_i\}$ of complete datasets is obtained. Unfortunately, Rubin (2000) notes that, first, nonmonotone missing data patterns arise frequently in practice, and, second, they can significantly complicate multiple imputation analysis, frequently requiring iterative procedures. As an alternative, Rubin (2000) notes that it may be reasonable to fill in a subset of missing values via single imputation to *create* a monotone pattern of missing values. A second alternative is to *omit* a subset of data records to obtain a monotone pattern of missing data (Rubin, 1987, p. 189). Note that if the number of records that must be omitted to achieve a monotone pattern of missing data is small, the influence of this omission on analytical results may be negligible. Also, note that this strategy represents a less extreme version of omitting all incomplete records to obtain a complete (and hence monotone) dataset.

	Variable 1	Variable 2	Sum
Respondent 1	x	y	204
Respondent 2	z	w	9
Total	204	9	213

Table 4.2. *Table with missing data values and known constraints.*

In some applications—especially those involving medical data records and other types of confidential information—it is vitally important to protect certain types of data entries (e.g., patient identities) from unauthorized access. Multiple imputation has been proposed as one way of accomplishing this task, effectively breaking the link between certain response variables that are to be made widely available and other variables that could be used to determine precise values for sensitive variables (Robertson, 2000; Rubin, 2000). If constraints are imposed on the variables in a dataset, they can sometimes be used to compute approximate values for missing variables. As Robertson (2000) notes, in cases of sensitive variables, it is important not to allow these approximations to be too precise. As a specific example, he considers the 2×2 data table shown in Table 4.2. If x, y, z, and w are constrained to be nonnegative, the results presented in this table are sufficient to establish the following bounds on the unknown variables:

$$195 \leq x \leq 204,$$
$$0 \leq y,\ z,\ w \leq 9. \tag{4.27}$$

These constraints correspond to the set-theoretic variable description discussed further in Chapter 5. One of the points Robertson (2000) emphasizes is that if these ranges are too narrow, we can effectively infer the missing/unknown variables from the constraints. In fact, in this particular example, we can reconstruct all variables exactly from any one of the four missing entries. In the context of disguising sensitive data, these observations represent an unwelcome complication, but in the case of interest here—missing data imputation—this example illustrates that constraints can be extremely useful.

Conversely, it is important to incorporate these constraints in a consistent fashion in multiple imputation. This point is illustrated by the problem of indefinite covariance matrix estimates discussed at the end of Sec. 4.2.1, which is a direct consequence of inadequately coordinating missing value imputations for associated variables. An example in which constraints were incorporated explicitly into a multiple imputation procedure is the collection of tree-based methods described by Barcena and Tusell (2000). There, one of the applications considered involved the number of hours per day devoted to different activities, where the total had to sum to 24 hours.

4.2.4 Unmeasured and unmeasurable variables

Sometimes, certain key variables are absent entirely from the available dataset because they have not been measured. This situation can arise for either of two reasons:

1. the importance of the variables was not recognized at the time the dataset was assembled, or

2. the variable in question is either difficult or impossible to measure directly.

One possible solution to the first of these problems is to obtain measurements of the missing variable once its importance is recognized, but this solution is not always practical. In particular, it may be difficult or impossible to obtain new measurements under the same experimental conditions as those under which the original dataset was obtained. Specifically, this problem is inherent in the analysis of destructive testing of materials since the sample from which the original measurements were obtained is destroyed in the final step of the testing process. In both of the cases cited above, it may be desirable to construct *surrogates* for these missing variables, an idea illustrated by the following example.

Levitt and Snyder Jr. (1997) considered the problem of estimating the influence of federal fundraising on the outcomes of U.S. House of Representatives elections. They begin by noting that, although it is widely believed by "academics, politicians, and the popular press" that candidates' ability to raise federal money for their constituencies positively influences their reelection probability, empirical evidence tends not to support this belief. Levitt and Snyder Jr. (1997) argue that the basis for this difficulty is an omitted variable bias that arises because previously developed models did not include an "electoral vulnerability" term, reflecting the idea that an incumbent was likely to work harder to bring in federal money for his or her constituency when facing a more difficult reelection battle. Unfortunately, this quantity can depend strongly on a number of factors that are difficult or impossible to measure reliably (e.g., the quality of the challenger, relative campaign funds, local scandals, etc.). To address this problem, the authors considered models of the general form

$$V_{sdt} = \beta_1 X_{sdt} + \beta_2 Z_{sdt} + \epsilon_{sdt},$$
$$X_{sdt} = \theta Z_{sdt} + \eta_{st} + \mu_{sdt}. \tag{4.28}$$

Here, V_{sdt} denotes the incumbent's share of the vote in the congressional election in state s at time t in district d and X_{sdt} represents the corresponding amount of federal money flowing into the incumbent's district. The term Z_{sdt} represents the unmeasurable electoral vulnerability, which influences both the election outcome (adversely, implying $\beta_2 < 0$) and the incumbent's fundraising efforts (positively, implying $\theta > 0$). The terms ϵ_{sdt} and μ_{sdt} represent independent random variations across states, times, and districts, and η_{st} represents a statewide random variation, assumed to be the same over all districts d within state s at time t. The detailed models considered by Levitt and Snyder Jr. (1997) include additional terms on the right-hand side, but the simplified model shown in (4.28) illustrates the key ideas.

First, note that since Z_{sdt} is not directly measurable, the model defined in (4.28) cannot be fit directly to the available data. Hence, Levitt and Snyder Jr. (1997) consider three alternatives, all of which can be fit to the data. The first is the model obtained by simply omitting the unmeasurable variable Z_{sdt}, corresponding to the traditional models that generally failed to find significant influences of X_{sdt} on V_{sdt} (recall that these models also include other explanatory variables). The second alternative replaces the district-specific spending X_{sdt} with the statewide average spending across all D districts in the state:

$$\bar{X}_{st} = \frac{1}{D} \sum_{d=1}^{D} X_{sdt}. \tag{4.29}$$

The third alternative considered uses the average federal spending in all *other* districts in the incumbent's state s to estimate X_{sdt} in a way that does not depend on the unobservable variable Z_{sdt}:

$$R_{sdt} = \frac{1}{D-1} \sum_{j \neq d} X_{sjt}. \qquad (4.30)$$

The key motivation here was to find a variable that is associated with the federal spending X_{sdt} but *not* with the unmeasurable electoral vulnerability Z_{sdt}. In particular, note that $X_{sdt} - R_{sdt}$ represents a plausible measure of the incumbent's electoral vulnerability. The authors show that this third model yields an asymptotically unbiased result and that the bias in the first model is strictly larger than that of the second model, which they note is often easier to work with than the third model. Overall, their results support the belief that federal fundraising has a positive influence on the incumbent's vote share (i.e., that $\beta_1 > 0$), as was generally believed but not apparently supported by the available data. The two key points here are, first, that this example provides a real illustration of the problem of omission bias, and, second, that it illustrates a clever way of imputing missing (in this case, unmeasurable) variables that are important in the analysis.

4.3   Cleaning time-series

The problem of dynamic data characterization arises frequently in areas as diverse as industrial process monitoring, financial data analysis, and the characterization of biomedical data sequences. An important practical aspect of dynamic data characterization is that standard methods are often quite sensitive to the presence of outliers. This observation has motivated the development of various nonlinear *data-cleaning filters* to remove outliers from the observed data sequences, thus improving the quality of the results obtained via standard dynamic analysis methods. The general question of how different types of data anomalies influence the results of time-series analysis is a complex one that has not been as widely explored in the statistics literature as have the problems of anomalous data in less-structured settings (e.g., multivariate outlier detection). A detailed treatment of this topic lies outside the scope of this book, but it is useful to briefly consider some of the issues that arise and some of their possible treatment strategies. A brief introduction to time-series outliers was given in Chapter 2, and the following subsections present some results concerning the practical treatment of time-series outliers.

4.3.1   The nature of the problem

In dynamic data characterizations such as spectral analysis, correlation analysis, and system identification, different types of outliers can have different kinds of influence on the results. In particular, a key characteristic of dynamic analysis that distinguishes it from static characterizations such as location estimation and regression analysis is that the sequence index k for the data value x_k conveys important information (specifically, time order). As a consequence, arbitrarily reordering the sequence $\{x_k\}$ will, in general, radically alter dynamic characterization results. In contrast, static characterizations such as the mean or standard deviation of the sequence are completely unaffected by such reorderings. Consequently, whereas location and scale estimators such as the mean and standard deviation are influenced

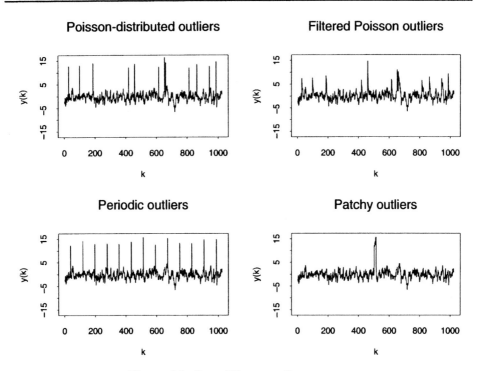

Figure 4.1. *Four different outlier patterns.*

by the *concentration* and *distribution* of the outliers in a sample, they are not influenced by the *pattern* or *dependence structure* of the outliers in the sample. This observation stands in marked contrast to dynamic data characterizations, where different patterns of outliers can have profoundly different effects on the results.

Four different time-series outlier examples are shown in Figure 4.1. In all four cases, the observed sequence $\{y_k\}$ is of length $N = 1{,}024$ and has the general form

$$y_k = \eta_k + o_k. \tag{4.31}$$

In these examples, $\{\eta_k\}$ represents the nominal (random) data sequence we wish to characterize and $\{o_k\}$ is a sequence of additive outliers described further below. In all four of the examples considered here, $\{\eta_k\}$ is a dependent Gaussian nominal data sequence generated by the *first-order autoregressive model* (Brockwell and Davis, 1991; Priestley, 1981)

$$\eta_k = a\eta_{k-1} + \epsilon_k, \tag{4.32}$$

where $\{\epsilon_k\}$ is a zero-mean, i.i.d., Gaussian sequence with variance σ^2. Here, the first-order autoregressive coefficient is $a = 0.8$ and the variance of $\{\epsilon_k\}$ is $\sigma^2 = 1 - a^2 = 0.36$, chosen so that the sequence $\{\eta_k\}$ has unit variance. The objective in typical time-series analyses is to characterize the nominal data sequence $\{\eta_k\}$, but as the following examples illustrate, most common time-series characterizations are quite sensitive to the presence of outliers (Pearson, 2001b).

In the upper left plot in Figure 4.1, the outlier sequence $\{o_k\}$ corresponds approximately to a *Poisson point process* (Grimmett and Stirzaker, 1982, Sec. 6.8), a model commonly used to describe the occurrence of rare events. In particular, a Poisson point process describes discrete events whose interarrival times are exponentially distributed; here, the sequence $\{o_k\}$ consists of 12 nonzero values, all of magnitude $+12$, with an intersample spacing that is approximately exponentially distributed. A variation on this outlier model is shown in the upper right plot in Figure 4.1. There, the outlier sequence o_k represents a *filtered version* of the Poisson outlier sequence shown in the upper left plot. That is, let $\{p_k\}$ denote the sequence of outliers in the upper left plot; the sequence $\{o_k\}$ of outliers in the upper right plot is obtained as the output of the *first-order linear filter*

$$o_k = 0.8 o_{k-1} + 0.2 p_k. \tag{4.33}$$

Note that this filter is described by essentially the same equation as (4.32) discussed above for the first-order autoregressive model. Here, the effect of this filter is to smooth the Poisson outlier sequence $\{p_k\}$, which exhibits only the two values 0 and $+12$ in this example, into a sequence that varies more smoothly, decaying toward 0 following each input shock (i.e., each nonzero value of p_k). The effect of this smoothing is both to reduce the amplitude of the outliers and to broaden them from isolated outliers like those in the Poisson outlier example into patches of successive anomalous value. Motivation for this model comes from the fact that the decaying behavior generated by this first-order filter approximates many different types of physical phenomena.

The lower left plot in Figure 4.1 shows 13 *periodic* outliers, uniformly spaced every 80 samples. Here, as in the case of the Poisson outliers in the plot above, the outliers may generally be regarded as *isolated*, since they are (mostly) well-separated. The significance of this observation is that all of the dynamic data-cleaning filters discussed in detail here involve a moving data window and, for isolated outliers, this data window generally contains either a single outlier or no outliers at all, rarely more. In contrast, the bottom right plot shows an example of *patchy outliers*, where 13 outliers are grouped into a single cluster. As the following discussion illustrates, the influence of patchy outliers can be quite different from that of isolated outliers. Also, note that the filtered Poisson outlier example shown in the upper right plot represents a more subtle case since, although it exhibits patchy character, the magnitude of the outliers is also smaller, which can make them less severe in their influence, more difficult to detect, or both.

To illustrate the different consequences of these different time-series outlier patterns on a simple data analysis result, Figure 4.2 shows a collection of model parameter estimates computed from contaminated data sequences like those shown in Figure 4.1. More specifically, 100 statistically independent data sequences $\{y_k\}$ were generated for each of the following scenarios:

N: the nominal data sequence $\{\eta_k\}$ defined by (4.32) without contamination;

A: $\{\eta_k\}$ with Poisson-distributed outliers;

B: $\{\eta_k\}$ with patchy outliers;

C: $\{\eta_k\}$ with periodic outliers;

D: $\{\eta_k\}$ with filtered Poisson outliers.

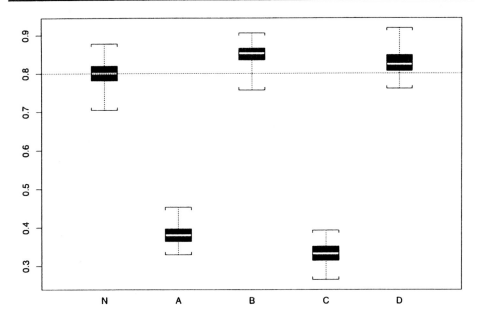

Figure 4.2. *Estimated a parameters versus outlier scenario.*

In all cases, the contamination level is the same (0.1%), so the differences seen in the results reflect either the influence of the outliers (comparing scenario N against the others) or the influence of different outlier patterns (scenarios A, B, C, and D), mostly with the same distribution (specifically, the single value $+12\sigma$ for all cases except the filtered Poisson outliers). For each individual sequence $\{y_k\}$, the data model

$$y_k = ay_{k-1} + e_k \qquad (4.34)$$

was fit by OLS to obtain an estimate $\hat{a}$ of the parameter a. Note that this model corresponds to the first-order autoregressive model (4.32) that describes the uncontaminated nominal data sequence $\{\eta_k\}$, and it should provide an adequate characterization in the absence of outliers.

It may be seen from the uncontaminated results (the boxplot designated N) that the least squares estimation procedure used here is approximately *unbiased*, meaning that its mean value is approximately equal to the correct value $a = 0.8$. (Since the boxplot is approximately symmetric, the median indicated in the boxplot is approximately equal to the mean.) In contrast, this estimation procedure gives *biased* results for all four of the contamination scenarios considered here. In particular, the results for the isolated outliers (scenarios A and C) are severely biased, exhibiting mean values that underestimate the true parameter by 50% or more. In marked contrast, both the patchy outlier scenario (B) and the filtered Poisson outlier scenario (D) exhibit much smaller biases, but in the opposite direction, both overestimating the a parameter. Although the magnitude of this effect is much smaller, it is still potentially serious since the value $a = 1$ represents the stability margin for first-order autoregressive models: models with $a > 1$ are unstable (i.e., nonstationary), exhibiting a variance that grows without bound as $k \rightarrow \infty$. The key points here are, first,

AIC Order	None N	Poisson A	Patchy B	Periodic C	Filtered D
1	64%	0%	43%	0%	62%
2	15%	2%	7%	5%	19%
3	5%	37%	2%	46%	8%
> 3	16%	61%	48%	49%	11%

Table 4.3. *AIC model orders versus outlier scenario.*

that outliers can have a significant effect on the results of dynamic analysis procedures, and, second, that this effect can depend strongly on the pattern of the outliers involved. Note also that in this particular example, the outliers have no obvious influence on the *variability* of the results since both the IQDs and the total range of variation seen in these results appear to be about the same in all cases.

The results shown in Figure 4.2 were obtained under the assumption that the order of the autoregressive model that generated the nominal data sequence was known. In practice, the determination of a reasonable model order is an important aspect of building time-series models, and a variety of methods have been developed to address this question. One of the most popular is the *Akaike information criterion* (AIC) (Box, Jenkins, and Reinsel, 1994; Brockwell and Davis, 1991), which represents a complexity-penalized goodness-of-fit measure: models are sought that minimize the AIC with respect to model order and the result is used to estimate both the model order and the model parameters. Even in the absence of outliers, the AIC does not always estimate the correct model order, but it is instructive to briefly consider the influence of outliers on this estimated model order for the different scenarios considered in Figures 4.1 and 4.2. These results are summarized in Table 4.3, which gives the percentage of 100 simulation runs for which the AIC model order assumed the value 1 (the correct value), 2, 3, or some value greater than 3. Inspection of this table shows that, even in the absence of outliers, the estimated AIC value is only correct 64% of the time. Conversely, in the presence of isolated outliers (i.e., either Poisson-distributed or periodic), the AIC value is *never* correct, with almost all estimated model orders (98% and 95%, respectively) being 3 or more. As with the estimated *a* parameters, the results are better for the patchy outliers (scenario B) and better still for the filtered Poisson outliers (scenario D).

Other examples illustrating the influence of outliers on dynamic data characterizations are discussed in the paper by Pearson (2001b). One of these examples shows the profound differences that different outlier patterns can have on spectrum estimation (Pearson, 2001b, Figure 3). There, patchy versus isolated outliers are compared, both for the case of outliers that all assume the same value (unipolar outliers) and for the case where they alternate in sign (bipolar outliers, lying ±8 standard deviations from the mean). For the case of isolated outliers, unipolar and bipolar outliers give the same results, consistent with the observations of others: isolated outliers "raise the noise floor" of the estimated spectrum, obscuring high-frequency details (Martin and Thomson, 1982). For patchy outliers, the effects of unipolar and bipolar outliers are substantially different, both from each other and from the case of isolated outliers. In the unipolar case, the patchy outliers cause an almost uniform upward shift of the estimated spectrum at all frequencies, whereas in the bipolar case, the effect at low frequencies is negligible; the effect at intermediate frequencies is moderate, but less severe than the effect of isolated outliers; but the effect at high frequencies is dramatically larger, reflecting the oscillatory character of the bipolar outlier patch. Overall, the key point is that the pattern of outliers can profoundly influence the results of standard dynamic analysis procedures such as spectrum estimation and system identification.

4.3.2 Data-cleaning filters

The intent of the previous section was to illustrate the consequences of undetected time-series outliers. The following paragraphs briefly survey the variety of approaches that have been proposed to deal with time-series outliers, ranging from techniques that are generally quite effective when they work, but also quite complicated and not always applicable, to techniques that are much simpler and always applicable, and whose effectiveness varies from marginal to as good as or better than the more complicated techniques.

Before proceeding to a detailed discussion of these filters, it is worth noting that the data-cleaning problem is one that requires a nonlinear solution. In particular, an effective data-cleaning filter is one that satisfies two important criteria. First, it replaces outliers with data values that are more consistent with the local variation of the nominal sequence. Second, it causes little or no change (distortion) in the nominal data sequence itself. To see that linear filters are inadequate to this task, consider the case of a single additive outlier:

$$o_k = \begin{cases} \lambda, & k = k_0, \\ 0, & k \neq k_0. \end{cases} \tag{4.35}$$

Linear filters are characterized by their *impulse response* $\{h_k\}$, a (generally infinite) sequence of values that defines the response $\{y_k\}$ to any input sequence $\{x_k\}$ via the *discrete convolution* operation, denoted with the symbol $\star$:

$$y_k = h_k \star x_k \equiv \sum_{j=0}^{\infty} h_{k-j} x_j. \tag{4.36}$$

For a linear filter with impulse response $\{h_k\}$, the response to the contaminated data sequence $\{x_k\} = \{\eta_k + o_k\}$ is

$$y_k = h_k \star (\eta_k + o_k) = h_k \star \eta_k + h_k \star o_k = h_k \star \eta_k + \lambda h_{k-k_0}. \tag{4.37}$$

Since λ is typically large and k_0 can be arbitrary, good outlier suppression requires $h_k \simeq 0$ for all k. Conversely, to minimize distortion effects, we want $h_k \star \eta_k \simeq \eta_k$, implying that $h_k \simeq 1$ for $k = 0$ and $h_k \simeq 0$ for $k \neq 0$. Since these requirements are strongly conflicting, it follows that linear filters are inadequate to the task of data cleaning. In contrast, a large class of nonlinear filters exist that are capable of completely rejecting isolated outliers in a dataset while preserving all sequences in a large set of *root sequences* (Astola and Kuosmanen, 1997), defined as those input sequences that are invariant under the action of the filter. The practical challenge, then, is to select a simple nonlinear filter that exhibits desirable outlier rejection characteristics and for which the root set contains most of the nominal sequences we wish to preserve.

One of the best examples of a data-cleaning procedure is that of Martin and Thomson (1982), developed for spectrum estimation. This procedure is based on the assumption that the nominal part of the data sequence is approximately Gaussian and leads to the following

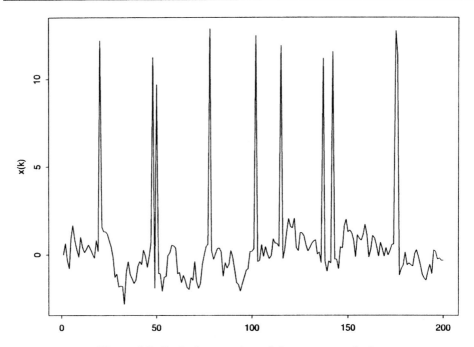

Figure 4.3. *Typical contaminated data sequence* $\{x_k\}$.

sequence of steps. First, a low-order autoregressive model is fit to the data sequence using an outlier-resistant procedure (specifically, a generalized M-estimator). Next, this model is converted into an equivalent state-space model and used to build an outlier-resistant Kalman filter. Finally, this Kalman filter is applied to the original data sequence to give an estimate of the nominal part $\{\eta_k\}$. In practice, this data-cleaning procedure often works extremely well, but it suffers from two practical limitations. First, it is quite complicated to implement and, although it is available commercially as part of the S-PLUS package (Insightful, 2001), circumstances frequently arise in which we want to implement our own, simpler, procedure. In fact, much simpler filters do exist that sometimes perform about as well as the Martin–Thomson procedure (Pearson, 2001b). The second practical limitation is the iterative character of the generalized M-estimator used in the initial model-building procedure. In particular, if the essential working assumptions on which this procedure is based (i.e., approximately Gaussian nominal data sequence) are violated too badly, it can fail to converge. In addition, there are other cases where the covariance matrix on which the Kalman filter is based becomes singular, causing it to fail (Pearson, 2001b). These observations motivate the problem of designing *simple* nonlinear digital filters, such as those discussed next, for use in data-cleaning applications.

The following discussions compare the performance of three simple nonlinear data-cleaning filters applied to contaminated data sequences like that shown in Figure 4.3. These simulated data sequences are based on the additive outlier model introduced in Chapter 3, where the nominal part of each data sequence is generated by the first-order autoregressive model

$$\eta_k = 0.8\eta_{k-1} + \epsilon_k, \tag{4.38}$$

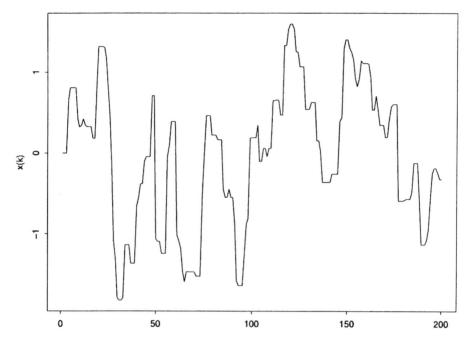

Figure 4.4. *Median filter ($K = 2$) applied to $\{x_k\}$ from Figure* 4.3.

where $\{\epsilon_k\}$ is a zero-mean Gaussian white noise sequence with variance $\sigma^2 = 0.36$, chosen so the variance of $\{\eta_k\}$ is 1. These sequences are of length $N = 200$ and are each contaminated with a sequence of 10 additive outliers, each of magnitude $+12$.

The first example considered is the historically important median filter, originally proposed by J.W. Tukey (Nodes and Gallagher, 1982), which maps a finite-length input sequence $\{x_k\}$ into an output sequence $\{w_k\}$ of the same length. Specifically, the filter output at time k is equal to the median of the values in the moving data window from time $k - K$ to time $k + K$:

$$w_k = \text{median} \{x_{k-K}, \ldots, x_k, \ldots, x_{k+K}\}. \tag{4.39}$$

Because this filter depends on future data values, it is not suitable for real-time applications, but it is quite useful in off-line data analysis applications; also, note that filter responses near the beginning and end of the input data sequence require special handling, as discussed in Chapter 7 (Sec. 7.5.1). For further discussion, see the book by Astola and Kuosmanen (1997), which also discusses a wide range of other nonlinear filters that may be useful in dynamic data-cleaning applications.

The result of applying a five-point median filter ($K = 2$) to the data sequence from Figure 4.3 is shown in Figure 4.4. It is clear from this result that the median filter has indeed eliminated the outliers from this data sequence, but it is also clear that the price of this outlier rejection is a substantial distortion of the nominal part of the data sequence. The "blocky" appearance of this filtered data sequence is typical of median filter responses, a consequence of the following observation. A *root sequence* for a filter $\mathcal{F}$ is a sequence

$\{r_k\}$ that is invariant under the action of the filter, that is, $\mathcal{F}\{r_k\} = \{r_k\}$. A characteristic of median filters is that they reduce any finite data sequence to a root sequence in a finite number of repeated applications (Gallagher and Wise, 1981). As a practical consequence, median filter outputs tend to resemble root sequences for the filter. A complete characterization of these sequences is known (Gallagher and Wise, 1981; Astola, Heinonen, and Neuvo, 1987): they consist of monotone segments separated by constant segments of width at least $K + 1$. Unfortunately, this root class does not include most nominal data sequences of interest in practice so the median filter tends to introduce significant distortion.

4.3.3 The center-weighted median filter

One useful generalization of the median filter is the *center-weighted median filter* (CWMF) defined by

$$\mathcal{F}\{x_k\} = \text{median } \{x_{k-K}, \ldots, w \diamond x_k, \ldots, x_{k+K}\}, \tag{4.40}$$

where w is a positive integer and $w \diamond x_k$ indicates that the central sample x_k is *replicated* w times before the indicated median is computed. The survey paper by Yin et al. (1996) gives a detailed discussion of these filters, where it is noted that there exist only a finite number of distinct CWMFs. In particular, the filter reduces to the standard median filter for $w = 1$, and it becomes an identity filter for $w \geq 2K+1$ since the replicated central value $w \diamond x_k$ then always constitutes the majority in the augmented data window in (4.40). Also, to keep the number of data points in this augmented window odd, the integer w is usually required to be odd. Finally, the CWMF with $w = 2K - 1$ is *idempotent*, meaning that it reduces any input sequence to a filter root in one pass (Haavisto, Gabbouj, and Neuvo, 1991). The significance of this observation is that, like the standard median filter, CWMFs also reduce any finite-length sequence $\{x_k\}$ to a root sequence in a finite number of steps. Since the CWMF with center weight $w = 2K - 1$ accomplishes this task in a single pass, it represents the most aggressive of the family of CWMFs with fixed window half-width K. An advantage of the CWMF over the corresponding standard median filter is that the CWMF root set is larger, meaning that the CWMF generally introduces less distortion in nominal data sequences than standard median filters do.

Figure 4.5 shows the results of applying the CWMF with $K = 2$ and $w = 3$ to the sequence shown in Figure 4.3. The best performance of the standard median filter is obtained for this example with $K = 2$, motivating this particular choice of K. Here, there are only two distinct CWMF structures: $w = 1$, corresponding to the standard median filter just examined, and $w = 3$, corresponding to the idempotent case. The feature that is most immediately obvious in Figure 4.5 is that the weighted median filter does not reject all of the outliers present in the data sequence. This behavior is a consequence of the fact that the outliers appearing at $k \sim 50$ and $k \sim 175$ in the original data sequence are not isolated, but constitute closely spaced pairs. Hence, the augmented data window is not wide enough to reject these outliers. More specifically, when $k = 48$ in this example, the augmented moving data window on which this filter is based contains the following values:

$$\{x_{46}, x_{47}, 3 \diamond x_{48}, x_{49}, x_{50}\} = \{-0.43, -0.71, 11.25, 11.25, 11.25, -1.92, 9.70\}. \tag{4.41}$$

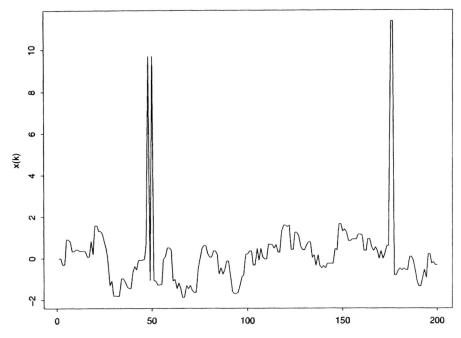

Figure 4.5. *CWMF response, K = 2, w = 3.*

Rank-ordering this augmented data window yields the following sequence, for which the median value is 9.70:

$$\{-1.92, -0.71, -0.43, 9.70, 11.25, 11.25, 11.25\}. \tag{4.42}$$

The behavior of this CWMF is analogous for the successive outlier pair in the original data sequence at $k = 175$ and $k = 176$.

To overcome this difficulty, it is necessary to increase K, and the results obtained for this same data sequence using a CWMF with $K = 5$ and $w = 7$ are shown in Figure 4.6. Comparing this result with the standard median filter result in Figure 4.4 shows that the CWMF exhibits significantly reduced distortion, a consequence of the fact noted above that the CWMF has a larger root set than the standard median filter. In particular, it can be shown that, for fixed half-width parameter K, the root sequence sets for the CWMF contain those for the standard median filter (Yin et al., 1996). Hence, for a given filter width, the distortion introduced by the CWMF should decrease with increasing center weight values w, but this occurs at the expense of increased sensitivity to closely spaced (e.g., patchy) outliers.

This point is illustrated in Figure 4.7, which shows the results obtained for the CWMF with half-width parameter $K = 5$ as in Figure 4.6, but with the center weight increased from $w = 7$ to its maximum useful value, $w = 9$. Here, the augmented window width is wide enough that this filter passes not only the closely spaced outlier pairs at $k \sim 50$ and

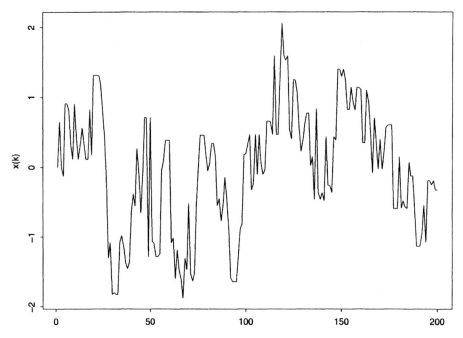

Figure 4.6. *CWMF response,* $K = 5$, $w = 7$.

$k \sim 175$ but also the more widely separated outlier pair at $k \sim 140$. Further, since this filter is idempotent (Haavisto, Gabbouj, and Neuvo, 1991), it follows that the sequence shown in Figure 4.7 is a root sequence for this particular CWMF, meaning that it is invariant to further applications of this filter. Hence, although the root set for this filter is clearly larger than that for the standard median filter, it is still not the root set we desire since it does not contain the undistorted nominal data sequence, but it does contain sequences like the one shown in Figure 4.7 that include closely spaced outliers.

To give a more complete assessment of the performance of this filter, Figure 4.8 shows a comparison of the root mean square (RMS) differences Δ between the CWMF response to the contaminated sequence $\{x_k\}$ and the nominal data sequence $\{\eta_k\}$ we wish to recover for $K = 1, 2$, and 3. The best of these results correspond to $K = 3$ and $w = 3$, representing a slight improvement over the best standard median filter result, obtained for $K = 2$ and corresponding to $K = 2$, $w = 1$ in this plot. The poor results seen here for large center weights (specifically, the idempotent filters $K = 2$ with $w = 3$ and $K = 3$ with $w = 5$) reflect the failure of these filters to reject the closely spaced outliers discussed in the preceding paragraphs. Overall, these results make it clear that, for this example at least, there exist optimal values for the tuning parameters K and w for the CWMF, and this filter exhibits at least somewhat better performance than the standard median filter for data-cleaning applications. Indeed, in some cases involving only isolated outliers, CWMF performance is much better than that of the standard median filter (Haavisto, Gabbouj, and Neuvo, 1991).

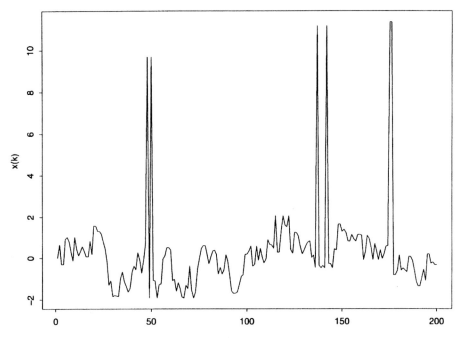

Figure 4.7. *CWMF response,* $K = 5$, $w = 9$.

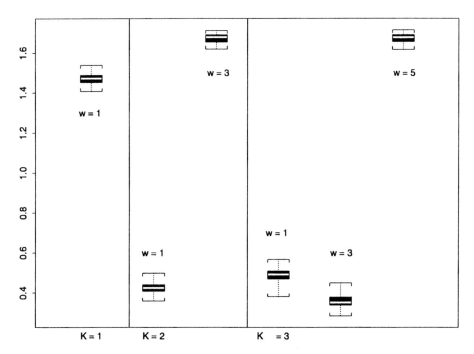

Figure 4.8. *CWMF RMS differences,* η_k *versus* $\mathcal{F}\{x_k\}$ *for* $K = 1, 2, 3$.

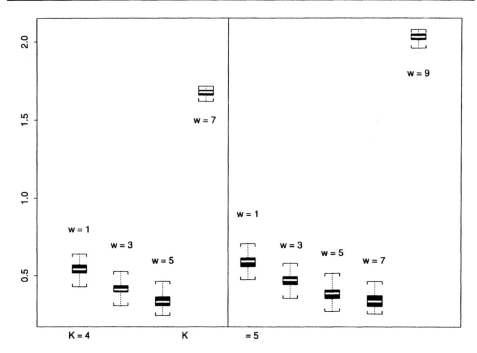

Figure 4.9. *CWMF RMS differences, η_k versus $\mathcal{F}\{x_k\}$ for $K = 4$ and 5.*

Analogous results for half-width parameters $K = 4$ and $K = 5$ are shown in Figure 4.9, again for the complete range of possible weight parameters. As before, making the center weight too large results in sensitivity to closely spaced outlier pairs, causing a dramatic increase in the RMS difference between the filter output and the nominal data sequence. Careful examination of the ranges of variation and the median values for these results leads to the conclusion that the optimum tuning parameters for this example appear to be $K = 4$ with $w = 5$. In particular, the median RMS deviation for this tuning parameter is approximately 0.333, versus 0.425 for the best standard median filter ($K = 2$) and 0.335 for the CWMF with $K = 5$ and $w = 7$. Note also that the breakdown of this filter in response to closely spaced outliers becomes worse with increasing K values, as seen in the increase in the RMS differences for $w = 2K - 1$ with increasing K.

4.3.4 The Hampel filter

The Hampel filter (Pearson, 1999, 2001b) is based on a moving-window implementation of the Hampel identifier discussed in Chapter 3. That is, like the median filter and the CWMF, the Hampel filter constructs a moving data window centered at the current value x_k that includes K previous values, x_{k-K} through x_{k-1}, and K future values, x_{k+1} through x_{k+K}. The Hampel identifier is then applied to the central point x_k in this moving window based on the median of the $2K + 1$ data values in the window and the MAD scale estimate computed from these data values. If x_k is declared to be an outlier, it is replaced with the median value from the data window; otherwise, it is not modified. Like the CWMF, this filter has two tuning parameters: the window half-width K and the threshold parameter t.

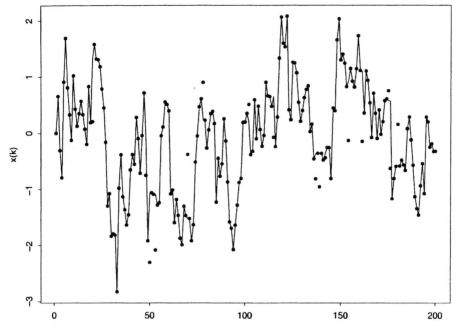

Figure 4.10. *Hampel filter response, $K = 3$, $t = 3$.*

This threshold parameter is extremely important because it determines the aggressiveness of the Hampel filter in rejecting outliers. In particular, note that the filter remains well defined for $t = 0$, for which it reduces to the median filter since x_k is always replaced with the median value from the data window. At the other extreme, note that if t is sufficiently large, x_k will never be modified *unless the MAD scale estimate is zero.* Although this condition only occurs when a majority of values in the moving data window $\mathbf{w}_k$ are exactly equal, it can arise when processing coarsely quantized data. As a consequence, the Hampel filter may perform poorly in such circumstances.

The response of the Hampel filter with $K = 3$ and $t = 3$ to the contaminated data sequence shown in Figure 4.3 is plotted as the solid line in Figure 4.10. In addition, the uncontaminated nominal data points are shown as solid circles, demonstrating that the Hampel filter leaves most of the data points unmodified. Conversely, at least for this example, all of the outliers in the data sequence have been eliminated and replaced with more reasonable values. Comparisons of this plot with those presented earlier for the standard median filter and the CWMF show that this filter introduces significantly less distortion into the nominal data sequence than the other filters do. Conversely, as the following results demonstrate, if the window width is made too narrow or the threshold parameter is made too large, the Hampel filter will also fail to reject outlier pairs that are too closely spaced in the data sequence, just like the CWMF examples considered previously.

A summary of Hampel filter performance for $K = 2$ is given in Figure 4.11. The case $t = 0$ corresponds to the standard median filter with $K = 2$, the optimum choice for this example. Increasing the threshold value to $t = 1$ and $t = 2$ gives uniformly better results, and increasing the threshold value further to $t = 3$ gives results that are generally better

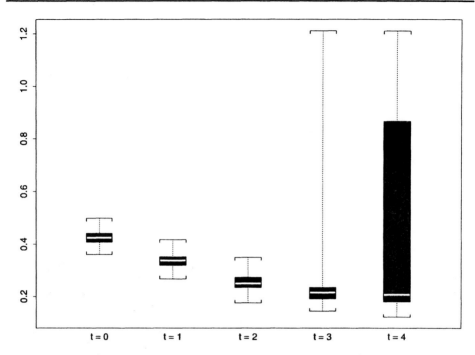

Figure 4.11. *Hampel filter RMS differences, η_k versus $\mathcal{F}\{x_k\}$ for $K = 2$ and* $t = 0, 1, 2, 3, 4.$

(in particular, note that both the median value and the upper and lower quartiles for $t = 3$ lie below the corresponding values for $t = 2$), but there are clearly special cases where the Hampel filter begins to break down, as seen in the dramatically increased maximum RMS difference for this case. Increasing the threshold parameter still further to $t = 4$ results in a much more complete breakdown of filter performance. As with the CWMF, this breakdown occurs because the five-point Hampel filter begins to pass closely spaced outlier pairs when t is large enough.

Finally, Figure 4.12 summarizes the results obtained using the Hampel filter with window half-width parameters $K = 3$, 4, and 5 and threshold parameters $t = 0$ (the standard median filter), $t = 2$, and $t = 4$. As in the results shown in Figure 4.11, for each K value, there appears to be an optimum t value somewhere between $t = 2$ and $t = 4$, and the filter begins to show signs of breaking down (i.e., passing some outlier pairs) for $t = 4$. Also, as in the case of the standard median filter and the CWMF, there appears to also be an optimum window width.

4.4 Multivariate outlier detection

There are at least three basic approaches to multivariate outlier detection: model-based, deletion-based, and visualization-based. Like the univariate outlier detection procedures discussed in Chapter 3, model-based multivariate outlier detection procedures adopt—either explicitly or implicitly—a data model that describes, first, how the nominal data values are

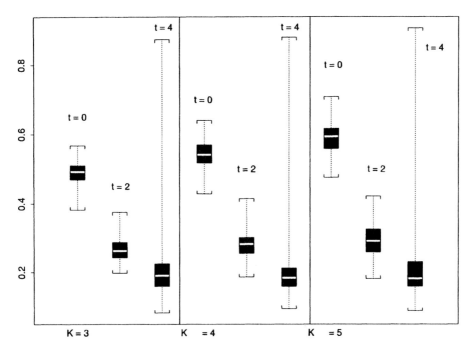

Figure 4.12. *Hampel filter RMS differences, η_k versus $\mathcal{F}\{x_k\}$ for $K = 3, 4, 5$ and $t = 0, 2, 4$.*

characterized, and, second, how the outliers differ from the nominal data values. Different data models lead to different outlier detection procedures, and the following discussions consider three classes of model-based procedures: covariance-based, regression-based, and depth-based. The second general class of outlier detection approaches is the class of deletion diagnostics discussed further in Chapter 7: there, "suspicious" points are those whose deletion results in a large change in a data analysis result (e.g., estimated model parameter or goodness-of-fit measure). As emphasized in Chapter 7, an important limitation of deletion-based approaches is their potential combinatorial complexity. Finally, while simple visualization-based methods are generally not practical for detecting outliers in large, high-dimensional datasets, they do provide an extremely useful basis for examining a number of important issues in the bivariate case, so the following discussions begin with a brief consideration of these methods.

4.4.1 Visual inspection

The bivariate outlier example shown in Figure 1.2 in Chapter 1 exhibits a single visually obvious outlier that is not extreme with respect to either data variable individually but that clearly violates the dominant nonlinear relationship between these variables. This example illustrates that visual examination of data plots *can* be an extremely effective method of detecting outliers, although it is clearly not practical as a systematic outlier detection method for large, multivariable datasets. It is, however, worth briefly considering visual outlier detection for two reasons.

First, visual displays provide a very useful means of confirming suspected data anomalies that are detected by other means. In particular, it is important to emphasize that while outlier *detection* represents a mathematical problem, outlier *interpretation* does not, and visual examination of informative data plots containing outliers can be very useful in suggesting interpretations. Further, plots like Figure 1.2 that clearly show both the dominant pattern in a dataset and anomalous data points that depart from this dominant pattern are extremely useful in presenting results to others. This is particularly the case if subsequent analysis is performed with these outliers omitted or replaced with alternative values, as some may hold the original dataset to be sacrosanct.

The second reason for considering visual outlier detection methods before moving on to more systematic procedures is that some of the basic difficulties associated with visual detection are in fact more fundamental and extend to many automated outlier detection procedures. For example, effective visual detection of outliers or other significant patterns in a multivariable dataset depends on taking an informative view of the data. This point is illustrated in the two plots shown in Figure 4.13. The plot on the left shows log intensity ratios from a microarray dataset plotted against the spot index. More specifically, the vertical axis of this plot corresponds to $M_k = \log_2(I_k/J_k)$, where I_k is the measured fluorescence intensity for a Cy3-labelled mRNA sample at spot k on the microarray and J_k is the corresponding Cy5-labelled fluorescence intensity for the *same* mRNA. There are no biological differences between these responses and the underlying hope behind two-dye microarray experiments like this one is that there are no systematic dye-specific effects. Under this assumption, M_k should correspond to a zero-mean random sequence, ideally with a small variance, whose distribution characterizes experimental measurement noise. It is clear from the left-hand plot in Figure 4.13, however, that these expectations do not hold: the mean is clearly not zero and the variance is not small. The right-hand plot in Figure 4.13 is a view advocated by Altman and Bland (1983) for comparing alternative measurement methods called an *MA*-plot. Here, the vertical axis is the same as before, $M_k = \log_2(I_k/J_k)$, but the horizontal axis is

$$A_k = \frac{\log_2 I_k + \log_2 J_k}{2} = \log_2 \sqrt{I_k J_k}. \tag{4.43}$$

The variable A_k represents an average response (here, $\log_2$ of the geometric mean optical intensity), and its use is advocated for detecting systematic intensity-dependent differences between alternative measurement methods. The right-hand plot in Figure 4.13 shows dramatic evidence for an intensity-dependent differential dye effect, whereas the left-hand plot only shows that our initial expectations that $M_k \simeq 0$ for all k were incorrect.

There are two key points of this example. First, the effectiveness of visual pattern detection strategies in a multivariable dataset is strongly dependent on what we choose to plot. This point has a direct analogy in the model-based outlier detection strategies discussed in Secs. 4.4.2, 4.4.3, and 4.4.4: the effectiveness of these procedures can depend strongly on the variables, combinations of variables, and transformations incorporated in the models on which the methods are based. The second key point is that the number of potential views we can take of a dataset is generally unlimited. For example, given a collection of n variables, the number of scatterplots of one variable against another that we *could* examine is $n(n-1)/2$. For $n = 10, 20$, and 30, these numbers are 45, 190, and 435, respectively. Further, the example shown in Figure 4.13 illustrates the utility of composite plots involving multivariate transformations, of which there are an uncountable number.

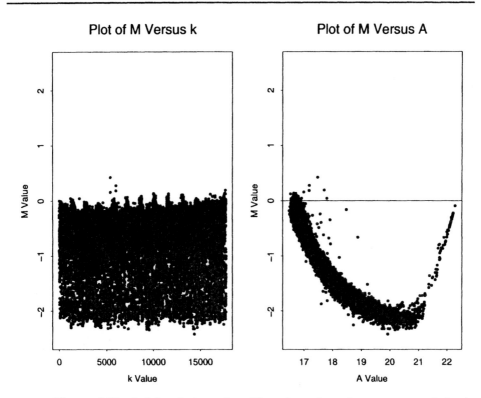

Figure 4.13. *Left-hand plot: plot of* $\log_2$ *intensity ratios versus spot index k.* *Right-hand plot: MA-plot of* $\log_2$ *intensity ratios versus* $\log_2$ *geometric mean intensities.*

4.4.2 Covariance-based detection

The simplest data model adopted in Chapter 3 for univariate outliers was the *location model*, which essentially represented a sequence $\{x_k\}$ of contaminated real values as

$$x_k = x_0 + e_k + o_k, \tag{4.44}$$

where x_0 is a constant nominal reference value, $\{e_k\}$ is a sequence of i.i.d. random variables with mean zero and finite variance σ^2, and $\{o_k\}$ is a sequence of anomalous perturbations responsible for the outliers, equal to zero for most k, but with magnitude typically large compared to σ when they are nonzero. In fact, the most common nominal data model assumes $e_k \sim N(0, \sigma^2)$. Under this univariate data model, a typical outlier detection method proceeds by first attempting to estimate the location parameter x_0 and the scale σ, leading to an outlier detection rule of the general form

$$|x_k - \hat{x}_0| > t\hat{\sigma} \;\;\Rightarrow\;\; x_k \text{ is an outlier.} \tag{4.45}$$

In particular, the three main outlier detection rules discussed in Chapter 3 corresponded to two different choices of $\hat{x}_0$ (the mean in the 3σ edit rule and the median in the Hampel and boxplot identifiers) and three different choices of $\hat{\sigma}$ (the usual standard deviation estimate in the 3σ edit rule, the MAD scale estimate in the Hampel identifier, and the IQD in the symmetric boxplot rule). Direct extensions of this idea to the multivariate case replace the scalar location estimate $\hat{x}_0$ with a vector-valued location estimate and the estimated variance with an estimate of the covariance matrix.

More specifically, consider the situation where $\{\mathbf{x}_k\}$ is a sequence of N observed data vectors, each of dimension p, with components x_{ki} for $i = 1, 2, \ldots, p$. The univariate data model of (4.44) then generalizes to

$$\mathbf{x}_k = \mathbf{x}_0 + \mathbf{e}_k + \mathbf{o}_k, \tag{4.46}$$

where $\mathbf{x}_0 \in R^p$ is a constant reference vector, $\{\mathbf{e}_k\}$ is a sequence of nominal multivariate fluctuations with mean $\mathbf{0} \in R^p$ and $p \times p$ covariance matrix Σ, and $\{\mathbf{o}_k\}$ is a sequence of multivariate outliers of dimension p. As in the univariate case, these values are assumed to be zero for most k and "large" when they are nonzero. Because multivariate non-Gaussian distributions are substantially more complicated to define and work with than univariate non-Gaussian distributions are, the nominal data values are almost always assumed to be Gaussian, meaning that $\mathbf{e}_k$ has a multivariate Gaussian distribution with mean $\mathbf{0}$ and covariance Σ. Under these assumptions, the appropriate extension of the 3σ edit rule is the outlier detection rule

$$d_k = \sqrt{(\mathbf{x}_k - \bar{\mathbf{x}})^T \hat{\Sigma}^{-1} (\mathbf{x}_k - \bar{\mathbf{x}})} > t \;\Rightarrow\; \mathbf{x}_k \text{ is an outlying observation.} \tag{4.47}$$

Here, d_k represents the Mahalanobis distance introduced in Chapter 2 for the observation $\mathbf{x}_k$ relative to the mean $\bar{\mathbf{x}}$, based on the covariance estimate $\hat{\Sigma}$.

As in the univariate case, the outlier detection rule just described is itself quite sensitive to the presence of outliers in the data. In particular, note that the standard estimators for $\bar{\mathbf{x}}$ and $\hat{\Sigma}$ are the following generalizations of their univariate counterparts:

$$\bar{\mathbf{x}} = \frac{1}{N} \sum_{k=1}^{N} \mathbf{x}_k, \quad \hat{\Sigma} = \frac{1}{N-1} \sum_{k=1}^{N} (\mathbf{x}_k - \bar{\mathbf{x}})(\mathbf{x}_k - \bar{\mathbf{x}})^T. \tag{4.48}$$

To achieve better outlier-resistance, it is necessary to replace these estimators of $\mathbf{x}_0$ and Σ with outlier-resistant alternatives, exactly as in the univariate case.

One set of alternatives is the pair of *minimum covariance determinant (MCD)* estimators (Rousseeuw and Leroy, 1987, p. 262), defined as follows. Given a set S of N data points $\mathbf{x}_k$, let S^h denote a subset of $h < N$ points, let $\bar{\mathbf{x}}^h$ denote the mean computed from S^h according to (4.48), and let $\hat{\Sigma}^h$ denote the covariance estimate $\hat{\Sigma}$ computed from S^h. The MCD estimator is the pair $(\bar{\mathbf{x}}^h, \hat{\Sigma}^h)$ computed from the set S^h that gives the minimum determinant for $\hat{\Sigma}^h$ over all subsets of size h. The subset size h is taken somewhere between $N/2$ and N, with $h \simeq 0.75N$ being one popular choice (Rousseeuw and Van Driessen, 1999). In practice, it has been found that the *reweighted MCD estimator* usually gives better performance: this estimator uses the initial MCD estimates to identify outliers, which are then removed and the mean and a scaled version of the standard covariance matrix are computed from the nonoutlying observations. A computationally efficient algorithm for evaluating the reweighted MCD estimator is available (Rousseeuw and Van Driessen, 1999) that has been applied to datasets as large as $N = 132{,}402$ with dimension $p = 27$.

A detailed discussion of the breakdown characteristics and statistical efficiency of the MCD estimator is given by Croux and Haesbroeck (1999). These authors also give a reasonably detailed discussion of several reweighting strategies and show that they yield significant performance improvements, consistent with the results reported by Rousseeuw and Van Driessen (1999).

A particularly useful application of the MCD estimator is the *distance-distance plot* described by Rousseeuw and Van Driessen (1999). This diagnostic tool plots a robust Mahalanobis distance MD_k^*, computed using the MCD estimator, for each point in the dataset on the vertical axis, against the classical Mahalanobis distance MD_k^0 as the horizontal axis. In addition, the reference line $MD_k^* = MD_k^0$ is also plotted, along with horizontal and vertical lines at the same threshold, typically computed as the square root of the 97.5% limit of the χ_p^2 distribution, where p is the dimension of the vectors in the dataset. (Note that this is the distribution of the standard Mahalanobis distance for an uncontaminated multivariate Gaussian dataset.) In the absence of outliers, the data points should lie near the reference line $MD_k^* = MD_k^0$, while significant departures from this line provide evidence for outliers in the dataset. In particular, extreme outliers will often exceed the detection thresholds for both distances, while less extreme outliers not detectable with the standard Mahalanobis distance due to masking effects will generally exceed the MD_k^* threshold but not the MD_k^0 threshold.

Two examples of distance-distance plots are shown in Figure 4.14. The upper left plot is a scatter plot of the two components of $N = 100$ independent random samples drawn from an uncontaminated bivariate Gaussian distribution, where each component has mean zero and standard deviation one and the correlation coefficient between the components is $\rho = 0.8$. The upper right plot shows the corresponding distance-distance plot: the horizontal axis corresponds to the classical Mahalanobis distance for each observation and the vertical axis corresponds to the outlier-resistant Mahalanobis distance computed from the MCD estimator. As expected, most of the points fall quite close to the reference line for this example. Also, note that only two points clearly exceed the 97.5% cutoff limit for the χ_2^2 distribution for the MCD distance, and only one exceeds this threshold for the classical distance. The lower left plot shows the same dataset, modified by replacing 15 of the original data points with the small cluster shown as solid circles in the lower right corner of the plot. The lower right plot shows the corresponding distance-distance diagnostic for this contaminated dataset. Here, note the substantial departures from the reference line and the large number of points exhibiting suspiciously large robust Mahalanobis distances. Here again, all of the outlying points are shown as solid circles and it is clear that the distance-distance plot declares them all suspicious, along with two other points that slightly exceed the χ_2^2 threshold. In contrast, note that only a few of these points exceed this threshold for the classical Mahalanobis distance. Also, note that the outlying points that do exceed this threshold are not the most extreme with respect to the classical Mahalanobis distance: one of the nonoutlying points is substantially farther from the center of the data with respect to this measure.

Since the covariance matrix Σ is central to a variety of popular multivariate data characterizations, the MCD estimator $\hat{\Sigma}^h$ provides the basis for outlier-resistant extensions of these characterizations. For example, multivariate hypothesis tests that generalize the classical t-test are based on Hotelling's T^2 statistic (Johnson and Wichern, 1988), which is essentially the Mahalanobis distance between the sample mean $\bar{x}$ and some reference mean

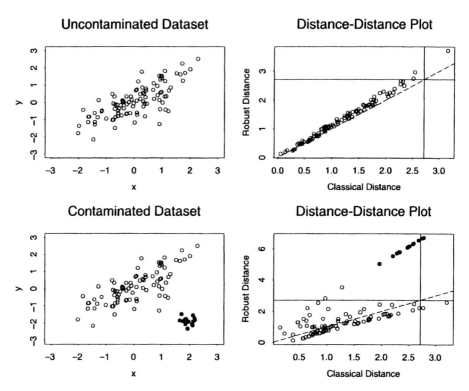

Figure 4.14. *Bivariate scatterplots (left) and distance-distance plots (right) for two datasets, one uncontaminated Gaussian and the other with a cluster of outliers.*

(e.g., **0**). The utility of this statistic is that, if the data sequence $\{x_k\}$ exhibits a multivariate normal distribution, the Hotelling T^2 statistic exhibits an F-distribution. An important practical limitation, however, is that like most other Gaussian-based data characterizations, this statistic is highly outlier-sensitive. Willems et al. (2002) describe an extension of Hotelling's T^2 statistic based on the MCD estimator that extends its utility to datasets that are reasonably approximated by contaminated Gaussian distributions. Similarly, principal component regression (PCR) is a multivariate analysis method that attempts to address collinearity problems by first performing a PCA to obtain a (typically small) set of linear combinations of the original predictor variables that are better conditioned (i.e., less collinear) than the full set of original variables, following this with a regression–model-building step. Verboven and Hubert (2002) describe an outlier-resistant formulation of this procedure that uses MCD estimators as the basis for an outlier-resistant PCA. Similarly, the MCD also forms the basis for the PCA diagnostic plots discussed by Pison and Van Aelst (2002), quite similar to that described by Rousseeuw and Van Zomeron (1990) for analyzing outlier-resistant regression residuals. In both cases, a robust Mahalanobis distance based on the MCD estimator is used to measure the "extremeness" of each data point. Finally, covariance matrix estimators are also central to the problem of canonical correlation analysis (CCA), which attempts to quantify the relationship between a set $\{x_k\}$ of p-dimensional vectors and a second set $\{y_k\}$ of q-dimensional vectors (Basilevsky, 1994, p. 300). The result of the simplest form of

CCA is a pair of constant vectors $\mathbf{a} \in R^p$ and $\mathbf{b} \in R^q$ such that the univariate sequences $\{\mathbf{a}^T \mathbf{x}_k\}$ and $\{\mathbf{b}^T \mathbf{y}_k\}$ are maximally correlated. Filzmoser, Dehon, and Croux (2000) describe an MCD-based CCA procedure that is much less sensitive to outliers than standard CCA procedures.

Other outlier-resistant covariance estimators also exist besides the MCD estimator. For example, the *minimum volume ellipsoid (MVE) estimator* (Rousseeuw and Leroy, 1987, p. 258) is based on the smallest ellipsoid $\mathcal{E}$ in R^p that contains a fixed fraction h of the data points (taking $h = 50\%$ gives the estimator a 50% breakdown point). The center of this ellipsoid defines the location estimator $\bar{\mathbf{x}}$, and the ellipsoid $\mathcal{E}$ is described by the quadratic inequality

$$\mathbf{x} \in \mathcal{E} \iff (\mathbf{x} - \bar{\mathbf{x}})^T \bar{\Sigma}^{-1} (\mathbf{x} - \bar{\mathbf{x}}) \leq 1. \tag{4.49}$$

The MVE covariance estimate corresponds to an appropriately scaled version of $\bar{\Sigma}$. Disadvantages of the MVE estimator relative to the MCD estimator include its poorer statistical efficiency and its greater computational complexity (Rousseeuw and Van Driessen, 1999). Conversely, there is some evidence to suggest that the practical choice between the MVE and MCD estimators depends on the dimension of the multivariate dataset and the contamination level. In particular, Becker (2000) compares the performance of the MVE, the MCD, and two other outlier-resistant covariance estimators for a collection of simulation examples involving $p = 10$ variables with $N = 500$. For contamination levels between 10% and $\sim 20\%$, the MCD estimator gives better results in these examples, but the MVE estimator rapidly becomes the better choice at higher contamination levels. Croux and Haesbroeck (1999) find that more complex S-estimators such as those considered by Becker (2000) perform better than the MCD estimator. Overall, it is clear that the problem of developing highly outlier resistant covariance estimators is still a topic of active research and one where algorithm developments are fundamentally changing the range of practical approaches to this problem.

4.4.3 Regression-based detection

The multivariate location model defined by (4.46) is not appropriate in all situations. In particular, this model assumes that the nominal data values lie within elliptical contours of "reasonable" Mahalanobis distance from the center of the data and that outliers are extreme relative to these contours. Conversely, the bivariate examples discussed in Chapter 2 to illustrate the problem of multivariate outliers were not of this form: the nominal data points were characterized by some visually obvious relationship between the components, and outliers were points that clearly violated this relationship. To detect multivariate outliers of this type, it is necessary to specify a more flexible data model than (4.46). The simplest regression-based alternative model for the bivariate case is of the form

$$y_k = \alpha_0 + \alpha_1 x_k + e_k + o_k, \tag{4.50}$$

where (x_k, y_k) represent the two components of the bivariate data vector and $\{e_k\}$ and $\{o_k\}$ are defined as in (4.44). If we can estimate the model parameters α_0 and α_1 accurately in the face of the contaminating outliers, we can transform our original bivariate data sequence (x_k, y_k) into the univariate sequence of residuals

$$r_k = y_k - \hat{\alpha}_0 - \hat{\alpha}_1 x_k \simeq e_k + o_k. \tag{4.51}$$

If $\{e_k\}$ is well approximated by a zero-mean, finite-variance i.i.d. sequence, this process of forming the residuals reduces the problem from a highly structured multivariate outlier detection problem to a much simpler univariate outlier detection problem, which may be approached using the methods discussed in Chapter 3. More typically, however, outlier detection occurs as a side effect of the process of estimating the model parameters α_0 and α_1 using methods such as those discussed in the next paragraphs. Before proceeding to this discussion, however, it is useful to generalize from the bivariate example described in (4.50) to the general p-variate case. There, the data model is of the form

$$y_k = \alpha_0 + \sum_{j=1}^{p-1} \alpha_j x_{kj} + e_k + o_k, \qquad (4.52)$$

where y_k is one of the p data variables that is predicted from the other $p - 1$ variables x_{kj} for $j = 1, 2, \ldots, p - 1$. As in the bivariate case, if we can reliably estimate the model parameters α_j for $j = 0, 1, \ldots, p - 1$, we can reduce the original, highly structured multivariate outlier detection problem to a univariate outlier detection problem by forming the residuals

$$r_k = y_k - \hat{\alpha}_0 - \sum_{j=1}^{p-1} \hat{\alpha}_j x_{kj} \simeq e_k + o_k. \qquad (4.53)$$

Again, the identification of outlying points normally emerges as a biproduct of the outlier-resistant regression procedure used to estimate the model coefficients $\{\alpha_j\}$.

An important practical point is the need to use an outlier-resistant procedure for estimating the regression model coefficients $\{\alpha_i\}$. In particular, estimating these coefficients by OLS regression generally leads to biased parameter estimates that obscure the presence of the outliers. Many different approaches have been proposed for outlier-resistant regression analysis (see Rousseeuw and Leroy (1987, Chapter 1) for a brief survey of some of these approaches), but the following discussion restricts attention to two: the *least median of squares* (LMS) (Rousseeuw, 1984) and *least trimmed squares* (LTS) methods. The idea behind the LMS method is to replace the outlier-sensitive minimization of the sum of squared residuals on which OLS regression is based with the median of the squared residuals

$$J = \text{median } \{r_k^2\}. \qquad (4.54)$$

Unlike OLS regression, the LMS regression problem does not have a simple analytic solution, and numerical solution poses some significant practical problems. In addition, the LMS regression estimator exhibits $1/N^{1/3}$ convergence to its limiting distribution, as opposed to the more usual $1/N^{1/2}$ convergence of the OLS regression estimator. This undesirable feature of the LMS estimator was one of the motivations for the LTS estimator, which replaces the median in (4.54) with a trimmed mean to obtain an estimator that converges like $1/N^{1/2}$ (Rousseeuw and Leroy, 1987, p. 15). Recently, a computationally efficient LTS regression procedure has been described and demonstrated for a dataset containing 56,744 astronomical observations with 8 predictor variables (Rousseeuw and Van Driessen, 2000). An important advantage of LMS and LTS estimators over many other outlier-resistant regression estimators (such as, for example, the regression M-estimators discussed by Huber (1981, Chapter 7)) is the fact that they can tolerate outliers in the predictor variables $\{x_{kj}\}$ as well as in the response variables $\{y_k\}$.

Analogous to the distance-distance plots discussed in Sec. 4.4.2 are the robust regression diagnostic plots discussed by Rousseeuw and Van Zomeron (1990). There, the vertical axis corresponds to the residuals r_k obtained from the LTS regression fit to the data, while the horizontal axis corresponds to the MCD-based Mahalanobis distance MD_k^* of the predictor variables $\{x_{ki}\}$ from their center. The idea behind this plot is that it permits separate identification of nominal observations (for which neither $|r_k|$ nor MD_k^* is excessively large), outliers that are not leverage points (for which $|r_k|$ is unusually large but MD_k^* is not), "good leverage points" that improve the regression fit (for which MD_k^* is large but $|r_k|$ is not), and "bad leverage points" that cause serious masking effects (for which both $|r_k|$ and MD_k^* are large). As a dramatic illustration of the effectiveness of this plot in revealing hidden structure, Rousseeuw and Van Driessen (2000) compare the results obtained using this diagnostic plot with those obtained using the corresponding OLS-based plot (i.e., OLS regression model residuals versus the standard Mahalanobis distance) for a large astronomical dataset. The LTS/MCD version of this plot clearly reveals a cluster of bad leverage points in this dataset, which were found to correspond to a group of giant stars. In contrast, the OLS version of this plot shows no evidence at all of this distinct cluster of points.

Other regression-based outlier detection procedures have been proposed and the area remains one of very active research in the statistics community, so no attempt is made here to survey this topic in detail. One approach based on LMS regression does seem particularly relevant, however, since it makes substantial use of comparisons and subset selection somewhat like the GSA framework described here. This approach is based on the idea of *forward search* using initial LMS estimates proposed by Atkinson (1994) and described in detail in the books by Atkinson and Riani (2000) and Atkinson, Riani, and Cerioli (2004). The basic idea is to use LMS regression to obtain an initial, highly outlier resistant fit to the dataset. Regression residuals are then computed and the p points with the residuals of smallest magnitude are chosen as a first data subset. This subset corresponds to a regression model (i.e., the model $\mathcal{M}_p$ that exactly fits the p data observations) and the residuals r_k^p from this model are evaluated for the complete N-observation dataset. The $p+1$ observations with the residuals of smallest magnitude are then fit to a model $\mathcal{M}_{p+1}$ using OLS regression. This process is then repeated iteratively to obtain models $\mathcal{M}_{p+2}$ through $\mathcal{M}_N$, where $\mathcal{M}_N$ corresponds to the OLS model fit to the complete dataset. Parameter values, prediction error standard deviations, or other OLS-based characterizations are then plotted against the number of data points n on which the model $\mathcal{M}_n$ is based. The essential idea is that, for $n \simeq p$, the datasets used to obtain $\mathcal{M}_n$ should be outlier-free, while for $n \simeq N$, these datasets may be highly contaminated. Monitoring the dependence of these characterizations on n can give useful indications of the presence of outliers. In particular, plotting the individual residuals r_k^n obtained from model $\mathcal{M}_n$ against n can be used to identify outlying observations $(\mathbf{x}_k, y_k)$ since these residuals should be large for small n but they may diminish substantially with increasing n as they become masked by other outliers in the dataset. Because this approach is based on OLS fits to the data subsets, many of the auxiliary tools developed for OLS regression can be used in connection with this analysis method. For a detailed exposition, refer to the books by Atkinson and Riani (2000) and Atkinson, Riani, and Cerioli (2004).

Finally, the robust regression ideas just discussed have also provided the motivation and the basis for the development of outlier-resistant extensions of some of the important

adjuncts to OLS regression analysis. As a specific example, Dehon and Croux (2002) note
that an important adjunct to classical regression analysis is a characterization of goodness-
of-fit, often together with significance results for the individual model terms. Both of these
ideas are based on Gaussian model error assumptions, and the standard characterizations exhibit undesirably strong outlier-sensitivities. To address these difficulties, Dehon and Croux
(2002) describe two useful outlier-resistant characterizations: an alternative to the R^2 coefficient and an alternative to the classical F-test for comparing two different models. The
classical R^2 statistic is computed from the model residuals defined in (4.53) as a way of comparing them to the prediction of the response variable y_k by its mean value $\bar{y}$. Specifically,
this statistic is given by

$$R^2 = 1 - \frac{\sum_{k=1}^{N} r_k^2}{\sum_{k=1}^{N} (y_k - \bar{y})^2}. \tag{4.55}$$

The idea is that if the regression model defined in (4.52) is a good approximation, the ratio
in (4.55) should be small, leading to a large R^2 value. Dehon and Croux (2002) generalize
this quantity as follows. First, they select a robust scale estimator $S(\cdot)$ satisfying the positive
homogeneity condition (see Chapter 5 for a more detailed discussion of this condition)

$$S(\alpha x_1, \alpha x_2, \ldots, \alpha x_N) = |\alpha| S(x_1, x_2, \ldots, x_N). \tag{4.56}$$

Given this scale estimator, they then determine the constant model $\hat{y}_k = \alpha_0$ that minimizes

$$J_0(\alpha_0) = S(y_1 - \alpha_0, y_2 - \alpha_0, \ldots, y_N - \alpha_0) \tag{4.57}$$

along with the regression model defined by (4.52) that minimizes

$$J_{p-1}(\alpha_0, \ldots, \alpha_{p-1}) = S\left(y_1 - \alpha_0 - \sum_{j=1}^{p-1} \alpha_j x_{1j}, \ldots, y_N - \alpha_0 - \sum_{j=1}^{p-1} \alpha_j x_{Nj}\right). \tag{4.58}$$

The modified R^2 statistic is then given by

$$R_S^2 = 1 - \frac{J_{p-1}^2(\alpha_0, \ldots, \alpha_{p-1})}{J_0^2(\alpha_0)}. \tag{4.59}$$

Different choices of scale estimators $S(\cdot)$ correspond to different regression methods, and the
authors present a summary of the results obtained for a simple example under four different
outlier scenarios using seven different regression methods, including OLS, LMS, and LTS.
As with the univariate outlier detection procedures discussed in Chapter 3, the relative
performance of these methods depends on both the outlier scenario and the contamination
level, but the only case where OLS results were better than LTS and LMS results was the
uncontaminated case.

4.4.4 Depth-based detection

The covariance-based multivariate outlier detection procedures discussed in Sec. 4.4.2 assume an approximate multivariate Gaussian nominal data model, with outliers exhibiting
unusually large Mahalanobis distances relative to this nominal data model. A more flexible

alternative is to describe multivariable datasets in terms of *data depth*, which provides a basis for rank-ordering data from "most representative" to "least representative/most outlying." While a detailed treatment of data depth lies beyond the scope of this book, the idea does appear extremely promising, motivating a brief introduction here. For more complete introductions, refer to the papers cited in the following paragraphs, particularly those by Liu, Parelius, and Singh (1999), Rousseeuw and Hubert (1999), and Tian, Vardi, and Zhang (2002).

Data depth is a characterization of an arbitrary vector $\mathbf{z} \in R^p$ that may be defined with respect to either a finite dataset $\{\mathbf{x}_k\}$ of observations in R^p or a p-variate probability distribution $F(\cdot)$. In the case of a finite dataset, the essential idea is that the vector $\mathbf{z}$ is "deep" if it lies near the "center" of the dataset and "not deep" if it lies at or beyond the "periphery" of this dataset. This idea can be made precise in different ways, leading to different quantitative measures of data depth. The fundamental idea is illustrated nicely by the bivariate case of *simplicial depth* described by Liu (1990). Suppose $\{\mathbf{x}_k\}$ is a set of N points in the plane and let $\Delta(\mathbf{x}_i, \mathbf{x}_j, \mathbf{x}_k)$ denote the closed triangle formed by any three distinct points $\mathbf{x}_i$, $\mathbf{x}_j$, and $\mathbf{x}_k$. The number of triangles we can form this way is $\binom{N}{3}$, and the simplicial depth of any vector $\mathbf{z} \in R^2$ is the fraction of these triangles containing $\mathbf{z}$ in their interior. Similarly, given a bivariate probability distribution $F(\cdot)$, the corresponding simplicial data depth is defined as

$$D(\mathbf{z}) = \mathcal{P}_F \{\mathbf{z} \in \Delta(\mathbf{x}_i, \mathbf{x}_j, \mathbf{x}_k)\}, \qquad (4.60)$$

where $\mathbf{x}_i$, $\mathbf{x}_j$, and $\mathbf{x}_k$ are three independent random samples drawn from the distribution $F(\cdot)$. The basic idea extends from the bivariate case to the general case by replacing triangles in the plane with simplices in R^p. Conversely, it is also instructive to examine the univariate analogue of this notion

$$D(z) = \mathcal{P}_F \{x_i < z < x_j\} = 2F(z)[1 - F(z)] \qquad (4.61)$$

for any continuous distribution function $F(\cdot)$. It is easy to see that the maximum value of $D(z)$ is $1/2$, which occurs when $F(z) = 1/2$ and corresponds to the median of the distribution $F(\cdot)$. This observation leads to the definition of a *multivariate simplicial median* as any point $\mathbf{z} \in R^p$ that maximizes the simplicial depth $D(\mathbf{z})$. In cases where this minimizer is not unique, a unique median is typically obtained by averaging over the deepest points.

Other definitions of data depth include the Mahalanobis depth, the half-space depth, the convex hull peeling depth, the Oja depth, the majority depth, and the likelihood depth, all discussed by Liu, Parelius, and Singh (1999), and the L_1 depth discussed further in the following paragraphs. Under any of these definitions of data depth, a dataset $\{\mathbf{x}_k\}$ can be ranked to obtain the depth-ordered dataset $\{\mathbf{x}_{[i]}\}$, where $\mathbf{x}_{[1]}$ is the *deepest* or *most central* point in the original dataset and $\mathbf{x}_{[N]}$ is the most extreme point. The deepest point then provides a basis for defining a multivariate median with respect to the given data depth. Alternatively, the direction of this association can be reversed, defining a data depth from a specified multivariate median, an idea illustrated by Tian, Vardi, and Zhang (2002) and Vardi and Zhang (2000) in their discussions of the L_1 median and the L_1 depth.

The (weighted) L_1 median $\mathbf{x}^\dagger$ of the dataset $\{\mathbf{x}_k\}$ is the vector $\mathbf{z} \in R^p$ that minimizes the following weighted sum of Euclidean distances from the data observations (Vardi and Zhang, 2000):

$$C(\mathbf{z}) = \sum_{k=1}^{N} w_k \|\mathbf{z} - \mathbf{x}_k\|, \tag{4.62}$$

where $\{w_k\}$ is a set of positive numbers and $\{\mathbf{x}_k\}$ is a set of N *distinct* vectors in R^p. One useful way of thinking about the weights w_k is as "multiplicities": if $\{\mathbf{x}_k\}$ appears r times in the dataset, remove $r - 1$ copies and set $w_k = r$. The L_1 median can also be defined with respect to a multivariate probability distribution $F(\cdot)$, essentially by replacing the weighted sum over data points in (4.62) with an expectation over $F(\cdot)$, giving

$$C_F(\mathbf{z}) = E_F(\|\mathbf{z} - \mathbf{x}\|) = \int \|\mathbf{z} - \mathbf{x}\| dF(\mathbf{x}). \tag{4.63}$$

That is, the L_1 multivariate median $\mathbf{x}^\dagger$ for the distribution $F(\cdot)$ is defined as the value of $\mathbf{z}$ that minimizes $C_F(\mathbf{z})$. The corresponding L_1 data depth function $D(\mathbf{y})$ is then defined as the smallest probability mass w that must be given to $\mathbf{y} \in R^p$ such that $\mathbf{y}$ becomes the L_1 median of the mixture distribution of this point mass (i.e., $\mathcal{P}(\mathbf{x} = \mathbf{y}) = w$) and the original distribution $F(\cdot)$. This mixture distribution may be written as

$$M(\mathbf{z}) = \frac{w\delta_\mathbf{y}(\mathbf{z}) + F(\mathbf{z})}{w + 1}, \tag{4.64}$$

where $\delta_\mathbf{y}(\mathbf{z})$ is the Dirac delta function that assigns infinite density to $\mathbf{z} = \mathbf{y}$ (i.e., concentrates all probability at this point). The L_1 data depth function is then given explicitly as

$$D(\mathbf{y}) = 1 - \inf \left\{ w \geq 0 \ \middle| \ \mathbf{x}^\dagger \left(\frac{w\delta_\mathbf{y} + F}{1 + w} \right) = \mathbf{y} \right\}. \tag{4.65}$$

Note that since w is a probability, it satisfies $0 \leq w \leq 1$ for all $\mathbf{y} \in R^p$. Also, if $\mathbf{y}$ corresponds to the L_1 median of $F(\cdot)$, the right-hand side condition is satisfied with no additional probability mass (i.e., with $w = 0$), so $D(\mathbf{y}) = 1$ for this case. Alternative definitions of data depth may be obtained by replacing the L_1 median $\mathbf{x}^\dagger$ in (4.65) with other multivariate median definitions. For example, the *marginal median* $\tilde{\mathbf{x}}$ is defined as the vector in R^p whose components are each equal to the univariate median of the corresponding component of $\mathbf{x}_k$, that is,

$$\tilde{\mathbf{x}}_j = \text{median}_k \{\mathbf{x}_{kj}\}, \quad j = 1, 2, \ldots, p. \tag{4.66}$$

Tian, Vardi, and Zhang (2002) note that most multivariate medians reduce to the standard univariate median for $p = 1$, but the results for $p > 1$ are often "vastly different."

An advantage of the L_1 data depth over most of the alternative definitions of data depth is the existence of a simple expression for $D(\mathbf{y})$ relative to a dataset $\{\mathbf{x}_k\}$. Specifically, Tian, Vardi, and Zhang (2002) give the result

$$D(\mathbf{z}) = 1 - \left(\left\| \frac{1}{N} \sum_{k=1}^{N} \frac{\mathbf{z} - \mathbf{x}_k}{\|\mathbf{z} - \mathbf{x}_k\|} I\{\mathbf{x}_k \neq \mathbf{y}\} \right\| - \frac{1}{N} \sum_{k=1}^{N} I\{\mathbf{x}_k = \mathbf{y}\} \right)^+, \tag{4.67}$$

where $I\{\mathbf{x} = \mathbf{y}\}$ is equal to 1 if the condition $\mathbf{x} = \mathbf{y}$ holds and 0 otherwise, and $x^+ = $ max $(0, x)$. The authors note that $D(\mathbf{z})$ exhibits its maximum possible value of 1 when $\mathbf{z}$ is the L_1 median and that $D(\mathbf{z}) \rightarrow 0$ as $||\mathbf{z}|| \rightarrow \infty$. Conversely, unlike the simplicial data depth and a number of others, the L_1 data depth is not affine-invariant, an important condition discussed further in Chapter 5.

The notion of data depth has also been extended to other multivariate data characterizations, including the regression setting discussed in Sec. 4.4.3. As a specific example, Tian, Vardi, and Zhang (2002) introduce two depth-based outlier-resistant regression approaches. The first is called the *dual space median (DSM)* estimator, defined as follows. The set of all p-point subsets that each uniquely determine a regression model of the desired form is characterized. This set corresponds to a set $\mathbf{L}$ of regression model parameter p vectors and the DSM estimate is the L_1 median of this parameter vector set. The second depth-based approach consists of the following three steps:

a. Determine the *depth relative to the regression (DRR) model* of each observation in the dataset.

b. Trim the α most outlying points from the dataset relative to DRR.

c. Fit the model to the trimmed dataset.

The DRR value for a data observation $\mathbf{x}_k$ is obtained by determining the p-point subsets containing $\mathbf{x}_k$ in $\mathbf{L}$, computing the L_1 data depth of each of the corresponding parameter vectors in $\mathbf{L}$, and averaging the result to obtain the depth of $\mathbf{x}_k$ relative to the regression model under consideration. Tian, Vardi, and Zhang (2002) compare the performance and computational complexity of a range of trimming percentages α and regression methods for Step c of this sequence.

Rousseeuw and Hubert (1999) describe another depth-based regression approach, where the basic idea is to assign depth values to the regression models themselves (i.e., the parameter vectors θ_i) rather than to the data points. To accomplish this, Rousseeuw and Hubert (1999) define a *nonfit* as a candidate parameter vector θ that satisfies the following condition: there exists a hyperplane $\mathbf{H}$ in the data space R^p that does not contain any of the points in $\{\mathbf{x}_k\}$ such that $r_k(\theta) < 0$ for all points in one of the open half-spaces defined by $\mathbf{H}$ and $r_k(\theta) > 0$ for all points in the other open half-space. Here, $r_k(\theta)$ represents the model residual evaluated at data point k for model parameter vector θ. The regression depth of a parameter vector θ is then defined as the smallest number of observations that must be removed from the dataset to make θ satisfy the nonfit conditions just described. The *deepest regression* is defined as the value of θ that maximizes the regression depth, and Rousseeuw and Hubert (1999) present a number of results and conjectures concerning the largest achievable regression depth. The resulting estimator exhibits a number of interesting properties, including invariance under monotone transformations of the response variables y_k. That is, since the regression depth depends only on the signs of the regression residuals, any model transformations that leave these signs invariant will not change the regression depth. As a consequence, this approach to depth-based regression exhibits considerable tolerance to certain unpleasant violations of distributional assumptions, including asymmetry and heteroscedasticity (i.e., nonconstant variances). Conversely, it is clear from the commentaries and rejoinder published with the paper of Rousseeuw and Hubert (1999) that a number of issues associated with this definition of regression depth are novel, controversial, and not yet fully understood.

The various notions of data depth just described have been used as the basis for many other extensions of traditional multivariate analysis methods, including the descriptive statistics (e.g., location, scale, skewness, and kurtosis measures) described by Liu, Parelius, and Singh (1999), extensions of cluster analysis (Jörnsten, Vardi, and Zhang, 2002), extensions of the classical Hotelling T^2 statistic discussed in Sec. 4.4.2, and multivariate statistical process control charts described by Liu (2003). In addition, data depth provides the foundation for the multivariate data partitioning approach called *DataSpheres* (Dasu and Johnson, 2003) discussed briefly in Chapter 7. Overall, these results suggest that depth-based analysis methods are rapidly evolving and potentially very useful, and hence worthy of continued attention.

4.5   Preliminary analyses and auxiliary knowledge

As the CAMDA normal mouse example discussed in Chapter 1 illustrates, one preprocessing strategy that is sometimes quite effective in detecting data anomalies—even quite severe ones—is to perform a preliminary data analysis whose outcome is believed to be known in advance. Observations of radical departures from these expectations can indicate the presence of data anomalies. Like the microarray dataset discussed in Sec. 4.1.2, the CAMDA normal mouse dataset contains several variables, including the optical intensity values obtained from organ-specific tissue samples and a reference sample that was common to all microarrays. Since these optical intensities are related to gene expression levels, which are expected to differ significantly between the three tissue types considered in this study, it was expected that the tissue-specific optical intensities would cluster into three distinct groups. Similarly, since the same genetic material was used in the reference sample for all microarrays, it was expected that all of these reference intensities would cluster in a fourth group, distinct from the three tissue-specific clusters. Stivers et al. (2003) performed a preliminary PCA to test this hypothesis, but they did not obtain the expected result. (For a more detailed discussion of this analysis, refer to the paper of Stivers et al. (2003).)

The results these authors did obtain raised the suspicion that an error had occurred in assembling the three data files provided to the CAMDA participants (one dataset for each tissue type, including both tissue-specific and reference intensity data from all microarrays). Besides the optical intensity data, these datasets also included the position of each spot on the microarray, along with an annotation for the gene spotted on the array at each position. The suspicion that something was wrong was initially confirmed by the observation that the pairings of spot position and gene identifier did not match across the three datasets. The original analysis was done on the basis of gene identifiers, so a second analysis was performed after reordering the dataset so that the spot positions agreed across the three datasets. This second analysis yielded different results that were better with respect to the clustering of the reference intensities, but the expected single cluster still exhibited two well-separated components and the main component overlapped significantly with one of the tissue-specific clusters. This result suggested that *neither* of the two possible alignments considered was correct because a misalignment had occurred in the middle of building one of the three datasets. Further investigation led to the conclusion that 1,932 of 5,304 genes had been misaligned in one of the three datasets, and a third analysis of the data based on this hypothesis ultimately led to a clustering of the results that was in reasonable agreement with expectations.

This example illustrates three important practical points. First is the utility of performing simple preliminary analysis to assess data quality. Unusual discrepancies, as in the example just described, can give useful indications of serious but possibly quite subtle anomalies. The second key point is the utility of auxiliary variables in confirming suspicious results. Often, these variables are of little inherent interest (e.g., the spot locations of the different genes on each microarray in the example just discussed), but they can still be extremely useful both in confirming initial suspicions and in formulating alternative analysis strategies to correct for the data anomalies. Another example of the effective use of ancillary variables in confirming suspicious observations is that discussed by Barnett and Lewis (1994, p. 12), who describe the regression analysis of a small dataset of auricular pressure and coronary flow in cats published by Rahman (1972). Although most of the data points appear consistent with a linear relation between these variables, four observations are visually inconsistent with this linear relationship. In addition, these data points all correspond to the *same* value of auricular pressure, and a subsequent examination of the original dataset reveals that these four points represent a sequence of *consecutive* measurements that decay monotonically to zero with time, which may be viewed as an auxiliary variable in the original analysis. Overall, these observations led Barnett and Lewis (1994) to speculate that the cat had died during these experiments.

Finally, the third key point of this example is the utility of comparing results obtained from a possibly contaminated dataset with those obtained after one or more attempts at correcting the assumed data anomaly have been made. In the case of simple data anomalies like outliers, the original results may be compared with those obtained by either omitting the suspicious values or replacing them with more reasonable alternative values. In the case of missing data values, this idea leads naturally to the multiple imputation strategies discussed in Sec. 4.2.

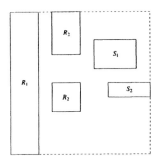

Chapter 5

What Is a "Good" Data Characterization?

Based on a set of simple axioms characterizing voting systems, Arrow's impossibility theorem establishes that "dictatorships, which are undesirable, are a consequence of desirable properties" (Day and McMorris, 2003, p. 17). One of the key points of this chapter is that somewhat similar conclusions apply to data characterizations: simple, desirable criteria such as finite breakdown can lead to unexpected behavior such as the exact fit property (EFP) discussed in Sec. 5.2.6, which some regard as a serious limitation (Hettmansperger and Sheather, 1992). More generally, this chapter is concerned with the interpretation and consequences of the following idea:

> A "good" characterization $\mathcal{K}$ of a dataset $\mathcal{D}$ should depend *predictably* on certain simple, systematic modifications of $\mathcal{D}$.

As a specific example, one of the fundamental criteria imposed on all location estimators $T(\cdot)$ considered in the Princeton Robustness Study (Andrews et al., 1972) is that the following invariance property hold for all real constants α and β:

$$T\{\alpha x_k + \beta\} = \alpha T\{x_k\} + \beta. \tag{5.1}$$

The practical importance of this particular condition is discussed further in Sec. 5.1, but an important general observation is that (5.1) belongs to the class of *functional equations*, which can yield extremely useful insight into the behavior of data characterizations. This point is illustrated in Sec. 5.2, which also includes a brief general introduction to the subject of functional equations, since they do not appear to be nearly as familiar to nonspecialists as, say, linear algebra is.

In addition to functional equations like (5.1), another extremely useful way of assessing "goodness" is through inequalities, a point illustrated in Sec. 5.3. There, four different applications of inequalities in data characterization are briefly considered: aiding interpretation, comparing different data characterizations, obtaining bounds on results that are not directly computable from the available data, and alternatively describing uncertainty (i.e., the set-theoretic model as opposed to the random variable model).

There are, of course, other important "goodness criteria" for a data characterization, and some of these are examined briefly in Sec. 5.4. One of the key points of that discussion is that the various ways of assessing goodness are often in conflict, forcing us to examine trade-offs and comparisons.

5.1   A motivating example

To see the practical importance of conditions like (5.1), consider the following example. Suppose we are given a sequence $\{x_k\}$ of temperatures measured at sample times t_k by a computer-based data collection system that occasionally failed, introducing a few gross outliers into the data sequence. Naturally, we would like to be able to apply outlier detection procedures like those discussed in Chapter 3 to this problem, *and we expect the performance of the selected outlier detection procedure not to depend on the measurement units chosen.* That is, regardless of whether our dataset contains temperatures in degrees Celsius or degrees Fahrenheit, we would expect that a "good" outlier detection procedure would declare the *same* set of points as outliers.

More specifically, consider the class of univariate outlier detection schemes discussed in Chapter 3:

$$|x_k - x_0| > t\zeta \ \Rightarrow \ x_k \text{ is an outlier,}$$

where x_0 is a nominal reference value and ζ is a measure of the spread of the nominal data values around this reference value. To simplify the following discussion, let $x_0 = \mu(\mathbf{x})$ and $\zeta = S(\mathbf{x})$, where $\mathbf{x}$ represents the vector of the available N data values. The general mathematical statement of the unit-independence condition described above is that, for any "good" location estimator $\mu(\cdot)$, any "good" scale estimator $S(\cdot)$, and any threshold parameter $t > 0$ that we choose to consider, the data observation x_k should be an outlier with respect to the data vector $\mathbf{x}$ if and only if the rescaled observation $\alpha x_k + \beta$ is an outlier with respect to the rescaled data vector $\alpha \mathbf{x} + \beta$. That is, we want the equivalence

$$|x_k - \mu(\mathbf{x})| > t S(\mathbf{x}) \ \Leftrightarrow \ |\alpha x_k + \beta - \mu(\alpha \mathbf{x} + \beta)| > t S(\alpha \mathbf{x} + \beta) \tag{5.2}$$

to hold for all real numbers α and β and all $t > 0$. Alternatively, note that this condition— which classifies points x_k into either "outliers" or "nominal points"—is equivalent to the following scaling of the decision boundaries:

$$x_k - \mu(\mathbf{x}) = \pm t S(\mathbf{x}) \ \Leftrightarrow \ \alpha x_k + \beta - \mu(\alpha \mathbf{x} + \beta) = \pm t S(\alpha \mathbf{x} + \beta). \tag{5.3}$$

For simplicity, assume $\alpha > 0$ and take the positive sign in (5.3), corresponding to consideration of the upper outlier decision boundary. It then follows that

$$x_k = \mu(\mathbf{x}) + t S(\mathbf{x}) \ \Rightarrow \ \alpha x_k + \beta = \alpha\mu(\mathbf{x}) + t\alpha S(\mathbf{x}) + \beta. \tag{5.4}$$

Combining this result with the desired scaling behavior in (5.3) then gives

$$\alpha\mu(\mathbf{x}) + t\alpha S(\mathbf{x}) + \beta = \mu(\alpha\mathbf{x} + \beta) + t S(\alpha\mathbf{x} + \beta). \tag{5.5}$$

Since this condition must hold for all real β, it is useful to first consider the special case $\beta = 0$, which gives

$$\alpha\mu(\mathbf{x}) + \alpha t S(\mathbf{x}) = \mu(\alpha\mathbf{x}) + t S(\alpha\mathbf{x})$$
$$\Rightarrow \ \alpha\mu(\mathbf{x}) - \mu(\alpha\mathbf{x}) = t[S(\alpha\mathbf{x}) - \alpha S(\mathbf{x})]. \tag{5.6}$$

Since this condition must hold for all $t > 0$ and only the right-hand side of the bottom equation depends on t, both sides of this equation must vanish, giving

$$\mu(\alpha\mathbf{x}) = \alpha\mu(\mathbf{x}),$$
$$S(\alpha\mathbf{x}) = \alpha S(\mathbf{x}) \tag{5.7}$$

for all $\alpha > 0$. This requirement corresponds to *positive-homogeneity*, an important notion discussed further in Sec. 5.2.2. Also, considering the case $\alpha < 0$ shows that this homogeneity condition must hold for all real α for the function $\mu(\cdot)$, but that $S(\cdot)$ satisfies the slightly different scaling condition $S(\alpha\mathbf{x}) = |\alpha|S(\mathbf{x})$ for all real α.

Next, consider (5.5) for $\beta \neq 0$ and $\alpha = 1$, which yields

$$\mu(\mathbf{x}) + \beta + tS(\mathbf{x}) = \mu(\mathbf{x} + \beta) + tS(\mathbf{x} + \beta)$$
$$\Rightarrow \mu(\mathbf{x}) + \beta - \mu(\mathbf{x} + \beta) = t[S(\mathbf{x} + \beta) - S(\mathbf{x})]. \tag{5.8}$$

Since this condition must hold for all $t > 0$, it again follows that both sides of the second equation must vanish, implying

$$\mu(\mathbf{x} + \beta) = \mu(\mathbf{x}) + \beta,$$
$$S(\mathbf{x} + \beta) = S(\mathbf{x}) \tag{5.9}$$

for all real β. Combining these results with (5.7) then gives the necessary conditions for the desired invariance of outlier detection under affine measurement unit rescalings

$$\mu(\alpha\mathbf{x} + \beta) = \alpha\mu(\mathbf{x}) + \beta,$$
$$S(\alpha\mathbf{x} + \beta) = |\alpha|S(\mathbf{x}) \tag{5.10}$$

for all real α and β. Note that the first of these conditions is the invariance condition (5.1) required of location estimators for inclusion in the Princeton Robustness Study. The second condition is significantly different and represents a natural "goodness condition" for scale estimators that is discussed further in Sec. 5.2.3. In fact, we have just proved the (harder) "only if" part of the following theorem; the "if" part follows immediately on substituting (5.10) into the outlier detection rule.

Theorem 5.1. *The decisions of the outlier detection rule*

$$|x_k - \mu(\mathbf{x})| > tS(\mathbf{x}) \implies x_k \text{ is an outlier}$$

are invariant under affine rescalings $x_k \to \alpha x_k + \beta$ *for all real* α *and* β *if and only if conditions* (5.10) *hold.*

5.2 Characterization via functional equations

Theorem 5.1 establishes the practical importance of the invariance properties given in (5.10), which represent simple examples of *functional equations*. In favorable cases, these equations can be solved to yield much useful insight into the behavior of different classes of data characterizations. Since, as noted earlier, functional equations are not as well known to non-mathematicians as other useful branches of mathematics, Sec. 5.2.1 provides a brief general introduction to the subject, after which Secs. 5.2.2 through 5.2.6 describe the application of functional equations to characterize a variety of important classes of data characterization procedures, including the outlier detection procedures discussed in Sec. 5.1.

5.2.1 A brief introduction to functional equations

The term *functional equation* is somewhat difficult to define precisely (Aczél, 1966, p. 1), but the fundamental idea is that functional equations characterize unknown functions in terms of their mathematical behavior. A set of simple but very instructive examples are the four functional equations considered by Cauchy. The simplest of these is *Cauchy's basic equation* (Aczél, 1966, p. 31)

$$f(x + y) = f(x) + f(y). \tag{5.11}$$

In this equation, $f(\cdot)$ is an unknown function to be determined and x and y can assume any real values. It follows by induction from (5.11) that

$$f\left(\sum_{k=1}^{N} x_k\right) = \sum_{k=1}^{N} f(x_k) \tag{5.12}$$

for all $x_k \in R$ and any finite N. Taking $x_k = x$ for all k then leads to the result that

$$f(Nx) = Nf(x) \tag{5.13}$$

for all integers N. Substituting $z = Nx$ into (5.13) leads immediately to the result that $f(z/N) = f(z)/N$ for all $z \in R$ and all integers N. Combining this observation with (5.13) then leads to the result that

$$f\left(\frac{M}{N}x\right) = \frac{M}{N}f(x) \tag{5.14}$$

for all integers N and M. Also, note that (5.13) implies

$$f(0) = f(N \cdot 0) = Nf(0) \Rightarrow f(0) = 0 \tag{5.15}$$

since this result must hold for all integers N. Also, taking $y = -x$ in (5.11) leads to the result that

$$0 = f(0) = f(x + (-x)) = f(x) + f(-x) \Rightarrow f(-x) = -f(x). \tag{5.16}$$

Combining (5.14), (5.15), and (5.16) leads to the conclusion that if $f(\cdot)$ satisfies Cauchy's basic functional equation, then $f(\cdot)$ is *homogeneous* with respect to *rational* scale factors:

$$f(rx) = rf(x) \quad \text{for all rational } r. \tag{5.17}$$

Further, taking $x = 1$ in this result implies that $f(r) = cr$ for all rational r, where $c = f(1)$ is a constant. In other words, all solutions of Cauchy's basic equation are linear when restricted to the rationals.

To go beyond this result requires additional assumptions on $f(\cdot)$, but remarkably weak ones. Specifically, Aczél and Dhombres (1989, p. 15) show that the only solution to Cauchy's basic functional equation (5.11) is the linear solution

$$f(x) = cx \quad \text{for all } x \in R, \tag{5.18}$$

provided the function $f(\cdot)$ is continuous at any point; monotone on any interval, no matter how small; or bounded on any interval, no matter how small. Conversely, nonlinear solutions that do not satisfy any of these conditions do exist, although they are so badly behaved mathematically that they are not practical for modelling physical systems or for analyzing data. Hence, for all practical purposes, the linear solution given in (5.18) represents the only solution of (5.11).

The second of the four Cauchy functional equations considered here is *Cauchy's exponential equation* (Aczél and Dhombres, 1989, p. 28), which requires that $f(\cdot)$ satisfy

$$f(x + y) = f(x)f(y) \tag{5.19}$$

for all real x and y. In fact, this equation can easily be reduced to Cauchy's basic equation by the following sequence of steps. First, suppose that $f(x_0) = 0$ for some real x_0. It then follows from (5.19) that, for any $y \in R$,

$$f(y) = f(x_0 + [y - x_0]) = f(x_0)f(y - x_0) = 0. \tag{5.20}$$

Consequently, any solution of (5.19) that is not identically zero is never equal to zero. Also, taking $x = y = z/2$ in (5.20) gives, for all $z \in R$,

$$f(z) = f\left(\frac{z}{2} + \frac{z}{2}\right) = \left[f\left(\frac{z}{2}\right)\right]^2 > 0. \tag{5.21}$$

Thus, since $f(x) > 0$ for all $x \in R$, the function $g(x) = \ln f(x)$ is well-defined for all x and satisfies Cauchy's basic functional equation:

$$g(x + y) = \ln f(x + y) = \ln[f(x)f(y)] = \ln f(x) + \ln f(y) = g(x) + g(y). \tag{5.22}$$

It then follows from the results presented above for this equation that the only practical solution to (5.22) is $g(x) = cx$, so the only practical solutions of (5.19) are

$$f(x) = e^{g(x)} = e^{cx} \quad \text{and} \quad f(x) = 0 \quad \text{for all } x \in R. \tag{5.23}$$

The third functional equation considered here is *Cauchy's logarithmic equation* (Aczél and Dhombres, 1989, p. 25), which requires that the function $f(\cdot)$ satisfy

$$f(xy) = f(x) + f(y) \quad \text{for all } x \neq 0. \tag{5.24}$$

The exclusion of the point $x = 0$ is important here since if (5.24) must hold for $x = 0$, it follows that

$$f(0) = f(0 \cdot y) = f(0) + f(y) \Rightarrow f(y) = 0 \tag{5.25}$$

for all $y \in R$, implying that $f(\cdot)$ is identically zero. Next, taking $x = y = \pm z$, (5.24) implies that

$$2f(z) = f(z^2) = 2f(-z) \Rightarrow f(-z) = f(z) \quad \text{for all } z > 0$$
$$\Rightarrow f(z) = f(|z|) \quad \text{for all } z \neq 0. \tag{5.26}$$

Hence, it is enough to consider (5.24) for $x > 0$ and $y > 0$, which permits the following substitutions: define $u = \ln x$, $v = \ln y$, and $g(u) = f(e^u) = f(x)$. We may then write (5.24) as

$$f(xy) = f(e^u \cdot e^v) = f(e^{u+v}) = g(u+v) = f(e^u) + f(e^v) = g(u) + g(v). \quad (5.27)$$

Again, this is Cauchy's basic functional equation, implying that the only practical solution is $g(u) = cu$. Hence, the only useful, nontrivial solution of (5.24) for $x > 0$ is given by $f(x) = g(u) = cu = c \ln x$. Combining this result with the second line of (5.26) and the trivial solution yields the complete practical solution to (5.24), which is

$$f(x) = c \ln |x| \quad \text{for all } x \neq 0 \quad \text{or} \quad f(x) = 0 \quad \text{for all } x \in R. \quad (5.28)$$

Finally, the fourth functional equation considered here is *Cauchy's power equation* (Aczél and Dhombres, 1989, p. 29), which requires $f(\cdot)$ to satisfy

$$f(xy) = f(x)f(y) \quad \text{for all } x \neq 0. \quad (5.29)$$

As in the previous example, the exclusion $x \neq 0$ is necessary to avoid trivial solutions: if (5.29) must be satisfied for $x = 0$, it follows that either $f(x) = 0$ or $f(x) = 1$ for all $x \in R$. As in the previous example, it is instructive to consider the special case $x = y = \pm z$, from which it follows that

$$[f(z)]^2 = f(z^2) = [f(-z)]^2 \Rightarrow f(-z) = \pm f(z). \quad (5.30)$$

Again restricting consideration to $x > 0$, $y > 0$ permits the use of logarithmic transformations: define $u = \ln x$, $v = \ln y$, and $g(u) = f(e^u) = f(x)$, reducing (5.29) to

$$f(xy) = f(e^{u+v}) = g(u+v) = f(e^u)f(e^v) = g(u)g(v). \quad (5.31)$$

This equation is simply (5.19), for which the practical solution was shown to be $g(u) = e^{cu}$. Hence, the solution to (5.29) for $x > 0$ is

$$f(x) = g(u) = e^{cu} = e^{c \ln x} = x^c. \quad (5.32)$$

Combining this result with (5.30) leads to the following general solution for practical applications, for all $x \neq 0$:

$$f(x) = |x|^c, \quad f(x) = |x|^c \text{sign} \{x\}, \quad f(x) = 0. \quad (5.33)$$

In summary, the four Cauchy functional equations just discussed illustrate a number of important general characteristics of functional equations. First, these examples illustrate that, in favorable cases, a simple functional equation can completely characterize the form of an unknown function, subject only to extremely mild regularity conditions. Another important point, illustrated by Cauchy's logarithmic and power equations, is that domain restrictions can be critical in determining the range of admissible solutions for a particular functional equation. In fact, Cauchy's exponential equation provides a further illustration of this point: if (5.19) is only required to hold for $x, y \geq 0$, an additional solution is given by $f(0) = 1$ and $f(x) = 0$ for all $x > 0$. For a more complete introduction to the subject of functional equations, see the references, particularly the books by Aczél (1966, 1987) and Aczél and Dhombres (1989), and the further references cited there.

5.2.2 Homogeneity and its extensions

The notion of homogeneity has already been introduced, both in the solution of Cauchy's basic functional equation in Sec. 5.2.1 in the restricted form of rational homogeneity and in connection with the outlier detection example discussed in Sec. 5.1. In its simplest form, a function $f : R^N \to R$ is *homogeneous* if it satisfies

$$f(\alpha x_1, \alpha x_2, \ldots, \alpha x_N) = \alpha f(x_1, x_2, \ldots, x_N) \tag{5.34}$$

for all $\mathbf{x} \in R^N$ and all $\alpha \in R$. Perhaps not surprisingly in view of the results presented in Sec. 5.2.1, the theory of functional equations provides a complete characterization of this class of functions. First, however, it is useful to briefly consider the following much more general notion of homogeneity.

A *generalized homogeneous function* $f : R^N \to R$ must satisfy the condition (Aczél, 1966, p. 304)

$$f(\alpha x_1, \alpha x_2, \ldots, \alpha x_N) = g(\alpha) f(x_1, x_2, \ldots, x_N) \tag{5.35}$$

for some function $g(\cdot)$ for all $\mathbf{x} \in R^N$ and all $\alpha \neq 0$. Clearly, a trivial solution is $f(\mathbf{x}) = 0$ for all $\mathbf{x} \in R^N$. To characterize the nontrivial solutions, assume there exists some $\mathbf{x} \in R^N$ for which $f(\mathbf{x}) \neq 0$ and note that $f(\cdot)$ must satisfy both of the conditions

$$f(\alpha \beta x_1, \alpha \beta x_2, \ldots, \alpha \beta x_N) = g(\alpha) f(\beta x_1, \beta x_2, \ldots, \beta x_N)$$
$$= g(\alpha) g(\beta) f(x_1, x_2, \ldots, x_N),$$
$$f(\alpha \beta x_1, \alpha \beta x_2, \ldots, \alpha \beta x_N) = g(\alpha \beta) f(x_1, x_2, \ldots, x_N) \tag{5.36}$$

for all real α and β. Since $f(\mathbf{x}) \neq 0$, we can divide it out of both of the equations in (5.36) to obtain the following functional equation for $g(\cdot)$:

$$g(\alpha \beta) = g(\alpha) g(\beta). \tag{5.37}$$

This equation is simply Cauchy's power equation, whose complete practical solution was given in Sec. 5.2.1. Nontrivial solutions correspond to $g(\alpha) = |\alpha|^c$ and $g(\alpha) = |\alpha|^c \text{sign} \{\alpha\}$. Taking $c = 1$, the second of these solutions reduces to $g(\alpha) = \alpha$, corresponding to homogeneity as defined in (5.34). The first of these solutions for arbitrary c corresponds to *homogeneity of order c* (Davis, 1962, p. 36):

$$f(\alpha x_1, \alpha x_2, \ldots, \alpha x_N) = |\alpha|^c f(x_1, x_2, \ldots, x_N). \tag{5.38}$$

The second corresponds to the following variation of this idea:

$$f(\alpha x_1, \alpha x_2, \ldots, \alpha x_N) = |\alpha|^c \, \text{sign} \{\alpha\} \, f(x_1, x_2, \ldots, x_N). \tag{5.39}$$

Also, it is important to note that we obtain a slightly different result if the generalized homogeneity condition is only required to hold for $\alpha > 0$, leading to the notion of *positive-homogeneity of order c*. There, since sign $\{\alpha\} = 1$, both (5.38) and (5.39) reduce to the same result:

$$f(\alpha x_1, \alpha x_2, \ldots, \alpha x_N) = \alpha^c f(x_1, x_2, \ldots, x_N) \quad \text{for } \alpha > 0. \tag{5.40}$$

Clearly, every function satisfying either condition (5.38) or (5.39) for all $\alpha \in R$ also satisfies condition (5.40) for $\alpha > 0$, but the converse is not true. This difference may be seen most easily by considering the scalar case $N = 1$. There, condition (5.38) reduces to

$$f(\alpha x) = |\alpha|^c f(x) \Rightarrow f(z) = A|z|^c, \tag{5.41}$$

a result obtained by taking $z = \alpha x$ and letting $x = 1$. Similarly, this argument reduces condition (5.39) to

$$f(\alpha x) = |\alpha|^c \, \text{sign} \, \{\alpha\} f(x) \Rightarrow f(z) = A|z|^c \, \text{sign} \, \{z\}. \tag{5.42}$$

In contrast, it is easy to show that the following more general functions exhibit positive-homogeneity of order c:

$$f(z) = \begin{cases} A_+ z^c & z > 0, \\ A_- |z|^c & z < 0, \end{cases} \tag{5.43}$$

where the two constants A_+ and A_- are arbitrary. Note that conditions (5.41) and (5.42) correspond to special cases of this result: for (5.41), $A_- = A_+$, while for (5.42), $A_- = -A_+$.

For $c \neq 0$, the following general result is sometimes extremely useful. Suppose $f(\cdot)$ is positive-homogeneous of order c and note that, for $\mathbf{x} = \mathbf{0}$,

$$f(0, 0, \ldots, 0) = f(\alpha \cdot 0, \alpha \cdot 0, \ldots, \alpha \cdot 0) = \alpha^c f(0, 0, \ldots, 0). \tag{5.44}$$

Since this condition must hold for all $\alpha > 0$, the only possible solutions are $f(\mathbf{0}) = 0$, $+\infty$, or $-\infty$. Hence, any positive-homogeneous function of order $c \neq 0$ that is bounded at $\mathbf{x} = \mathbf{0}$ necessarily satisfies $f(\mathbf{0}) = 0$. Also, note that if $c \leq 0$, requiring condition (5.38) or (5.39) to hold for all real α causes difficulties since $|\alpha|^c$ is singular at $\alpha = 0$ for $c < 0$ and indeterminate for $c = 0$. Hence, for $c \leq 0$, these conditions will only be required to hold for $\alpha \neq 0$.

For $\mathbf{x} \neq \mathbf{0}$, it is easy to show that the following general construction leads to positive-homogeneous functions of order c, a result closely related to those given by Aczél and Dhombres (1989, p. 346) and Aczél, Gronau, and Schwaiger (1994, Theorem 11):

$$f(x_1, x_2, \ldots, x_N) = ||\mathbf{x}||^c \, G\left(\frac{x_1}{||\mathbf{x}||}, \frac{x_2}{||\mathbf{x}||}, \ldots, \frac{x_N}{||\mathbf{x}||}\right). \tag{5.45}$$

Here, the function $G(\cdot)$ is *any* map from R^N into R and $|| \cdot ||$ denotes any norm on R^N. In particular, note that the replacement $x_i \rightarrow \alpha x_i$ means that $||\mathbf{x}|| \rightarrow \alpha||\mathbf{x}||$ for any $\alpha > 0$, leaving all of the arguments of $G(\cdot)$ unmodified, while scaling the term in front of $G(\cdot)$ by α^c. Note that for any norm, $||\mathbf{x}|| > 0$ unless $\mathbf{x} = \mathbf{0}$, so that $f(\cdot)$ is well-defined everywhere except $\mathbf{x} = \mathbf{0}$, but this value may be taken as zero by the arguments presented above. Further, note that if the stronger homogeneity condition (5.38) is imposed, (5.45) still holds, but now the function $G(\cdot)$ must satisfy the *even symmetry* condition

$$G(-x_1, -x_2, \ldots, -x_N) = G(x_1, x_2, \ldots, x_N) \tag{5.46}$$

for all $\mathbf{x} \in R^N$. Similarly, if condition (5.39) is required, $G(\cdot)$ must satisfy the following *odd symmetry* condition for all $\mathbf{x} \in R^N$:

$$G(-x_1, -x_2, \ldots, -x_N) = -G(x_1, x_2, \ldots, x_N). \tag{5.47}$$

Note that the function $G(\cdot)$ appearing in (5.45) is positive-homogeneous of order zero by construction: the arguments in this function are modified so that scaling each component of the data vector $\mathbf{x}$ by the same positive constant leaves the arguments of $G(\cdot)$ unmodified. This result may be viewed as a special case of the following two more general results. First, note that if $\phi(\mathbf{x})$ and $\psi(\mathbf{x})$ are two positive-homogeneous functions of the same order $c \neq 0$ and $\psi(\mathbf{x}) \neq 0$ for all $\mathbf{x} \neq \mathbf{0}$, the following function is positive-homogeneous of order zero for all $\mathbf{x} \neq \mathbf{0}$:

$$F(\mathbf{x}) = \frac{\phi(\mathbf{x})}{\psi(\mathbf{x})}. \qquad (5.48)$$

The second key result here is that if $f(\mathbf{x})$ is positive-homogeneous of order zero and $g : R \to R$ is any function at all, then the function $h(\mathbf{x}) = g(f(\mathbf{x}))$ is also positive-homogeneous of order zero. More generally, if $\{\phi_i(\mathbf{x})\}$ is a set of N positive-homogeneous functions of order zero and $G : R^N \to R$ is any mapping, the following function is positive-homogeneous of order zero:

$$f(\mathbf{x}) = G(\phi_1(\mathbf{x}), \phi_2(\mathbf{x}), \ldots, \phi_N(\mathbf{x})). \qquad (5.49)$$

To obtain the specific function considered in (5.45), let $\mathbf{e}_i$ denote the unit vector in the ith component direction and note that the functions $\mathbf{e}_i^T \mathbf{x}$ and $||\mathbf{x}||$ are both positive-homogeneous of order one. Hence, the functions $\phi_i(\mathbf{x}) = \mathbf{e}_i^T \mathbf{x}/||\mathbf{x}||$ are positive-homogeneous of order zero by (5.48), and substituting this result into (5.49) leads to the function appearing in (5.45). Also, as a generalization of (5.48), note that if $\phi(\mathbf{x})$ is positive-homogeneous of order c_1 and $\psi(\mathbf{x})$ is positive-homogeneous of order c_2, then the product $f(\mathbf{x}) = \phi(\mathbf{x})\psi(\mathbf{x})$ is positive-homogeneous of order $c_1 + c_2$ and the quotient $g(\mathbf{x}) = \phi(\mathbf{x})/\psi(\mathbf{x})$ is positive-homogeneous of order $c_1 - c_2$, provided $\psi(\mathbf{x}) \neq 0$. Similarly, sums or differences of positive-homogeneous functions of order c are also positive-homogeneous of order c. The key point here is that positive-homogeneous functions are often useful data characterizations because they behave predictably with respect to data rescalings. This observation is particularly pertinent to positive-homogeneous characterizations of order zero, which are *scale-independent*.

Finally, the following observation regarding positive-homogeneous functions of order zero is useful and is related to a number of results discussed subsequently. Suppose $f : R^N \to R$ is positive-homogeneous of order zero and continuous at $\mathbf{x} = \mathbf{0}$. It then follows from the definition of continuity that, given $\epsilon > 0$, there exists $\delta > 0$ such that

$$||\mathbf{x} - \mathbf{0}|| = ||\mathbf{x}|| < \delta \;\Rightarrow\; |f(\mathbf{x}) - f(\mathbf{0})| < \epsilon. \qquad (5.50)$$

Next, suppose $\mathbf{y} \in R^N$ is arbitrary and note that there exists $\alpha > 0$ small enough that $||\alpha \mathbf{y}|| = \alpha ||\mathbf{y}|| < \delta$. Hence, it follows by positive-homogeneity of order zero that

$$|f(\mathbf{y}) - f(\mathbf{0})| = |f(\alpha \mathbf{y}) - f(\mathbf{0})| < \epsilon. \qquad (5.51)$$

Since both $\mathbf{y}$ and $\epsilon > 0$ are arbitrary, it follows that $f(\mathbf{y}) = f(\mathbf{0})$ for all $\mathbf{y} \in R^N$. *As a consequence, it follows that any nonconstant, positive-homogeneous function of order zero is necessarily discontinuous at $\mathbf{x} = \mathbf{0}$.*

5.2.3 Location-invariance and related conditions

A function $f : R^N \to R$ is *location-invariant* if it satisfies the condition

$$f(x_1 + c, x_2 + c, \ldots, x_N + c) = f(x_1, x_2, \ldots, x_N) + c \qquad (5.52)$$

for all $\mathbf{x} \in R^N$ and all real c. Note that any function $f(\cdot)$ that is of the form

$$f(x_1, x_2, \ldots, x_N) = x_i + \phi(x_1 - x_i, x_2 - x_i, \ldots, x_N - x_i) \qquad (5.53)$$

satisfies this location-invariance condition, where i is any integer between 1 and N and $\phi(\cdot)$ is *any* function of the $N - 1$ arguments $x_j - x_i$ for $j \neq i$. Another useful representation is

$$f(x_1, x_2, \ldots, x_N) = \bar{x} + \Phi(x_1 - \bar{x}, x_2 - \bar{x}, \ldots, x_N - \bar{x}),$$
$$\bar{x} = \frac{1}{N} \sum_{k=1}^{N} x_k, \qquad (5.54)$$

where $\Phi(\cdot)$ is any arbitrary function of N arguments. Like the homogeneous function classes discussed in Sec. 5.2.2, it is clear from these results that the class of location-invariant functions is extremely large.

Also as in the case of the class of homogeneous functions considered in Sec. 5.2.2, it is instructive to consider generalizing the notion of location-invariance. In particular, suppose we require the following condition to be satisfied for all $\mathbf{x} \in R^N$ and all real β for some unspecified function $g(\cdot)$:

$$f(\mathbf{x} + \beta) = f(\mathbf{x}) + g(\beta). \qquad (5.55)$$

Defining $\mathbf{e}$ as the N vector whose components are all one, it follows from (5.55) that

$$f(\beta \mathbf{e}) = f(\mathbf{0} + \beta) = f(\mathbf{0}) + g(\beta). \qquad (5.56)$$

Similarly, for any real γ, it follows that

$$f([\beta + \gamma]\mathbf{e}) = f(\mathbf{0}) + g(\beta + \gamma), \qquad (5.57)$$

but it also follows from (5.55) and (5.56) that

$$\begin{aligned} f([\beta + \gamma]\mathbf{e}) &= f(\beta \mathbf{e} + \gamma) = f(\beta \mathbf{e}) + g(\gamma) \\ &= f(\mathbf{0}) + g(\beta) + g(\gamma). \end{aligned} \qquad (5.58)$$

Combining (5.57) and (5.58) then yields the following functional equation for $g(\cdot)$:

$$g(\beta + \gamma) = g(\beta) + g(\gamma), \qquad (5.59)$$

which we recognize from Sec. 5.2.1 as Cauchy's basic equation. Since the only practical solution of this equation is $g(z) = \lambda z$ for some real λ, it follows that the generalized location-invariance condition posed in (5.55) reduces to

$$f(\mathbf{x} + \beta) = f(\mathbf{x}) + \lambda \beta \qquad (5.60)$$

for some real constant λ. Probably the two most important special cases are $\lambda = 1$, corresponding to the location-invariance condition (5.52), and $\lambda = 0$, corresponding to the *location-insensitivity* condition imposed on "good" scale estimators $S(\cdot)$ in Sec. 5.1. This condition is examined further in Sec. 5.2.4, where the outlier detection problem introduced in Sec. 5.1 is revisited.

If we require $f(\cdot)$ to be *equivariant*—i.e., both location-invariant and homogeneous so that it satisfies (5.1)—we obtain a common refinement of both (5.54) and the homogeneous function characterization presented in Sec. 5.2.2. First, recall from Sec. 5.2.2 that if $f : R^N \to R$ is homogeneous, then $f(\mathbf{0}) = 0$. Hence, it follows directly from (5.52) that

$$f(x, x, \ldots, x) = f(0, 0, \ldots, 0) + x = x \tag{5.61}$$

for all $x \in R$. Aczél (1966, p. 236) shows that the following construction leads to an equivariant function $f(\cdot)$:

$$f(x_1, x_2, \ldots, x_N) = \bar{x} + \hat{\sigma} G\left(\frac{x_1 - \bar{x}}{\hat{\sigma}}, \frac{x_2 - \bar{x}}{\hat{\sigma}}, \ldots, \frac{x_N - \bar{x}}{\hat{\sigma}}\right),$$

$$\hat{\sigma} = \left[\frac{1}{N-1} \sum_{k=1}^{N} (x_k - \bar{x})^2\right]^{1/2}, \tag{5.62}$$

where $G : R^N \to R$ is arbitrary if only positive-homogeneity is required and $G(\cdot)$ must satisfy the odd symmetry condition (5.47) if homogeneity with respect to all real scalings is required. (Actually, Aczel proves this result using the biased standard deviation estimate $\hat{\sigma} = [(1/N) \sum_{k=1}^{N} (x_k - \bar{x})^2]^{1/2}$, but the same arguments may be applied to obtain (5.62).) Note that $\hat{\sigma} \neq 0$ unless $x_k = x$ for all k, in which case the function is defined by (5.61). Again, it follows from this result that the class of equivariant functions is extremely large, but the following observations provide some important perspective.

First, the special case $N = 2$ leads to the following surprising result. Note that if $N = 2$, $x_1 - \bar{x} = (x_1 - x_2)/2$ and $x_2 - \bar{x} = -(x_1 - x_2)/2$. Substituting these results into the expression for $\hat{\sigma}$ in (5.62) then gives the result that $\hat{\sigma} = (\sqrt{2}/2)|x_1 - x_2|$, so the general expression for $f(\cdot)$ reduces to

$$f(x_1, x_2) = \frac{x_1 + x_2}{2} + |x_1 - x_2| \cdot (\sqrt{2}/2) \cdot G(\pm\sqrt{2}/2, \mp\sqrt{2}/2). \tag{5.63}$$

Since the arguments of the arbitrary function $G(\cdot)$ in this expression do not depend on the values of x_1 and x_2, it may be regarded as an arbitrary constant, reducing (5.63) to

$$f(x_1, x_2) = ax_1 + bx_2, \tag{5.64}$$

subject to the constraint that $f(x, x) = x$, which implies that $a + b = 1$. In other words, for $N = 2$, the very general result given in (5.62) reduces to an expression for the weighted arithmetic mean of x_1 and x_2. This result is proved separately by Aczél (1966, p. 234), who notes that it does not extend to the general case $N > 2$ unless additional constraints are imposed on $f(\cdot)$. One such constraint is differentiability at $\mathbf{x} = \mathbf{0}$, as shown by Aczél, Gronau, and Schwaiger (1994, Proposition 14). Conversely, since all of the 68 location estimators discussed in the Princeton Robustness Study (Andrews et al., 1972) satisfy (5.1), it follows from this differentiability result that of these estimators, only the arithmetic mean is a *smooth* function of the data observations.

Finally, another useful condition often imposed on data characterizations is *permutation-invariance*, meaning that $f(\mathcal{P}\mathbf{x}) = f(\mathbf{x})$ for any permutation $\mathcal{P}$ of the components of $\mathbf{x}$. This condition is a natural one for data sequences where individual observations are

assumed exchangeable and should therefore be treated equivalently. In particular, note that
this condition was satisfied by all of the 68 location estimators considered in the Princeton
Robustness Study (Andrews et al., 1972). If we require the function $f : R^N \to R$ considered
here to satisfy both (5.1) and permutation-invariance, it follows that the function $G : R^N \to R$
R appearing in (5.62) must also be permutation-invariant. In the case of differentiable
characterizations where $f(\cdot)$ reduces to a weighted average, permutation-invariance requires
that all weights be equal (hence equal to $1/N$), further reducing $f(\cdot)$ to the arithmetic average
μ of the data observations. A closely related result noted by Rousseeuw (1994) is discussed
in Sec. 5.2.6.

5.2.4 Outlier detection procedures

Sec. 5.1 concluded with necessary and sufficient conditions for the class of univariate outlier
detection rules introduced in Chapter 3 to be invariant under affine changes of measurement
units. These conditions took the form of functional equations characterizing the location
estimator $\mu(\cdot)$ and the scale estimator $S(\cdot)$ on which this outlier detection procedure is based.
It follows from the results presented in Sec. 5.2.3 that any admissable location estimator
$\mu(\cdot)$ may be represented as in (5.62):

$$\mu(x_1, x_2, \ldots, x_N) = \bar{x} + \hat{\sigma} G(z_1, z_2, \ldots, z_N), \tag{5.65}$$

where $z_k = (x_k - \bar{x})/\hat{\sigma}$ represents the z-score corresponding to data observation x_k. For
a given location estimator $\mu(\cdot)$, we can solve this equation for the corresponding function
$G(\cdot)$, giving

$$
\begin{aligned}
G(z_1, z_2, \ldots, z_N) &= \frac{\mu(x_1, x_2, \ldots, x_N) - \bar{x}}{\hat{\sigma}} \\
&= \frac{\mu(x_1 - \bar{x}, x_2 - \bar{x}, \ldots, x_N - \bar{x})}{\hat{\sigma}} \\
&= \mu\left(\frac{x_1 - \bar{x}}{\hat{\sigma}}, \frac{x_2 - \bar{x}}{\hat{\sigma}}, \ldots, \frac{x_N - \bar{x}}{\hat{\sigma}}\right) \\
&= \mu(z_1, z_2, \ldots, z_N).
\end{aligned}
\tag{5.66}
$$

As the following discussion demonstrates, the advantage of this result is that it leads to an
interesting interpretation of the class of unit-invariant outlier detection procedures. Substituting (5.65) into the general outlier detection criterion gives

$$
\begin{aligned}
|x_k - \mu(\mathbf{x})| > t S(\mathbf{x}) &\Rightarrow |x_k - \bar{x} - \hat{\sigma} G(\mathbf{z})| > t S(\mathbf{x}) \\
&\Rightarrow \hat{\sigma} \left| \frac{x_k - \bar{x}}{\hat{\sigma}} - G(\mathbf{z}) \right| > t S(\mathbf{x}) \\
&\Rightarrow |z_k - G(\mathbf{z})| > t \frac{S(\mathbf{x})}{\hat{\sigma}}.
\end{aligned}
\tag{5.67}
$$

Next, note that the admissibility condition on the scale estimator $S(\mathbf{x})$—i.e., the second line
of (5.10)—implies that

$$S(\mathbf{x}) = S(\hat{\sigma}\mathbf{z} + \bar{x}) = \hat{\sigma} S(\mathbf{z}). \tag{5.68}$$

Combining (5.67) and (5.68) then gives the following reformulation of the outlier detection rule in terms of z-scores:

$$|z_k - G(\mathbf{z})| > t S(\mathbf{z}) \;\Rightarrow\; x_k \text{ is an outlier.} \qquad (5.69)$$

To see the utility of this result, consider two important examples from Chapter 3: the ESD identifier and the Hampel identifier. For the ESD identifier, we have

$$G(\mathbf{z}) = \mu(\mathbf{z}) = \bar{z} = \frac{1}{N} \sum_{k=1}^{N} z_k = \frac{1}{N} \sum_{k=1}^{N} \frac{x_k - \bar{x}}{\hat{\sigma}} = \frac{1}{N\hat{\sigma}} \sum_{k=1}^{N} (x_k - \bar{x}) = 0 \qquad (5.70)$$

and

$$S(\mathbf{z}) = \left[\frac{1}{N-1} \sum_{k=1}^{N} (z_k - \bar{z})^2 \right]^{1/2} = \left[\frac{1}{N-1} \sum_{k=1}^{N} \left(\frac{x_k - \bar{x}}{\hat{\sigma}} \right)^2 \right]^{1/2}$$

$$= \frac{1}{\hat{\sigma}} \left[\frac{1}{N-1} \sum_{k=1}^{N} (x_k - \bar{x})^2 \right]^{1/2} = 1. \quad (5.71)$$

Combining these results leads to the standard z-score interpretation of the ESD identifier:

$$|z_k| > t \;\Rightarrow\; x_k \text{ is an outlier.} \qquad (5.72)$$

Examination of other outlier detection rules leads to more significant conclusions. In particular, for median-based detection rules like the Hampel identifier or the symmetric boxplot rule, we have

$$\mu(\mathbf{z}) = \text{median } \{z_1, z_2, \ldots, z_N\} = \text{median } \left\{ \frac{x_1 - \bar{x}}{\hat{\sigma}}, \frac{x_2 - \bar{x}}{\hat{\sigma}}, \ldots, \frac{x_N - \bar{x}}{\hat{\sigma}} \right\}$$

$$= \frac{x^{\dagger} - \bar{x}}{\hat{\sigma}}, \qquad (5.73)$$

where $x^{\dagger} = \text{median } \{x_1, x_2, \ldots, x_N\}$. This result corresponds to *Hotelling's skewness measure*, which is known to satisfy the bounds $|(x^{\dagger} - \bar{x})/\hat{\sigma}| \leq 1$ for all data sequences (Rohatgi and Szekely, 1989). Hence, it follows that for all median-based outlier detection rules, the detection criterion is

$$\left| z_k - \frac{x^{\dagger} - \bar{x}}{\hat{\sigma}} \right| > t S(\mathbf{z}) \;\Rightarrow\; x_k \text{ is an outlier.} \qquad (5.74)$$

This result suggests the following interpretation: median-based outlier detection rules apply a skewness correction to the classical z-scores in identifying outliers.

The scale estimator $S(\cdot)$ on which the Hampel identifier is based is the MAD, normalized so that

$$E\{S(\mathbf{x})\} = \sigma \;\Rightarrow\; E\{S(\mathbf{z})\} = 1 \qquad (5.75)$$

for Gaussian nominal data. For outlier-contaminated data, the MAD scale estimate is typically smaller than $\hat{\sigma}$, implying $S(\mathbf{z}) < 1$. Hence, $S(\mathbf{z})$ may be regarded as a factor that reduces the threshold in the ESD identifier to account for outlier-induced variance inflation.

Overall, these results suggest the following interpretation for the unit-invariant outlier detection rule in (5.69):

- $\mu(\mathbf{z})$ represents a skewness correction to the classical z-scores.

- $S(\mathbf{z})$ represents a correction for variance inflation in the standard deviation estimate on which the classical z-scores are based.

It is a consequence of (5.62) that the function $\mu(\mathbf{z})$ can be chosen arbitrarily—*as a function of the z-scores* $\{z_k\}$—subject only to the restriction that $\mu(\mathbf{0}) = 0$, a consequence of the positive-homogeneity of the location estimator $\mu(\mathbf{x})$ expressed in the original variables. Similarly, the function $S(\mathbf{z})$ can also be chosen arbitrarily—*again, as a function of the z-scores*—subject only to the constraint that $S(\mathbf{0}) = 0$. Conversely, to obtain *useful* outlier detection procedures, it is important to restrict consideration to functions for which $S(\mathbf{z}) \geq 0$ for all $\mathbf{z}$ since if $S(\mathbf{z}) < 0$ and $t > 0$, *all* points x_k will be declared outliers.

5.2.5 Quasi-linear means

A useful family of data characterizations that has played an important role in both the theory of functional equations and the classical theory of inequalities is the family of *quasi-linear means* (Aczél and Dhombres, 1989, p. 270):

$$L(x_1, x_2, \ldots, x_N) = \phi^{-1}\left(\sum_{i=1}^{N} a_i \phi(x_i)\right), \quad a_i > 0, \ \sum_{i=1}^{N} a_i = 1. \tag{5.76}$$

Here, $\phi(\cdot)$ is a continuous, strictly increasing function (which is therefore invertible (Klambauer, 1975, p. 181)), typically defined on either the real line R or the positive reals R^+. If $L(\cdot)$ is required to be permutation-invariant, all of the weights a_i must be equal, reducing $L(\cdot)$ to the corresponding *quasi-arithmetic mean* (Aczél and Dhombres, 1989, p. 245)

$$A(x_1, x_2, \ldots, x_N) = \phi^{-1}\left(\frac{1}{N} \sum_{i=1}^{N} \phi(x_i)\right). \tag{5.77}$$

Practically important special cases of $A(\cdot)$ include the ordinary arithmetic mean, obtained by taking $\phi(x) = x$; the RMS value, obtained by taking $\phi(x) = x^2$ for $x \geq 0$; the *geometric mean*

$$G(x_1, x_2, \ldots, x_N) = \left[\prod_{i=1}^{N} x_i\right]^{1/N}, \tag{5.78}$$

obtained by taking $\phi(x) = \ln x$ for $x > 0$; and the *harmonic mean*

$$H(x_1, x_2, \ldots, x_N) = \left[\frac{1}{N} \sum_{i=1}^{N} \frac{1}{x_i}\right]^{-1}, \tag{5.79}$$

obtained by taking $\phi(x) = 1/x$ for $x > 0$. All of these quasi-arithmetic means, along with their corresponding quasi-linear means, satisfy the extended *arithmetic-geometric mean (AGM) inequality* discussed in Sec. 5.3.

The quasi-linear means are also closely related to a functional equation called the *bisymmetry equation* (Aczél, 1966; Aczél and Dhombres, 1989; Aczél, 1997). Suppose $\{x_{ij}\}$

is an array of N^2 numbers, defined for $i, j = 1, 2, \ldots, N$, and suppose $F(\cdot)$ is a function mapping R^N into R. The bisymmetry equation requires $F(\cdot)$ to satisfy the condition

$$F(F(x_{11}, \ldots, x_{1N}), \ldots, F(x_{N1}, \ldots, x_{NN})) = F(F(x_{11}, \ldots, x_{N1}), \qquad (5.80)$$
$$\ldots, F(x_{1N}, \ldots, x_{NN}))$$

for all real x_{ij}. Conceptually, if we regard $\{x_{ij}\}$ as an $N \times N$ table of numbers and $F(\cdot)$ as a data characterization, the bisymmetry equation establishes a compatibility relationship between the row-ordered summary of column summaries and the column-ordered summary of row summaries. In particular, the bisymmetry equation generalizes the idea that the sum of column totals across a table is equal to the sum of row totals down the table, a useful arithmetic check for contingency tables or bookkeeping ledgers. More generally, it is not difficult to show that the quasi-linear mean $L(\cdot)$ defined by (5.76) satisfies the bisymmetry equation:

$$L(L(x_{11}, \ldots, x_{1N}), \ldots, L(x_{N1}, \ldots, x_{NN})) \qquad (5.81)$$
$$= \phi^{-1} \left(a_1 \sum_{j=1}^{N} a_j \phi(x_{1j}) + \cdots + a_N \sum_{j=1}^{N} a_j \phi(x_{Nj}) \right)$$
$$= \phi^{-1} \left(\sum_{i=1}^{N} \sum_{j=1}^{N} a_i a_j \phi(x_{ij}) \right)$$
$$= \phi^{-1} \left(a_1 \sum_{i=1}^{N} a_i \phi(x_{i1}) + \cdots + a_N \sum_{i=1}^{N} a_i \phi(x_{iN}) \right)$$
$$= L(L(x_{11}, \ldots, x_{N1}), \ldots, L(x_{1N}, \ldots, x_{NN})).$$

Conversely, if the function $F(\cdot)$ in (5.80) is continuous and increasing in each variable and if $F(x, x, \ldots, x) = x$ for all real x, then the quasi-linear mean $L(\cdot)$ is the *only* solution of this equation (Aczél, 1997). In addition, motivated at least in part by its utility in economics, mathematicians have generalized the bisymmetry equation to rectangular $m \times n$ tables with possibly distinct row and column summaries (Aczél and Maksa, 1996; Aczél, 1997). An important result of this generalization is that the functional equation may not have a solution if one or more of these functions is specified a priori.

Finally, it follows as a generalization of the results presented by Aczél (1966, p. 153) that the only *equivariant* quasi-linear mean (i.e., the only quasi-linear mean satisfying (5.1)) is the linear weighted average obtained by taking $\phi(x) = x$ in (5.76). Conversely, if we only require scale-invariance, this condition may be reduced to Cauchy's power equation, yielding the generalized means $M_r(x_1, x_2, \ldots, x_N)$ discussed in Sec. 5.3.2.

5.2.6 Results for positive-breakdown estimators

Many of the functional equation results presented in the previous examples are closely related to a useful collection of results for positive-breakdown estimators presented by Rousseeuw (1994). Recall that an estimator T exhibits a finite sample breakdown point of m/n if m outliers in a dataset of size n can be chosen in a way that causes T to exhibit arbitrarily extreme values. Recall also that classical OLS estimators like the arithmetic mean exhibit finite sample breakdown points of $1/n$, which goes to zero in the limit of infinitely large sample sizes. Hence, these estimators are called zero-breakdown estimators, while estimators with finite sample breakdown points $m/n \geq \gamma > 0$ for all n are called positive-breakdown estimators.

The results considered here mostly pertain to regression estimators $T\{(\mathbf{x}_i^T, y_i)\}$ that depend on a vector $\mathbf{x}_i^T$ of p explanatory variables and predict a response variable y_i, although univariate location estimators that do not depend on $\mathbf{x}_i^T$ may be regarded as a special case. The transpose here arises from the convention of denoting the vector $\mathbf{x}_i^T$ of explanatory variables as a row vector, corresponding to the ith row of the independent variable matrix $\mathbf{X}$ appearing in the regression model $\mathbf{y} = \mathbf{X}\theta + \mathbf{e}$. Further, the estimators considered here all exhibit one or more important transformation invariance properties, typically called *equi-variance properties* in the robust regression literature. Specifically, Rousseeuw and Leroy (1987, p. 116) define an estimator to be *scale-equivariant* if it satisfies the homogeneity condition $T\{(\mathbf{x}_i^T, \alpha y_i)\} = \alpha T\{(\mathbf{x}_i^T, y_i)\}$, and they define $T\{(\mathbf{x}_i^T, y_i)\}$ to be *regression-equivariant* if it satisfies the condition

$$T\{(\mathbf{x}_i^T, y_i + \mathbf{x}_i^T \mathbf{v})\} = T\{(\mathbf{x}_i^T, y_i)\} + \mathbf{v} \qquad (5.82)$$

for any vector $\mathbf{v} \in R^p$. The significance of this requirement is that it means the qualitative behavior of the estimator $T\{(\mathbf{x}_i^T, y_i)\}$ is invariant under changes of the true value θ of the unknown regression parameter. In particular, Rousseeuw and Leroy (1987, p. 116) note that statements like, "there is no loss of generality in assuming $\theta = \mathbf{0}$," commonly invoked in simulation studies, are invalid if the estimator considered is not regression-equivariant.

Finally, the estimator $T\{(\mathbf{x}_i^T, y_i)\}$ is *affine-equivariant* if it satisfies the condition

$$T\{([\mathbf{A}\mathbf{x}_i]^T, y_i)\} = \mathbf{A}^{-T} T\{(\mathbf{x}_i^T, y_i)\} \qquad (5.83)$$

for any $n \times n$ nonsingular matrix $\mathbf{A}$. Motivation for this requirement comes from the fact that the predicted response values $\hat{y}_i$ associated with the regression estimator $T\{(\mathbf{x}_i^T, y_i)\}$ are $\hat{y}_i = \mathbf{x}_i^T T\{(\mathbf{x}_i^T, y_i)\}$. Consequently, affine-equivariance implies that these predictions are invariant under nonsingular rescalings of the independent variables $\mathbf{x}$ since

$$\hat{y}_i = \mathbf{x}_i^T T\{(\mathbf{x}_i, y_i)\} = (\mathbf{A}\mathbf{x}_i)^T (\mathbf{A}^{-T} T\{(\mathbf{x}_i, y_i)\}) = (\mathbf{A}\mathbf{x}_i)^T T\{([\mathbf{A}\mathbf{x}_i]^T, y_i)\}. \qquad (5.84)$$

Unfortunately, the term *affine-equivariant* is also applied with a different meaning to univariate location estimators, a fact that can cause some confusion: a univariate location estimator is said to be affine-equivariant if it satisfies (5.1) (Rousseeuw and Leroy, 1987, p. 159).

The n data observations $\{(\mathbf{x}_i^T, y_i)\}$ are said to be in *general position* if any subset of size p uniquely determines a p-dimensional parameter vector θ. Essentially, this condition means that the available data exhibit no collinearity problems. Given n data observations in general position, a regression estimator $T\{(\mathbf{x}_i^T, y_i)\}$ satisfies the EFP if, whenever there exists some regression parameter β such that $y_i = \mathbf{x}_i^T \beta$ holds exactly for at least $n - m + 1$ of the observations, then $T\{(\mathbf{x}_i^T, y_i)\} = \beta$ regardless of the value of the other m observations (Rousseeuw, 1994). An extremely useful observation is the following (Rousseeuw and Leroy, 1987, p. 123; Rousseeuw, 1994, Proposition 1):

> If $T\{(\mathbf{x}_i^T, y_i)\}$ is regression and scale equivariant and has a breakdown point of m/n for n data observations in general position, it satisfies the exact fit property for the same value of m.

Because this objection is somewhat unexpected, Rousseeuw (1994) notes that it has some-times been raised to the EFP as an unnatural or undesirable characteristic (Hettmansperger and Sheather, 1992), but the result presented above implies that the EFP is a necessary condition for nonzero-breakdown regression estimators. In addition, Rousseeuw notes that this result extends to other estimators such as multivariate location estimators, univariate scale estimators such as the MAD scale estimate (which must necessarily be equal to zero if more than $n - m + 1$ observations have the same value), and outlier-resistant covariance estimators such as the MCD and MVE estimators discussed in Chapter 4.

The EFP results just presented are closely related to the issues of continuity and monotonicity of the estimator $T\{(\mathbf{x}_i^T, y_i)\}$. Specifically, Rousseeuw (1994, Proposition 2) observes:

> The only affine-equivariant, permutation-invariant multivariate location esti-mator that is continuous in the data observations is the arithmetic mean.

Note that this result extends those presented earlier for differentiable location- and scale-invariant univariate estimators (Sec. 5.2.3) and for location- and scale-invariant quasi-linear means (Sec. 5.2.5). Also, note that it follows immediately as a converse that any positive-breakdown multivariate location estimator is necessarily discontinuous. Rousseeuw (1994) notes that, as a practical matter, this observation means that there exist special configurations where positive-breakdown estimators can "jump" from one value to another in response to arbitrarily small changes in the data configuration. In fact, Hettmansperger and Sheather (1992) used a simple nine-point regression example to show that LMS regression estimators can switch between two very different models in response to small changes in one critical data value. Specifically, this critical data point lies on the exact fit lines for two very different five-point subsets of the data, so that small changes in the position of this point move it off one or the other of these competing exact fit lines, leading to very different regression models. Rousseeuw refers to this behavior as "mode seeking" and notes that it can be extremely useful in the context of exploratory data analysis, since it can be used to detect significant substructures in heterogeneous datasets. Conversely, Hettmansperger and Sheather (1992) use this result to argue against the use of the LMS estimator. In addition, Rousseeuw (1994) discusses analogous critical configurations for other positive-breakdown estimators such as the MCD and MVE covariance estimators discussed in Chapter 4.

A univariate location estimator $\mu : R^N \to R$ is *monotone* if

$$x_k \geq y_k \text{ for all } k \implies \mu(\mathbf{x}) \geq \mu(\mathbf{y}). \tag{5.85}$$

While this restriction may sound like a reasonable one, Rousseeuw (1994, Proposition 4) cites the following result of Bassett (1991):

> The only univariate location estimator with a 50% breakdown point that is location- and scale-invariant and monotone with respect to all data observa-tions is the median.

As a consequence, it follows that most high-breakdown estimators will *downweight* obser-vations once they become sufficiently extreme. Rousseeuw gives a simple example of an M-estimator where increasing the most extreme observation from 17 to 18 actually reduces the location estimate from 10.49 to 9.86. Although this behavior may seem counterintuitive,

Rousseeuw (1994) also quotes a comment from John Tukey, who argued that he would never use a monotone estimator, making the case that ridiculously extreme observations should be discounted entirely.

Finally, Rousseeuw (1994) also considers the question of whether the lack-of-fit criterion minimized by a regression estimator should be a norm, arriving at a simple conclusion: no. In particular, he considers the development of regression estimators that minimize some function $J(\mathbf{e})$ of the prediction error vector and poses the question of whether this function should be a norm, as it is in both OLS and LAD regression. In support of his answer, he establishes the following result (Rousseeuw, 1994, Proposition 3):

> If $J(\mathbf{e})$ is a pseudonorm, the corresponding regression estimator has a breakdown point of at most $1/n$ for any dataset in general position.

Recall that a norm satisfies the following defining conditions (Haaser and Sullivan, 1991, p. 160):

1. $\|\mathbf{x}\| \geq 0$ for all $\mathbf{x} \in R^N$;

2. $\|\alpha \mathbf{x}\| = |\alpha| \cdot \|\mathbf{x}\|$ for all real α and all $\mathbf{x} \in R^N$;

3. $\|\mathbf{x} + \mathbf{y}\| \leq \|\mathbf{x}\| + \|\mathbf{y}\|$ for all $\mathbf{x}, \mathbf{y} \in R^N$;

4. $\|\mathbf{x}\| = 0$ if and only if $x_1 = x_2 = \cdots = x_N = 0$.

A *pseudonorm* weakens Condition 4 to

4.' $\|\mathbf{x}\| = 0$ if and only if $x_1 = x_2 = \cdots = x_N = c$ for some real c.

Also, note that a *seminorm* dispenses with Condition 4 altogether, requiring only that Conditions 1 through 3 hold (Haaser and Sullivan, 1991, p. 162). In particular, note that every norm and every pseudonorm is also a seminorm, but the converse does not hold.

Since the EFP must hold for some $m > 1$ if the estimator is to exhibit a breakdown point greater than $1/n$, the essence of the proof is to show that the EFP cannot hold for even a single sufficiently extreme data observation. To establish this result, Rousseeuw considers any set $\{\mathbf{x}_i^T\}$ of $n-1$ observations in general position, each of dimension p, and takes $y_i = 0$ for $i = 1, 2, \ldots, n-1$ so that the EFP holds with $\beta = \mathbf{0}$. The final data point is then taken as $\mathbf{x}_n^T = [\delta, \delta, \ldots, \delta]$ with $y_n = p\delta$ for arbitrary $\delta > 0$. For $\theta = \beta = \mathbf{0}$, the lack-of-fit criterion is

$$J(\mathbf{e}) = J([0, 0, \ldots, 0, p\delta]^T) = \delta p J([0, 0, \ldots, 0, 1]^T) \qquad (5.86)$$

if $J(\cdot)$ is any seminorm. If $J(\cdot)$ is a pseudonorm, it follows that $J(\mathbf{e}) > 0$ and can be made arbitrarily large by taking δ large enough. Conversely, if we now consider the estimator $\hat{\theta} = [1, 1, \ldots, 1]^T$, it follows that the corresponding lack-of-fit measure is

$$J(\mathbf{e}') = J([y_1 - \mathbf{x}_1^T \hat{\theta}, \ldots, y_{n-1} - \mathbf{x}_{n-1}^T \hat{\theta}, 0]), \qquad (5.87)$$

which does not depend on δ. Hence, we can always choose $\delta > 0$ large enough to force $J(\mathbf{e}) > J(\mathbf{e}')$, so the estimator that minimizes $J(\mathbf{e})$ does not satisfy the EFP, further implying that this estimator cannot exhibit a positive breakdown point.

As Rousseeuw notes, the fact that $J([0, 0, \ldots, 0, 1]^T) > 0$ is the key to this result, since to satisfy the EFP for $m > 1$ it is necessary to have $J([e_1, e_2, \ldots, e_n]^T) = 0$ whenever at least $n - m + 1$ of the e_i values are zero. If we now suppose $J(\mathbf{e})$ is a seminorm, this lack-of-fit measure is necessarily nonnegative and must satisfy the triangle inequality, implying

$$0 \leq J(\mathbf{e}) \leq J([e_1, 0, \ldots, 0]^T) + \cdots + J([0, 0, \ldots, e_n]^T) = 0. \qquad (5.88)$$

Hence, it follows that no regression estimator that minimizes any seminorm of the regression error vector can exhibit a positive breakdown point.

5.3 Characterization via inequalities

Inequalities arise naturally in data analysis for a number of reasons. One of the most important is that they can provide useful guidance in interpreting certain data characterizations, a point discussed in detail in Sec. 5.3.1. Similarly, inequalities can also provide useful insight into the relationships between different data characterizations, as in the AGM inequality discussed in Sec. 5.3.2. Another important use for inequalities is the estimation of bounds on data characterizations that cannot be computed exactly because the complete dataset is not available, but certain summary statistics are known. Specific examples of this application of inequalities are discussed in Sec. 5.3.3. Finally, a fourth application of inequalities discussed here is their use as an uncertainty description in the *set-theoretic* or *unknown-but-bounded* error model, introduced in Sec. 5.3.4.

The literature associated with inequalities is enormous and cannot be surveyed in detail here. Instead, the intent of the following subsections is to present a few key results that are closely related to the data analysis problems considered in this book. For more detailed treatments of the general subject of inequalities, refer to the excellent references by Hardy, Littlewood, and Polya (1952) and Mitrinovic, Pecaric, and Fink (1993).

5.3.1 Inequalities as aids to interpretation

Despite their practical limitations—discussed at some length in previous chapters—the mean and standard deviation remain extremely useful standard data characterizations in many applications. One reason for this utility is a direct consequence of Chebyshev's inequality (Billingsley, 1986, p. 75)

$$\mathcal{P}\{|x - \mu| > a\} \leq \frac{\sigma^2}{a^2}, \qquad (5.89)$$

where x is any random variable with finite mean μ and finite variance σ^2. Taking $a = t\sigma$ in this inequality leads to the equivalent inequality

$$\mathcal{P}\left\{\frac{|x - \mu|}{\sigma} > t\right\} \leq \frac{1}{t^2}. \qquad (5.90)$$

It follows from this result that the mean μ represents the "typical" value of the random variable x, and the standard deviation σ gives a measure of the "spread" of x about this typical value. Conversely, since the inequality (5.90) must hold for *all* distributions with finite μ and σ, this bound is necessarily quite conservative. For example, taking $t = 3$, the bound (5.90) gives a probability of at most 11% for all distributions in this class, compared with the Gaussian bound of approximately 0.3%. Conversely, it is also important to note that this bound is not always applicable, as distributions with infinite variance do sometimes arise—often unwittingly—as data models. As a specific example, if x is assumed to have a normal distribution, the reciprocal transformation $y = 1/x$ yields a random variable with infinite variance. Consequently, if we adopt the popular working assumption that two variable sequences $\{x_k\}$ and $\{y_k\}$ are statistically independent Gaussian random variables, then the ratio x_k/y_k exhibits an infinite variance regardless of the means and variances assumed for x_k and y_k. Hence, the inequality (5.90) does not apply under this data model. As a practical matter, this difficulty is a direct consequence of poor problem formulation and can be overcome by replacing the assumed Gaussian distribution for the denominator variable y_k with a more suitable alternative.

Perhaps a more familiar application of inequalities to data characterizations is the *Cauchy–Schwarz inequality* (Haaser and Sullivan, 1991, p. 278), which holds for any two real-valued sequences $\{x_k\}$ and $\{y_k\}$ of common length N:

$$\left| \sum_{k=1}^{N} x_k y_k \right| \leq \left[\sum_{k=1}^{N} x_k^2 \right]^{1/2} \left[\sum_{k=1}^{N} y_k^2 \right]^{1/2}. \tag{5.91}$$

Recall that the product-moment correlation coefficient $\hat{\rho}_{xy}$ between the two sequences $\{x_k\}$ and $\{y_k\}$ is given by

$$\hat{\rho}_{xy} = \frac{\sum_{k=1}^{N} (x_k - \bar{x})(y_k - \bar{y})}{\left[\sum_{k=1}^{N} (x_k - \bar{x})^2 \right]^{1/2} \left[\sum_{k=1}^{N} (y_k - \bar{y})^2 \right]^{1/2}}, \tag{5.92}$$

where $\bar{x}$ and $\bar{y}$ are the arithmetic means of the two sequences $\{x_k\}$ and $\{y_k\}$, respectively. It follows on replacing x_k with $x_k - \bar{x}$ and y_k with $y_k - \bar{y}$ in the Cauchy–Schwarz inequality that

$$|\hat{\rho}_{xy}| \leq 1. \tag{5.93}$$

In addition, it is a standard result that the Cauchy–Schwarz inequality is strict unless $y_k = \alpha x_k$ for some real number α, from which it follows that

$$\hat{\rho}_{xy} = +1 \text{ if and only if } y_k = \alpha x_k + \beta \text{ for some real } \beta \text{ and some } \alpha > 0 \tag{5.94}$$

and

$$\hat{\rho}_{xy} = -1 \text{ if and only if } y_k = \alpha x_k + \beta \text{ for some real } \beta \text{ and some } \alpha < 0. \tag{5.95}$$

Taken together, these results establish that the product-moment correlation coefficient is a measure of linear association that varies between -1, representing perfect negative association, and $+1$, representing perfect positive association.

To emphasize the utility of this last observation, it is worth contrasting two asymmetry measures: the standard third–moment-based skewness discussed in Chapter 2 and Hotelling's skewness measure introduced in Sec. 5.2.4. In particular, recall that the standard skewness measure is a normalized third moment, where the normalization makes the result both location- and scale-invariant but the skewness itself can assume any real value. Hence, we require results in using this measure with various reference distributions to answer questions such as, "Is 0.8 a large skewness value or a small one?" Conversely, it was noted in Sec. 5.2.4 that Hotelling's skewness measure is bounded between -1 and $+1$, like the product-moment correlation coefficient, giving us a basis for interpretation: 0.8 represents a large value for Hotelling's skewness measure.

5.3.2 Relations between data characterizations

One of the key points of this book has been the utility of comparisons of "similar" results, either those that arise from what should be exchangeable datasets or those that arise using what should be "equivalent" or "comparable" methods. In considering this latter class of comparisons, it is important to recognize that fundamental inequalities sometimes relate different data characterizations of the same data sequence. The following discussion illustrates this point for a few simple examples.

One important classical inequality with many extensions and applications is the *AGM inequality* (Hardy, Littlewood, and Polya, 1952, p. 17)

$$G(x_1, \ldots, x_N) = \left[\prod_{i=1}^{N} x_i \right]^{1/N} \leq \frac{1}{N} \sum_{i=1}^{N} x_i = A(x_1, \ldots, x_N), \qquad (5.96)$$

where it is assumed that $x_i \geq 0$ for all i. This inequality is strict unless $x_i = x$ for all i, in which case both means simply reduce to the common value x. In addition, this inequality extends to weighted arithmetic and geometric means, which are most conveniently viewed as members of the quasi-linear means family discussed in Sec. 5.2.5. Specifically, note that the quasi-linear mean $L(x_1, \ldots, x_N)$ with $\phi(x) = x$ is simply the linear weighted average

$$L_A(x_1, \ldots, x_N) = \sum_{i=1}^{N} a_i x_i, \quad a_i \geq 0, \quad \sum_{i=1}^{N} a_i = 1, \qquad (5.97)$$

while taking $\phi(x) = \ln x$ yields the weighted geometric mean

$$L_G(x_1, \ldots, x_N) = \prod_{i=1}^{N} x_i^{a_i}, \quad a_i \geq 0, \quad \sum_{i=1}^{N} a_i = 1, \qquad (5.98)$$

where, by convention, x_i^0 is defined as one when $x_i = 0$. Assuming the weights $\{a_i\}$ are the same in both cases, the basic AGM inequality (5.96) generalizes to (Hardy, Littlewood, and Polya, 1952, p. 17)

$$L_G(x_1, \ldots, x_N) \leq L_A(x_1, \ldots, x_N), \qquad (5.99)$$

where again the inequality is strict unless all of the x_i values are identical.

In fact, the AGM inequality corresponds to an important special case of a more general inequality between the *generalized means*

$$M_r(x_1, \ldots, x_N) = \left[\sum_{i=1}^{N} a_i x_i^r \right]^{1/r}, \quad a_i \geq 0, \quad \sum_{i=1}^{N} a_i = 1, \qquad (5.100)$$

defined for all $r \neq 0$ and all $x_i > 0$. An important observation is that $M_r(\mathbf{x})$ approaches the weighted geometric mean $L_G(\mathbf{x})$ as $r \to 0$ (Hardy, Littlewood, and Polya, 1952, p. 15), so we may regard $M_0(\mathbf{x})$ as the geometric mean in what follows. Specifically, the family of generalized means satisfies the inequality (Hardy, Littlewood, and Polya, 1952, p. 26)

$$r < s \quad \Rightarrow \quad M_r(x_1, \ldots, x_N) \leq M_s(x_1, \ldots, x_N), \tag{5.101}$$

and the inequality is strict unless $x_i = x$ for all i, in which case both generalized means simply reduce to the common value x. The special case $r = -1$ corresponds to the weighted harmonic mean

$$M_{-1}(x_1, \ldots, x_N) = \left[\sum_{i=1}^{N} \frac{a_i}{x_i} \right]^{-1}, \quad a_i \geq 0, \quad \sum_{i=1}^{N} a_i = 1. \tag{5.102}$$

It follows from inequality (5.101) that the harmonic, geometric, and arithmetic means are related by

$$\left[\sum_{i=1}^{N} \frac{a_i}{x_i} \right]^{-1} \leq \prod_{i=1}^{N} x_i^{a_i} \leq \sum_{i=1}^{N} a_i x_i, \quad a_i \geq 0, \quad \sum_{i=1}^{N} a_i = 1, \tag{5.103}$$

provided $x_i > 0$ for all i. As before, both inequalities are strict unless all x_i values are equal.

An interesting application of the inequality (5.103) is the bounding approach to computing the roots $x^{1/p}$ for positive integers p proposed by Cohen (1985). Specifically, Cohen (1985) considers this inequality with $N = p$ and $a_i = 1/p$ for all i, with $x_i = r_k$ for $i = 1, 2, \ldots, p-1$, where r_k is an approximation of the desired root $x^{1/p}$ and $x_p = x/r_k^{p-1}$. The harmonic, geometric, and arithmetic means of these values are given by

$$H_p = \left\{ \frac{1}{p} \left[\frac{p-1}{r_k} + \frac{r_k^{p-1}}{x} \right] \right\}^{-1} = \frac{p}{\left[\frac{p-1}{r_k} + \frac{r_k^{p-1}}{x} \right]},$$

$$G_p = \left[r_k^{p-1} \cdot \frac{x}{r_k^{p-1}} \right]^{1/p} = x^{1/p},$$

$$A_p = \frac{1}{p} \left[(p-1) r_k + \frac{x}{r_k^{p-1}} \right]. \tag{5.104}$$

In particular, since the geometric mean G_p is always equal to the desired root in this case, it follows that the harmonic mean H_p defines a lower bound and the arithmetic mean A_p defines an upper bound on the result, and that both of these bounds are computable using only ordinary arithmetic operations. Cohen (1985) notes that taking $r_{k+1} = A_p$ gives a well-known sequence $\{r_k\}$ that converges monotonically from above to the desired root $x^{1/p}$ (specifically, this iteration scheme corresponds to Newton's method (Kreyszig, 1978, p. 306)). In addition, Cohen (1985) also notes that taking $r_{k+1} = H_p$ yields a sequence $\{r_k\}$ that converges monotonically to $x^{1/p}$ from below. More importantly, he notes that taking $r_{k+1} = (A_p + H_p)/2$ gives a sequence that converges more rapidly to $x^{1/p}$. The key point here is that the basis for this simple and highly effective iterative procedure is the extended AGM inequality (5.103).

5.3.3   Bounds on means and standard deviations

Since the mean $\bar{x}$ and standard deviation $\hat{\sigma}_x$ are imperfect but nevertheless extremely useful characterizations of a data sequence $\{x_k\}$, it is sometimes useful to have bounds on these quantities that can be computed when the complete dataset is not available. The following paragraphs briefly describe some computable bounds on the mean $\bar{z}$ and standard deviation $\hat{\sigma}_z$ of a transformed data sequence $\{z_k = t(x_k)\}$ for cases where the transformation $t(\cdot)$ is known but neither of the complete data sequences $\{x_k\}$ nor $\{z_k\}$ is available. Instead, it is assumed that some or all of the following summary statistics are available for the original data sequence $\{x_k\}$:

- the mean: $\bar{x} = (1/N) \sum_{k=1}^{N} x_k$;

- the standard deviation: $\hat{\sigma} = \sqrt{(1/N) \sum_{k=1}^{N} (x_k - \bar{x})^2}$;

- the sample minimum: $m = \min\{x_k\}$;

- the sample maximum $M = \max\{x_k\}$.

Alternatively, in cases where m and M are not available, they can be replaced with lower and upper bounds on the data values, say x_L and x_U, respectively. The principal cost of this replacement is a widening of the computed bounds on the mean and standard deviation of the transformed data sequence by an amount that depends on how far x_L and x_U are from m and M, respectively.

The results that follow are taken from a paper by Rowe (1988), who derives bounds based on the restriction that the first three derivatives of $t(\cdot)$ exist and have constant algebraic signs on their entire domain. For the first derivative, this condition implies that the function is either increasing (if $t'(x) > 0$ for all x) or decreasing (if $t'(x) < 0$ for all x). As a further consequence, these restrictions imply that $t(\cdot)$ is continuous and strictly monotone, hence invertible (Klambauer, 1975, p. 181). The detailed results given by Rowe explicitly assume $t''(x) > 0$, but he notes that the corresponding results for any function satisfying $t''(x) < 0$ may be obtained by considering $g(x) = -t(x)$ instead, since then $g''(x) > 0$. The assumption that $t''(x) > 0$ for all x in the domain of $t(\cdot)$ implies that $t(\cdot)$ is a *convex function* (Rockafellar, 1970, p. 26), a very useful class of functions that can be defined in several different ways. One definition of a convex function is one satisfying *Jensen's inequality* (Rockafellar, 1970, p. 25):

$$t\left(\sum_{i=1}^{m} \lambda_i x_i\right) \leq \sum_{i=1}^{m} \lambda_i t(x_i), \quad \lambda_i \geq 0, \quad \sum_{i=1}^{m} \lambda_i = 1. \tag{5.105}$$

The integral extension of this inequality is also extremely useful (Hardy, Littlewood, and Polya, 1952, p. 151):

$$\phi\left(\int_a^b f(x)p(x)dx\right) \leq \int_a^b \phi(f(x))p(x)dx \tag{5.106}$$

for every convex function $\phi : [a, b] \to R$, provided $f : [a, b] \to [a, b]$, $p(x) \geq 0$ for all $x \in [a, b]$, and the normalization condition

$$\int_a^b p(x)dx = 1 \tag{5.107}$$

holds. Since the restrictions on $p(x)$ are those of a probability density function, taking $f(x) = x$ in (5.107) yields the following expectation result for any convex function $\phi(\cdot)$:

$$\phi(E\{x\}) \leq E\{\phi(x)\}. \tag{5.108}$$

In fact, this result is the basis for several of the results presented here.

Although Rowe's restrictions are fairly strong, the class of functions satisfying them is large enough to include many important examples that arise frequently in data analysis applications. Specific examples of transformations $t : R^+ \rightarrow R$ satisfying these conditions are

$$t(x) = x^r \quad \text{for } r > 1 \text{ or } r < 0,$$
$$t(x) = -x^r \quad \text{for } 0 < r < 1,$$
$$t(x) = e^x,$$
$$t(x) = -\ln x. \tag{5.109}$$

The simplest of Rowe's results is the following pair of inequalities on the mean of the transformed data sequence $\{t(x_k)\}$, given only the mean $\bar{x}$, the minimum value m, and the maximum value M of the original data sequence:

$$t(\bar{x}) \leq \frac{1}{N}\sum_{k=1}^{N} t(x_k) \leq t(m) + \left(\frac{\bar{x} - m}{M - m}\right)[t(M) - t(m)]. \tag{5.110}$$

Note that if we take $t(x) = x$, both of these bounds collapse to the mean value $\bar{x}$. As a nontrivial application, Rowe (1988) notes that taking $t(x) = (x - \bar{x})^2$ gives the following bounds on the variance of the sequence $\{x_k\}$, computable from the mean and sequence bounds alone:

$$0 \leq \frac{1}{N}\sum_{k=1}^{N}(x_k - \bar{x})^2 \leq (\bar{x} - m)(M - \bar{x}). \tag{5.111}$$

This bound is also given by Bhatia and Davis (2000), who generalize it to the much more abstract setting of positive unital maps between C^* algebras. In addition, these authors also show that necessary and sufficient conditions for the upper bound to be achieved are that x_k take only the extreme value m or M. Further, Bhatia and Davis (2000) note that inequality (5.111) strengthens the following bound of Popoviciu:

$$0 \leq \frac{1}{N}\sum_{k=1}^{N}(x_k - \bar{x})^2 \leq \frac{(M - m)^2}{4}. \tag{5.112}$$

The authors note that this upper bound is achieved if and only if N is even and $x_k = m$ for $N/2$ observations and $x_k = M$ for the remaining $N/2$ observations.

As another application of the inequality (5.110), note that $t(x) = 1/x$ satisfies Rowe's criteria, giving the bounds

$$\frac{1}{M} \leq \frac{1}{\bar{x}} \leq \frac{1}{N}\sum_{k=1}^{N}\frac{1}{x_k} \leq \frac{M + m - \bar{x}}{mM} \leq \frac{1}{m}. \tag{5.113}$$

Note that taking the reciprocal of these bounds gives the following bounds on the harmonic mean:

$$m \ \le \ \frac{mM}{M+m-\bar{x}} \ \le \ \left[\frac{1}{N}\sum_{k=1}^{N}\frac{1}{x_k}\right]^{-1} \ \le \bar{x} \ \le M. \qquad (5.114)$$

In this case, the upper bound follows directly from the extended AGM discussed in Sec. 5.3.2, but the lower bound is not related to the classical generalized means.

Another interesting extension of this reciprocal transformation result is related to the ratio characterization problem mentioned in Sec. 5.3.1. Specifically, note that the statistical independence of two sequences $\{x_k\}$ and $\{y_k\}$ is a very common working assumption, often justified on the basis of the physical independence of error sources. An important consequence of statistical independence is that the variables involved are uncorrelated, meaning that

$$E\{(x - E\{x\})(y - E\{y\})\} = 0. \qquad (5.115)$$

The finite sample version of this lack of correlation is the orthogonality condition

$$\sum_{k=1}^{N}(x_k - \bar{x})(y_k - \bar{y}) = 0, \qquad (5.116)$$

where $\bar{x}$ and $\bar{y}$ represent the means of the sequences $\{x_k\}$ and $\{y_k\}$. Since the sum of the deviations from the mean is zero, condition (5.116) reduces to

$$\sum_{k=1}^{N}(x_k - \bar{x})y_k = \sum_{k=1}^{N}x_k y_k \ - \ N\bar{x}\bar{y} = 0 \Rightarrow \sum_{k=1}^{N}x_k y_k = N\bar{x}\bar{y}. \qquad (5.117)$$

Now, suppose we are given $\bar{x}$ and $\bar{y}$, we are interested in obtaining bounds on the ratio $z_k = y_k/x_k$, and we are willing to assume x_k and y_k are statistically independent. The quantity of interest is then the average ratio

$$\bar{R} = \frac{1}{N}\sum_{k=1}^{N}\frac{y_k}{x_k} \ = \ \bar{y}\bar{z}, \qquad (5.118)$$

where $z_k = 1/x_k$. Combining (5.118) with the inequalities (5.113) immediately gives the desired bounds

$$\frac{\bar{y}}{M} \ \le \ \frac{\bar{y}}{\bar{x}} \ \le \ \bar{R} \ \le \ \left(\frac{M+m-\bar{x}}{mM}\right)\bar{y} \ \le \ \frac{\bar{y}}{m}. \qquad (5.119)$$

Note that these bounds show that the ratio of the individual sequence means, $\bar{y}/\bar{x}$, is a lower bound on $\bar{R}$, suggesting that the simple, intuitive estimation strategy of taking the ratio of the means is likely to underestimate the true ratio. It is possible to extend these results to cases where the data sequences $\{x_k\}$ and $\{y_k\}$ are not statistically independent, but this would require specification of the form of association between the variables, significantly complicating the results. In particular, statistical independence is a very useful simplifying assumption, implying that y_k is uncorrelated with both x_k and $1/x_k$, while alternative assumptions require detailed descriptions of the nature and extent of the association between the variables involved.

The bounds on the mean of the transformed sequence given in (5.110) depend only on knowledge of m, M, and $\bar{x}$, but Rowe (1988) shows convincingly that much better bounds can usually be obtained if the standard deviation $\hat{\sigma}$ of the original data sequence is also known. Specifically, these bounds are given by

$$\phi_L = \min\{\beta_1, \beta_2\} \leq \frac{1}{N}\sum_{k=1}^{N} x_k \leq \max\{\beta_1, \beta_2\} = \phi_U, \qquad (5.120)$$

where β_1 and β_2 are defined by

$$\beta_1 = p_m t(m) + (1 - p_m)t\left(\bar{x} + \frac{\hat{\sigma}^2}{\bar{x} - m}\right),$$

$$\beta_2 = p_M t(M) + (1 - p_M)t\left(\bar{x} + \frac{\hat{\sigma}^2}{M - \bar{x}}\right),$$

$$p_m = \frac{\hat{\sigma}^2}{\hat{\sigma}^2 + (\bar{x} - m)^2},$$

$$p_M = \frac{\hat{\sigma}^2}{\hat{\sigma}^2 + (M - \bar{x})^2}. \qquad (5.121)$$

Further improvements are sometimes possible if order statistics are also available for the original data sequence, but the improvements appear to be quite small in most cases, and order statistics are not always available.

Finally, Rowe (1988) also presents some bounds for the standard deviation τ of the transformed sequence $\{t(x_k)\}$ given the values of m, M, $\bar{x}$, and $\hat{\sigma}$ for the original data sequence, but these bounds are generally more complicated and harder to derive, failing to exist in some circumstances. The simplest and apparently most useful of these bounds are defined separately for increasing and decreasing transformations:

$$\left[\frac{\phi_L - t(m)}{v_L - m}\right]\sqrt{\hat{\sigma}^2 + (v_L - \bar{x})^2} \leq \tau \leq \left[\frac{\phi_U - t(M)}{v_U - M}\right]\sqrt{\hat{\sigma}^2 + (v_U - \bar{x})^2}, \qquad (5.122)$$

$$\left[\frac{\phi_U - t(M)}{v_U - M}\right]\sqrt{\hat{\sigma}^2 + (v_U - \bar{x})^2} \leq \tau \leq \left[\frac{\phi_L - t(m)}{v_L - m}\right]\sqrt{\hat{\sigma}^2 + (v_L - \bar{x})^2}. \qquad (5.123)$$

Here, $v_L = t^{-1}(\phi_L)$ and $v_U = t^{-1}(\phi_U)$, where ϕ_L and ϕ_U are the bounds on the mean of the transformed sequence $\{t(x_k)\}$ defined in (5.120). Numerical results presented by Rowe (1988) suggest that these bounds are much more conservative than the mean bounds discussed above. Still, the availability of easily computed bounds on τ can be very useful in cases where only summary statistics are available for the original data sequence $\{x_k\}$.

5.3.4 Inequalities as uncertainty descriptions

The results presented in Sec. 5.3.3 demonstrate that it is sometimes possible to obtain simple bounds on results that cannot be computed explicitly due to a lack of detailed data. The following discussion considers an alternative but closely related idea: the use of inequalities to describe uncertain or unknown data. The basic idea considered here is that of the *set-theoretic* or *unknown-but-bounded* data model (Milanese et al., 1996; Schweppe, 1973) as an alternative to the more popular random data model. The set-theoretic model is closely related to the ideas of *interval arithmetic* (Moore, 1979), in which real numbers are replaced with intervals of possible values to account for effects such as roundoff errors in finite-precision computer arithmetic. In interval arithmetic, real data values x are replaced with closed, bounded intervals $X = [X^-, X^+]$ for some $X^+ \geq X^-$. Taking $X^+ = X^- = x$ reduces the interval data model to the real data model, but the more general interval data model provides the basis for an interesting variety of novel computational and data analysis procedures. These ideas also have some important similarities and differences with the random variable uncertainty model, a point discussed briefly in the following paragraphs.

The essential idea behind the interval data model is to work with intervals $[X^-, X^+]$ that are known to contain the "correct" value of an imprecisely known real data variable x. As Rowe (1988) notes, in favorable cases, these bounds can be both tight (i.e., $X^+ - X^- \geq 0$ is small) and easily computed. In addition, bounds on data characterizations computed from interval-valued data sequences $\{X_k\}$ do not depend on *distributional* assumptions, but instead on strictly weaker bounding assumptions. Since this point is often the source of significant misunderstanding, it is worth illustrating with the following simple example. First, note that the *midpoint* of the interval X is given by (Moore, 1979, p. 10)

$$m(X) = \frac{X^- + X^+}{2} \tag{5.124}$$

and the *width* is given by

$$w(X) = X^+ - X^-. \tag{5.125}$$

It follows from these definitions that the interval X may be represented as

$$X = m(X) + \left(\frac{w(X)}{2}\right) \cdot [-1, 1], \tag{5.126}$$

where $a \cdot [Z^-, Z^+]$ represents the product of the real number a and the interval $Z = [Z^-, Z^+]$, giving the new interval $[aZ^-, aZ^+]$ for any $a \geq 0$. (Note that if $a < 0$, it is necessary to reverse the order of these terms: $a \cdot [Z^-, Z^+] = [aZ^+, aZ^-]$, since then $aZ^+ \leq aZ^-$.) Representation (5.126) for the interval X is analogous to the normalization of a random variable x with mean μ and standard deviation σ to obtain a zero-mean, unit-variance random variable z:

$$z = \frac{x - \mu}{\sigma} \Rightarrow x = \mu + \sigma z. \tag{5.127}$$

In particular, note that the interval midpoint $m(X)$ in (5.126) is analogous to the mean μ in (5.127) and the interval half-width $w(X)/2$ in (5.126) is analogous to the standard deviation σ in (5.127).

Confusion sometimes arises as a consequence of the mistaken belief that the interval variable $X = [a, b]$ is equivalent to a random variable uniformly distributed on $[a, b]$. To see that these data models are not equivalent, compare the following two scenarios. First, suppose $\{x_k\}$ is a sequence of real numbers described by the unknown-but-bounded uncertainty model $x_k \in [a, b]$ for $k = 1, 2, \ldots, N$. Next, suppose $\{u_k\}$ is a sequence of i.i.d. random variables with uniform distribution on $[a, b]$. Given this description of the variables x_k, it follows only that their mean satisfies $\bar{x} \in [a, b]$. In particular, note that while $\bar{x} \simeq m(X)$ is certainly possible, this condition is not necessary since $x_k = a$ or $x_k = b$ for all k is equally consistent with the unknown-but-bounded uncertainty description. In contrast, it follows from the central limit theorem (Billingsley, 1986, p. 367) that the mean $\bar{u}$ of the sequence $\{u_k\}$ approaches a Gaussian limiting distribution as $N \to \infty$ with mean $(a+b)/2$ and variance $(b-a)^2/12N$. More generally, note that since $u_k \in [a, b]$ for all k, the sequence $\{u_k\}$ is consistent with the unknown-but-bounded model, but so are an uncountably infinite variety of other data sequences, including *any* random variable sequence restricted to the interval $[a, b]$ (e.g., suitably scaled beta distributions (Johnson, Kotz, and Balakrishnan, 1995, Chapter 25)), simple deterministic bounded models such as exponential decays or sinusoids, and complicated deterministic models such as chaotic sequences (Guckenheimer and Holmes, 1983).

The interval data model provides the basis for *interval arithmetic*, which is defined by the following operations (Moore, 1979, p. 11):

A: addition: $[X^-, X^+] + [Y^-, Y^+] = [X^- + Y^-, X^+ + Y^+]$;

S: subtraction: $[X^-, X^+] - [Y^-, Y^+] = [X^- - Y^+, X^+ - Y^-]$;

M: multiplication: $[X^-, X^+] \cdot [Y^-, Y^+] = [\min(X^-Y^-, X^-Y^+, X^+Y^-, X^+Y^+),$
$\max(X^-Y^-, X^-Y^+, X^+Y^-, X^+Y^+)]$;

D: division: $[X^-, X^+]/[Y^-, Y^+] = [X^-, X^+] \cdot (1/[Y^-, Y^+])$, where $1/[Y^-, Y^+] = [1/Y^+, 1/Y^-]$ provided $0 \notin [Y^-, Y^+]$.

Note that while these operations reduce to the familiar four operations of real arithmetic when the intervals shrink to real numbers, in the general case they are more complicated and exhibit some fundamentally different algebraic characteristics. The added complexity is perhaps most clearly evident in the expression for interval multiplication, which is a direct consequence of the fact that multiplication by negative numbers reverses the direction of inequalities, so it is not possible to say a priori which of the four individual products of $X^\pm$ with $Y^\pm$ will be the smallest or the largest. Similarly, the requirement that $0 \notin [Y^-, Y^+]$ in the definition of interval division is a simple extension of the restriction that $y \neq 0$ if the ratio x/y of two real numbers is to be well-defined.

The interval addition operation defined above corresponds to *Minkowski addition* of two sets (Berger, 1987, p. 334) and, unlike with the case of ordinary addition and subtraction, the subtraction operation defined above is *not* the inverse of Minkowski addition. In particular, note that

$$(X + Y) - Y = [X^- + Y^-, X^+ + Y^+] - [Y^-, Y^+]$$
$$= [X^- + Y^- - Y^+, X^+ + Y^+ - Y^-], \qquad (5.128)$$

which is *not* equal to X unless $Y^+ = Y^-$, reducing the interval Y to a single real number. A closely related result is the fact that

$$X - X = [X^- - X^+, X^+ - X^-] = w(X) \cdot [-1, 1], \qquad (5.129)$$

which is not zero unless $w(X) = 0$, again meaning that the interval X reduces to a single real value. More generally, it is easy to show that both interval addition and interval multiplication are associative, like ordinary addition and multiplication:

$$X + (Y + Z) = (X + Y) + Z,$$
$$X \cdot (Y \cdot Z) = (X \cdot Y) \cdot Z. \tag{5.130}$$

They are also commutative, again like ordinary addition and multiplication:

$$X + Y = Y + X,$$
$$X \cdot Y = Y \cdot X. \tag{5.131}$$

Conversely, while ordinary addition and multiplication are also distributive, these interval operations are only *subdistributive* (Moore, 1979, p. 13):

$$X \cdot (Y + Z) \subset X \cdot Y + X \cdot Z. \tag{5.132}$$

The key point here is that, although similar, interval arithmetic operations are *not* fully equivalent to their real-number counterparts, so interval computations must be considered carefully to avoid errors or misinterpretations.

In the context of more specific data analysis problems, the interval variable formulation provides the foundation for *set-theoretic parameter estimation* (Milanese et al., 1996), which in its simplest form replaces the Gaussian error model that leads to OLS regression procedures with the unknown-but-bounded error model. Specifically, consider the general linear regression model

$$y_i = \sum_{j=1}^{p} X_{ij}\theta_j + e_i, \quad i = 1, 2, \ldots, N, \tag{5.133}$$

where $\{y_i\}$ is a sequence of N observed response variables, $\{X_{ij}\}$ is an $N \times p$ matrix of explanatory variables, $\{\theta_j\}$ is a collection of p unknown model parameters to be determined, and $\{e_i\}$ is a sequence of N data-modelling errors. In the usual regression problem, the sequence $\{e_i\}$ is assumed to be an i.i.d. sequence of zero-mean Gaussian random variables. Maximum likelihood estimation under this model assumption then leads to the OLS regression estimator discussed in Chapter 4. If instead we invoke the unknown-but-bounded error model $|e_i| \leq \epsilon$ for all i, we obtain the set-theoretic regression problem, which converts (5.133) into the N pairs of simultaneous inequalities

$$y_i - \epsilon \leq \sum_{j=1}^{p} X_{ij}\theta_j \leq y_i + \epsilon. \tag{5.134}$$

The exact solution of these inequalities defines a *convex polytope* (Ziegler, 1995), but these exact solution sets are, unfortunately, quite complicated in general, motivating the use of *bounding sets* like ellipsoids or parallelepipeds that contain the exact solution of the inequalities as a subset but are much easier to parameterize (Milanese et al., 1996; Pearson, 1988).

Although it is not identified as such, Buzzigoli and Giusti (2000) describe a set-theoretic procedure they call the "shuttle algorithm" to compute upper and lower bounds on

	Characterization A	Characterization B	Class Total
Class 1	n_{1A}	n_{1B}	$n_{1.}$
Class 2	n_{2A}	n_{2B}	$n_{2.}$
Characterization Total	$n_{.A}$	$n_{.B}$	N

Table 5.1. *General* 2×2 *contingency table.*

the elements of an n-way data array from a complete set of its $(n-1)$-way marginals. A key working assumption of this algorithm is that all entries are positive, providing the basis for the set-theoretic data model since the $(n-1)$-way marginals define upper bounds on the table entries. In fact, it is useful to briefly consider the problem of reconstructing a contingency table (i.e., a table of counts n_{ij}) from its marginals. Specifically, consider the general 2×2 table shown in Table 5.1, summarizing two mutually exclusive characterizations, denoted Characterization A and Characterization B, for two groups of experimental units, denoted Class 1 and Class 2. The entries n_{ij} in the table specify the number of units from Class i that exhibit Characterization j, and the marginals constitute the Class Totals $n_{1.}$ for Class 1 and $n_{2.}$ for Class 2, and the Characterization Totals $n_{.A}$ for Characterization A and $n_{.B}$ for Characterization B. The problem considered here is that of reconstructing some or all of the individual table entries n_{ij} from whatever individual entries may be known, together with the marginals.

It is fair to ask how far we can go with this problem. In particular, note that the individual entries and the marginals are related by the following four equations:

$$n_{1A} + n_{1B} = n_{1.},$$
$$n_{2A} + n_{2B} = n_{2.},$$
$$n_{1A} + n_{2A} = n_{.A},$$
$$n_{1B} + n_{2B} = n_{.B}. \tag{5.135}$$

Attempting to compute the individual entries from the marginals alone is equivalent to attempting to solve the following system of linear equations:

$$\begin{bmatrix} 1 & 1 & 0 & 0 \\ 0 & 0 & 1 & 1 \\ 1 & 0 & 1 & 0 \\ 0 & 1 & 0 & 1 \end{bmatrix} \begin{bmatrix} n_{1A} \\ n_{1B} \\ n_{2A} \\ n_{2B} \end{bmatrix} = \begin{bmatrix} n_{1.} \\ n_{2.} \\ n_{.A} \\ n_{.B} \end{bmatrix}. \tag{5.136}$$

The difficulty is that the 4×4 matrix appearing in this equation is singular, meaning that the individual entries cannot be reconstructed from the marginals alone. Conversely, note that if any one of the four individual entries is known, together with the marginals, all three of the other individual entries may be constructed exactly from (5.135). For example, if n_{1A} is the only individual entry known, n_{1B} can be reconstructed as $n_{1B} = n_{1.} - n_{1A}$, n_{2A} can be reconstructed as $n_{2A} = n_{.A} - n_{1A}$, and, finally, n_{2B} can be reconstructed from either n_{1B} or n_{2A} using the appropriate marginal. Conversely, for more general $I \times J$ contingency tables that describe I mutually exclusive classes and J mutually exclusive characterizations, more individual entries are required for a complete reconstruction of the table.

The utility of the set-theoretic data model in this problem arises from the fact that even an $I \times J$ contingency table with none of the individual entries known immediately provides

	Characterization A	Characterization B	Characterization C	Class Total
Class 1	12	?	?	23
Class 2	?	6	9	22
Class 3	?	?	?	15
Characterization Total	27	14	19	60

Table 5.2. *Example* 3×3 *contingency table with missing entries.*

	Characterization B	Characterization C	Class Total
Class 1	?	?	11
Class 3	?	?	7
Characterization Total	8	10	18

Table 5.3. 2×2 *subtable of missing entries derived from the incomplete* 3×3 *contingency table in Table* 5.2.

bounds on all individual entries. Specifically, for a traditional contingency table whose entries are integer counts, admissible values for n_{ij} are integers satisfying the set-theoretic constraints

$$0 \leq n_{ij} \leq \min\{n_{i\cdot}, n_{\cdot j}\}. \tag{5.137}$$

Typically, these bounds are too wide to be interesting, but if values for or tighter bounds on a subset of the individual entries are available, they can be combined with the marginal definitions

$$\sum_{j=1}^{J} n_{ij} = n_{i\cdot}, \quad i = 1, 2, \ldots, I,$$

$$\sum_{i=1}^{I} n_{ij} = n_{\cdot j}, \quad j = 1, 2, \ldots, J \tag{5.138}$$

to obtain a set-theoretic characterization of the remaining entries.

As a specific example, consider the 3×3 contingency table shown in Table 5.2, with missing entries marked as "?" appearing in six of the nine table entries. The entry n_{2A} for Class 2 and Characterization A can be computed immediately from the Class 2 marginal $n_{2\cdot} = 22$, implying $n_{2A} = 7$. Similarly, the entry n_{3A} can be determined from this result, together with the Characterization A marginal $n_{\cdot A} = 27$, implying $n_{3A} = 8$. These results then leave us with four missing entries, which may be extracted as the 2×2 subtable shown in Table 5.3. The following preliminary set-theoretic bounds follow immediately from (5.137):

$$0 \leq n_{1B} \leq 8,$$
$$0 \leq n_{1C} \leq 10,$$
$$0 \leq n_{3B} \leq 7, \tag{5.139}$$
$$0 \leq n_{3C} \leq 7. \tag{5.140}$$

It is possible to refine these bounds, as follows. First, note that since $n_{1B} \leq 8$ and $n_{1B}+n_{1C} = 11$, it follows that $n_{1C} \geq 3$. Similarly, since $n_{1C} \leq 10$ and $n_{1B}+n_{1C} = 11$, it also follows that $n_{1B} \geq 1$. Together, these conditions reduce (5.139) to the following system of inequalities:

$$1 \leq n_{1B} \leq 8,$$
$$3 \leq n_{1C} \leq 10,$$
$$0 \leq n_{3B} \leq 7,$$
$$0 \leq n_{3C} \leq 7. \tag{5.141}$$

Note that each of these inequalities has eight possible integer solutions. In fact, they define eight consistent contingency tables, obtained by requiring any one of these four unknown entries to assume one of its eight possible values. Given this constraint, the marginal conditions then determine consistent values for the other three table entries, yielding a consistent contingency table.

For this example, two of the six missing contingency table entries can be determined precisely from the marginals, while the inequality-based analysis described here permits us to determine a family of eight possible sets of values for the remaining four table entries. If additional information is available, it may be possible to refine these results further by eliminating solutions that are inconsistent with this information. For example, if it is known that none of the cells are empty in the original contingency table, the family of admissible entries for the indeterminate 2×2 subtable shown in Table 5.3 is reduced from eight members to six, since two of the original solutions correspond to either $n_{3B} = 0$ or $n_{3C} = 0$.

5.4   Coda: What is a "good" data characterization?

Although they do provide some very useful insight into various "goodness criteria," the preceding discussions have not really answered the question posed in the title of this chapter: What *is* a "good" data characterization? The following paragraphs briefly examine this original question further from a somewhat broader perspective. Specifically, the following discussion considers six alternative viewpoints from which "goodness" may be judged:

1. predictable qualitative behavior,

2. ease of interpretation,

3. appropriateness to the application,

4. historical acceptance,

5. availability,

6. computational complexity.

Because these viewpoints are often in conflict, it is important in practice to consider how they should be balanced, and the primary conclusion of this discussion is that there is rarely a unique "best" approach, so several different approaches should be compared to help us select a reasonable compromise or a reasonable set of alternatives, all of which may be presented for further consideration.

   The first criterion—predictable qualitative behavior—was examined in detail in Secs.
5.1 and 5.2, so it will not be discussed further here, except to reiterate that it is practically
important and can lead to some useful insight. Similarly, the second criterion—ease of
interpretation—was examined in Sec. 5.3.1, where it was noted that the use of normalized criteria such as Hotelling's skewness measure, which is bounded in magnitude by
one, leads to easier interpretation than nonnormalized measures such as the more familiar
third–moment-based skewness measure introduced in Chapter 2. More generally, ease of
interpretation usually also has a strong application-specific component, related in part to the
criterion of historical acceptance discussed further below.
   The third criterion—appropriateness to the application—is obviously crucial, but it
may not be met in practice if the working assumptions on which the selected characterization
is based are violated badly enough. Historically, one of the primary motivations for the
development of robust statistical procedures was the need to have practical alternatives in
cases where the Gaussian distributional assumptions underlying many (if not most) classical
analysis procedures were violated badly enough to give questionable results. Indeed, it is
not difficult to find introductory-level treatments of many data analysis topics that do not
even state the underlying assumptions on which the specific methods described are based.
As a specific example, the t-test for the hypothesis that two sample means are equal is
explicitly based on the assumption that the two samples represent i.i.d. sequences of random
variables drawn from Gaussian distributions with the same variance but possibly different
means. Despite these working assumptions, in practice the t-test is still widely used in
circumstances where they are not even approximately satisfied.
   This point is illustrated in Figure 5.1, which contrasts two t-test results. The upper
two plots show two Gaussian sequences of the same length and the same variance but with
different means. This difference is detected by the t-test, which associates a p value of
0.0061 with the null hypothesis that the means are equal. Hence, this hypothesis may
be rejected at the 1% significance level. In contrast, the lower two plots show two data
sequences that again have means zero and one, respectively, but here the deviations of both
sequences from their mean values have the very heavy-tailed Student's t distribution with
two degrees of freedom. Here, the null hypothesis cannot be rejected even at the 10%
significance level, since the computed p value for the t-test is 0.1984.
   The fourth criterion—historical acceptance—is an important one to recognize, even
when we have significant grounds for believing it is inappropriate in the particular case under consideration. Specifically, many types of analysis are so frequently approached using
one or more methods with strong historical acceptance that it may require substantial justi-
fication to present results obtained by any other method. Again, Gaussian statistics underlie
many analysis methods with strong historical acceptance, but—as several of the examples
discussed in previous chapters demonstrate—these methods often fail spectacularly in the
presence of outliers or other significant deviations from Gaussianity. As a practical matter,
it is often best to include one or more standard methods among those considered, both to
confirm our suspicions of weakness in the historically accepted methods and to demonstrate
these weaknesses to others. Further, such comparisons head off the question of why standard
methods were not considered.
   The fifth criterion—accessibility—refers to the availability of the computational
software to implement a particular analysis method. Recent and ongoing advances in
computational resources and the development of "freeware" packages like the R statistical

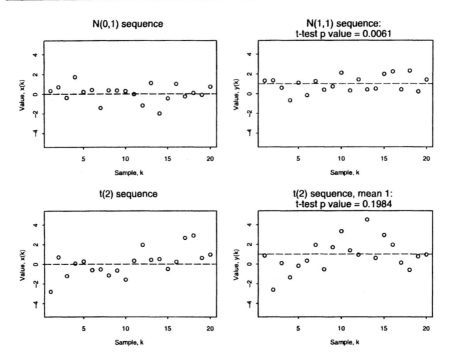

Figure 5.1. *Comparison of two classical t-test results: the upper two plots compare two Gaussian sequences, correctly shown to have different means, while the lower two plots compare two Student's t sequences with two degrees of freedom, incorrectly suggesting the means are not different.*

programming platform (Venables and Ripley, 2002) have greatly enhanced the availability of a very wide range of analysis methods. As a consequence, this criterion—once a significant barrier to the application of sophisticated methods—is steadily becoming less and less significant. Conversely, the widespread availability of increasingly complicated analytical tools does increase the danger of their inappropriate application. *In particular, it is important to emphasize that many analytical characterizations are available that can be applied to most or all datasets and that will return numerical results, even in cases where the method's working assumptions are so badly violated that these results are meaningless.*

The sixth criterion—computational efficiency—continues to represent a significant limitation of the utility of certain data characterizations despite the advances in computing resources. For example, Rousseeuw (1994) notes that for some high-breakdown estimators based on exhaustive subset searches, computational considerations limit applicability to datasets of size $N \lesssim 25$ for the foreseeable future. Conversely, this is an area where precise problem formulations are extremely important. As a specific example, Hansen, Jaumard, and Mladenovic (1995) discuss the inherent computational complexity of a number of different partition-based clustering procedures. In all cases, the objective is to assign the objects o_k in a set S to a fixed number of clusters $C_i \subset S$ such that $o_k \in C_i$ if o_k is closer to other objects in C_i than it is to objects in clusters C_j for $j \neq i$. This basic objective may be translated into several different optimization problems, and the complexity of these optimization problems can be radically different. In particular, the authors note that *minimum diameter clustering*, which minimizes the objective function

$$J(C) = \max_{o_k \in C} \left\{ \max_{o_l \in C} \ d_{k\ell} \right\}, \tag{5.142}$$

where $d_{k\ell}$ is a dissimilarity measure between objects o_k and o_ℓ, is NP-hard. Interestingly, these authors also note that if the attribute vectors on which the clustering is based correspond to points in a Euclidean space (a constraint on the data types considered), a computationally efficient algorithm is available. Further, if the criterion $J(C)$ defined in (5.142) is replaced with the following *minimum radius criterion*, the problem can be solved easily in polynomial time:

$$J(C) = \min_{o_k \in C} \left\{ \max_{o_l \in C} \ d_{k\ell} \right\}. \tag{5.143}$$

Differences in performance between these criteria can be expected to vary from one application to another, but the key point here is that the computational consequences of such changes in problem formulation can be profound, nonobvious, and data-dependent.

The overall conclusion to be drawn from this discussion is that only rarely is one method "best" with respect to all of these criteria, and sometimes no single method is even "acceptably good" with respect to all of them, at least at first glance. As a consequence, it is important to take a broader view, comparing and evaluating a *set* of methods, each of which is—or at least appears to be—highly desirable with respect to a subset of these criteria. Such comparisons can be extremely useful. First, they can quantify the uncertainty in our results. Second, they can suggest directions for refinement of the analysis that may ultimately lead to a more complete and generally satisfactory result. This conclusion motivates the detailed discussion of GSA presented in the next two chapters as a framework for setting up and managing systematic comparisons between methods and datasets.

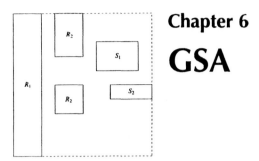

Chapter 6
GSA

The basic notion of GSA was introduced in Chapter 1, and examples presented in Chapters 2, 3, and 4 illustrated the idea further. This chapter is devoted to a more complete discussion of GSA, and additional examples are presented in Chapter 7, which considers GSA sampling schemes in detail.

6.1 The GSA metaheuristic

GSA may be viewed as a *metaheuristic* for characterizing the quality of data analysis results and the datasets on which they are based. A metaheuristic is a systematic procedure for generating *heuristics*, which are defined by Pearl (1984, p. 3) as

> ... *criteria, methods, or principles for deciding which among several alternative courses of action promises to be the most effective in order to achieve good results.*

Further, Pearl notes that heuristics represent compromises between the need to keep selection criteria simple and the need to keep them effective in distinguishing between good and bad alternatives. One of the most common applications of heuristics is to the search for good approximate solutions to optimization problems that have been shown to be NP-hard (Hansen and Mladenovic, 2002; Papadimitriou and Steiglitz, 1982). In contrast, data analysis problems generally belong to the class of *vague problems* for which no "exact" solution exists. Hence, the heuristics of interest here are practical procedures for deciding between good and bad analysis options, and the effectiveness of these heuristics will be judged on the basis of either simulation-based case studies for which exact answers are known or post hoc assessments of the "reasonableness" of real data results.

The GSA metaheuristic generates graphical heuristics to compare the performance of different analysis results across application-specific scenarios. The essential idea is embodied in the following informal statement, which may be taken as the basic principle underlying the GSA metaheuristic:

> A "good" data analysis result should be insensitive to small changes in either the methods or the datasets on which the analysis is based.

Clearly, this condition is not *sufficient* for goodness, since it is satisfied by "characterizations" that are completely independent of the available data. ("The answer is six: What was the question?") Conversely, the results of a GSA can also reveal these difficulties, since the basic idea is to compare results that should be "about the same" but not "identical, independent of the datasets involved." The results obtained with the GSA metaheuristic help us to choose between analysis methods, to assess the degree to which different datasets appear to be similar or dissimilar, or to address some combination of these objectives. As discussed in Chapter 1, this procedure consists of four steps, repeated here for convenience:

1. Select a collection $\{\Sigma_\ell\}$ of *scenarios* to be compared, corresponding to different choices of data sources, analysis methods, or both.

2. Select a *sampling scheme* that generates, for each scenario Σ_ℓ, a collection $\{S_j\}$ of datasets, each of which is expected to give comparable analysis results.

3. Select a common, real-valued *descriptor* $d(\cdot)$ that may be used to compare analysis results, both within and across scenarios.

4. Construct a boxplot summary of the descriptor values for each scenario.

The notion of *small changes* on which this procedure is based may be discussed more precisely in terms of the notion of *exchangeability* as defined by Draper et al. (1993) and introduced in Sec. 6.2. Some general advice on the selection of scenarios Σ_ℓ in Step 1 is given in Sec. 6.3, and the problem of specifying a sampling scheme in Step 2 is considered briefly in Sec. 6.4, primarily to distinguish among three important classes of sampling schemes, of which one (subset-based sampling schemes) will be of primary interest here. A detailed discussion of this class of sampling schemes forms the basis for Chapter 7. Selection of a useful descriptor $d(\cdot)$ in Step 3 is strongly method-dependent, but this topic is discussed briefly in general terms in Sec. 6.5. More detailed discussions accompany GSA-based examples presented elsewhere in this book. Finally, the problems of displaying and interpreting the results of a GSA procedure are discussed in Sec. 6.6 and illustrated further in the case study example presented in Sec. 6.7.

Hansen and Mladenovic (2002) offer the following eight desirable properties for a good metaheuristic:

1. *simplicity:* metaheuristics should be based on a simple, broadly applicable principle;

2. *precision:* the steps of the metaheuristic should be formulated in precise, mathematical terms;

3. *coherence:* all steps for heuristics derived from the metaheuristic should follow naturally from its underlying principle;

4. *efficiency:* heuristics obtained should be optimal or near-optimal for most realistic problems;

5. *effectiveness:* heuristics obtained should take moderate computing time;

6. *robustness:* performance of the heuristics should not depend too strongly on individual datasets;

7. *user-friendliness:* heuristics should be clearly expressed, easy to understand, and easy to use;

8. *innovation:* the metaheuristic's principle and/or the efficiency and effectiveness of the heuristics derived from it should lead to new types of applications.

One of the objectives of this chapter is to show that the GSA framework described here satisfies most of these criteria. The basic statement given above is certainly simple, and subsequent sections of this chapter attempt to make it precise and illustrate its coherence. Examples presented in Chapters 2, 3, and 4; the case study considered in Sec. 6.7; and further examples presented in Chapter 7 all provide evidence of the effectiveness, user-friendliness, and innovation of the GSA metaheuristic, and the motivation for considering sampling schemes that generate a collection of exchangeable subsets in Step 2 is precisely to ensure robustness. As far as efficiency is concerned, assessment is difficult since—in contrast to the optimization problems considered by Hansen and Mladenovic (2002)—most of the data analysis problems considered here do not exhibit demonstrably optimal solutions.

6.2 The notion of exchangeability

The essential idea on which the GSA framework is based is that of comparing results obtained for different datasets that are "distinct but not essentially different." To discuss the "equivalence" desired in Step 2 of the GSA procedure between the m datasets generated by the specified sampling scheme, it is useful to have a formal definition of *equivalent datasets*. As defined by Draper et al. (1993), *exchangeability* is a judgment we make concerning distinct sources of data. Loosely speaking, two data sources (or datasets) are exchangeable if important characterizations of both give approximately the same results. To make this definition more precise, Draper et al. (1993) introduce the following five mathematical components:

1. a set $\mathcal{U}$ of *units,* which may be any sources of data;

2. a collection $\Omega = \{(S_i, S_j)\}$ of pairs of distinct datasets S_i and S_j, obtained from the units in $\mathcal{U}$;

3. a *descriptor* $\delta(\cdot)$ mapping the sets S_i into R^n for some $n \geq 1$;

4. a *norm* $||\cdot||$ on the space R^n;

5. a positive constant C called a *caliper.*

Under this definition, exchangeability is a judgment made regarding the units in $\mathcal{U}$ based on the pairs of datasets contained in the collection Ω. The authors call these pairs of datasets *comparisons* and it is important to note that, although the sets involved must be distinct (i.e., $S_i \neq S_j$), they need not be disjoint (i.e., $S_i \cap S_j \neq \emptyset$ is allowed). Taken together, the descriptor $\delta(\cdot)$ and the norm $||\cdot||$ permit us to make quantitative comparisons of the sets S_i and S_j. In particular, $||\delta(S_i) - \delta(S_j)||$ is a positive number, defined for all comparisons (S_i, S_j) in the collection Ω, that may be interpreted as a measure of distance or dissimilarity between these two datasets. Draper et al. (1993) define the units in $\mathcal{U}$ to be exchangeable (or, more precisely, $(\Omega, \delta(\cdot), || \cdot ||, C)$-exchangeable) if the following condition holds:

$$||\delta(S_i) - \delta(S_j)|| \leq C \quad \text{for all } (S_i, S_j) \in \Omega,$$

where the constant $C > 0$ is the caliper defined in the above list. This constant represents a threshold parameter, quantifying the allowed mismatch between $\delta(S_i)$ and $\delta(S_j)$ for equivalent datasets S_i and S_j.

In the GSA framework proposed here, each scenario Σ_ℓ corresponds to a set $\mathcal{U}$ of data-generating units, and the nominal working assumption invoked in constructing specific implementations of the GSA framework is that these units are exchangeable. That is, our expectation is that, *in the absence of data anomalies,* the m datasets generated in Step 2 of the GSA procedure are exchangeable. As a practical matter, this exchangeability requirement reduces to something like an experimental design specification. The question of how we meet this requirement is discussed further in Sec. 6.4 and illustrated in the examples discussed subsequently. Here, the key point is that we regard exchangeable datasets S_i and S_j to be "small changes" of each other, and the objective of the GSA procedure is to assess whether these small changes cause correspondingly small changes in the results obtained using a specified analysis method $\mathcal{M}$. In particular, note that each of the boxplots constructed using the GSA procedure may be regarded as an informal assessment of the range of variation of $\{d(\mathcal{M}_i S_j)\}$ for fixed i over the subsets S_j generated by the sampling scheme specified in GSA Step 2. Indeed, the objective of Step 2 is to generate a collection $\{S_i\}$ of $\{\Omega, \delta(\cdot), || \cdot ||, C\}$-exchangeable subsets for some (usually informally specified) descriptor $\delta(\cdot)$, and the objective of the GSA procedure as a whole is to determine whether each analysis method $\mathcal{M}_i$ generates results $\mathcal{M}_i S_j$ that are exchangeable with respect to the (generally quite different) descriptor $d(\cdot)$ explicitly specified in GSA Step 3. By restricting consideration to scalar-valued descriptors $d(\cdot)$ and constructing graphical representations of the results, we eliminate the need for the norm and the caliper in this assessment of the exchangeability of the analysis results.

6.3 Choosing scenarios

One of the most important decisions to be made in formulating a useful GSA study is the choice of scenarios $\{\Sigma_\ell\}$ to be compared. For example, since the sampling scheme inherent in this method provides a basis for assessing within-scenario variability, there is no advantage in repeating scenarios. Conversely, the differences between the scenarios chosen should be meaningful with respect to the application at hand. Thus, characterizations of the drugstore purchases of vegetarian baseball fans and nonvegetarian dog owners might show interesting patterns of differences, but it is not obvious how an understanding of these differences would be useful. The focus of the following three subsections is the selection of useful scenarios for GSA comparisons. First, Sec. 6.3.1 gives some guidelines for defining scenarios based on a few general principles. Since the number of potentially interesting scenarios is often too large to permit a complete comparison, Sec. 6.3.2 considers the problem of decomposing scenarios into subscenarios and managing comparisons across subscenarios. Finally, since one basis for defining scenarios and subscenarios is often one or more auxiliary variables, several of the basic ideas from the theory of experimental design can be quite useful in specifying scenarios or subscenarios. Consequently, Sec. 6.3.3 presents a brief introduction to some of these ideas and their applicability to scenario selection.

6.3.1 Some general guidelines

Broadly speaking, there are three general ways to define scenarios:

1. by analysis methods,

2. by data characteristics,

3. by both analysis methods and data characteristics.

Since the third of these approaches builds on the first two and leads naturally to stratified scenario/subscenario structures like those discussed in Sec. 6.3.2, the following discussion considers only the first two of these three general strategies.

In the first strategy, scenarios differ only with respect to analysis method, so the results obtained by different methods are compared for the same dataset. Insight gained from the GSA results then depends on the methods chosen for comparison and the nature of the dataset on which these comparisons are based. In particular, if the dataset represents a well-characterized benchmark dataset (e.g., either a dataset obtained by simulation or a dataset that has been extensively characterized by a variety of methods), the results may give useful insight into differences in the behavior of the methods. The utility of this idea is illustrated here with a variety of simulation-based case studies, such as the one presented in Chapter 1 to illustrate the differences in sensitivity of specific trimmed means to three different types of data anomalies. Conversely, if the methods exhibit well-known characteristics and the dataset is not well-characterized, the results of the GSA comparison can give useful insight into the character of the dataset. In such cases, it is generally most useful to compare methods for which results are expected to be similar under some plausible set of working assumptions. A particularly important example of this strategy is the comparison of closely related data characterizations with dramatically different outlier-sensitivities, since small observed differences between results support the working hypothesis of an uncontaminated nominal dataset, while large differences suggest the possibility of outliers in the dataset.

Often, it is useful to distinguish between two versions of the analysis-based scenario development strategy, namely:

1a. scenarios defined by a discrete set of analysis methods,

1b. scenarios defined by a single method with different tuning parameter values.

The first of these approaches is illustrated by the comparisons presented in Chapter 3 of the 3σ edit rule, the Hampel identifier, and the boxplot identification rule. The second approach is illustrated by the trimmed mean comparison presented in Chapter 1, which compared one location estimator (the trimmed mean) as its tuning parameter (the trimming percentage) varied from 0 to 12.5% to 25% to 50%. An important difference between these two cases is that, in Case 1a, the method options considered are finite in number and generally not a priori ordered. In contrast, in Case 1b, the number of possible tuning parameter values is generally uncountably infinite, but if the performance of the method depends continuously on the tuning parameter, it may be possible to achieve a reasonable assessment of the method's behavior as a function of this parameter by examining a few well-chosen cases. The question of how to select these points is closely related to the notion of experimental design discussed in Sec. 6.3.3.

The second general strategy noted above—defining scenarios based on data characteristics—typically starts with a large collection of data values, datasets, or databases and partitions it into a finite number of subcollections. Each of these subcollections then defines a scenario, which is subjected to the same type of analysis. As the following discussions illustrate, this partitioning can be done in many different ways, but first it is useful to note that good partitionings generally exhibit some or all of the following four characteristics:

1. interpretability,

2. distinctness,

3. balance across scenarios,

4. homogeneity within scenarios.

The first criterion means that scenarios should be chosen so that any similarities or differences that are seen between scenarios have a potentially useful interpretation in the context of the application. In particular, interpretability implies that the criteria used in defining scenarios for analysis should be clear and meaningful to the end-users of the results. The second criterion—distinctness—means that the collections defining the different scenarios considered are disjoint. A possible exception arises when a special group is being compared with the general population, although even here, the analysis results will be cleaner if the comparison is made between the special group and the group drawn from the general population that specifically excludes members of the special group. This idea is closely related to the fact that data characterizations of overlapping subsets tend to be positively correlated, a point discussed in detail in Chapter 7.

The third criterion—balance across scenarios—means that the different scenarios considered should be as similar as possible with respect to characteristics that are not of primary interest. As a simple but specific example, if different scenarios correspond to different datasets, it is desirable that the number of records in each dataset be as similar as possible. More generally, it is desirable to match scenarios as well as possible with respect to observed variables that might have a significant influence on our analysis results. In the statistical literature on observational studies, the influence of imbalance in these auxiliary variables (i.e., covariates) on analysis results is called *overt bias*, and compensation for these effects is one of the primary concerns of the analysis of observational study results. As a specific example, Rosenbaum (1970, p. 72) discusses an analysis of the relationship between smoking and mortality published by Cochran (1968) that compared three groups of men: nonsmokers, cigarette smokers, and cigar and pipe smokers. Simple computation of mortality rates for these three groups gave 20.2 deaths per 1000 per year for the nonsmokers, 20.5 for the cigarette smokers, and 35.5 for the cigar and pipe smokers. Naive acceptance of these results would suggest that smoking cigarettes was not particularly hazardous to your health, but that smoking cigars and pipes was quite hazardous. These initial results do not account for differences in the ages of the men in these groups, however, which were, on average, 54.9 for the nonsmokers, 50.5 for the cigarette smokers, and 65.9 for the cigar and pipe smokers. Partitioning the dataset into groups on the basis of age and comparing mortality rates for groups of approximately age-matched subgroups led to a very different conclusion: age-adjusted mortality rates were 20.3 per 1000 per year for the nonsmokers, 28.3 for the cigarette smokers, and 21.2 for the cigar and pipe smokers. The key point of this example is to emphasize the importance of balancing scenarios with respect to potentially significant auxiliary variables. For a much more detailed discussion of this idea and its implementation in the statistical analysis of observational data, refer to the book by Rosenbaum (1970).

Alternatively, in cases where balancing across scenarios on the basis of certain potentially important variables is not feasible, it may still be feasible to examine the importance of these variables by including additional *control scenarios*. That is, if two scenarios of primary interest differ with respect to some key variable that is of interest (e.g., business segments that appear to be in trouble versus those that appear to be doing well, patients with cancer versus those without cancer, good versus bad batches of an industrial product), it may be feasible to construct several scenarios that are identical with respect to the primary outcome of interest but differ with respect to the auxiliary variables that we are concerned with. In the context of the previous example, if we had abundant data on nonsmokers and sparse data on cigarette smokers, one way of detecting the influence of age on our original results would be to construct multiple nonsmoker datasets on the basis of age and compare results across these different scenarios. In this case, we would see a clear increase in mortality rate as the group age increased. Note that while this analysis would not by itself lead to age-corrected mortality rates, it would provide clear evidence of the importance of age as an influential auxiliary variable that should be included in our analysis.

Finally, the fourth criterion—homogeneity within scenarios—is what Thompson (2002) calls the *stratification principle:* within each stratum (here, scenario), the individual units should be as similar as possible. This notion is closely related to the stratified sampling notions discussed in Chapter 7 that are widely used in the design of survey samples; there, it is suggested that the best results (i.e., most accurate data models) are obtained when the internal homogeneity of the subgroups is maximized (i.e., the within-group variance is minimized) (Govindarajulu, 1999, p. 92). In GSA, this idea is closely related to the problem of designing a good sampling scheme for creating subsets for comparison within a scenario, a topic discussed further in Sec. 6.4 and forming the basis for Chapter 7.

To define scenarios that satisfy some or all of these goodness criteria, we have at least two general options: analysis-based scenario selection and knowledge-based scenario selection. One practically important analysis-based approach to defining scenarios is through partition-based cluster analysis. There, the objective is to find a partitioning of a given dataset $\mathcal{D}$ into disjoint subsets such that data observations within each subset are highly similar, while data observations in different subsets are highly dissimilar (Gordon, 1999; Kaufman and Rousseeuw, 1990). In such cases, the clusters obtained from this analysis can be used to define distinct analysis scenarios Σ_ℓ. Note that since the groups defined by a partition-based clustering are disjoint and as similar as possible with respect to the clustering criterion, these results are well-aligned with the second and fourth criteria presented above for good scenarios, although it is worth noting that traditional cluster analysis algorithms can and frequently do lead to highly imbalanced partitions with respect to cluster size. Conversely, there has been some recent work in the area of developing balanced clustering algorithms, specifically for applications where it is necessary or desirable to have groups of approximately the same size (Zhong and Ghosh, 2003). Ideally, these subsets should also correspond to groups that are distinguishable on the basis of some secondary data characteristic, providing a useful interpretation of the results.

A fascinating example of the use of cluster analysis to define scenarios in the analysis of demographic data is the book *The Clustering of America* by Michael J. Weiss (1988). Essentially, each ZIP code in the U.S. is treated as an object with 34 attributes extracted from U.S. Census data and other sources that characterize social rank, mobility, ethnicity, family lifestyle, and housing style. Applying partition-based cluster analysis to these attributes ultimately yielded 40 ZIP-code clusters, each accounting for between 0.5% and 6.0% of the total U.S. population at the time of the analysis. One of the key points of Weiss's book is the high degree of homogeneity within these clusters with respect to everything from what we read to how we travel or how likely we are to join the armed services, despite the extreme *geographic* heterogeneity of these "neighborhoods." For example, the most affluent cluster, dubbed "Blue Blood Estates," includes both Beverly Hills, California (ZIP 90212), and Scarsdale, New York (ZIP 10583), and is characterized by higher than average tendencies to own U.S. Treasury notes, read *Barron's* magazine, own Rolls Royces, and drink bottled water. Conversely, occupants of these neighborhoods are less likely than average American citizens to watch wrestling or purchase home pregnancy tests, groin irritation remedies, or TV dinners. In contrast, the cluster ranked 39th of the 40 in terms of affluence is called "Hard Scrabble" and includes New Milton, West Virginia (ZIP 26411), and Montezuma, Utah (ZIP 84534). Residents of this cluster are three times more likely than the national average to purchase chewing tobacco but are extremely unlikely to ever go downhill skiing, read *Modern Bride* magazine, or purchase frozen yogurt. The key point of this example is that cluster analysis can be used to obtain a partitioning into scenarios that meet all four of the criteria given above: the names given to the 40 clusters give an approximate interpretation to each (e.g., cluster names include "Money and Brains," "Young Suburbia," "Blue Collar Nursery," and "Small Town Downtown"); the clusters are disjoint, consisting of different ZIP code groups; they are roughly balanced in size; and again, one of the main points of Weiss's book is the internal homogeneity of these clusters.

Knowledge-based scenarios are necessarily application-specific, but often there are certain "natural" scenarios that may be of particular interest to compare. It is instructive to consider a few specific examples, both for clarification and because some of the ideas that emerge are much more broadly applicable. For example, in the analysis of business data, natural scenarios might include

1. data partitioned by business organization,

2. data partitioned by product type,

3. data partitioned by customer type,

4. data partitioned by geographic region.

In the analysis of industrial process operating data, natural scenarios might include

1. data partitioned by manufacturing batch,

2. data partitioned by operating condition,

3. data partitioned by raw material characteristics,

4. data partitioned by time (e.g., week, month, quarter, or year).

Similarly, medical data are often usefully partitioned on the basis of various factors, including

1. demographic information (age, sex, race, etc);

2. medical history (e.g., smoker versus nonsmoker, hypertensive versus nonhypertensive, diabetic versus nondiabetic, etc.);

3. disease outcome (e.g., biopsy cancerous or noncancerous).

In fact, defining scenarios on the basis of binary outcomes (e.g., cancer patient versus healthy patient) provides the foundation for *case-control studies* (Collett, 2003, p. 217), also known as *case-referent studies* (Rosenbaum, 1970, p. 7). While this idea appears to be mainly used in the analysis of medical data, the basic notion is one that is applicable to any situation involving two scenarios of interest, one of which can be designated as the "case" (binary outcome one, e.g., "biopsy cancerous" or "product defective") and the other as the "control" or "referent" (binary outcome zero, e.g., "biopsy noncancerous" or "product nondefective").

Case-control studies are particularly useful when we are interested in uncovering reasons for important differences, especially where the events of interest are rare. As a specific example, Rosenbaum (1970, p. 7) describes a study by Herbst, Ulfelder, and Poskanzer (1971) on cancer of the vagina in young women. The basis of their study was 8 women between the ages of 15 and 22 who had developed this form of cancer, which is rare, especially in women this young. Each of these patients (the "cases" in the case-control terminology) was matched to four "controls" or "referents," who were born within five days of the case to whom they were matched, in the same hospital with the same type of service (i.e., ward or private). Of the eight cases, seven were born to mothers who had received the drug diethylstilbestrol (DES), while none of the matched controls were born to mothers who had received DES. Clearly, these results provide strong evidence for a link between maternal DES therapy and the development of vaginal cancer in young women. While confirmation of this hypothesis requires additional analysis (see the book by Rosenbaum (1970) for further discussion of this analysis), this example clearly illustrates the exploratory utility of the case-control methodology in identifying putative causes of important events, particularly rare ones.

Finally, another knowledge-based approach to defining scenarios that sometimes leads to very interesting insight is the adoption of a strongly nontraditional partitioning of the data. An extremely interesting example of this approach is that taken by Garreau (1981) in his analysis of the social, political, and economic character of North America. The traditional view divides North America into the three nations of Canada, the U.S., and Mexico, and then further subdivides each of these countries into states or provinces. Garreau's view, however, is that this traditional partitioning does not account for people's views on major social, political, and economic issues. Hence, he defines nine regions that exhibit clear intraregional similarities and clear interregional differences. For example, he defines "Ecotopia" as a thin region along the west coast, from approximately San Francisco, California, through Vancouver, British Columbia, to Homer, Alaska. This region is bounded on the east by mountains and consists of the only rain forest in North America. As a consequence, many of the prevailing views of this region differ profoundly from those of its two neighbors: "the Empty Quarter" to the east, and "MexAmerica" to the south. For example, because MexAmerica, which includes southern California, is a region largely made inhabitable by water brought in from elsewhere, views on environmental issues are strongly divergent (Garreau, 1981, p. 5):

> *Thus, in MexAmerica, the idea of a freshwater supply flowing unchecked into the sea is considered a crime against nature—a sin. In Ecotopia, leaving a river wild and free is viewed as a blow struck for God's original plan for the land.*

All in all, Garreau makes a compelling argument for his nontraditional regional view of North America as a way of understanding local views and some of the difficulties inherent in developing rational, broadly acceptable national policies. The point here is that nontraditional partitionings that deliberately violate certain traditional notions can sometimes lead to very useful views of a large, complicated dataset.

6.3.2 Managing subscenarios

Frequently, we wish to examine the influence of multiple factors on the results of a data analysis procedure, and in such cases it may be useful to divide scenarios Σ_ℓ into subscenarios $\Sigma_{\ell,\ell'}$. This was the case, for example, in the GSA analysis of trimmed means presented in Chapter 1: the main scenarios Σ_ℓ corresponded to four different classes of data sequences (uncontaminated nominal, bimodal, anomalous zeros, and outliers), while the subscenarios $\Sigma_{\ell,\ell'}$ corresponded to four different trimming percentages (0%, corresponding to the ordinary arithmetic mean; 12.5%; 25%; and 50%, corresponding to the median). It is, of course, possible to take this subdivision further, defining subsubscenarios $\Sigma_{\ell,\ell',\ell''}$ and so forth, but if we pursue this nesting too far, it becomes increasingly difficult to interpret the results. Since the primary motivation of GSA is to generate easily interpreted graphical comparisons, allowing the subscenario structure to become too complex defeats its purpose. This observation raises the question of how subscenarios should be managed, especially in cases where we wish to examine the influence of several different factors and their potential interactions. To address this question, the following discussion considers some useful general ideas in defining subscenarios, after which Sec. 6.3.3 gives a brief introduction to the closely related topic of experimental design.

The decomposition of scenarios into subscenarios described in the preceding paragraph represents a simple *stratification*, in which the top-level stratum corresponds to the main scenarios Σ_ℓ and the subscenarios $\Sigma_{\ell,\ell'}$ represent the second-level strata. Ideally, this stratification should be *balanced*, meaning that subscenarios should be identical across scenarios, as in the trimmed mean example discussed in Chapter 1. There, the main scenarios corresponded to different datasets and each subscenario corresponded to the same four trimming percentages for all of the trimmed means compared. This structure has the advantage of highlighting both interscenario and intrascenario contrasts, and it is particularly useful when subscenarios correspond to different analysis methods (e.g., means versus medians, regression based on linear versus quadratic models, or least-squares versus LAD regression, etc.). If we know the main factors that can be responsible for differences between the results obtained by these different methods, intrascenario comparisons can point to the existence of certain types of data anomalies, either in all scenarios or in a few isolated scenarios.

Sometimes, balanced stratification is not possible. A specific example is the assessment presented in Chapter 4 of the performance of the CWMF as a data cleaner for time-series outliers. There, the main scenario is defined by one of two tuning parameters associated with the filter (specifically, the moving data window width), and subscenarios correspond to values of a second tuning parameter (the filter center weight). Both of these parameters take positive integer values, and the case study presented in Chapter 4 compares the performance of CWMF data cleaners for a small but useful range of these parameters. Since the range of admissible center weight parameters depends on the window width parameter, each scenario has a different number of possible subscenarios associated with it, leading to an unbalanced subscenario structure. Still, there are few enough subscenarios compared in this case study and their conceptual interrelations are clear enough that a graphical comparison of the results quickly yields useful insight into how best to select these tuning parameters, at least for datasets like the one on which this case study is based. In contrast, it is probably best to avoid situations where each scenario has a different number of associated subscenarios and no obvious logical relationships exist between these subscenarios.

Two relevant notions discussed by Singer (1991, Sec. 4B) are *crossing* and *nesting*. In a crossed data layout (i.e., scenario stratification), strata $\Sigma_{\ell_1,\dots,\ell_p}$ are defined by p *factors* $f_1, \dots, f_p$, where each factor f_i assumes one of n_i discrete values, corresponding to the fully balanced stratification just discussed. This stratification scheme has the advantage of providing the most complete data summary possible, but it also has the disadvantage of generating a very large number L of scenarios to be considered:

$$L = \prod_{i=1}^{p} n_i.$$

In particular, note that if each factor involves $n_i = n$ possible levels, we have $L = n^p$, which grows very rapidly with both n and p.

An alternative data layout that often leads to a useful organization of factors while generating many fewer scenarios is the *nested* stratification. There, factors defining individual substrata are only varied for fixed values of the other factors. As a specific example, suppose we wish to examine the influence of two tuning parameters, t_1 and t_2, for a data analysis method $\mathcal{M}$ over a collection $\{\mathcal{D}_i\}$ of datasets. If t_1 and t_2 can assume eight and five possible values, respectively, and we have six datasets to consider, a fully crossed stratification generates $L = 240$ scenarios. A nested alternative would be to first select a nominal pair (t_1^0, t_2^0) from the 40 possible tuning parameter pairs and compare the performance of method $\mathcal{M}$ with these tuning parameters over the 6 datasets, giving a preliminary indication of the sensitivity of method $\mathcal{M}$ to the variations in data characteristics represented by the collection $\{\mathcal{D}_i\}$. Next, we select, say, two of the datasets $\mathcal{D}_i$ (e.g., those giving the best and worst performance), fix the second tuning parameter at its nominal value t_2^0, and vary the parameter t_1 over its eight possible values. This strategy gives 16 second-level comparisons representing a partial summary of the influence of the tuning parameter t_1. Finally, we select one of the two datasets considered in this second-level comparison, together with three of the eight possible values for t_1 (e.g., t_1^0 together with the best and worst t_1 values from the previous comparisons), and vary the second tuning parameter t_2 over its five possible values.

This choice gives 15 third-level comparisons, which summarize the influence of the second tuning parameter t_2 for 3 different choices of t_1. Although the results are much less complete than those obtained from the fully crossed stratification, the number of scenarios considered has been reduced from 240 to 37, organized into sets in which only 1 factor is varied at a time. Alternatively, stratification can also be based on the ideas of experimental design, discussed next.

6.3.3   Experimental design and scenario selection

One of the key points noted in the preceding discussion was the rapid growth of the total number of scenarios in a balanced (i.e., fully crossed) stratification based on many levels. Analogous practical concerns underlie the theory of optimum experimental design in classical statistics, which attempts to minimize the number of experiments required to adequately characterize some phenomenon or system of interest by maximizing the unique information contributed by each experiment. Although this theory is based on specific working assumptions that are not appropriate to the GSA scenario selection problem considered here, some of the results turn out to be quite useful in this context. Hence, the following paragraphs give a very brief introduction to this theory.

Atkinson (1991) gives a useful summary of the history, objectives, and key results in the theory of optimum experimental design. The basic motivating problem is the collection of useful datasets for linear regression models, closely related to the classical ANOVA problem. That is, suppose we wish to determine the unknown coefficients $\{\theta_i\}$ in the data model

$$y_k = \sum_{i=1}^{p} \theta_i x_{ki} + e_k, \quad k = 1, 2, \ldots, N, \tag{6.1}$$

where $\{y_k\}$ is a vector of N observed experimental outcomes, $\{x_{ki}\}$ is an $N \times p$ matrix consisting of N observations for each of p explanatory variables, and $\{e_k\}$ is a vector of N prediction errors, arising from random effects not explainable by the variables x_{ki}. If, as is sometimes but not always the case, we have freedom to choose the values of the explanatory variables $\{x_{ki}\}$ that define the N experiments, how should we make this choice?

To see the importance of this question, note that the most popular approach historically to estimating the parameters θ_i is the method of least squares, which minimizes the sum of squared prediction errors:

$$J(\theta) = \sum_{k=1}^{N} e_k^2 = (\mathbf{y} - \mathbf{X}\theta)^T (\mathbf{y} - \mathbf{X}\theta). \tag{6.2}$$

Here, $\theta \in R^p$ is the p vector of unknown parameters $\{\theta_i\}$, $\mathbf{y}$ is the N vector of experimental responses $\{y_k\}$, and $\mathbf{X}$ is the $N \times p$ matrix of controllable experimental conditions. A convex optimization problem with the unique solution

$$\hat{\theta} = (\mathbf{X}^T \mathbf{X})^{-1} \mathbf{X}^T \mathbf{y} \tag{6.3}$$

is defined by (6.2) *provided that the $p \times p$ matrix $\mathbf{X}^T\mathbf{X}$ is nonsingular.* This result provides a necessary condition for useful experimental designs: the $\{x_{ki}\}$ values must be chosen so that this matrix is nonsingular.

If this basic solvability condition is satisfied and if the sequence $\{e_k\}$ represents an i.i.d. sequence of random variables with mean zero and finite variance σ^2, it is not difficult to show that $\hat{\theta}$ is an unbiased estimate of the parameter vector θ with covariance matrix

$$\text{cov } \{\hat{\theta}\} = \sigma^2(\mathbf{X}^T\mathbf{X})^{-1}. \tag{6.4}$$

This result underlies much of the theory of optimum experimental design, which attempts to achieve precise parameter estimates by making $(\mathbf{X}^T\mathbf{X})^{-1}$ "small" in some useful sense. Specific strategies include D-optimum designs, which minimize the determinant of this matrix, corresponding to the volume of the parameter confidence regions if the sequence $\{e_k\}$ is normally distributed, and A-optimum designs, which minimize the trace of this matrix, corresponding to the average variance of the parameter estimates $\hat{\theta}_i$.

As a specific example, consider the historically important simple linear regression model

$$y_k = \theta_0 + \sum_{i=1}^{p} \theta_i x_{ki} + e_k, \quad k = 1, 2, \dots, N. \tag{6.5}$$

If the p independent variables can assume any real value in the range $-1 \le x_{ki} \le 1$, a good design for this problem is the 2^p *factorial design* (Atkinson and Donev, 1992, Chapter 7), which uses all 2^p possible combinations of the extreme values $x_{ki} = \pm 1$. This design is D-optimal for this problem (Atkinson and Donev, 1992, Chapter 7), it leads to uncorrelated parameter estimates (i.e., the matrix $\mathbf{X}^T\mathbf{X}$ is diagonal), and it is also D-optimal for estimating the parameters of models involving all possible *interaction terms*, corresponding to products of the individual terms x_{ki} in which no single variable is repeated (e.g., $x_{ki}x_{kj}$ is an interaction term for $i \ne j$, but the terms x_{ki}^2 and $x_{ki}x_{kj}^2$ are not). If *curvature terms* like x_{ki}^2 are included in the model, 2^p factorial designs are no longer D-optimal. As a specific example, Atkinson and Donev (1992, pp. 166–167) give D-optimal designs for the two-variable second-order model

$$y_k = \theta_0 + \theta_1 x_{k1} + \theta_2 x_{k2} + \theta_3 x_{k1}x_{k2} + \theta_4 x_{k1}^2 + \theta_5 x_{k2}^2 + e_k. \tag{6.6}$$

Note that this model includes a constant term, linear terms in both explanatory variables, the interaction term $x_{k1}x_{k2}$ in both variables, and the curvature terms x_{k1}^2 and x_{k2}^2. Because this model involves six parameters, nonsingularity of the matrix $\mathbf{X}^T\mathbf{X}$ requires $N \ge 6$ observations, and Atkinson and Donev give the D-optimal design points (x_{k1}, x_{k2}) for $N = 6$, 7, 8, and 9 as follows:

6: $(-1, -1), (1, -1), (-1, 1), (-0.1315, -0.1315), (1, 0.3945), (0.3945, 1)$;

7: $(-1, -1), (-1, 1), (1, -1), (1, 1), (-0.092, 0.092), (1, -0.067), (0.067, -1)$;

8: $(-1, -1), (-1, 1), (1, -1), (1, 1), (1, 0), (0.082, 1), (0.082, -1), (-0.215, 0)$;

9: $(-1, -1), (-1, 1), (1, -1), (1, 1), (-1, 0), (0, -1), (0, 0), (0, 1), (1, 0)$.

The D-optimal design for $N = 9$ here corresponds to a 3^p *factorial design*, which assigns all possible combinations of the values $\{-1, 0, 1\}$ to the variables involved. A practical disadvantage of the 2^p or 3^p factorial design is that its complexity increases rapidly with the number of variables p. To address this problem, *fractional factorial designs* have been developed that reduce the number of design points required. Since this reduction comes at the expense of our ability to estimate certain model parameters (e.g., higher-order interaction terms like $x_{k1}x_{k2}x_{k3}$), these designs are somewhat more involved to develop. For details, refer to the book by Atkinson and Donev (1992) and the references cited there.

Although the GSA problem formulation does not involve minimization of parameter variability, the examples just considered do suggest a useful strategy for selecting scenarios and subscenarios. Specifically, both the specific D-optimal designs just described and optimal experimental designs more generally tend to spread the design points fairly evenly over the range of possible variation for all of the variables involved, generally concentrating on extreme values, possibly with interior points if curvature terms are included in the regression model of interest. In the context of choosing GSA scenarios and/or subscenarios, note that these choices often correspond to choices of values for one or more scenario-distinguishing variables. The basic message here is to generally spread these choices out as much as possible. In particular, by focusing on extreme values of the factors defining scenarios rather than on clusters of nearby values, we maximize the likelihood of seeing evidence for the factor's influence on the results. Certainly, there are cases (e.g., quadratic responses) where differences in results between extreme factor values can be negligible while differences between extreme and central values are large—and this is precisely why 3^p factorial designs are needed here instead of 2^p factorial designs—but the key point is that if we are looking for evidence of influence, basing different scenarios on factor values that are too similar is likely to be wasted effort. Also, it is worth noting that these ideas often steer us away from inherently poor choices. In the case of optimum experimental designs for regression models, poor choices of x_{ki} values are automatically avoided because they cause near-singularity of the $\mathbf{X}^T\mathbf{X}$ matrix, making its inverse "large" and thus far from optimal.

6.4   Sampling schemes

In the GSA framework, sampling schemes provide the basis for assessing nominal variability due to effects like sampling variation or low-level measurement errors and unexpected variability caused by data anomalies. In practice, different sampling strategies are appropriate to different circumstances, depending on the data generation mechanisms involved. Here, it is useful to distinguish three situations:

1. Each dataset S_i results from a separate data generation experiment.

2. Each dataset S_i is a subset of a single larger dataset $\mathcal{D}$.

3. Each dataset S_i is generated by a simulation procedure.

The first situation represents the fundamental working assumption behind traditional experimental design results in classical statistics (Atkinson and Donev, 1992), introduced briefly in Sec. 6.3.3. These results generally assume a specific form for the data distribution (most commonly Gaussian), specify an analysis to be performed, and determine how data values should be collected so that they are maximally informative for that analysis. Historically, strong motivation for these results came from the fact that manual experiments are relatively difficult and/or expensive, so the total number of experimental runs performed was minimized subject to the constraint that the resulting datasets provided an adequate basis for subsequent analysis. Since these results are obtained for a *fixed* analysis procedure specified before any data values are acquired, they are generally not applicable to the situation of primary interest here, where several different analysis results are to be compared for one or more previously acquired datasets. Traditional experimental design is quite appropriate to setting up clinical trials to determine drug effectiveness, for example, since different treatments may be assigned to suitably chosen clinical subjects, but we do not have the level of control necessary to apply these approaches to the analysis of historical records of financial transactions, adverse drug effects reported to the FDA, or industrial process operating data. In cases where designed experiments are feasible, they have much to recommend them, but the primary focus of this book is on the analysis of datasets that were not (and generally cannot be) collected on the basis of an experimental design for a prespecified type of data analysis. Consequently, the sampling schemes of primary interest here belong to the second class listed above: each scenario Σ_ℓ corresponds to a fixed dataset $\mathcal{D}_\ell$, and sampling schemes correspond to subset selection strategies. Because these strategies are central to the procedures and results discussed in this book, Chapter 7 examines them in detail. Conversely, in situations like deciding how to define and organize scenarios to give meaningful comparisons, experimental design ideas are more directly applicable, as discussed in Sec. 6.3.3.

Another common practical problem is the comparison of different analysis methods in one or more simulation-based case studies, leading to the third sampling strategy listed above. This idea has already been illustrated in Chapters 1 through 4 in connection with the effects of known data anomalies on specific data characterizations. In particular, recall for the kurtosis example discussed in Chapter 1 that kurtosis estimates were compared across nine scenarios corresponding to three different data distributions (Gaussian, uniform, and Student's t) and three different contamination levels (0%, 1%, and 5% outliers). All datasets generated were of fixed size ($N = 100$), and exchangeability within each scenario corresponded to an assumption that the statistical character of each dataset was the same. In more specific terms, exchangeability within scenarios represents the assumption that the random number generator used to create the uncontaminated datasets gives a reasonable approximation to an i.i.d. sequence with the specified distribution, together with the fact that the same set of outliers is used in contaminating all datasets within a given scenario. Since the results presented for that example clearly demonstrated that the standard kurtosis estimator exhibits a pronounced, distribution-dependent outlier-sensitivity, it follows that the different collections of datasets $\{S_i^\ell\}$ are *not* exchangeable across the nine scenarios Σ_ℓ. Conversely, the fact that all of these datasets were the same size does guarantee that the results are *comparable* in the sense of providing a basis for comparisons across scenarios that do not reflect sampling-related differences such as sample size. A further illustration of simulation-based sampling schemes is provided in Sec. 6.7, where a simulation-based GSA procedure is used to compare the approximation quality of a very diverse collection of approximate discretizations of an ordinary differential equation describing the dynamic relationship between two variables.

Although it is not strictly necessary for exchangeability of the datasets $\{S_i\}$, it is desirable that these datasets all be the same size. Hence, most of the sampling schemes considered in this book meet this requirement: all of the m subsets S_i generated within a fixed scenario Σ_ℓ are of the same size N. Since it is also desirable that the datasets considered across scenarios be as comparable as possible, the sampling schemes considered here usually also generate constant-sized datasets across scenarios, although there are cases where this is not possible.

6.5   Selecting a descriptor $d(\cdot)$

In the strict formulation described here, the GSA descriptor $d(\cdot)$ is required to be a map from the results generated by the analysis methods considered into the set of real numbers. This restriction has important practical consequences since it permits us to construct the boxplot generated in Step 4 of the GSA procedure. Alternatively, it is possible to replace this graphical characterization with other univariate data descriptions, including quantile-quantile (Q-Q) plots (D'Agostino and Stephens, 1986), to informally assess the distributional character of the results, or more formal tests of the hypothesis that results differ across scenarios. Since the primary focus of this book is exploratory analysis of datasets that may contain significant anomalies, formal hypothesis tests will generally not be considered here to avoid strong dependence on distributional assumptions. The use of Q-Q plots and other informal univariate data characterizations in the GSA framework is discussed further in Sec. 6.6. Finally, although the general definition of exchangeability admits vector-valued descriptors, the use of such descriptors would require replacement of the boxplots considered here with something more complicated, a topic considered further in Sec. 6.8.

An important class of scalar descriptors for the applications considered here are *figure-of-merit descriptors*, which have the following practical interpretation: if $d(\mathcal{M}_i S) > d(\mathcal{M}_j S)$, then the results obtained from dataset S by method $\mathcal{M}_i$ are either clearly better than or clearly worse than those obtained by method $\mathcal{M}_j$. Similarly, for comparisons using the same method $\mathcal{M}$ across different datasets S_i and S_j based on a figure-of-merit descriptor, if $d(\mathcal{M}S_i) > d(\mathcal{M}S_j)$, then again, the results obtained for dataset S_i are either clearly better or clearly worse than those obtained for dataset S_j. Probably the most common figure-of-merit descriptors are prediction error measures such as the RMS data-cleaning errors considered in the CWMF case study presented in Chapter 4 and the prediction error standard deviations considered in the model approximation case study presented in Sec. 6.7, both of which have the interpretation that "smaller is better."

It is, of course, not necessary to restrict consideration to figure-of-merit descriptors, but the use of other descriptors generally only allows us to assess *relative variability* across methods or scenarios and not *relative quality*. The requirement that *is* fundamental is that whatever descriptor we choose be comparably suitable as a summary of the different analysis methods obtained across all scenarios and subscenarios, particularly in cases where certain characteristics of the results obtained for the different scenarios can be quite different. As a specific example, consider the problem of partition-based clustering, which seeks to classify a group of N objects into k distinct classes based on measured attributes of each object. Many different methods have been developed to solve this problem (Kaufman and Rousseeuw, 1990, Chapter 2), and it is natural to ask how these methods compare. Various comparison measures have been proposed, including those such as *cluster diameter*, which characterizes individual clusters, or *separation*, which characterizes the relationship between individual clusters. One measure that attempts to combine both of these characteristics is the *silhouette coefficient* (Kaufman and Rousseeuw, 1990, p. 85), defined for each object i as

$$s(i) = \frac{b(i) - a(i)}{\max\{a(i), b(i)\}}. \tag{6.7}$$

Here, $a(i)$ is the average dissimilarity between object i and all other objects included in the same cluster, and $b(i)$ is the average dissimilarity between object i and all objects of the closest neighboring cluster (i.e., the closest cluster of objects that does not contain object i). In a good clustering, we generally want small dissimilarities between objects within each cluster and large dissimilarities between clusters. It follows from this observation that the silhouette coefficients for the objects in a good clustering should be as large as possible. Further, it can be shown that $s(i)$ is bounded between -1 and $+1$ for all objects provided that there are at least two clusters and that each cluster contains at least two elements. Hence, the average of the individual silhouette coefficients $s(i)$ over all objects i is a scalar figure-of-merit descriptor that is applicable to all such clusterings. In particular, note that this descriptor may be used to compare partition-based clusterings obtained by radically different methods, possibly involving different numbers of clusters.

Finally, note that the requirement that the same descriptor be applicable across all methods may be viewed as a restriction on the classes of methods that can be compared. Specifically, define a collection $\{\mathcal{M}_i\}$ of methods to be $d(\cdot)$-*equivalent* if $d(\mathcal{M}_i S)$ is well-defined for any dataset S to which the methods $\{\mathcal{M}_i\}$ can all be applied. In the clustering example just described, methods are $d(\cdot)$-equivalent with respect to the average silhouette coefficient if they are dissimilarity-based methods that generate at least two clusters, each containing more than one object.

6.6   Displaying and interpreting the results

The basic GSA framework described here facilitates the exploratory comparison of results across scenarios. As discussed in Chapter 1, boxplots provide a useful graphical summary of possibly diverse results in a format that does not depend on details of the number m of datasets $\{S_i\}$ considered in each scenario, the sizes of the datasets, or the number of scenarios compared. In particular, boxplots provide useful indications of the typical descriptor value obtained from the datasets $\{S_i\}$ in each scenario (specifically, the median value of $d(S_i)$) and the range of variation seen around this typical value (i.e., the interquartile range represented by the central boxes in each boxplot). Hence, side-by-side boxplots give clear indications of systematic variations of either the median values or the range of variation across scenarios. More importantly in the context of this book, these graphical displays can also reveal anomalous scenarios that violate either a general pattern of consistency or a clear pattern of regular variation across the other scenarios, which can lead to important discoveries. Similarly, identification of anomalous subsets S_i within a scenario can also be extremely useful.

Conversely, while most of the GSA examples in this book do employ boxplot summaries, it is worth noting that a number of useful alternatives also exist. For example, Emerson (1991, p. 42) discusses *dotplots*, in which the m values $\{d(S_i)\}$ are represented as individual dots, plotted vertically above a scenario label. Because these displays represent more information than boxplots, they can be advantageous (e.g., when significant gaps exist between subsets of closely spaced values), but dotplots generally become less useful as m increases. Since the GSA results presented here typically involve $m > 50$ subsets in each scenario, boxplots are usually easier to interpret visually, providing direct comparisons of simple summary statistics such as the median and the interquartile range. Two other data summaries that may be particularly useful for large collections of datasets, especially for a second look at GSA results, are Q-Q plots, discussed in Sec. 6.6.1, and the direct interscenario comparison strategies discussed in Sec. 6.6.2.

6.6.1 Normal Q-Q plots

Q-Q plots are graphical displays that provide informal distributional assessments for real-valued data sequences based on the following two key observations. First, if $\{u_k\}$ is a sequence of N independent random numbers, uniformly distributed on the unit interval $[0, 1]$, their rank-ordered samples $u_{(1)} \leq u_{(2)} \leq \cdots \leq u_{(N)}$ should be uniformly spaced over this interval. That is, we should have $u_{(i)} \simeq i/N$, although this approximation tends to break down when $i \simeq 1$ or $i \simeq N$. Second, a random variable x with any absolutely continuous cumulative distribution function $\Phi(x)$ may be transformed to uniformity by the transformation $u = \Phi(x)$ (Port, 1994, p. 99). Combining these observations, note first that if $\{x_k\}$ is an i.i.d. sequence with common distribution $\Phi(x)$, then $u_k = \Phi(x_k)$ defines a uniform i.i.d. sequence on $[0, 1]$. Further, since $\Phi(\cdot)$ is a strictly increasing function, it follows that $u_{(i)} = \Phi(x_{(i)})$, where $x_{(1)} \leq x_{(2)} \leq \cdots \leq x_{(N)}$. Hence, we expect that $\Phi(x_{(i)}) \simeq i/N$ or, equivalently, $x_{(i)} \simeq \Phi^{-1}(i/N)$. This result means that if we plot the rank-ordered data sequence $\{x_{(i)}\}$ against $\Phi^{-1}(i/N)$, we should obtain an approximately straight line.

Without question, the most common practical implementation of this idea is the normal Q-Q plot, where we take the standard normal distribution as our reference, $\Phi(x)$. As noted, the approximation $x_{(i)} \simeq \Phi^{-1}(i/N)$ breaks down for values of i near 1 and N, and this breakdown is usually dealt with by replacing the argument i/N with a modified argument like $(i-1/3)/(N+1/3)$ (Emerson, 1991, p. 187). Also, note that if $\{x_k\}$ is normally distributed with mean μ and standard deviation σ, the transformed variable $z_k = (x_k - \mu)/\sigma$ has the standard normal distribution (i.e., zero mean and unit variance). Hence, the normal Q-Q plot for the sequence $\{x_k\}$ will still be linear, satisfying $x_{(i)} \simeq \mu + \sigma \Phi^{-1}([i-1/3]/[N+1/3])$.

One practical motivation for examining normal Q-Q plots of GSA results is that many popular summary statistics are asymptotically normal. That is, even if the data values in the dataset S_i from which the descriptor $d(S_i)$ is computed are not normally distributed, the results $\{d(S_i)\}$ often approach a normal limiting distribution as the size N of the individual datasets becomes sufficiently large. For example, the Princeton Robustness Study was a detailed comparison of 68 different location estimators (i.e., the arithmetic mean and 67 proposed outlier-resistant alternatives), and the vast majority of these were shown to exhibit approximately normal behavior for samples of size $N = 20$ (Andrews et al., 1972, Sec. 5J). Even when asymptotic normality is known to hold for a particular data characterization $d(\cdot)$, however, this last observation raises an important practical question: How large must the dataset be for the Gaussian approximation to be valid? Since the GSA framework described here generates m replicated results, normal Q-Q plots provide an informal method of addressing this question.

The following example illustrates these ideas. Figure 6.1 shows four normal Q-Q plots, each derived from a dataset of size 200. The upper left plot was computed from a sample of $N = 200$ gamma-distributed data values with shape parameter $\alpha = 2$. This probability distribution is defined by the density function (Johnson, Kotz, and Balakrishnan, 1994, p. 337)

$$p(x) = \frac{x^{\alpha-1}e^{-x}}{\Gamma(\alpha)}, \tag{6.8}$$

where $\Gamma(\alpha)$ is the gamma function that appears commonly in statistics and mathematical physics (Abramowitz and Stegun, 1972). This distribution is strongly asymmetric, a fact

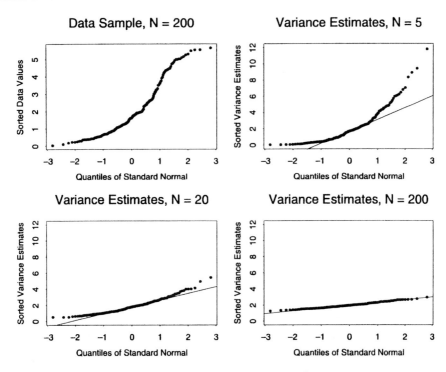

Figure 6.1. *Four normal Q-Q plots.*

reflected in the systematic deviations from linearity seen in the upper left plot in Figure 6.1, with the sorted data values lying consistently above the reference line in both the upper and lower tails of the distribution. The variance estimated from $m = 200$ samples, each of size $N = 5$, is shown in the upper right plot, and it is clear that these estimates also exhibit a markedly asymmetric distribution. The lower left plot in Figure 6.1 shows the corresponding results for $m = 200$ variance estimates, computed from independent samples of size $N = 20$, plotted on the same scale as the upper right plot for $N = 5$. It is clear that the results for $N = 20$ are much more linear than those for $N = 5$, although distributional asymmetry remains evident. Increasing the sample size to $N = 200$ gives the plot shown in the lower right: there, linearity appears nearly perfect, consistent with the fact that the limiting distribution for the variance estimator is known to be Gaussian. Note also that the range of the variance estimates and the slopes of the reference lines in the normal Q-Q plots for the estimated variances both decrease with increasing N, a point emphasized by the fact that all three of the variance Q-Q plots shown here are plotted on the same vertical scale. These systematic changes reflect the fact that the standard deviation of these variance estimates decays like $1/\sqrt{N}$ as $N \to \infty$.

6.6.2 Direct comparisons across scenarios

Often, there is a natural one-to-one correspondence between the datasets $\{S_i\}$ in one scenario Σ_ℓ and the datasets $\{S_i'\}$ in another scenario $\Sigma_{\ell'}$. As a simple but important example, this condition holds if Σ_ℓ and $\Sigma_{\ell'}$ correspond to the application of two different analysis methods, $\mathcal{M}$ and $\mathcal{M}'$, to the same collection of datasets $\{S_i\}$. Specific examples of such formulations include the trimmed mean and scale estimator comparisons presented in Chapter 1 and the moment versus order statistic estimator comparisons presented in Chapter 2. In such cases, it may be useful to examine the differences $\Delta_i = d(\mathcal{M}S_i) - d(\mathcal{M}'S_i)$ between the results obtained under the two scenarios. The advantage of such direct comparisons over the indirect comparison provided by side-by-side boxplots is that direct comparisons can reveal *systematic* differences between the scenarios. In particular, if $d(\cdot)$ is a figure-of-merit descriptor, direct comparisons can provide evidence in support of the hypothesis that method $\mathcal{M}'$ is either consistently better than method $\mathcal{M}$ or consistently poorer, while indirect comparisons can only say whether these methods differ "on average."

In fact, the difference between direct and indirect interscenario comparisons lies in the relationship between the *intrascenario* variations within the two different scenarios. In particular, suppose that the individual intrascenario results $\{d(S_i)\}$ and $\{d(S_i')\}$ are described by the random variable models

$$d(S_i) = \mu + \epsilon_i, \qquad d(S_i') = \mu' + \nu_i. \tag{6.9}$$

Further, suppose the fluctuation sequences $\{\epsilon_i\}$ and $\{\nu_i\}$ are i.i.d. random variables, but not necessarily independent from each other. Without loss of generality, assume that $E\{\epsilon_i\} = E\{\nu_i\} = 0$; let σ_ϵ and σ_ν denote the standard deviations of ϵ_i and ν_i, respectively; and let ρ denote the correlation coefficient between ϵ_i and ν_i. It is easy to show that the variance of the difference $\Delta_i = d(S_i) - d(S_i')$ is

$$\mathrm{var}\,\{\Delta_i\} = \sigma_\epsilon^2 - 2\rho\sigma_\epsilon\sigma_\nu + \sigma_\nu^2. \tag{6.10}$$

Since $|\rho| \leq 1$, it follows that the variance of Δ_i must lie between a minimum possible value of $(\sigma_\epsilon - \sigma_\nu)^2$ and a maximum possible value of $(\sigma_\epsilon + \sigma_\nu)^2$. If $\sigma_\epsilon = \sigma_\nu = \sigma$, this range becomes $0 \leq \mathrm{var}\,\{\Delta_i\} \leq 4\sigma^2$ as ρ varies from $+1$ to -1. In this case, if the fluctuation sequences $\{\epsilon_i\}$ and $\{\nu_i\}$ are strongly positively correlated, direct comparisons (i.e., examining the differences Δ_i) can give much more precise results than indirect comparisons (i.e., side-by-side boxplots) since the variance of the differences $\{\Delta_i\}$ can be much smaller than the common variance of the scenario results $\{d(S_i)\}$ and $\{d(S_i')\}$.

This point is illustrated in Figure 6.2, which takes a closer look at two of the results presented in Sec. 2.2.1. Specifically, the leftmost of the three boxplots in Figure 6.2 summarizes Galton's skewness measure γ_G^0 computed from $m = 200$ uncontaminated Gaussian data sequences, each of length $N = 100$. The central boxplot shows the corresponding result γ_G^c computed from the same data sequence with a single outlier at $+8\sigma$ added, representing a 1% contamination level. Since these boxplots are visually indistinguishable, it is not possible to assess the differences between these results to get an idea of the magnitude of the contamination effect. In particular, the total range of variation of this difference could be anywhere between zero (corresponding to $\gamma_G^c = \gamma_G^0$ for all cases, implying no effect) and twice the common range of variation for these two skewness measures (corresponding to $\gamma_G^c = -\gamma_G^0$, representing a strong, counterintuitive effect that would be difficult to explain). The rightmost boxplot shows the actual range of variation for these differences. While this range of variation is not zero, it is significantly smaller than the common range of γ_G^0 and γ_G^c variations, suggesting (correctly) a weak sensitivity of Galton's skewness measure to low-level contamination.

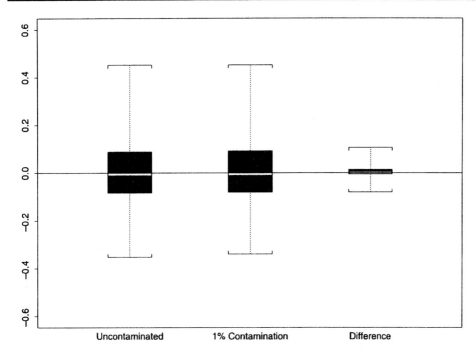

Figure 6.2. *Boxplots of results for two scenarios and their difference.*

Finally, note that this difference summary also suggests that the computed values for γ_G^0 and γ_G^c have a high positive correlation. In fact, the product-moment correlation coefficient between these two sequences is 0.980 and the Spearman rank correlation coefficient is 0.974, further supporting this suggestion. This high correlation is due in part to the high degree of overlap between the data sequences from which γ_G^0 and γ_G^c were computed, a point discussed further in Chapter 7.

6.7 The model approximation case study

The following example illustrates the application of the GSA metaheuristic to a problem of evaluating nonlinear dynamic models. This example also illustrates that $d(\cdot)$-equivalent methods can be very different in character, underscoring the generality of the GSA framework. Specifically, the basic problem considered here is that of developing a "good" discrete-time approximation of the general form

$$y_k = f(y_{k-1}, \dots, y_{k-p}, u_k, \dots, u_{k-q}) + e_k \qquad (6.11)$$

to the simple continuous-time, nonlinear ordinary differential equation

$$\frac{dy(t)}{dt} = -\alpha y(t) + \beta y(t)u(t) + \gamma u(t). \qquad (6.12)$$

Here, $u(t)$ represents the value of an input variable u at time t that can be deliberately manipulated, while $y(t)$ represents the value of an observable response variable y at time t. The sequences $\{u_k\}$ and $\{y_k\}$ represent discrete-time samples of the continuous-time variables $u(t)$ and $y(t)$, sampled uniformly every T time units. In this example, the parameters α, β, γ, and T are all assumed to have the value one for convenience. Motivation for this problem comes from the field of industrial process control, where discrete-time models of the form (6.11) are required for implementing model-based control strategies such as non-linear model predictive control (Qin and Badgwell, 2000). A more detailed discussion of this example is given in the book by Doyle III, Pearson, and Ogunnaike (2002, Sec. 5.6.4).

For simple models like (6.12), one feasible strategy is to work directly with the equations, replacing derivatives with finite-difference approximations. Here, if we assume $y_k = y(t_0 + kT)$ and $u_k = u(t_0 + kT)$, we obtain the following *Euler discretization*, designated as Model E in subsequent discussions:

$$\frac{dy(t)}{dt} \simeq \frac{y_k - y_{k-1}}{T} \qquad (6.13)$$
$$\Rightarrow y_k \simeq [1 - \alpha T]y_{k-1} + \beta T y_{k-1}u_{k-1} + \gamma T u_{k-1}.$$

Alternatively, we can develop approximate models empirically, generating a finite-length input sequence $\{u_k\}$, simulating the response of the continuous-time model (6.12) to this input sequence, and choosing model parameters that minimize some measure of goodness-of-fit between the response of the continuous-time model and the approximating empirical model. In the example considered here, this approach was used to fit approximate models of the following four forms:

$$
\begin{aligned}
\text{A:} \quad & y_k = y_0 + ay_{k-1} + bu_{k-1}, \\
\text{B:} \quad & y_k = y_0 + ay_{k-1} + bu_{k-1} + cy_{k-1}u_{k-1}, \\
\text{H:} \quad & y_k = y_0 + ay_{k-1} + bu_{k-1} + cu_{k-1}^2, \\
\text{Q:} \quad & y_k = y_0 + ay_{k-1} + bu_{k-1} + cy_{k-1}^2.
\end{aligned} \qquad (6.14)
$$

The abbreviations here designate the model structures compared, which are *affine* (A), *bilinear* (B), *Hammerstein* (H), and *quadratic NARX* (Q).

An important, inherent feature of nonlinear dynamic models is that answers to questions such as, "which approximation is best?" can depend strongly on the range and general character of the input sequences considered. Hence, a useful choice of scenario Σ_ℓ in evaluating these approximate models is *input sequence type*. In the results presented here, all sequences $\{u_k\}$ belong to the general class of random step inputs (Pearson, 1999, Sec. 8.4.3), generated as follows. First, a sequence $\{z_k\}$ of n i.i.d. random variables is generated, uniformly distributed over a specified range. An input sequence $\{u_k\}$ of length n is then generated by first setting $u_1 = z_1$ and then generating u_k for $k > 1$ according to the random selection procedure

$$u_k = \begin{cases} z_k & \text{with probability } p, \\ u_{k-1} & \text{with probability } 1 - p. \end{cases} \qquad (6.15)$$

The resulting input sequence $\{u_k\}$ consists of random steps whose average duration is determined by the switching probability p and whose instantaneous values are uniformly distributed over a specified range.

In the example considered here, this range is $[-0.5, 0.5]$, and four scenarios are considered, corresponding to $p = 1.00$, $p = 0.30$, $p = 0.10$, and $p = 0.05$. Note that for $p = 1.00$, we recover the uniformly distributed white noise sequence $\{z_k\}$ that changes value at every time step, and the number of transitions in $\{u_k\}$ decreases as p decreases. The sampling strategy considered here consists of generating $m = 100$ statistically independent sequences $\{u_k\}$, each of length $n = 200$. This strategy is implemented by generating 100 independent uniform random sequences $\{z_k\}$ and applying the random selection rule (6.15) to generate the input sequences $\{u_k\}$. Note that here, the exchangeability assumption on which the equivalence of these sequences is based corresponds to quality assumptions on the uniform random number generator used in generating the sequences $\{z_k\}$ and on the binary random number generator used to implement the selection procedure (6.15).

The descriptor $d(\cdot)$ considered in this example is the prediction error standard deviation for each model, computed as

$$\hat{\sigma}_p = \left(\frac{1}{n} \sum_{i=1}^{n} [y_k - \hat{y}_k]^2 \right)^{1/2}, \tag{6.16}$$

where $\{y_k\}$ represents the simulated response of the continuous-time model (6.12) to the input sequence $\{u_k\}$ and $\{\hat{y}_k\}$ represents the response of one of the approximating models to this input sequence. Note that this descriptor is of figure-of-merit type, since better models are those for which $\hat{y}_k$ more accurately predicts y_k, resulting in a smaller value of $\hat{\sigma}_p$.

The models compared here are the Euler discretization (E) defined in (6.13) and the four empirical models A, B, H, and Q defined in (6.14). Note that these models are $d(\cdot)$-equivalent since, given the predictions $\{\hat{y}_k\}$ generated by any of them, we may evaluate the descriptor $d(\cdot)$ according to (6.16). The importance of this observation is that these models are obtained by radically different methods. In particular, Model E is computed directly from the continuous-time model equation (6.12), independently of the datasets $\{u_k\}$ used in its evaluation. In contrast, the four other models cannot be obtained directly from the original model equation, but are identified from the response of this model to a fixed input sequence $\{u_k\}$.

In fact, two important aspects of these latter four models should be noted. First, whereas Model E represents a *single model*, to be evaluated with respect to each of 100 input sequences generated for each scenario Σ, the other four cases actually represent *sets of models*, one obtained for each input sequence. The second point is that the criterion used to obtain these models appears similar to the descriptor $\hat{\sigma}_p$ defined in (6.16), *but it is not the same*. Specifically, each of the models of types A, B, H, and Q considered here is obtained by minimizing the *one-step prediction error sum of squares* or, equivalently, the *one-step prediction error standard deviation*

$$\tau_p(a, b, c) = \left(\frac{1}{n} \sum_{i=1}^{n} [y_k - \tilde{y}_k(a, b, c)]^2 \right)^{1/2}, \tag{6.17}$$

where $\tilde{y}_k(a, b, c)$ is the prediction of y_k from the previous input u_{k-1} *together with the previous output* y_{k-1}. Given any input sequence $\{u_k\}$ and the corresponding sequence $\{y_k\}$ of simulated responses for the continuous-time model, we obtain the empirical model that best matches this input/output data by choosing parameters a, b, and c to minimize $\tau_p(a, b, c)$.

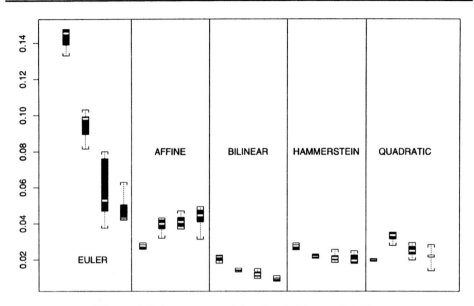

Figure 6.3. $\hat{\sigma}_p$ *versus model and switching probability.*

To illustrate the difference between $\tilde{y}_k$ and $\hat{y}_k$, consider the bilinear model B:

$$\tilde{y}_k(a, b, c) = ay_{k-1} + bu_{k-1} + cy_{k-1}u_{k-1},$$
$$\hat{y}_k = a\hat{y}_{k-1} + bu_{k-1} + c\hat{y}_{k-1}u_{k-1}. \tag{6.18}$$

The quantities $\hat{\sigma}_p$ and $\tau_p(a, b, c)$ can be significantly different, and in problems such as model-based control where predictions beyond one time step into the future are required (Qin and Badgwell, 2000), this difference can be important. The key point here is that, since $\hat{\sigma}_p$ is a practically important measure of model quality that, unlike $\tau_p(a, b, c)$, is not directly minimized in the empirical model-fitting procedure, $\hat{\sigma}_p$ represents a reasonable quantity to evaluate with an approach like the GSA metaheuristic.

Figure 6.3 shows the GSA results obtained for the five different approximations (Models E, A, B, H, and Q, respectively) to the observed responses of the continuous-time nonlinear dynamic model for four different input sequence scenarios defined by the switching probabilities $p = 1.00, 0.30, 0.10,$ and 0.05. Results for the different model structures are labelled and separated by vertical lines, and the input scenarios appear in order of decreasing switching probability p: the leftmost boxplots for each model correspond to $p = 1.00$, while the rightmost boxplots correspond to $p = 0.05$. Because these boxplots represent summaries of a figure-of-merit descriptor, it is clear that the Euler discretization generally exhibits both the poorest performance in terms of $\hat{\sigma}_p$ values and the least consistent performance: the range of variation seen in these values is significantly larger than that seen for the other four model types. Further, the dependence of this performance on the input scenario (the switching probability p) is also quite dramatic, further supporting the general conclusion that Model E is a poor one, violating the informal statement of the GSA metaheuristic given in Sec. 6.1 more severely than any of the other models.

In terms of consistency across input scenarios, the best models appear to be B and H, with Models A and Q exhibiting a wider range of variation than Models B and H, but a much narrower range than Model E. Also, note that the input sequence sensitivity appears to be slightly better for Model H than for Model B. However, because the descriptor considered here is of figure-of-merit type, we are led to prefer Model B, since it appears only slightly more sensitive than Model H, but exhibits consistently better (i.e., smaller) descriptor values. Similarly, comparing the performance of the five different models within a fixed input scenario generally also leads to the conclusion that Model E is significantly poorer than all of the others, that Models B and H are the best, and that Models A and Q are of intermediate quality. As a specific case, note that we obtain the following model ranking within the scenario $p = 0.30$ (the second-from-the-left boxplot for each model):

$$B > H > Q > A >> E.$$

In this particular example, this preference ordering generally holds across most input scenarios, based on both the median values (a conclusion related to the fact that $\hat{\sigma}_p$ is a figure-of-merit descriptor) and the ranges of variability. Finally, when we compare results across input scenarios for each model structure, we obtain a nice illustration of the point made earlier that the extent to which a particular nonlinear dynamic model approximates another one exhibits a significant input dependence, even for the best approximations.

6.8 Extensions of the basic GSA framework

Essentially, the GSA framework described in this book provides a systematic approach to making useful comparisons between different datasets that are believed to be similar, different analysis methods that are believed to be comparable, or both. In practice, this is typically an iterative procedure, as emphasized in the summary presented in Chapter 8 of the *data-based prototyping* approach to large-scale data analysis projects described by Huber and Nagel (1996). Since iteration is not inherent in the basic GSA framework as described here, Sec. 6.8.1 briefly considers some of the ways that iteration is commonly used in detecting and treating data anomalies and some simple iteration-based extensions of the basic GSA framework. Also, another limitation of the basic GSA formulation presented up to now has been the restriction to real-valued descriptors $d(\cdot)$. Sec. 6.8.2 briefly considers some possible multivariate alternatives.

6.8.1 Iterative analysis procedures

In practice, data analysis typically involves iteration at many levels. For example, one way of implementing outlier-resistant M-estimators is to employ *iteratively reweighted least squares* (Huber, 1981, Chapter 7), beginning with an OLS fit to the data, computing weights for each data point from this result, and solving a weighted least squares problem to obtain a refined estimate. This process is then repeated until further refinements are insignificant. More explicit iterations typically also occur at higher levels, where we take a preliminary analysis result, examine it, and use our insight to guide subsequent analysis. Although the basic GSA framework discussed here is noniterative, it is possible to extend it in several ways to incorporate iteration, as the following two examples illustrate.

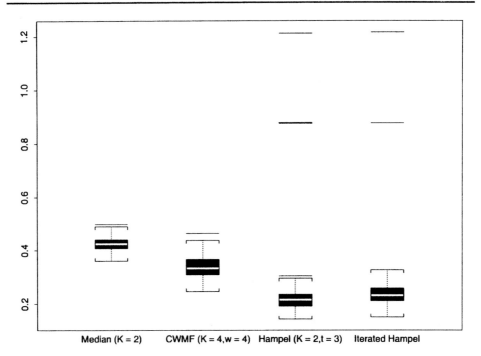

Figure 6.4. *A GSA comparison of four data-cleaning filters: the standard median filter, the CWMF, the Hampel filter, and a two-pass iteration of the Hampel filter.*

Inward testing procedures consist of the iterative application of an outlier detection procedure, followed by outlier removal, repeating the process until no further outliers are found, as discussed by Davies and Gather (1993). These authors note that inward testing procedures based on the Hampel identifier improve effectiveness (i.e., the ability to detect outliers) at the cost of a slight increase in swamping effects (i.e., the tendency to declare nominal points outliers). This point is illustrated in Figure 6.4, which compares the performance of four nonlinear data-cleaning filters for contaminated time-series. The format of this figure is analogous to those presented in Chapter 4, where the standard median filter, the CWMF, and the Hampel filter were discussed. Figure 6.4 shows the results obtained by the best of each of these filters for the additive outlier-contaminated $AR(1)$ time-series example considered in Chapter 4. That is, each boxplot summarizes the RMS data-cleaning error obtained for each of 100 independently generated time-series using this data model. The fourth boxplot shows the result obtained with a single iterative application of the Hampel filter. There, the Hampel filter with moving window half-width parameter $K = 2$ and threshold parameter $t = 3$ is applied twice: first to the original data sequence, generating the results summarized in the third boxplot, and then again to the output of this filter, generating the results summarized in the fourth boxplot. Careful examination of the results shows that this iteration strategy has three effects: it slightly improves outlier rejection in the second-worst case (i.e., the number of simulations with RMS error $e_{RMS} \sim 0.85$ is reduced, as indicated by the lighter outlier line above the boxplot), it slightly increases the variability of the majority of cases (i.e., the width of the central box in the fourth boxplot is slightly greater than that of the third boxplot), and it slightly increases the median RMS data-cleaning error. Overall, these results are in qualitative agreement with the observations of Davies and Gather (1993) for the inward testing Hampel procedure: since the Hampel filter is a moving-window implementation of the Hampel identifier, this iterative filtering procedure corresponds to a two-pass application of the inward testing procedure to this moving data window.

This example illustrates one possible iterative extension of the GSA framework. Specifically, the simplest extension for methods such as inward testing that typically involve only a few iterations is to take each iteration as a GSA scenario. In the example just discussed, the third and fourth boxplots in Figure 6.4 illustrate this idea: here, these results suggest a slight improvement in some respects due to iteration, but a slight degradation in other respects, and they do not make a compelling case for further iteration. Another situation where a small number of iterations is typical is that discussed by Rousseeuw (1994), who notes that the desirable combination of high breakdown, like that achieved by LTS estimators, and high efficiency (i.e., small estimation variance), like that achieved by good M-estimators, can be obtained with iterative procedures that combine the two approaches. The price paid for this improvement, however, is an increase in estimator bias with each iteration, providing another argument for keeping the number of iterations small (i.e., one or two). Note that a useful feature of the iterative GSA strategy just described is that, since each scenario yields results for a collection of individual datasets (here, the *same* datasets should be used for each iteration to facilitate comparison), the results obtained can give an indication of bias and variance effects from one iteration to the next.

Usually, iterative procedures are repeated until either some convergence criterion is achieved or a fixed iteration limit is exceeded, with this second condition often being taken as an indication of poor convergence. In such cases, the number of iterations is typically too large for the iterative GSA extension just described to be practical. A possibly useful alternative is to treat every rth iteration as a separate GSA scenario, although this may require some preliminary experience to assess the approximate rate of convergence so that r can be chosen reasonably. As a specific example, McLachlan and Krishnan (1997, Sec. 1.4) present results obtained with the iterative expectation maximization (EM) algorithm (discussed further in the next paragraphs) for three datasets, converging in 8, 22, and 27 iterations, respectively. Also, note that this example raises the possibility that the number of iterations required to achieve a given level of convergence could be a strong function of the individual datasets considered. In particular, it is easy to imagine troublesome cases where the different datasets generated within each scenario by the GSA sampling scheme require significantly different numbers of iterations to achieve a given level of convergence. In cases where this difficulty is suspected, an alternative GSA formulation would be to treat the number of iterations required to achieve a fixed level of convergence as the GSA descriptor $d(\cdot)$.

The EM algorithm (McLachlan and Krishnan, 1997) is a general procedure for iteratively computing maximum likelihood parameter estimates in the face of missing data. A detailed discussion of either maximum likelihood estimation or the EM algorithm lies beyond the scope of this book, but the idea is useful enough that a brief discussion is appropriate. McLachlan and Krishnan (1997) note that the EM algorithm grew out of ad hoc iterative schemes involving imputation and estimation, and they show that several of these procedures may be obtained as special cases of the EM algorithm. One specific example considered by these authors is a missing data regression approach proposed by Healy and Westmacott (1956), which consists of the following sequence of steps:

0. Perform an initial imputation of missing data values.

1. Solve the OLS regression problem for the imputed dataset.

2. Use this regression model to update imputations for the missing data values.

3. Iterate Steps 1 and 2 until convergence is achieved.

Note that convergence may be assessed in different ways, such as convergence of the imputed missing data values or convergence of some measure of regression model prediction accuracy (e.g., prediction error variance). Further, since convergence criteria are typically real-valued, they represent potential GSA descriptors $d(\cdot)$.

Although this example provides a simple illustration of the basic structure of typical EM algorithm implementations, it fails to show the broad applicability of this idea. More generally, part of the EM algorithm's utility arises from the possibility of cleverly recasting problems that do not obviously involve missing data in terms of related problems that do. As a specific example, recall from the discussion in Chapter 3 that mixture models postulate that a data observation x_i is drawn from one of p distinct distributions $p_j(x)$ for $j = 1, 2, \ldots, p$. The EM approach to fitting mixture models defines the indicator variable z_{ij} as one if x_i was drawn from distribution j and zero otherwise, and the algorithm then treats z_{ij} as missing data. For a detailed discussion of this approach to fitting mixture models, refer to the book by McLachlan and Bashford (1988); for a detailed introduction to the EM algorithm, refer to the book by McLachlan and Krishnan (1997).

6.8.2 Multivariable descriptors

One reason for emphasizing scalar-valued descriptors $d(\cdot)$ in the GSA framework is that they provide the basis for constructing simple boxplot summaries of the results for comparison across scenarios and methods. There are, however, circumstances where it is more natural or more desirable to consider multivariable descriptors $D(\cdot)$. One obvious approach to this problem, at least for descriptors of moderate dimension p, is to view $D(\cdot)$ as a collection $\{d_i(\cdot)\}$ of p univariate descriptors and summarize each component separately. This approach is often—perhaps "usually" is the better word here—unsatisfactory, since it takes no account of the relationships that typically exist between the individual components. In considering effective alternatives, it is useful to first examine the bivariate case, both because it is the simplest extension of the class of univariate descriptors and because some very useful ideas have been described in the literature for displaying bivariate data.

One of these ideas is what Rousseeuw, Ruts, and Tukey (1999) call *bagplots* and Liu, Parelius, and Singh (1999) call *starburst plots*, based on the concept of data depth discussed in Chapter 4. In the univariate case, the deepest data point represents the sample median, which defines the central value in the univariate boxplot. The "box" in these boxplots is then defined by the upper and lower quartiles and thus contains half of the sample data values. In the bivariate bagplot or starburst plot, the univariate median is replaced with the deepest point in the dataset with respect to a computable bivariate data depth. The interquartile range in the univariate boxplot is then replaced with a depth contour containing 50% of the observed data values. Finally, lines are drawn from this contour outward to the other data points. In this construction, all of the data points are represented in the plane, so the display corresponds to a bivariate scatterplot with additional markings to aid in interpretation (i.e., a symbol for the deepest data point, the 50% depth contour, and the lines extending outward from this curve to the more extreme data points). The advantage of this construction is that it clearly shows which points are most extreme and how these points are distributed relative to the others. In particular, as in the univariate boxplot, these bivariate extensions give clear visual indications of distributional asymmetry and clusters of extreme points.

Another closely related idea is the *clockwise bivariate boxplot* described by Corbellini (2002). As the author notes, the construction of any bivariate boxplot involves three steps: specification of an inner region (i.e., the "box"), definition of a robust centroid (i.e., a bivariate median), and the construction of the outer region (i.e., the division between "nominal" and "outlying" values). The essence of the clockwise bivariate boxplot is the use of a family of projections of the data values onto unit vectors at different orientation angles $\{\theta_i\}$ with respect to the coordinate axes. Thus, taking $\theta_i = 0$ gives the standard univariate boxplot with respect to one of the two data components, while taking $\theta_i = \pi/2$ gives the standard boxplot for the other component. Intermediate values of θ_i give different views of the data that preserve the natural association between components. To define a robust data centroid, Corbellini (2002) uses the average of the centroids (i.e., the univariate medians) obtained from each of these projections as θ_i varies from 0 to 2π. Finally, he also proposes two different ways of defining the outer boxplot region, representing two different extensions of the univariate boxplot outlier detection rule discussed in Chapter 3. The first of these approaches defines a constant scale factor K such that K times the inner region, nominally containing 50% of the data values, should contain a fixed fraction of the data under some distributional assumption. This idea is analogous to the univariate boxplot outlier detection rule, which should not flag more than 1% of Gaussian data values as outliers. The second approach is to apply the univariate boxplot rule separately to each projection θ_i and construct the outer curve from these limits. This second approach generally gives a different-shaped contour that seems to give information concerning the influence of the outliers on the bivariate data distribution (see, for example, Figures 3 and 4 of Corbellini (2002)).

All of the bivariate boxplot extensions just described may be viewed as "annotated bivariate scatterplots," providing lines and/or curves to help us visualize the bivariate data distribution. To extend these ideas to more than two dimensions would seem to require multivariate extensions of these bivariate scatterplots. Gower and Hand (1996) define *biplots* as "the multivariate analogue of scatter plots," and they give detailed discussions of a number of ways of constructing these plots. These constructions are themselves based on multivariate analyses such as PCA, multiple correspondence analysis (MCA), and canonical variate analysis (CVA). Thus, while these ideas represent a potential means of arriving at higher-dimensional extensions of the bivariate boxplots just described, this extension appears nontrivial. Another alternative is the use of DataSpheres and pyramids proposed by Dasu and Johnson (2003) and discussed in Chapter 7.

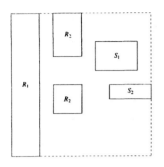

Chapter 7

Sampling Schemes for a Fixed Dataset

Since data-mining applications often deal with one or more large, fixed datasets, an important class of sampling schemes consists of those based on subset selection, as noted in Chapter 6. This chapter describes four general classes of subset selection strategies: random subset selection, subset deletion, comparison-based strategies, and systematic approaches that often use auxiliary knowledge about a dataset. Sec. 7.1 describes each of these four approaches in detail and Secs. 7.2 through 7.5 present GSA case studies that illustrate each strategy in turn. Besides their utility in the context of GSA sampling schemes, it is important to note that these subset selection strategies also play an important role in the development of computational algorithms for large datasets, the design of moving-window data characterizations for time-series data, and the stratification of composite datasets for simpler and often much more informative data analyses, relative to "large-scale" analyses of the entire dataset.

7.1 Four general strategies

Conceptually, one of the simplest ways of generating fixed-size subsets of a given dataset $\mathcal{D}$ is *random selection*, a term whose various possible interpretations are discussed briefly in Sec. 7.1.1. Sometimes, the selected subsets are mutually disjoint (i.e., $S_i \cap S_j = \emptyset$ if $j \neq i$), but in other cases they are not. This distinction is important since characterizations of overlapping datasets tend to be correlated, an issue examined in Sec. 7.1.2. The degree of overlap is most extreme in the case of deletion strategies, where small subsets are omitted from a larger dataset $\mathcal{D}$. These strategies can be quite useful in detecting various classes of outliers, an idea discussed in detail in Sec. 7.1.3. The philosophy behind deletion strategies is to make what should be small changes in a dataset and look for unusually large effects. This philosophy is opposite to that of comparison strategies such as the computational negative control idea discussed in Sec. 7.1.4, where we deliberately make what *should* be large (i.e., "structure-destroying") changes and examine the consequences: if the changes in computed results are large enough, they provide evidence in support of the hypothesized structure on which our data analysis is based. Finally, Sec. 7.1.5 describes a variety of systematic or partially systematic subset selection strategies that can incorporate explicit prior knowledge, related auxiliary data, or preliminary data characterizations such as cluster analysis results.

7.1.1   Strategy 1: Random selection

GSA comparisons based on random subset selection represent a useful approach to assessing the natural variability of *static* data characterizations such as location and scale estimates, regression models, and other characteristics that do not depend on the order of the elements in a dataset $\mathcal{D}$. The basic objective of random subset selection is to generate p subsets $\{S_i\}$ of $\mathcal{D}$, each of the same size M. The simplest version of random subset selection is probably *random selection with replacement*, in which each of the M elements of the subset S_i is randomly drawn from the size-N dataset $\mathcal{D}$ *independently*, with probability $1/N$. That is, the probability that any element of $\mathcal{D}$ is selected for element j of S_i does not depend on the values selected for element k of S_i for any $k \neq j$. Random sampling with replacement forms the basis for *bootstrap resampling schemes*, a topic discussed further below. An important feature of random sampling with replacement is that there is a nonzero probability that some of the original data values $x_i \in \mathcal{D}$ are *replicated* in S_i, appearing more than once in S_i even though they appear only once in $\mathcal{D}$. For example, once the first element x_1 has been chosen for S_i, the probability that this same observation is selected for x_2 remains $1/N$.

Unfortunately, replication is undesirable in many applications. For example, as in the single imputation schemes for missing data discussed in Chapter 4, replication reduces the inherent variability of S_i relative to $\mathcal{D}$. Since assessment of inherent variability is one of the main motivations for considering random subsamples, our primary focus here is *random sampling without replacement*, which does not lead to data replication. In this sampling scheme, each subset S_i is constructed as follows. Given a dataset $\mathcal{D}$ of N records, the first element of S_i is randomly selected from $\mathcal{D}$ with equal probability $p = 1/N$ for every element $x_k \in \mathcal{D}$. The second element of S_i is then selected from among the remaining $N - 1$ elements of $\mathcal{D}$, each with probability $p = 1/(N - 1)$. This process is continued until all M elements of S_i have been selected. Note that this construction guarantees that all elements of the set S_i are distinct.

It is a standard result that the number of distinct size-M subsets S_i of an N-element set $\mathcal{D}$ is (Brualdi, 1999; Riordan, 2002; van Lint and Wilson, 1992)

$$C(N, M) = \binom{N}{M} = \frac{N!}{M!(N - M)!}, \tag{7.1}$$

where $N!$ denotes the factorial function $N! = N \cdot (N - 1) \cdots 1$ for all integers $N \geq 1$. By convention, $0!$ is taken as 1 in expressions like (7.1). This result assumes we are considering sampling without replacement so that all elements of S_i are distinct. For sampling with replacement, each of the M elements of S_i can take any one of the N possible values from $\mathcal{D}$ with no restrictions, so the number of distinct subsets that can be generated under this sampling scheme is larger, equal to N^M.

It is important to note that the $C(N, M)$ distinct subsets S_i that can be generated by random sampling without replacement are not *disjoint*. That is, if we generate a collection of p distinct subsets $\{S_i\}$ by this sampling scheme, it does *not* generally follow that $S_i \cap S_j = \emptyset$ for $j \neq i$. In fact, the probability that S_i and S_j are disjoint for two randomly selected subsets is easily computed. Suppose $S_i = \{x_1, \ldots, x_M\}$ and $S_j = \{y_1, \ldots, y_M\}$, and proceed as follows. First, note that the probability that $y_1 \in S_i$ is M/N, since S_i contains M of the N possible values for y_1. Hence, the probability that $y_1 \notin S_i$ is $p_1 = 1 - M/N$. Next, since y_2 is distinct from y_1, it can be chosen from the $N - 1$ remaining elements of $\mathcal{D}$, a subset that includes all of the M elements of S_i if $y_1 \notin S_i$. Hence, the probability that $y_2 \notin S_i$ given that $y_1 \notin S_i$ is $p_2 = 1 - M/(N-1)$. More generally, it is easy to see that the probability that $y_k \notin S_i$ given that $y_\ell \notin S_i$ for $\ell = 1, 2, \ldots, k-1$ is $p_k = 1 - M/(N-k+1)$. Combining these results, it follows that

$$
\begin{aligned}
\mathcal{P}\{S_i \cap S_j = \emptyset\} &= \mathcal{P}\{y_1 \notin S_i\} \cdot \mathcal{P}\{y_2 \notin S_i \mid y_1 \notin S_i\} \\
&\quad \cdots \mathcal{P}\{y_M \notin S_i \mid y_1 \notin S_i, y_2 \notin S_i, \ldots, y_{M-1} \notin S_i\} \\
&= \prod_{\ell=1}^{M} \left(1 - \frac{M}{N-\ell+1}\right).
\end{aligned}
\tag{7.2}
$$

Note that if $M << N$, we obtain the approximation

$$
\mathcal{P}\{S_i \cap S_j = \emptyset\} \simeq \left(1 - \frac{M}{N}\right)^M,
\tag{7.3}
$$

which also represents an upper bound on $\mathcal{P}\{S_i \cap S_j = \emptyset\}$ for all M and N. It is not difficult to see that this probability bound decreases monotonically with increasing M for fixed N, and a few numerical results illustrate that it rapidly becomes very small. For example, for $N = 100$ and $M = 10$, the probability that the subsets S_i and S_j are disjoint is on the order of 30%, while for $M = 20$, this probability declines to about 1%. For $N = 1,000$ and $M = 100$, the probability that S_i and S_j are disjoint is on the order of 10^{-5}.

In cases where it is desirable to obtain p mutually disjoint random subsets $\{S_i\}$, each of size M, we can adopt the following simple scheme *provided* $pM \leq N$. Note that in the limiting case $pM = N$, the disjoint subsets $\{S_i\}$ form a *partition* of the original dataset $\mathcal{D}$ (Brualdi, 1999, p. 45). To obtain the desired subsets, we first generate a random permutation $\pi \mathcal{D}$ of the original dataset $\mathcal{D}$. The desired subsets $\{S_i\}$ are then obtained by taking p consecutive length-M subsequences of $\pi \mathcal{D}$. That is, if $\pi \mathcal{D} = \{z_k\}$, we have $S_i = \{z_{(i-1)M+1}, z_{(i-1)M+2}, \ldots, z_{iM}\}$. The total number of ways this objective can be accomplished may be determined as follows. First, note that there are $N!$ possible permutations π of the original dataset $\mathcal{D}$. Here, we are interested only in the contents of the subsets S_i and not in the order in which these elements appear. That is, we regard a subset S_i of M elements as equivalent to any of its $M!$ possible permutations. Hence, the $N!$ possible permutations of $\mathcal{D}$ correspond to $M!$ equivalent versions of each of the p distinct subsets S_i, so to correct for this degeneracy, it is necessary to divide the number of possible permutations by $(M!)^p$. Further, these p subsets may be relabelled in any one of $p!$ possible ways, leading to the following result for the total number of distinct collections of mutually disjoint subsets $\{S_i\}$:

$$
D(N; M, p) = \frac{N!}{(M!)^p p!} \quad \text{provided } pM \leq N.
\tag{7.4}
$$

As an instructive special case, suppose N is even, $M = N/2$, and $p = 2$. The pairs of disjoint subsets $\{S_1, S_2\}$ then correspond to partitions of the original dataset into distinct halves, and the number of ways we can form these pairs is $D(N; N/2, 2) = C(N, N/2)/2$. The reason for this particular relationship is that, while S_1 can be chosen in $C(N, N/2)$ different ways, S_2 is the complement of S_1 in $\mathcal{D}$, meaning that it is completely specified once we select S_1. This constraint reduces the number of choices for S_1 by a factor of two, leading to the relationship just noted.

As noted above, *bootstrap procedures* are based on random sampling with replacement, and they are very broadly applicable (Davison and Hinkley, 1997; Efron, 1982; Efron and Tibshirani, 1993). In the simplest cases, we are given a dataset $\mathcal{D}_0$ that consists of a sequence $\{x_k\}$ of N real numbers and the underlying idea is to generate a relatively large collection of B *resampled* datasets $\{\mathcal{D}_i\}$ that each correspond to a sequence of the same length as $\{x_k\}$, with the same distribution. The basic bootstrap procedure accomplishes this objective by sampling from the empirical distribution of $\{x_k\}$ with replacement, exactly as described above: each of the original data samples x_k can appear anywhere in the new data sequences with probability $1/N$. Given these B resampled datasets, we compute the characterization $\mathcal{K}_i$ of interest (e.g., the mean, median, standard deviation, or some more complex characterization) for each dataset $\mathcal{D}_i$. We can then estimate the variability of the characterization $\mathcal{K}$ as

$$\hat{\sigma}_B = \left[\frac{1}{B-1} \sum_{i=1}^{B} (\mathcal{K}_i - \bar{\mathcal{K}})^2 \right]^{1/2}, \tag{7.5}$$

where $\bar{\mathcal{K}}$ is the mean of the bootstrap estimates:

$$\bar{\mathcal{K}} = \frac{1}{B} \sum_{i=1}^{B} \mathcal{K}_i. \tag{7.6}$$

As noted, this idea is extremely general and can be extended to applications such as estimating confidence intervals (Davison and Hinkley, 1997, Chapter 5), selecting variables to include in linear regression models (Davison and Hinkley, 1997, Sec. 6.4), characterizing the variability of linear time-series models using the *moving-blocks bootstrap* (Efron and Tibshirani, 1993, p. 99), or assessing the stability of clustering results (Kerr and Churchill, 2001). For more detailed discussions of the bootstrap and illustrations of a wide range of bootstrap applications, refer to the books by Davison and Hinkley (1997) and Efron and Tibshirani (1993).

Although random subset selection is a simple, conceptually appealing idea, it is important to note that there are practical settings where this strategy does not perform well. For example, Davison and Hinkley (1997, pp. 42–44) note that bootstrap methods can perform poorly in the face of infinite-variance distributions such as the Cauchy distribution, certain types of missing data, dependent data such as the correlated sequences discussed in Sec. 7.4.1, or "dirty data" that contain outliers. These observations led the authors to advocate careful preprocessing and the use of diagnostic procedures following the bootstrap analysis.

A more compelling example where simple random sampling performs poorly is provided by Marron, Hernandez-Campos, and Smith (2002), who consider the practical problem of visualizing Internet traffic flow. Their results are based on a collection of Web-browsing response times collected during a four-hour period of heavy network traffic. The result was a dataset containing 6,870,022 response times, so practical visualization mandated the use of subsets. Marron, Hernandez-Campos, and Smith (2002) consider several different strategies. The first and simplest falls into the category of systematic stratification discussed in Sec. 7.1.5: the total number of records was reduced from over 6 million to 104,839 by selecting a 3.75-minute subset from the center of the 4-hour dataset. Because this sample was still too large to plot completely, a random subsample of 5,000 observations, or about 5% of the total, was chosen as the basis for visualizing the network response times. The visualization technique chosen was to plot line segments corresponding to the flow of network data as a function of time, and the result shows a very large number of short segments, termed *mice*, and a small number of very large segments, termed *elephants*. The authors note that, although random sampling is an appealing idea for finding "representative subsamples" of a dataset, this particular dataset is very heavy-tailed (like the infinite-variance Cauchy distribution), and the overall impression we get of this dataset depends very strongly on exactly how we select these subsamples. In particular, selecting 5,000 random samples from the complete 4-hour dataset (a sampling of less than 0.1%) yields a plot that does not exhibit *any* elephants, leading to the erroneous conclusion that the traffic consists entirely of mice. Conversely, selecting 5,000 random subsamples from the 6,910 records obtained during a 14-second subset from the center of the 3.75-minute segment leads to precisely the opposite conclusion: the plot is dominated by the presence of elephants, 163 of which cross the entire 14-second time window. To show clearly that these results are a consequence of the heavy-tailed character of the Internet flow data, Marron, Hernandez-Campos, and Smith (2002) also present the corresponding results obtained for a simulation based on an exponential response time model that is widely used in queueing theory: there, they find no elephants even though the mean response time was chosen to be the same as that of the Internet dataset. Based on these observations, the authors offer the following important practical caution:

> *A clear lesson is that random sampling is not an effective method for choosing a "representative sample" for internet data, or indeed data from heavy tail distributions that appear elsewhere, e.g., financial and environmental contexts.*

Overall, the authors conclude that the question of how to select a "representative sample" in these circumstances remains open, a point that is particularly relevant in the context of data anomalies, which may be quite rare and difficult to detect with simple random sampling strategies.

One alternative approach described by Marron, Hernandez-Campos, and Smith (2002) for their Internet dataset was to separately examine the 5,000 largest response times, giving an "elephants-only" characterization that was incomplete but useful over the entire 4-hour period examined. This idea represents a special case of the systematic sampling strategies discussed further in Sec. 7.1.5. This idea is also closely related to the concept of *importance sampling*, discussed by Davison and Hinkley (1997, Sec. 9.4) in connection with bootstrap methods. The essential idea is to recognize that, as in the elephants and mice example of Marron, Hernandez-Campos, and Smith (2002), data observations that occur only rarely can still have a disproportionately large effect on analysis results, leading us to deliberately increase their concentration in the random samples selected relative to their natural frequency of occurrence in the original dataset. In fact, the elephants-only characterization described above for the Internet dataset may be viewed as an extreme extension of this idea, where *only* the "most important" samples are retained in the subset. Clearly, to implement an importance sampling scheme, it is necessary to either implicitly or explicitly specify which samples are more important than others in order to increase their probability of being included in our random subsets. In certain situations, systematic procedures have been proposed to accomplish this, although they necessarily depend on the specific data characterization under consideration. For a more detailed discussion of this idea, refer to Davison and Hinkley (1997, Sec. 9.4).

Finally, it is useful to conclude this discussion with three observations. First, as noted at the beginning of this discussion, the basic working assumption underlying random subset selection is that individual observations may be regarded as exchangeable in the sense discussed in Chapter 4. It follows that the collection of p subsets S_i, each of the same size M, may also be regarded as exchangeable. As the examples presented in Sec. 7.2 illustrate, outliers in the dataset can cause violations of this working assumption, but in favorable cases, subsets containing more or fewer outliers will exhibit significantly different data characterizations, leading us to discover them in the dataset. In the absence of outliers or other significant data anomalies, the range of the random subset results provides a useful measure of the inherent variability of the data characterization of interest. Second, this idea has been used in various contexts in the statistics and data analysis literature. Connections with bootstrap methods were briefly discussed above, but a more direct application of the ideas discussed here is the use of random subsamples to characterize the *stability* of clustering results (Bolshakova and Azuaje, 2003; Dudoit and Fridlyand, 2002; Roth et al., 2002). There, we are given a dataset $\mathcal{D}$ of N objects to be partitioned into k nonoverlapping clusters, and the basic strategy of stability analysis is to compare the clustering results obtained from a collection $\{S_i\}$ of p subsamples of $\mathcal{D}$, each of size M. This idea is revisited briefly in Sec. 7.1.4, where it is contrasted with the use of structure-destroying permutations to assess the significance of clustering results. Third, the equivalance of subsets S_i under reordering invoked above (i.e., the exchangeability of individual data observations) is appropriate for static data characterizations but not for time-series characterizations such as those discussed in Sec. 7.3.2, an observation that is closely related to the comparison-based strategies discussed in Sec. 7.1.4.

7.1.2   Correlation and overlap

It was noted in Sec. 7.1.1 that random sampling without replacement generates a collection $\{S_i\}$ of datasets that are distinct but not disjoint. It follows that, even if our original dataset $\mathcal{D}$ consists of a sequence $\{x_k\}$ of i.i.d. random variables, the subsets $\{S_i\}$ generated by that sampling scheme will *not* be statistically independent for $i \neq j$. Since these correlations imply an association between data characterizations computed from these subsets, it is important to keep this fact in mind in GSA comparisons based on these subsets.

The following simple example illustrates the nature of this association between subsets and provides a useful rule of thumb for quantifying it. Consider two distinct but not disjoint subsets of real numbers, $S_i = \{x_k\}$ and $S_j = \{z_k\}$, both of the same size N. Further, define $A = S_i \cap S_j$ as the set of samples from $\mathcal{D}$ that are common to both S_i and S_j, define $B = S_i \setminus A$ as the set of values unique to S_i, and define $C = S_j \setminus A$ as the set of values unique to S_j. Note that since S_i and S_j are the same size, the sets B and C are also the same size. The mean of the subset S_i is the random variable

$$\bar{x}_N = \frac{1}{N} \sum_{k=1}^{N} x_k = \frac{1}{N} \left[\sum_{k \in A} x_k + \sum_{k \in B} x_k \right] = \frac{|A|}{N} \bar{x}_A + \frac{N - |A|}{N} \bar{x}_B, \qquad (7.7)$$

where $\bar{x}_A$ and $\bar{x}_B$ denote the mean values of the subsets A and B and $|A|$ and $|B|$ denote their sizes, which are related by $|B| = N - |A|$. Define $p = |A|/N$ as the fraction of common elements between S_i and S_j and note that the mean values of these data sequences are given by

$$\bar{x}_N = p\bar{x}_A + (1 - p)\bar{x}_B,$$
$$\bar{z}_N = p\bar{x}_A + (1 - p)\bar{x}_C. \tag{7.8}$$

Under the assumption that the original dataset $\mathcal{D}$ corresponds to an i.i.d. sequence of random variables with mean μ and variance σ^2, so do the subsets S_i and S_j and the derived sets A, B, and C. An immediate consequence of this observation is that the means $\bar{x}_N$ and $\bar{z}_N$ are unbiased estimators of the mean μ. To compute the correlation coefficient $\rho(\bar{x}_N, \bar{z}_N)$ between the subset means $\bar{x}_N$ and $\bar{z}_N$, we need the expectation

$$
\begin{aligned}
E\{(\bar{x}_N - \mu)(\bar{z}_N - \mu)\} &= E\{\bar{x}_N\bar{z}_N\} - \mu^2 \\
&= E\{p^2\bar{x}_A^2 + p(1 - p)\bar{x}_A(\bar{x}_B + \bar{x}_C) + (1 - p)^2\bar{x}_B\bar{x}_C\} - \mu^2 \\
&= p^2 E\{\bar{x}_A^2\} + p(1 - p)[E\{\bar{x}_A\bar{x}_B\} + E\{\bar{x}_A\bar{x}_C\}] \\
&\quad + (1 - p)^2 E\{\bar{x}_B\bar{x}_C\} - \mu^2.
\end{aligned}
\tag{7.9}
$$

Since the subsets A, B, and C are mutually disjoint, they are statistically independent, implying that $E\{\bar{x}_A\bar{x}_B\} = E\{\bar{x}_A\}E\{\bar{x}_B\} = \mu^2$, with the same result for the expectations $E\{\bar{x}_A\bar{x}_C\}$ and $E\{\bar{x}_B\bar{x}_C\}$. Hence, (7.9) simplifies to

$$E\{(\bar{x}_N - \mu)(\bar{z}_N - \mu)\} = p^2[E\{\bar{x}_A^2\} - \mu^2] = p^2\mathrm{var}\,\{\bar{x}_A\}. \tag{7.10}$$

It follows immediately from this result that the correlation between $\bar{x}_N$ and $\bar{z}_N$ is

$$\rho(\bar{x}_N, \bar{z}_N) = \frac{E\{(\bar{x}_N - \mu)(\bar{z}_N - \mu)\}}{\sqrt{\mathrm{var}\{\bar{x}_N\}\mathrm{var}\{\bar{z}_N\}}} = \frac{p^2\mathrm{var}\{\bar{x}_A\}}{\mathrm{var}\{\bar{x}_N\}}, \tag{7.11}$$

where we have made use of the fact that $\mathrm{var}\{\bar{x}_N\} = \mathrm{var}\{\bar{z}_N\}$. In fact, note that

$$\mathrm{var}\{\bar{x}_N\} = \frac{\sigma^2}{N}, \quad \mathrm{var}\{\bar{x}_A\} = \frac{\sigma^2}{|A|} = \frac{\sigma^2}{pN}. \tag{7.12}$$

Combining (7.11) and (7.12) yields the extremely simple result

$$\rho(\bar{x}_N, \bar{z}_N) = p. \tag{7.13}$$

The interpretation of this result is that the means of distinct but overlapping subsets S_i and S_j are positively correlated, with a correlation coefficient equal to their fractional overlap p. In fact, note that this result is more general than it appears since the derivation just presented needs no modification other than notation to show that the same conclusion holds for any static transformation of the data values $x_k \to f(x_k)$ and $z_k \to f(z_k)$ for any function $f(\cdot)$.

7.1.3 Strategy 2: Subset deletion

In contrast to random subset selection strategies, subset deletion strategies create a collection $\{S_i\}$ of p distinct subsets by *omitting* a collection $\{A_i\}$ of subsets, which may be either randomly or systematically chosen. Historically, there are two main motivations for this strategy. The first is the *jackknife* (Davison and Hinkley, 1997; Efron, 1982; Efron and Tibshirani, 1993), a computationally intensive procedure, like the bootstrap discussed in Sec. 7.1.1, for assessing nominal estimator variability that sometimes gives comparable results with less computation. In its simplest form, the jackknife is used to estimate either the bias or the standard error of a permutation-invariant estimator $\hat{\theta} = T\{x_k\}$ such as the mean or the standard deviation. Define the ith *jackknife sample* as the data sequence with the ith element omitted:

$$\mathbf{x}_{(i)} = \{x_1, x_2, \ldots, x_{i-1}, x_{i+1}, \ldots, x_N\}. \tag{7.14}$$

Then, define the ith *jackknife replication of* $\hat{\theta}$ as $\hat{\theta}_{(i)} = T\{\mathbf{x}_{(i)}\}$, the estimator of θ computed from the data sequence $\{x_k\}$ with the ith observation omitted. The *jackknife bias estimator* for $\hat{\theta}$ is

$$B = (N-1)(\hat{\theta}_{(\cdot)} - \hat{\theta}), \tag{7.15}$$

where $\hat{\theta}_{(\cdot)}$ is the average of the jackknife replications of $\hat{\theta}$, i.e.,

$$\hat{\theta}_{(\cdot)} = \frac{1}{N} \sum_{i=1}^{N} \hat{\theta}_{(i)}. \tag{7.16}$$

The jackknife can also be used to assess variability via the *jackknife standard error estimate*

$$S = \left[\frac{N-1}{N} \sum_{i=1}^{N} (\hat{\theta}_{(i)} - \hat{\theta}_{(\cdot)})^2 \right]^{1/2}. \tag{7.17}$$

In simple cases like the mean, these jackknife characterizations offer no practical advantage over more familiar standard results (e.g., the arithmetic mean is an unbiased estimator of μ with variance σ^2/N for any i.i.d. sequence of random variables with mean μ and variance σ^2), but the advantage of these characterizations is that they can be extended to much more complex settings. A specific example is the use of jackknife variance estimates in multiwindow spectrum estimation (Riedel, Sidorenko, and Thomson, 1994; Thomson, 1990) and various other closely related nonparametric dynamic data characterizations (e.g., coherence analysis and transfer function estimation (Chave, Thomson, and Ander, 1987)). In fact, Chave and Thomson (1989) note the following:

> *The jackknife offers many advantages over conventional approaches, including robustness to heterogeneity of residual variance, relative insensitivity to correlations induced by the spectral analysis of finite data sequences, and computational simplicity.*

Thomson (1990) takes this point further, recommending the computation of both conventional and jackknife variance estimates and comparing them: he notes that the jackknife estimator is rarely smaller than the conventional estimator, but that if the jackknife estimator is substantially larger than the standard estimator, this "usually suggests unresolved structure, non-stationarity or simply outliers." For small datasets, jackknife estimators are often regarded as a computationally simpler approximation of the corresponding bootstrap estimator (Efron and Tibshirani, 1993, p. 145), but jackknife estimators are known to fail in cases such as the median that are not smooth functions of the data (Efron and Tibshirani, 1993, p. 148). For more detailed accounts of the jackknife, including its history, applications, advantages, and disadvantages, refer to the books by Efron (1982), Efron and Tibshirani (1993), and Davison and Hinkley (1997).

The second main motivation for subset deletion strategies is that the effects of subset deletion can be computed efficiently for OLS regression models by exploiting the structure of their analytic solution (Belsley, Kuh, and Welsch, 1980; Chatterjee and Hadi, 1988). In particular, it is a standard result that the OLS estimator for the unknown parameter θ in the linear regression model $\mathbf{y} = \mathbf{X}\theta + \mathbf{e}$ is $\hat{\theta} = (\mathbf{X}^T\mathbf{X})^{-1}\mathbf{X}^T\mathbf{y}$. (See Chapter 4, Sec. 4.1.4 for a discussion of this problem and its solution.) Here, $\mathbf{X}$ represents an $N \times p$ matrix of explanatory variables, and the key to the existence of computationally efficient deletion diagnostics is the expression for the modified inverse $(\mathbf{X}_{(i)}^T\mathbf{X}_{(i)})^{-1}$ that results when the ith data observation is omitted from the dataset (Chatterjee and Hadi, 1988, p. 22):

$$(\mathbf{X}_{(i)}^T\mathbf{X}_{(i)})^{-1} = (\mathbf{X}^T\mathbf{X})^{-1} + \frac{(\mathbf{X}^T\mathbf{X})^{-1}\mathbf{x}_i\mathbf{x}_i^T(\mathbf{X}^T\mathbf{X})^{-1}}{1 - \mathbf{x}_i^T(\mathbf{X}^T\mathbf{X})^{-1}\mathbf{x}_i}, \tag{7.18}$$

where $\mathbf{x}_i$ represents the ith row of the data matrix $\mathbf{X}$. As a specific example, it follows from this result that the residual sum of squared errors, SSE, is reduced by the deletion of observation i to (Chatterjee and Hadi, 1988, p. 75)

$$SSE_{(i)} = SSE - \frac{e_i^2}{1 - \mathbf{x}_i^T(\mathbf{X}^T\mathbf{X})^{-1}\mathbf{x}_i} = \sum_{k=1}^{N} e_k^2 - \frac{e_i^2}{1 - \mathbf{x}_i^T(\mathbf{X}^T\mathbf{X})^{-1}\mathbf{x}_i}. \tag{7.19}$$

Here, $e_i = y_i - \mathbf{x}_i\hat{\theta}$ represents the ith residual (i.e., prediction error) from the unmodified least squares regression model. A variety of other closely related results may also be derived from (7.18), and Chatterjee and Hadi (1988, p. 79) suggest that one of the most useful of these diagnostic quantities is the ith *externally Studentized residual* given by

$$r_i^* = \frac{e_i}{\sqrt{\frac{(1-\mathbf{x}_i^T(\mathbf{X}^T\mathbf{X})^{-1}\mathbf{x}_i)SSE_{(i)}}{N-p-1}}}, \tag{7.20}$$

where p is the number of unknown model parameters to be estimated. The key point here is that it is sometimes possible to obtain special deletion-based results that avoid the necessity of recomputing the complete solution to the original problem for a range of modified datasets. In particular, note that here it is only necessary to solve *one* regression problem: all deletion-based results are directly computable from the solution of this problem with only modest added computational effort.

The correlation results presented in Sec. 7.1.2 have the greatest practical implications when the degree of overlap between subsets is large. This observation is particularly important here, since the most common subset deletion strategies are the *leave-one-out* strategies, in which a single data point x_i is omitted from the dataset $\mathcal{D}$ to obtain the subset $S_{(i)}$ of size $N - 1$. This can be done for each point in the dataset, giving a collection of N subsets, each of the same size; if the original data points can be regarded as exchangeable, so can the collection $\{S_{(i)}\}$ of subsets, although it follows from the results presented in Sec. 7.1.2 that these subsets will be very highly correlated. As a practical consequence, this observation means that deletion strategies are probably most useful when the deleted subsets are anomalous (i.e., *not* exchangeable with the rest of the dataset $\mathcal{D}$) and their omission causes large changes in the data characterization under consideration. As the examples discussed in Sec. 7.3 illustrate, this strategy can be extremely effective in the face of a single glaring outlier, but the use of deletion strategies becomes problematic if we must consider larger, arbitrary subsets. In particular, note that the number $O(N, M)$ of subsets $S_{(A)}$ we can obtain from a dataset $\mathcal{D}$ of size N by omitting subsets A of size M is equal to the number of distinct subsets of size M in $\mathcal{D}$:

$$O(N, M) = \binom{N}{N - M} = \frac{N!}{(N - M)!M!} = \binom{N}{M} = C(N, M). \qquad (7.21)$$

Thus, while leave-one-out deletion strategies are quite practical, complete leave-k-out subset deletion strategies rapidly become computationally infeasible. For example, complete leave-one-out deletion diagnostic results are presented in Sec. 7.3 for two datasets of size $N = 1{,}024$, but extending this idea even to leave-two-out deletion diagnostics would expand the number of subsets considered from 1,024 to 523,776. One possible solution to this computational dilemma is to randomly sample from the possible deletion subsets, obtaining a reasonably sized collection $\{S_{(A_i)}\}$. For characterizing nominal variability, this idea forms the basis for practical implications of the *delete-d jackknife* for $d > 1$ (Davison and Hinkley, 1997; Efron and Tibshirani, 1993; Shao and Wu, 1989), and it has been extended to more complex settings such as discriminant analysis (Weihs, 1995). The main practical difficulty with this approach for anomaly detection is that, in complicated cases, there may only be a few key subsets A_i whose deletion leads to a large change in the computed results. This problem is exactly analogous to the mice and elephants problem of Marron, Hernandez-Campos, and Smith (2002) discussed in Sec. 7.1.1.

In fact, this difficulty is closely related to the probability of randomly selecting a "good" subsample from a contaminated dataset. For a dataset of size N containing a fraction ϵ of outliers, the probability of selecting m samples of size p such that one of them is outlier-free is approximately (Rousseeuw and Leroy, 1987, p. 198)

$$\mathcal{P} = 1 - (1 - (1 - \epsilon)^p)^m \qquad (7.22)$$

provided p/N is sufficiently small. Rousseeuw and Leroy (1987) give a table of values for m such that $\mathcal{P} = 0.95$ for subsample sizes p between 1 and 10 and ϵ between 0.05 and 0.50 for $N >> 10$. If $p = 10$, these numbers are $m = 7$ for $\epsilon = 0.10$, $m = 52$ for $\epsilon = 0.25$, $m = 494$ for $\epsilon = 0.40$, and $m = 3{,}067$ for $\epsilon = 0.50$.

Another variation on the generic leave-k-out deletion strategy described above is the *successive leave-k-out deletion strategy* described by Bruce and Martin (1989) for time-series. There, since the basic problem of interest is the characterization of the relationship between successive data observations in the sequence $\{x_k\}$, it is sensible to restrict consideration to the effects of deleting *successive* subsets. This restriction dramatically reduces the number of subsets considered from $C(N, k)$ to $N - k + 1$, making the successive leave-k-out strategy comparable in terms of computational effort to the leave-one-out strategy. Further, Bruce and Martin (1989) demonstrate convincingly that this strategy can be used to detect a variety of time-series anomalies, including isolated outliers, patchy outliers, and other phenomena such as nonstationarity. Even better, in cases where popular least squares

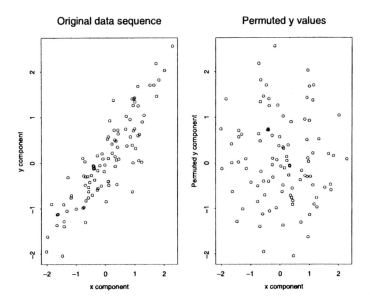

Figure 7.1. *Scatterplots of a bivariate Gaussian dataset (left) and the result of a random permutation applied to one of its components (right).*

characterizations are of interest, simple variants of the OLS regression diagnostics discussed above can be developed to substantially reduce computation times relative to brute-force implementations. It is worth noting, however, that brute-force implementations are feasible for most dynamic data characterizations, even when they are not least squares based, making this idea very broadly applicable.

7.1.4 Strategy 3: Comparisons

The basic GSA formulation described in Chapter 6 is built on sampling schemes that generate datasets $\{S_i\}$ that should, under ideal conditions, be exchangeable in the sense discussed in Chapter 6. In contrast, the sampling schemes described in the following paragraphs are based on the opposite notion: the deliberate creation of subsets $\{S_i\}$ that are *not* exchangeable with a given nominal set S_0. Typically, this nominal subset S_0 is simply the original dataset $\mathcal{D}$, but the ideas described here are equally applicable to any fixed subset $S_0 \subset \mathcal{D}$. Motivation for this approach comes from the observation that many data analysis procedures impose, either explicitly or implicitly, certain structural assumptions on the dataset under consideration. The sampling schemes described here use random permutations to destroy this structure—if it is present—generating a collection $\{S_i\}$ of p subsets that should be exchangeable with each other but *not* exchangeable with the nominal set S_0.

Perhaps the best way to clarify this idea is with the following simple example. The left-hand plot in Figure 7.1 is a scatterplot of 100 samples $\{(x_k, y_k)\}$ of a bivariate Gaussian random variable with correlation $\rho = 0.9$. This high positive correlation value is clearly reflected in the strong linear trend seen in this scatterplot. The right-hand plot in Figure 7.1 is the scatterplot that results when the $\{y_k\}$ values in this sample are reordered by a random

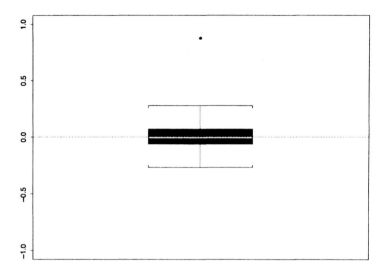

Figure 7.2. *Boxplot of the correlation estimates from* 200 *random permutations of the* {y_k} *values shown in Figure* 7.1. *The solid point in the center near the top indicates the correlation estimated from the original dataset.*

permutation π, replacing {y_k} with {$y_{\pi(k)}$}. The effect of this random permutation is to destroy the association between the sequences {x_k} and {$y_{\pi(k)}$}, making them statistically independent, hence uncorrelated.

This effect is illustrated nicely in Figure 7.2, which shows a boxplot summary of the correlation coefficients $\hat{\rho}_{xy}$ estimated from 200 independent randomizations of {y_k}. That is, 200 independent random permutations π_i were generated and applied to the {y_k} data sequence, and the correlation coefficient between the original {x_k} sequence and the ith randomized sequence {$y_{\pi_i(k)}$} was computed. As may be seen in Figure 7.2, the median correlation value is approximately zero, consistent with statistical independence, and the computed $\hat{\rho}_{xy}$ values appear symmetrically distributed about zero. The correlation coefficient computed from the original dataset is $\hat{\rho}_{xy} = 0.9029$, shown as the solid circle above the boxplot in Figure 7.2 and in excellent agreement with the correct value of $\rho = 0.9000$.

This example serves to illustrate the comparison-based GSA formulation proposed here and illustrated further in Sec. 7.4 in connection with dynamic auto- and cross-correlation analysis. Another application is the assessment of cluster analysis results (Pearson et al., 2004) where various cluster quality measures have been proposed, including the silhouette coefficient introduced in Chapter 6 and many others (Bolshakova and Azuaje, 2003). In the strategy considered here, one of these cluster quality measures is evaluated, both for a clustering computed from the original dataset and for a collection of clusterings computed from randomized versions of this dataset, using the same clustering algorithm. The intent of these randomizations is to destroy any cluster structure that existed in the original dataset, so if an inherent cluster structure exists, the effect of the randomizations should be to substantially reduce the cluster quality measure relative to the original dataset. Results obtained for simulation-based datasets demonstrate that this is indeed the case (Pearson et al., 2004).

Since it was noted in Sec. 7.1.1 that random subset selection has been used as a basis for assessing the inherent stability of clustering results (Bolshakova and Azuaje, 2003;

Dudoit and Fridlyand, 2002; Roth et al., 2002), it is worth emphasizing the difference between that strategy and the comparison-based cluster evaluation strategy just described. In cluster stability assessments based on random subset selection, the working assumption is that the subsets should be exchangeable for a stable clustering procedure, so the quality of the clustering results measured by a descriptor $d(\cdot)$ such as the silhouette coefficient discussed in Chapter 6 should be similar for the clusterings determined from these subsets. In contrast, the comparison-based *computational negative control (CNC) procedure* described by Pearson et al. (2004) attempts to assess the *significance* of the clustering result obtained for the nominal dataset S_0 by comparing it with those obtained from the randomized subsets $\{S_i\}$, which should be structureless. Motivation for this idea comes from experimental biology, where "negative controls" represent experimental units that are known not to respond to an experimental treatment. There, if the other experimental units do not exhibit noticeably stronger responses than the negative controls, the results do not give clear evidence for a biological response and are deemed nonsignificant.

Since it is often practical to generate and characterize a relatively large number M of randomized subsets (e.g., $M \gtrsim 100$), it is useful to formalize these significance statements. In the simplest case, if we observe fewer than q out of M of the randomized descriptors $\{d(S_i)\}$ that exceed the original value $d(S_0)$, the probability of observing a value this large or larger among exchangeable randomization results is less than q/M. This result is most useful in cases where $d(\cdot)$ belongs to the figure-of-merit descriptor class discussed in Chapter 6, like the silhouette coefficient, where larger values of $d(\cdot)$ are more desirable. Conversely, if $d(\cdot)$ is a figure-of-merit descriptor such as the prediction error standard deviation for which smaller values are better, the probability of observing a result better than $d(S_0)$ among the randomizations is less than q/M if $d(S_0)$ is smaller than q out of the M values for $d(S_i)$. Finally, in cases such as the correlation coefficient considered in Figure 7.2, it may be more reasonable to consider two-sided significance levels, which are more conservative by a factor of two. That is, if $d(S_0)$ lies outside the range of variation of q of the M $d(S_i)$ values, the observed value $d(S_0)$ is declared significant relative to the randomizations with probability $p = q/2M$. In the specific case shown in Figure 7.2, since the estimated correlation value $\hat{\rho}_{xy}$ for the original dataset S_0 lies outside the range of the 200 randomization values, we declare it significant at the 1% level.

The basis for this interpretation is the assumption that the randomized subsets $\{S_i\}$ are exchangeable (Good, 2000, p. 24). In particular, note that unlike traditional hypothesis tests (e.g., the t-test for the significance of the difference between the mean values of two data sequences), the permutation-based hypothesis tests just described do not rely on distributional assumptions for the descriptor values $\{d(S_i)\}$. Instead, these significance assessments are based completely on the ranks of the $d(S_i)$ and $d(S_0)$ values. While this distribution-independence is a very desirable practical characteristic, note that these rank-based significance assessments make no use of the distance between $d(S_0)$ and the reference values $\{d(S_i)\}$. In cases where this distance is large and we can say something about the distribution of the randomized values, we can usually make much stronger significance statements. In particular, it is often—but not always—true that the values $\{d(S_i)\}$ have an approximate Gaussian distribution. In practice, given $M \gtrsim 100$ randomizations, we can informally assess the quality of this normality assumption using the normal Q-Q plots discussed in Chapter 6. Figure 7.3 shows the normal Q-Q plot obtained for the randomized correlation values summarized in Figure 7.2, along with a reference line to aid in assessing

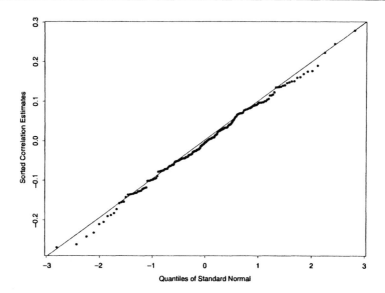

Figure 7.3. *Normal Q-Q plot of the correlations estimated from the* 200 *random permutations summarized in Figure* 7.2.

the linearity of this plot. The generally close agreement between the plotted points and this reference line suggests that the normality approximation is reasonable in this case. The mean of these randomized correlation values is $\bar{\rho} = 0.0096$ and the standard deviation is $\hat{\sigma} = 0.0965$, while the original correlation estimate is $\hat{\rho}_{xy} = 0.9029$, as noted above. Hence, the z-score or normalized deviation is

$$z = \frac{\hat{\rho}_{xy} - \bar{\rho}}{\hat{\sigma}} \simeq 9.25. \tag{7.23}$$

For the Gaussian distribution, the two-sided p value associated with this z-score is approximately 2×10^{-20}, giving overwhelming evidence in support of the hypothesis that the two components of the original dataset $S_0 = \{(x_k, y_k)\}$ are correlated.

It is important to emphasize that the Gaussian approximation for the randomized descriptors $\{d(S_i)\}$ is not always a reasonable one. This point is illustrated in Figure 7.4, which shows the normal Q-Q plot for a set of 200 randomized regression error standard deviations. Specifically, the dataset shown in the left-hand plot in Figure 7.1 was randomized 200 times, exactly as before, and the results were fit to the following linear regression model via OLS:

$$y_k = \alpha + \beta x_k + e_k. \tag{7.24}$$

For the original dataset, the estimated α parameter is approximately zero; the estimated β parameter is approximately equal to the correlation coefficient, $\rho = 0.9$; and the standard deviation of the model error sequence $\{e_k\}$ is approximately 0.44. The results for 200 randomizations give a slightly but consistently larger estimate for α, a wider range of estimated β values centered around zero, and prediction error standard deviations that become much larger, ranging from approximately 0.89 to approximately 0.94. Normal Q-Q plots (not shown) for the randomized parameter estimates support their approximate normality, but the corresponding Q-Q plot for the prediction error standard deviations shown in Figure 7.4

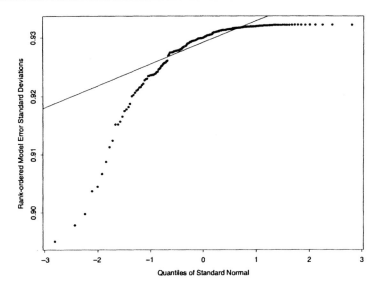

Figure 7.4. *Normal Q-Q plot of the regression model error standard deviations estimated from* 200 *random permutations of the dataset shown in Figure* 7.1.

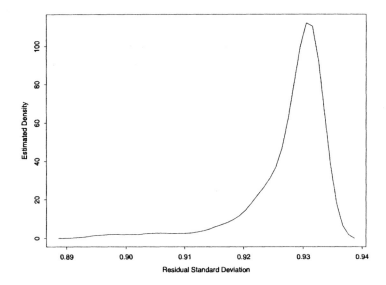

Figure 7.5. *Nonparametric density estimate of the distribution of residual standard deviations of the permutation results.*

exhibits markedly nonnormal behavior. In particular, note the pronounced downward curvature of this plot, which falls consistently below the reference line in both the upper and lower tails. The shape of this Q-Q plot suggests pronounced distributional asymmetry, which is supported by the nonparametric density estimate for these standard deviations shown in Figure 7.5.

Even in cases like this one where the normality assumption is untenable, the z-scores remain a useful basis for comparing results *provided it is reasonable to assume the distributions are approximately the same for the results being compared.* Note that this is a much weaker assumption than normality and it should be reasonable in cases where the same descriptor is applied across similar scenarios (e.g., comparison of different regression models on the basis of their prediction error standard deviations). Although the z-scores would not have the same probability interpretation as they do under a normality assumption, it remains true that the probability associated with z-scores of large magnitude is smaller than that associated with z-scores of smaller magnitude. This observation is a direct consequence of Chebyshev's inequality discussed in Chapter 5, which implies that the probability of observing a z-score larger than ζ is at most $1/\zeta^2$ for any distribution with finite mean and standard deviation. Hence, the probability of observing a z-score larger in magnitude than 10 is at most 1% under *any* finite-variance distribution and is negligibly small under most common distributions (e.g., it is on the order of 10^{-24} for the Gaussian distribution). Similarly, note that a z-score larger in magnitude than 31.7 has a probability of less than 0.1% under any finite-variance distribution. Again, the key point here is that the z-scores computed from permutation results like those considered here provide a useful basis for quantitative comparisons across scenarios, often substantially improving on the significance results obtained from the permutation ranks alone. This point is illustrated further in Sec. 7.4.

7.1.5   Strategy 4: Partially systematic sampling

Although the examples presented below in Secs. 7.2 through 7.4 demonstrate the utility of the three sampling schemes described in Secs. 7.1.1, 7.1.3, and 7.1.4, the discussions and examples also demonstrate that these three strategies do not always detect the anomalies present in a dataset. In the case of random subset selection discussed in Sec. 7.1.1, this point was illustrated by the mice and elephants example of Marron, Hernandez-Campos, and Smith (2002). There, the original Internet response dataset contained very large segments (elephants) that were not detected at all in randomly selected subsets of the complete dataset. Similarly, it was noted in Sec. 7.1.3 that deletion-based strategies must delete the right subsets to show the presence of anomalies. This is not difficult for the case of isolated outliers, but it becomes quite difficult for larger, more complex data anomalies where deletion of larger subsets is necessary. Finally, although they are intended to confirm the presence of a hypothesized dataset structure rather than to detect data anomalies per se, it is important to note that the comparison-based strategies discussed in Sec. 7.1.4 can be completely blind to even simple, isolated outliers. This point is illustrated in Sec. 7.4.1 in connection with the dynamic autocorrelation analysis problem introduced in Chapter 1.

How, then, do we find these data anomalies? While there is no universally effective procedure, there are two useful guiding principles. First is the use of comparison, inherent in the GSA framework: gross disagreements between attempts to analyze the same problem in different ways provide one of the most effective methods of detecting data anomalies, a point that has been emphasized repeatedly. The second guiding principle is the *appropriate use of auxiliary information.* This idea leads to the use of *partially systematic sampling schemes* that incorporate prior knowledge, auxiliary data, and/or tentative working hypotheses. A simple example is the elephants-only characterization of Marron, Hernandez-Campos, and Smith (2002) discussed in Sec. 7.1.1, where the knowledge (or suspicion) that the data exhibited a heavy-tailed distribution led to an examination of random samples of the largest data values. Similarly, the successive leave-k-out deletion strategy of Bruce and Martin (1989) for time-series was motivated by the recognition that time-series characterizations are based on the relationship between neighboring elements of the data sequence, so it is not sensible to consider random deletions that interrupt this structure. This idea is closely related to the notion of systematic segmentation by sample index, an idea illustrated in Sec. 7.5.1. In fact, such segmentations can be based on any totally ordered auxiliary variable, an idea closely related to the concept of stratified sampling discussed below.

One useful approach to characterizing a large dataset $\mathcal{D}$ is to treat the problem as one of *survey sampling* (Särndal, Swensson, and Wretman, 1992; Thompson, 2002), where we regard $\mathcal{D}$ as a *finite population* to be surveyed. This view leads naturally to *design-based* analyses in which the only random phenomena arise from the use of random subsamples of $\mathcal{D}$ (Thompson, 2002, p. 22). An important distinction is made in the survey sampling literature between a *complete enumeration* or *census*, which gives an exact, error-free characterization of the finite population, and a more typical sample-based survey that characterizes this population on the basis of one or more *samples* (here, subsets of $\mathcal{D}$). Substantial effort has gone into the development of survey sampling and analysis methods in the social sciences where complete enumeration is frequently impractical. Typical data analysis is more closely allied with the notion of *model-based* (Thompson, 2002, p. 22) or *model-assisted* (Särndal, Swensson, and Wretman, 1992) survey sampling, which assumes that the observations in the population (i.e., the dataset $\mathcal{D}$) are viewed as random variables rather than unknown deterministic constants as in design-based survey sampling. In either case, questions of how to obtain and characterize *representative* samples from a large population have been examined extensively in the survey sampling literature, and these results lead to some extremely useful ideas for GSA sampling schemes.

The two sampling schemes discussed in Sec. 7.1.1—random sampling with and without replacement—are both important in the theory of survey sampling (Särndal, Swensson, and Wretman, 1992; Thompson, 2002), but many variations have also been developed, motivated by a wide variety of practical considerations. One example is *systematic sampling* (Särndal, Swensson, and Wretman, 1992, Sec. 3.6), which in its simplest form generates a sample of fixed size n from a dataset $\mathcal{D}$ of size N as follows. The first sample is drawn with equal probability $p = 1/M$ from among the first M elements of $\mathcal{D}$, corresponding to $\{\mathbf{x}_k\}$ for $k \in \{1, 2, \ldots, M\}$. Subsequent samples are then $\mathbf{x}_{k+jM}$ for $j = 1, 2, \ldots, n-1$. In survey applications, the motivation for this form of systematic sampling is simplicity, but the key point here is that the introduction of systematic elements into a sampling scheme can have significant practical benefits. To illustrate this point, Figure 7.6 shows 384 successive monthly average atmospheric carbon dioxide concentrations in parts per million at Mauna Loa, Hawaii, collected by the Scripps Institute of Oceanography in La Jolla, California, and included as a built-in data object in the S-PLUS software package (Insightful, 2001). It is clear from this plot that the data sequence exhibits both a long-term increasing trend with time and shorter-term cyclic fluctuations. To examine this dataset further, the long-term trend was removed using the nonparametric *lowess* local regression smoother (Venables and Ripley, 2002, p. 231) popular in microarray data analysis. The results shown in Figure 7.7 are the residuals obtained after this trend estimate has been subtracted from the original data sequence. Little structure is evident in this sequence of residuals: in particular, the regular pattern of short-term variation seen in Figure 7.6 is not at all obvious in Figure 7.7.

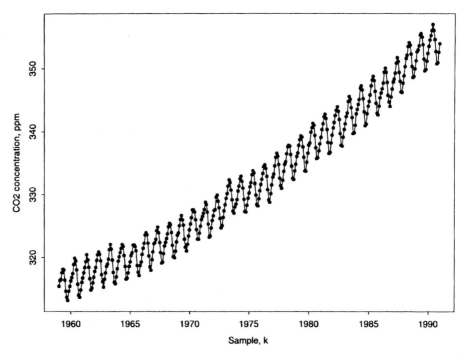

Figure 7.6. *Plot of* 384 *monthly atmospheric carbon dioxide concentration measurements from Mauna Loa, Hawaii.*

Figure 7.8 presents a very different view of the residuals shown in Figure 7.7. There, every 12th point has been combined into a subset of 32 monthly values, and the boxplots shown in Figure 7.8 characterize each of these subsets. The cyclic behavior seen in the original dataset is now very pronounced and its origin is clear: these cycles represent *seasonal variations* that occur quite repeatably. The key point of this example is to illustrate that the exploitation of known or suspected structure in selecting data subsets can be extremely informative.

An advantage of the simple random sampling schemes discussed in Sec. 7.1.1 is that they yield fixed sample sizes, specified by the user. Another important strategy in survey sampling is *Bernoulli sampling* (Särndal, Swensson, and Wretman, 1992, Sec. 3.2). In the context of sampling a fixed dataset $\mathcal{D}$, each record $\mathbf{x}_k$ in the dataset is randomly selected with a fixed probability p or not selected with probability $1 - p$. If the dataset $\mathcal{D}$ contains N records, the size of the Bernoulli sample is a random variable n assuming any value between 0 and N with probability

$$\mathcal{P}(n) = p^n (1 - p)^{N-n}. \tag{7.25}$$

The fact that the sample size is not fixed for Bernoulli sampling often has practical disadvantages, both in survey sampling applications and in the GSA sampling schemes considered here. Also, note that Bernoulli sampling assigns a constant inclusion probability p to all elements of $\mathcal{D}$, so it suffers from the same susceptibility to the "missing elephants problem"

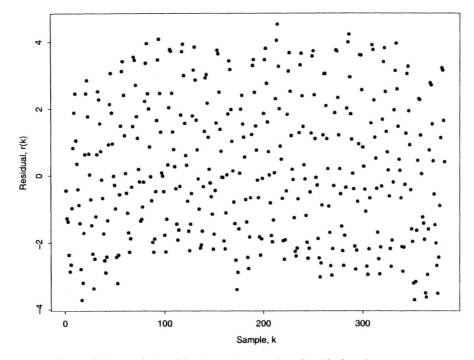

Figure 7.7. *Residuals of the Mauna Loa carbon dioxide data from a nonparametric trend model.*

that simple random sampling has in applications like that of Marron, Hernandez-Campos, and Smith (2002) discussed in Sec. 7.1.1.

Another general class of sampling schemes considered in the survey sampling literature is the class of *Poisson sampling schemes* (Särndal, Swensson, and Wretman, 1992, Sec. 3.5). These are random sampling schemes such as Bernoulli sampling that lead to random sample sizes, but they have the advantage of assigning distinct selection probabilities π_k to each record $\mathbf{x}_k \in \mathcal{D}$. Note that if we can somehow characterize the "important" samples $\mathbf{x}_k \in \mathcal{D}$, we can develop Poisson sampling schemes that are closely related to the notion of importance sampling discussed briefly in Sec. 7.1.1. One simple embodiment of this idea is *probability proportional-to-size sampling* (Särndal, Swensson, and Wretman, 1992, Sec. 3.6). There, the basic idea is that we are interested in a quantity Q_k that is difficult to characterize for data record $\mathbf{x}_k$, but we have some basis for believing that Q_k is strongly associated with some other auxiliary characteristic A_k that is much more readily determined. In such cases, it has been shown that making the sampling probability π_k proportional to A_k leads to improved (i.e., less variable) characterizations of Q_k. A specific case where size per se is a very relevant auxiliary variable is biology, where it has been shown that many important characteristics (e.g., skeletal mass, running speed, heart rate, and life span) are strongly associated with body mass (Calder, 1994).

A general strategy for systematic data partitioning is *stratified sampling*, in which the dataset $\mathcal{D}$ is partitioned into disjoint subsets called *strata* (Särndal, Swensson, and Wretman,

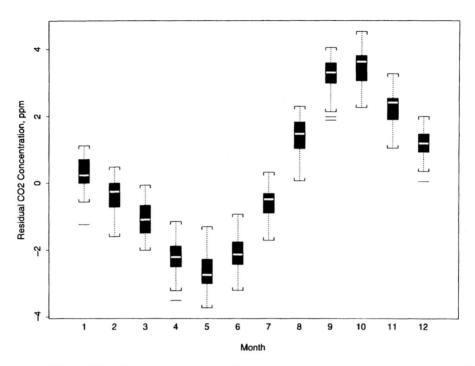

Figure 7.8. *Boxplot summary of the Mauna Loa carbon dioxide smooth trend residuals, organized by month.*

1992, Sec. 3.7), typically based on values for one or more auxiliary variables. In fact, it was noted in Chapter 6 that this idea can form the basis for defining scenarios and subscenarios. Within these scenarios or subscenarios, we can apply any sampling scheme that would be appropriate to the original dataset, a point discussed further below. Stratified sampling schemes are particularly useful in analyzing large datasets with many auxiliary variables that can serve as a basis for stratification. As a practical matter, such datasets often involve mixed data types, a point discussed further below.

To develop a practical stratified sampling scheme, Särndal, Swensson, and Wretman (1992, p. 101) note that the following three questions must be answered:

1. What variables are to be used for stratification?

2. How should the strata be demarcated?

3. How many strata should there be?

In fact, these questions are interrelated. For example, if a simple binary variable $\{z_k\}$ is chosen as a basis for stratification, there can only be two strata, demarcated by the two possible values for z_k. Usually, we have more flexibility than this, but it is typically true that questions 2 and 3 are answered together. One general strategy is data-driven, basing the stratification on a clustering of auxiliary variables, corresponding to the notion of

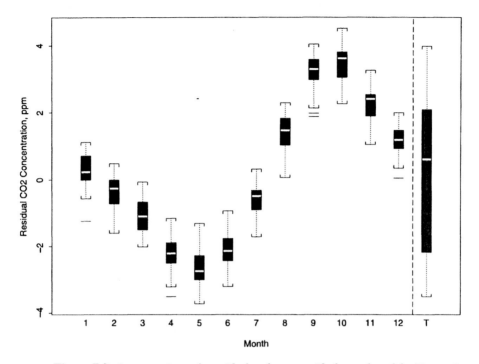

Figure 7.9. *A comparison of stratified and nonstratified samples of the Mauna Loa carbon dioxide trend residuals.*

cluster sampling discussed below. Conversely, it is important to note that stratified sampling represents an opportunity to bring prior knowledge, subject matter expertise, hunches, and conjectures into the analysis by selecting stratification variables on the basis of these factors.

The examples presented in Sec. 7.5 demonstrate the utility of stratified sampling, but it is also important to note that poorly chosen stratifications can lead to poor analysis results. This point is illustrated by Efron (1982, p. 63), who compares bootstrap, jackknife, and various other sampling schemes in assessing the variability of correlation estimates for a 14-point dataset. One of these schemes is based on sampling with replacement from seven strata, each consisting of two data observations. For this example, the bootstrap procedure discussed in Sec. 7.1.1 gave the best results, the jackknife procedure discussed in Sec. 7.1.3 gave poorer results, and the stratified sampling scheme just described gave very poor results. In the context of GSA sampling schemes, we can sometimes obtain an assessment of the quality of a stratification by comparing the boxplot summaries obtained for individual strata with those for comparable-sized unstratified random subsamples from $\mathcal{D}$. This idea is illustrated in Figure 7.9, which shows boxplots of each of the 32 monthly Mauna Loa carbon dioxide trend residuals summarized in Figure 7.8, along with the corresponding boxplot for a random sample of 32 residuals drawn from the complete dataset. This last boxplot is labelled "T" (for "total dataset") and separated from the 12 monthly boxplots by a vertical dashed line. It is clear from this figure that the stratification by month provides a useful partitioning of the data variability. In fact, one of the primary motivations for stratification in survey sampling is the reduction of within-stratum variability relative to between-strata or unstratified variability. To accomplish this objective, Thompson (2002, p. 22) offers the *stratification principle:* within each stratum, the individual units should be as similar as possible. In the context of the ideas presented in Chapter 6, this means the samples chosen within each stratum should be exchangeable.

As Särndal, Swensson, and Wretman (1992, p. 101) note, once a set of variables has been chosen, we are faced with the problem of partitioning these variables into strata. In cases like the binary example mentioned earlier, where only a small number of binary or nominal variables are involved, assuming only a few possible values, this question is not difficult to answer. Similarly, in the case of a single real-valued variable, it may be useful to base this partitioning on order statistics, as in the case of boxplots. For example, the lower quartile, the median, and the upper quartile provide a natural partitioning into four groups: bottom, lower-middle, upper-middle, and top. As the following three examples illustrate, extensions of these ideas to more complex settings can be made in many different ways.

The first idea is based on the notions of *DataSpheres* and *pyramids* described by Dasu and Johnson (2003, Sec. 3.4), which are in turn based on the concept of *data depth* discussed briefly in Chapter 4 (Sec. 4.4.4). The setting here assumes we seek a stratification based on p real-valued variables, for which observations $\{x_k^i\}$ are available for $k = 1, 2, \ldots, N$ and $i = 1, 2, \ldots, p$. As discussed in Chapter 6, the notion of data depth generalizes the ordering on which univariate boxplots are based, allowing us to partition p-variate data vectors such as $\mathbf{x}_k = [x_k^1, \ldots, x_k^p]$ into sets of increasing depth. In fact, these sets define DataSpheres, centered at the deepest point in the dataset. We could, for example, define three partitions by specifying two depth radii, $r_1 < r_2$, as follows: the inner sphere I, consisting of those points lying no farther than radius r_1 from the center; the middle region M, consisting of those points lying farther than r_1 but no farther than r_2 from the center; and the outer region O, consisting of those points lying farther than r_2 from the center. This stratification can be further refined by introducing *pyramids*, defined as follows. Let $\mathbf{x}^*$ denote the center of the dataset and define $\mathbf{z}_k = \mathbf{x}_k - \mathbf{x}^*$. Pyramids are defined by assigning each observation to one of the following $2p$ sets:

$$\mathbf{x}_k \in P_i^+ \text{ if } |z_i| > |z_j| \text{ for all } j \neq i \text{ and } y_i > 0,$$
$$\mathbf{x}_k \in P_i^- \text{ if } |z_i| > |z_j| \text{ for all } j \neq i \text{ and } y_i < 0. \qquad (7.26)$$

Since the DataSphere stratification is based on radial data depth, it does not give any orientation information that can distinguish the influence of the components of $\mathbf{x}_k$. This information is provided by the pyramids, which give the dataset an angular orientation. Taken together, an r-level radial DataSphere description and a pyramid decomposition lead to a stratification of the dataset into $2pr$ strata, where p is the number of real variables on which the stratification is based.

For the second example, suppose we want to stratify a dataset $\mathcal{D}$ based on a real-valued variable x and a nominal variable C designating one of L unordered categories. If it is reasonable to make approximate distributional assumptions about x, we can develop a stratification based on the ideas of ranking populations discussed by Gibbons, Olkin, and Sobel (1999). For example, if it is reasonable to assume, for $i = 1, 2, \ldots, L$, that $\{x_k^i\}$ is a sequence of N Gaussian random variables with distribution $N(\mu_i, \sigma^2)$, one possible stratification would be to order the L categories according to their mean values μ_i. Not surprisingly, this is accomplished by ordering the sample means $\{\bar{x}_N^i\}$, but Gibbons, Olkin, and Sobel (1999) present the results needed to select a sample size N large enough that the rankings computed for $\{\bar{x}_N^i\}$ agree with those for the underlying means μ_i with probability at least p. Related results are given for cases where we wish to rank the populations by variance or where we wish to partition the L categories into two groups: those with mean greater than that of some specified control population and those whose mean is less than that of a specified control population, again with specified probability p. Results are also given for selecting and ordering binomial, multinomial, gamma, and multivariate normal distributions; for details, refer to the book by Gibbons, Olkin, and Sobel (1999).

The third example is based on an idea described by Morgenthaler (2002). Assume we have three stratification variables: a nominal variable indexed by i and taking one of I possible values, a second nominal variable indexed by j and taking one of J possible values, and a real variable y. Further, suppose these variables are believed to be related so that it is reasonable to consider the ANOVA model (Sahai and Ageel, 2000, Chapter 4)

$$y_{ij} = m + a_i + b_j + c_{ij} + \epsilon_{ij}, \tag{7.27}$$

where m represents the overall mean y value, a_i describes the influence of the first nominal variable on y in the absence of interactions, b_j describes the corresponding influence of the second nominal variable, and c_{ij} describes their interaction. The term ϵ_{ij} represents the error in this model, which may be taken as zero-mean with no loss of generality. A useful simplification of (7.27) is *Tukey's one degree of freedom model for nonadditivity*, which assumes that $c_{ij} = ga_ib_j$, where g is an unknown parameter to be estimated from the available data along with m, $\{a_i\}$, and $\{b_j\}$. Morgenthaler (2002) describes the following stratification of this model. First, Tukey's nonadditivity model is fit to the original dataset to obtain estimates for m, $\{a_i\}$, $\{b_j\}$, and g. The nominal categories are then ordered by the estimated a_i and b_j values, analogous to the ranking of populations described in the previous example. Morgenthaler's motivation for this stratification is consistent with Thompson's stratification principle given above: by decomposing the original two-way table into a set of subtables and then refitting Tukey's two-way model to these subtables, he is able to obtain dramatically better fits to some of the subtables. The specific partitioning he considers is based on the median, upper and lower quartiles, and upper and lower octiles (i.e., $p = 0.125$ and $p = 0.875$), which subdivide both the a_i values and the b_j values into six segments. Overall, this leads to a partitioning of the original dataset into 36 strata. In the GSA applications considered here, this partitioning could provide the basis for a stratification of one large scenario into 36 subscenarios. Alternatively, we could obtain a coarser, 16-level stratification by applying the "bottom, lower-middle, upper-middle, top" partitioning defined above to the $\{a_i\}$ and $\{b_j\}$ parameters from Tukey's nonadditivity model.

The primary point of the three examples just discussed was to illustrate the enormous range of possibilities for stratification, particularly in the multivariate case. Once we have defined such a stratification scheme, there remains the question of how to draw samples from it. It should be clear that all of the ideas discussed previously (e.g., random sampling with or without replacement, probability proportional-to-size sampling, etc.) can be applied to each of the strata individually, as can the cluster-sampling ideas discussed at the end of this section. Before discussing cluster sampling, however, it is worth noting that there are sometimes advantages to stratifying the sampling process itself. This idea is particularly

useful in cases where computational considerations limit the size of the largest dataset we
can reasonably process directly. The fast MCD algorithm of Rousseeuw and Hubert (1999)
provides a nice illustration of this point. This algorithm is based on random subsamples
of the data and, for each subsample, it computes the p-dimensional mean and the $p \times p$
covariance matrix and uses these results to order the complete dataset on the basis of the
resulting Mahalanobis distances. For datasets with $N > 1,500$, Rousseeuw and Hubert
(1999) develop a two-stage sampling strategy: first, a random sample of size $n = 1,500$ is
drawn from the original dataset $\mathcal{D}$, and this dataset is *sequentially* partitioned into 5 disjoint
subsequences, each of length 300. The most complex computations are then performed on
these smallest datasets, the results are compressed and combined for the intermediate dataset
of size n, and these results are used as the basis for simpler final computations applied to
the original dataset $\mathcal{D}$. The key point here is that multilevel sampling schemes often have
significant practical advantages. For further discussion of related ideas, see survey sampling
books such as those by Särndal, Swensson, and Wretman (1992) and Thompson (2002).

The final idea considered here is that of *cluster sampling* (Särndal, Swensson, and
Wretman, 1992, Chapter 4), which is popular in survey sampling situations where simple
random sampling strategies such as those described in Sec. 7.1.1 would result in impracti-
cally expensive and time-consuming data collection efforts. Cluster sampling typically first
partitions the population of interest into *contiguous* clusters and then randomly selects a
collection of these clusters, which is then completely characterized. To see that this strategy
can lead to significant simplifications of the data collection effort, consider the difference
between conducting surveys at, say, 1,000 randomly selected houses spread over a large city,
and surveys of 20 respondents in each of 50 randomly selected neighborhoods. Here, the
motivation for using clustering ideas is somewhat different: it provides us with a data-driven
means for stratifying a large dataset. That is, if we can identify interesting "neighborhoods"
within a dataset; sample randomly, systematically, or completely within these neighborhoods; and compare the results between different neighborhoods, we may be able to identify either anomalous neighborhoods worthy of closer scrutiny or unexpected systematic
dependencies on the underlying characteristics used to define those neighborhoods.

Cluster analysis is a very broad subject, and it is not reasonable to attempt to survey
it here, but it is worthwhile to briefly discuss a few key ideas that may lead us to useful
stratification schemes for large datasets; for a more thorough introduction, refer to the books
by Gordon (1999) and Kaufman and Rousseeuw (1990) and the references cited there.
Broadly speaking, clustering procedures attempt to characterize the "local neighborhood
structure" within a given dataset, and they can be decomposed into a few general types.
Partition-based procedures operate as follows: given a dataset $\mathcal{D}$ and a specified number
of clusters k, the objective is to determine the "best" partitioning of the N objects in $\mathcal{D}$ into
k disjoint clusters C_i. In contrast, *hierarchical clustering procedures* construct a hierarchy
of partitionings, from a finest one in which each object defines its own cluster to a coarsest
one that corresponds to the original dataset $\mathcal{D}$. Since partition-based clustering leads to a
simple stratification of the dataset $\mathcal{D}$ while hierarchical methods lead to a more complex data
description, partition-based methods are probably most useful for stratifying a fixed dataset
$\mathcal{D}$. Alternatively, since cluster analysis remains an area of active research, other clustering
approaches have been developed, including *sequential clustering* (Hansen, Jaumard, and
Mladenovic, 1995), which is particularly interesting in the context of analyzing imperfect
data. There, clustering proceeds by first identifying and removing the "dominant" cluster,

then identifying and removing the next most prominent cluster, and so on until no further cluster structure is detected. Motivation for this idea comes from the fact that traditional partition-based clustering procedures must put *all* objects from the dataset $\mathcal{D}$ into one of the specified number of clusters, even if they are highly anomalous; sequential clustering attempts to avoid this difficulty. A closely related idea is the outlier detection procedure of Santos-Pereira and Pires (2002), which first applies a partition-based clustering procedure to the dataset $\mathcal{D}$ to obtain a specified number of clusters k. Then, a mean vector and covariance matrix are computed for each cluster and used as the basis for classifying every point in $\mathcal{D}$ as either an outlier or a nonoutlier with respect to each cluster. Points that are outliers with respect to all clusters are declared outliers and removed from the dataset, as are clusters below a certain minimum size. After all of these outliers have been removed, the procedure is repeated until no further outliers are detected.

Most clustering procedures are based on the notion of dissimilarity between objects. In particular, partition-based methods typically seek partitions such that the dissimilarity between objects within a cluster is small and the dissimilarity between objects in different clusters is large. This idea can be formulated in many different ways, leading to many different clustering algorithms (Hubert, Arabie, and Meulman, 2001) that can have profoundly different computational characteristics and can yield significantly different partitions for the same dataset. In addition, the performance for the same algorithm used with different dissimilarities can also yield substantially different results for the same dataset (Strehl, Ghosh, and Moody, 2000). Despite these dependencies, the notion of classifying data points into near or distant neighbors is an extremely useful one in many different applications, including nonparametric smoothing with k-nearest neighbor (kNN) smoothers (Härdle, 1990) and statistical file matching (Rässler, 2002).

Unfortunately, as with Bernoulli and Poisson random sampling schemes, we generally have no direct control over the *size* of the clusters we obtain using these clustering procedures. As a result, the clusters obtained from a given dataset are sometimes quite severely imbalanced, although there has been some recent work in the area of *balanced clustering*, which attempts to obtain a partitioning into clusters of approximately the same size (Zhong and Ghosh, 2003). In cases of large datasets, even with significant imbalance there may still be a large number of members of the underrepresented classes, but this imbalance is known to cause computational difficulties in a variety of settings (Japkowicz and Stephen, 2002), including cluster analysis (Pearson, Gonye, and Schwaber, 2003). Two popular solutions to this problem in the machine-learning community are *undersampling*, in which the smaller class is retained completely and a comparable-sized subset of the larger class is drawn by random sampling without replacement, and *oversampling*, in which the smaller class is sampled with replacement to make it comparable in size with the larger class. In the specific context of the C4.5 decision tree learning procedure, Drummond and Holte (2003) have shown that the undersampling strategy is to be preferred. The key point here is that these imbalance issues are extremely important in the context of stratified sampling based on clustering results.

7.2   Random selection examples

As noted in Sec. 7.1.1, random subset selection is most suitable for static data characterizations such as simple descriptive statistics (e.g., location and scale estimates) or regression models. If the individual observations in the dataset may be regarded as exchangeable, the range of variation seen across a collection of random subsets can give a useful indication of the natural range of variation of the data characterization of interest. The following two subsections illustrate the utility of this idea, first for two collections of simulation-based datasets and then for a collection of four industrial pressure measurement datasets. This idea is further illustrated in Sec. 7.3.1 in connection with the storage tank dataset introduced in Chapter 2.

7.2.1   Variability of kurtosis estimates

The following example is closely related to the one presented in Chapter 1 to illustrate the concept of a boxplot. There, two sets of $M = 100$ independent random sequences were generated, one with a uniform distribution and one with a Gaussian distribution, and kurtosis estimates were computed from each sequence. Side-by-side boxplots then provided a useful comparison of both the median kurtosis estimate and the range of variation seen around this median value. In the example considered here, a wider range of distributions is considered, but in each case it is assumed that we have only a *single* dataset for each distribution and the random subsampling ideas introduced in Sec. 7.1.1 are applied to generate $r = 200$ subsets of fixed size $M = 100$. Boxplot comparisons of the results computed from these subsamples then give analogous assessments of the bias and variability of these estimates over the range of distributions considered.

The term *platykurtic* refers to distributions with kurtosis $\kappa < 0$, traditionally interpreted as evidence for "light tails." The *beta distributions* (Johnson, Kotz, and Balakrishnan, 1995, Chapter 25) are a convenient family of platykurtic distributions defined by the density

$$p(x) = \frac{x^{p-1}(1-x)^{q-1}}{B(a,b)}, \quad 0 \le x \le 1. \tag{7.28}$$

Here, p and q are positive *shape parameters* and $B(a,b)$ is a normalization constant that depends on these parameters. If $p = q$, the beta distribution is symmetric, with mean $1/2$, skewness zero, and variance and kurtosis given by

$$\sigma^2 = \frac{1}{4(2p+1)}, \quad \kappa = -\frac{6}{2p+3}. \tag{7.29}$$

As $p \to 0$, the symmetric beta distribution approaches a discrete limiting distribution that takes the value zero or one with equal probability (i.e., $\mathcal{P}\{x = 0\} = \mathcal{P}\{x = 1\} = 1/2$), and the kurtosis approaches $\kappa = -2$, the minimum possible kurtosis value, achievable only for this distribution (Rohatgi and Szekely, 1989). Conversely, as $p \to \infty$, the symmetric beta distribution approaches a degenerate (i.e., zero-variance) Gaussian limit, with $\kappa = 0$. For all finite p, the symmetric beta distribution is platykurtic with $-2 < \kappa < 0$.

Figure 7.10 shows the results obtained by applying the random sampling strategy discussed in Sec. 7.1.1 to four different platykurtic datasets, together with a Gaussian dataset for comparison. Specifically, a single dataset of $N = 1,000$ samples was generated for each distribution, and 200 random subsets, each of size $M = 100$, were drawn from each of these original datasets. The first four datasets exhibit symmetric beta distributions with $p = q = 1/2$, 1, 2, and 4, and the fifth exhibits a zero-mean, unit-variance Gaussian

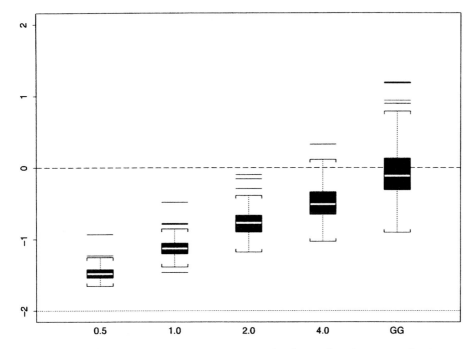

Figure 7.10. *Kurtosis estimates for four platykurtic distributions and a Gaussian reference distribution.*

distribution. Boxplot summaries of the standard moment-based kurtosis estimator discussed in Chapter 1 are compared in Figure 7.10. Two trends are clearly evident: first, the median kurtosis value increases (as it should) with increasing shape parameter p, and, second, the variability of these estimates also increases with increasing p. This point is further emphasized in Table 7.1, which presents the true kurtosis value κ for each case, the median $\hat{\kappa}^\dagger$ of the estimated kurtosis values, and the spread of these estimates (specifically, the unscaled IQD that describes the width of the central box in the boxplots). In addition, the results in this table also include the median bias $\beta = \hat{\kappa}^\dagger - \kappa$, which exhibits the following behavior. For negative kurtosis values, the bias tends to be small and positive, apparently exhibiting a maximum between $p = q = 2$ and $p = q = 4$. For the Gaussian case, the median kurtosis estimate is slightly negative, and this tendency to underestimate the kurtosis becomes more pronounced with increasing κ, a point discussed further below.

Table 7.1 also presents these same results for four examples of the *leptokurtic* (or "heavy tailed") Student's t-distribution (Johnson, Kotz, and Balakrishnan, 1995, Chapter 28), defined by the probability density function

$$p(x) = K(\nu)\left[1 + \frac{x^2}{\nu}\right]^{-(\nu+1)/2}. \tag{7.30}$$

Here, ν is a positive number called the *degrees of freedom*, typically taken as a positive integer, and $K(\nu)$ is a normalization constant that depends on ν. This distribution is zero-

Case	Distribution	κ	Median Estimate	Bias	Spread
1	Beta, $p = q = 0.5$	-1.50	-1.48	0.02	0.12
2	Beta, $p = q = 1.0$	-1.20	-1.13	0.07	0.15
3	Beta, $p = q = 2.0$	-0.86	-0.77	0.09	0.23
4	Beta, $p = q = 4.0$	-0.55	-0.51	0.04	0.31
5	Gaussian	0.00	-0.12	-0.12	0.44
6	Student's t_{24}	0.30	0.04	-0.26	0.61
7	Student's t_{12}	0.75	0.22	-0.53	0.85
8	Student's t_6	3.00	1.26	-1.74	2.30
9	Student's t_3	∞	4.48	—	3.53

Table 7.1. *Comparison of exact and estimated kurtosis values, along with their spread (unscaled IQD).*

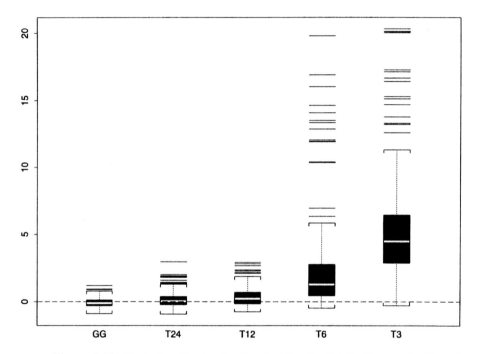

Figure 7.11. *Kurtosis estimates for four leptokurtic distributions and a Gaussian reference distribution.*

mean and symmetric for all $\nu > 0$, with standard deviation and kurtosis given by

$$\sigma = \frac{\nu}{\nu - 2} \text{ for } \nu > 2, \quad \kappa = \frac{6}{\nu - 4} \text{ for } \nu > 4. \tag{7.31}$$

Like the symmetric beta distribution, the Student's t-distribution approaches a Gaussian limit as $\nu \to \infty$.

Figure 7.11 compares the kurtosis estimates $\hat{\kappa}$ obtained for 200 random subsets of size $M = 100$ from a sequence of $N = 1,000$ random values drawn from a Gaussian distribution and from Student's t-distributions with $\nu = 24, 12, 6,$ and 3 degrees of freedom. Note that the kurtosis is infinite for this last example ($\nu = 3$), but the estimate remains well-defined since the individual samples drawn from this distribution are finite in number and in value. It is clear both from this figure and from the numerical results presented in Table 7.1 that the trends seen with the symmetric beta distribution also hold for the Student's t-distribution: both the median kurtosis estimate $\hat{\kappa}^\dagger$ and the variability of these estimates increase as the true kurtosis κ increases. In addition, the bias becomes more negative with increasing κ. This behavior is not surprising since the true kurtosis becomes infinite as $\nu \to 4$, while $\hat{\kappa}$ remains finite, as noted above.

The two main points of this example are the following. First, Figures 7.10 and 7.11 both clearly illustrate that the random sampling scheme described in Sec. 7.1.1 can provide a useful assessment of the natural variability of a data characterization, even when only a single dataset is available for analysis. As a practical matter, it is important for this dataset to be large enough that the individual random samples are not too highly correlated, as discussed in Sec. 7.1.2. This condition is satisfied here since the individual samples contain 10% of the total dataset, leading to a correlation of $\rho \simeq 0.1$ between distinct random samples. Second, random sampling schemes can easily give useful variability assessments even in cases where the corresponding analytical results would be very difficult to obtain. In particular, note that the simplest variability estimate for the estimated kurtosis values is the variance of the estimated kurtosis, a quantity that depends on the *eighth moments* of the underlying distribution. Even for relatively simple distributions such as the symmetric beta family, characterizations involving eighth moments are extremely complicated to work out.

7.2.2 The industrial pressure datasets

The following example is somewhat similar to the previous one, but is based on four real industrial pressure measurement datasets. The first two of these data sequences are shown in the upper two plots in Figure 7.12, with the normal Q-Q plots introduced in Chapter 6 shown beneath each of the data sequences. The general appearance of the left-hand Q-Q plot suggests that, aside from a clearly visible single isolated outlier, a Gaussian approximation to the data distribution may not be too bad. There is, however, some slight evidence of distributional asymmetry in the way the lower tail lies above the reference line in this Q-Q plot. This behavior is much more pronounced in the second pressure data sequence, shown in the upper right plot in Figure 7.12. In particular, the normal Q-Q plot for this second data sequence shows strong evidence for distributional asymmetry, with both the upper and lower tails showing systematic curvature above the reference line.

The corresponding plots for two more pressure sequences are shown in Figure 7.13. Specifically, the upper two plots show the original data sequences, with the corresponding normal Q-Q plots below. Here, the situation appears much more complicated, with the normal Q-Q plots each exhibiting the pronounced "knee" that is often associated with bimodal distributions.

Given the range of evidence for distributional asymmetry seen in the normal Q-Q plots for these four data sequences (very weak for Sequence 1, strong for Sequence 2, and highly ambiguous for Sequences 3 and 4), it is interesting to examine the standard–moment-based skewness estimates for these data sequences. These data sequences are all of the same length ($N = 1,024$), and the resulting skewness estimates are $\hat{\gamma}_1 = 0.26$, $\hat{\gamma}_2 = 1.56$, $\hat{\gamma}_3 = 1.36$, and $\hat{\gamma}_4 = 2.16$. While these results certainly support the suggestions inferred from the

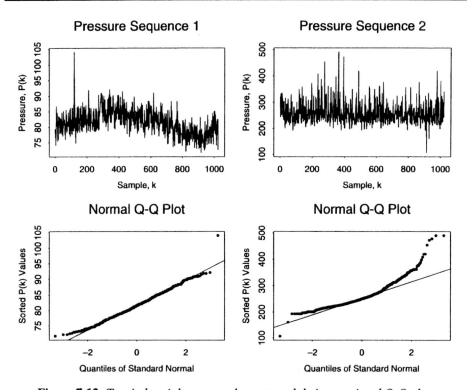

Figure 7.12. *Two industrial pressure datasets and their associated Q-Q plots.*

normal Q-Q plots for Sequences 1 and 2, they also suggest that the other two sequences have distributions that are either almost as asymmetric as Sequence 2 (specifically, Sequence 3) or even more strongly asymmetric (Sequence 4). To gain further insight into these results, it is instructive to examine their variability using the random sampling scheme discussed in Sec. 7.1.1.

Figure 7.14 shows boxplot summaries of the moment-based skewness estimates $\hat{\gamma}$ computed from 200 random subsets of size $M = 100$ taken from each of these four data sequences. Aside from some outlying large skewness values, Sequence 1 generally yields a small skewness estimate, consistent with the nearly linear normal Q-Q plot seen in Figure 7.12. These outlying skewness estimates correspond to the anomalously large values obtained for $\hat{\gamma}$ from subsets that include the single outlier in Sequence 1, clearly visible in the upper left plot in Figure 7.12. Note that since each randomly selected subsequence contains approximately 10% of the data values from the original sequence, the probability of including this outlier in any given subsequence is approximately 10%. Interestingly, note that the results for Sequence 2 are the least consistent of the four cases considered here, based on either the IQDs or the total ranges of variation. Specifically, the IQDs for these skewness estimates are 0.25 for Sequence 1, 0.83 for Sequence 2, 0.28 for Sequence 3, and 0.38 for Sequence 4. The results for Sequence 3 appear about as consistent as those for Sequence 1, with a median skewness estimate that is virtually identical to that for Sequence 2 (i.e., $\hat{\gamma}_2 = 1.38$ versus $\hat{\gamma}_3 = 1.32$). Finally, the results for Sequence 4 are clearly more variable than those for Sequences 1 and 3, but far less variable than those for Sequence 2. Overall,

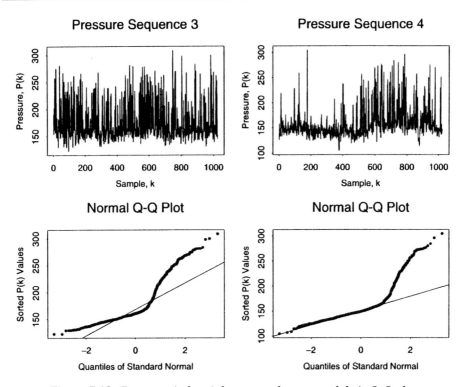

Figure 7.13. *Two more industrial pressure datasets and their Q-Q plots.*

the median results are in reasonably good agreement with the skewness values estimated from the complete dataset, but the differences seen in the normal Q-Q plots for these data sequences and those seen in the variability of the skewness estimates motivate the further examination of these datasets presented in Sec. 7.5.1.

7.3   Subset deletion examples

Sampling schemes based on subset deletion were discussed in Sec. 7.1.3, and the following subsections present two illustrations of this idea, both based on the storage tank dataset introduced in Chapter 2 to illustrate the concept of common-mode outliers. The first of these examples (Sec. 7.3.1) compares the results obtained for the same set of three descriptors (specifically, three different scale estimators) under two different sampling schemes: the random subset selection strategy discussed and illustrated in Secs. 7.1.1 and 7.2 and the leave-one-out deletion strategy discussed in Sec. 7.1.3. The second example applies this deletion strategy to the problem that originally motivated the collection of the storage tank dataset: dynamic characterization using traditional auto- and cross-correlation estimators.

7.3.1   The storage tank dataset

Two short sequences of physical property measurements were discussed in Chapter 2, first to illustrate the idea of time-series outliers and then to illustrate the phenomenon of common-

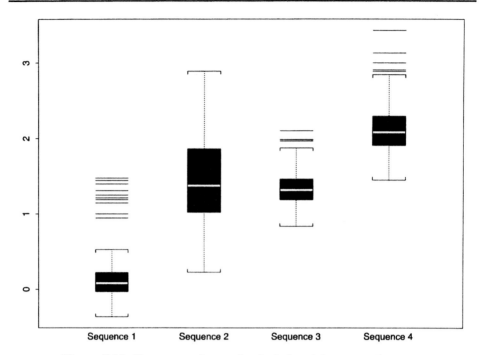

Figure 7.14. *Skewness estimates for the industrial pressure datasets.*

mode outliers. Figure 7.15 shows longer versions of these two data sequences, which
correspond to the same physical property measurements made at the inlet (left-hand plot)
and outlet (right-hand plot) of an intermediate product storage tank that is part of a larger
industrial manufacturing process. The gross common-mode outliers in this dataset discussed
in Chapter 2 are clearly evident in this plot at $k \sim 290$, and it is also clear that the median
physical property values are different at the inlet and outlet of the storage tank, but the range
of variation about these median values appears roughly the same in both cases. This last
observation motivates the GSA comparisons considered here based on the same three scale
estimates but using two different sampling schemes: the random sampling scheme discussed
in Secs. 7.1.1 and 7.2 and the leave-one-out deletion strategy discussed in Sec. 7.1.3.

Figure 7.16 shows the results obtained using the random subset-sampling scheme.
Specifically, the three boxplots to the left of the vertical dashed line compare the usual
standard deviation estimator $\hat{\sigma}$ (denoted STD in Figure 7.16), the MAD scale estimate
introduced in Chapter 1, and the scaled IQD estimator also introduced in Chapter 1 for the
inlet dataset shown in the left-hand plot in Figure 7.15. The three boxplots to the right of the
vertical dashed line in Figure 7.16 present the corresponding results for the outlet dataset
shown in the right-hand plot in Figure 7.15. In all cases, these boxplots summarize results
computed from 200 random subsets, each of size $M = 100$. The outlier-sensitivity of the
standard deviation estimator is clear from these results, since the isolated outlier in each
of these datasets is responsible for the cluster of extreme outliers at $\hat{\sigma} \sim 20$ for the inlet
dataset and the cluster of outliers at $\hat{\sigma} \sim 25$ for the outlet dataset. As with the first pressure
data sequence discussed in Sec. 7.2.2, the probability is approximately 10% of including the

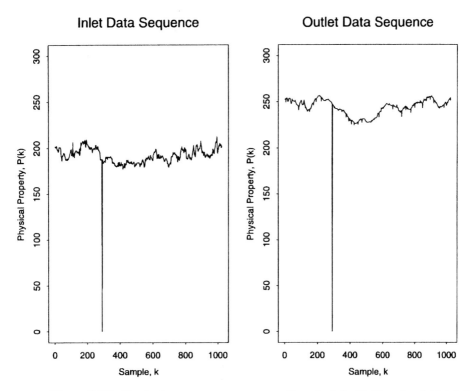

Figure 7.15. *Physical property measurements from the inlet (left) and outlet (right) of an industrial process storage tank.*

single outlier from the original dataset in the random subsample from which $\hat{\sigma}$ is computed in Figure 7.16. Due to the extreme magnitude of the outlier in each of these original datasets, its presence dominates the estimated standard deviation for any subsample in which it is included. In contrast, both the MAD and IQD scale estimates are essentially immune from the effects of this outlier, as reflected in the much narrower range of variation seen for these results relative to that for $\hat{\sigma}$. Also, note that both the median value and the interquartile spreads are essentially identical for the MAD and IQD scale estimates for both the inlet and outlet datasets. In contrast, the interquartile range is smaller for $\hat{\sigma}$ for both datasets, and the median scale estimates are slightly different. Further, the fact that most $\hat{\sigma}$ values are smaller than the MAD and IQD values for the inlet dataset but slightly larger than these values for the outlet dataset suggests possible distributional differences between these datasets.

The results shown in Figure 7.17 compare the same three scale estimates as in Figure 7.16, but under a different sampling scheme. Specifically, the boxplots in Figure 7.17 summarize the scale estimates obtained as each individual data point is omitted from the original dataset. As before, the standard deviation $\hat{\sigma}$, MAD scale estimate, and normalized IQD scale estimate are compared, and the results for the inlet dataset are shown to the left of the vertical dashed line while those for the outlet dataset are shown to the right of this line. As in Figure 7.16, the MAD and IQD scale estimates are completely insensitive to the presence of the extreme outlier in the original dataset. In particular, note the very small range of

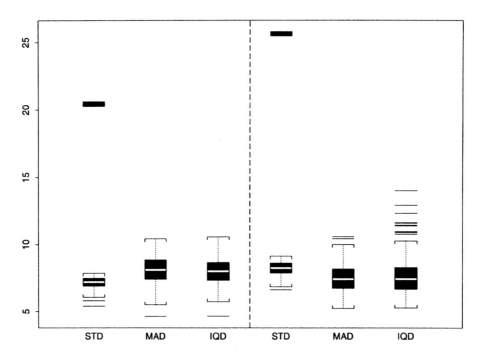

Figure 7.16. *Scale estimate comparison for the storage tank datasets.*

variation seen for these estimates and the lack of any outliers, independent of which point is deleted from the dataset. In contrast, the standard deviation estimate shows a dramatic decrease when the outlier is omitted from the original dataset, appearing as a clear lower outlier in the standard deviation estimates summarized in Figure 7.17.

The main point of this example was to illustrate the difference in the general behavior of GSA comparisons under two different sampling schemes. Both results highlight the significant difference in outlier-sensitivity of the $\hat{\sigma}$, MAD, and IQD scale estimates. The details of the resulting boxplots are quite different, however: deletion of the outlier from the inlet dataset reduces $\hat{\sigma}$ from approximately 9 to approximately 7, while including this outlier in a random subset increases $\hat{\sigma}$ from approximately 7 to approximately 20. In addition, the deletion-based results presented in Figure 7.17 provide much stronger evidence that $\hat{\sigma}$ is highly sensitive to the presence or absence of the gross outlier in these two datasets, while the MAD and IQD scale estimates essentially ignore this data point completely. Conversely, in more complicated settings where the omission of a specified subset does not fully remove the data anomaly, the random subset selection strategy may be more effective. Alternatively, systematic (i.e., nonrandom) partitioning strategies may be still more effective, an idea examined further in Sec. 7.5.1.

7.3.2 Dynamic correlation analysis

The original motivation for collecting the storage tank datasets shown in Figure 7.15 was to characterize the performance of the storage tank relative to its design objectives. These

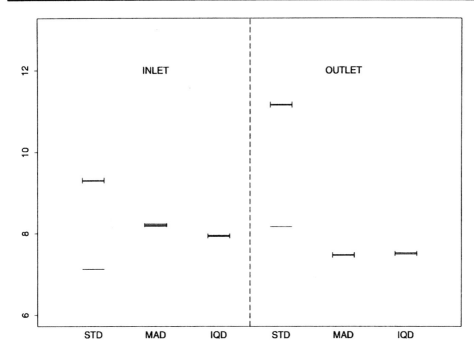

Figure 7.17. *Single deletion-based scale estimate comparison for the storage tank datasets.*

objectives were that material would enter the tank from an upstream manufacturing step and spend an average of $d \sim 16$ hours in the tank before exiting to a downstream physical processing step. During the time spent in the tank, significant mixing was expected to occur so that the product sent to the downstream processing facility would be more homogeneous than that coming from the upstream manufacturing step. The datasets shown in Figure 7.15 were collected to assess the average time the material actually spent in the storage tank.

The cross-correlation function is a generalization of the autocorrelation function introduced in Chapter 1 and it provides a basis for this assessment. Unfortunately, there are some important and confusing differences in how these terms are defined between the engineering and statistics literatures. For example, the definition of the autocorrelation function given in Chapter 1 corresponds to that commonly adopted in the engineering literature (see, for example, Papoulis (1965, p. 282)), while Brockwell and Davis (1991, p. 12) define the autocorrelation function as the correlation coefficient between x_k and x_{k+m}, which is

$$\rho_{xx}(m) = \frac{E\{(x_k - \mu_x)(x_{k+m} - \mu_x)\}}{\sigma_x^2}, \tag{7.32}$$

where $\mu_x = E\{x_k\}$ and $\sigma_x = \text{var}\{x_k\}$. The very common and often fairly reasonable assumption of *stationarity* has been made here, meaning that μ_x, σ_x, and $\rho_{xx}(m)$ do not depend on the time index k. An advantage of the autocorrelation function definition given in (7.32)—which is adopted in the following discussion—is that it is normalized: since $\rho_{xx}(m)$ represents the correlation coefficient between the original data sequence $\{x_k\}$ and the time-shifted data sequence $\{x_{k+m}\}$, it follows that $|\rho_{xx}(m)| \leq 1$ for all m and all stationary data sequences $\{x_k\}$. Further, note that $\rho_{xx}(0) = 1$ for all stationary data sequences. The cross-correlation function is defined analogously as

$$\rho_{xy}(m) = \frac{E\{(x_k - \mu_x)(y_{k+m} - \mu_y)\}}{\sigma_x \sigma_y}, \tag{7.33}$$

which represents the correlation coefficient between the data sequences $\{x_k\}$ and $\{y_{k+m}\}$. Hence, it also follows that $|\rho_{xy}(m)| \leq 1$ for all m and all jointly stationary data sequences $\{x_k\}$ and $\{y_k\}$, although it is *not* generally true that $\rho_{xy}(0) = 1$.

To see the relevance of these quantities to the storage tank data characterization problem, let x_k denote the measurement of a physical property P made at the tank inlet at time k, and let y_k denote the measurement of the *same* physical property made at the tank outlet at time k. The simplest model of the behavior of the storage tank is the *plug flow model*, which postulates that the material emerging from the tank is exactly the same as the material that went into the tank d time units earlier, i.e., $y_k = x_{k-d}$. A slightly more realistic model allows for the possibility of measurement noise, giving the noisy plug flow model

$$y_k = x_{k-d} + e_k, \tag{7.34}$$

where $\{e_k\}$ is an i.i.d. (or "white noise") sequence, statistically independent from $\{x_k\}$. For this model, note that

$$\mu_y = E\{y_k\} = E\{x_{k-d} + e_k\} = \mu_x \tag{7.35}$$

since $E\{e_k\} = 0$, and

$$\sigma_y^2 = \sigma_x^2 + \sigma_e^2 \tag{7.36}$$

since the sequences $\{x_k\}$ and $\{e_k\}$ are statistically independent. Substituting these results into (7.33) gives

$$\begin{aligned}
\rho_{xy}(m) &= \frac{E\{(x_k - \mu_x)(x_{k-d+m} + e_k - \mu_x)\}}{\sigma_x \sqrt{\sigma_x^2 + \sigma_e^2}} \\
&= \frac{E\{(x_k - \mu_x)(x_{k+m-d} - \mu_x)\}}{\sigma_x^2 \sqrt{1 + \sigma_e^2/\sigma_x^2}} \\
&= \frac{\rho_{xx}(m - d)}{\sqrt{1 + \sigma_e^2/\sigma_x^2}}.
\end{aligned} \tag{7.37}$$

The utility of this result lies in the observation that the maximum possible value of $\rho_{xy}(m)$ is $(1 + \sigma_e^2/\sigma_x^2)^{-1/2}$, which occurs when $m = d$. Hence, we can estimate $\rho_{xy}(m)$ as

$$\hat{\rho}_{xy}(m) = \frac{\sum_{k=1}^{N} (\tilde{x}_k - \bar{x})(\tilde{y}_k - \bar{y})}{\left[\sum_{k=1}^{N} (\tilde{x}_k - \bar{x})^2 \sum_{k=1}^{N} (\tilde{y}_k - \bar{y})^2\right]^{1/2}} \tag{7.38}$$

and look for the value of m that maximizes $\hat{\rho}_{xy}(m)$, which should occur at the average residence time of the material in the storage tank.

The left-hand plot in Figure 7.18 shows two plots of $\hat{\rho}_{xy}(m)$ for $0 \leq m \leq 43$: one (open circles) computed from the raw data sequences shown in Figure 7.15 and the other

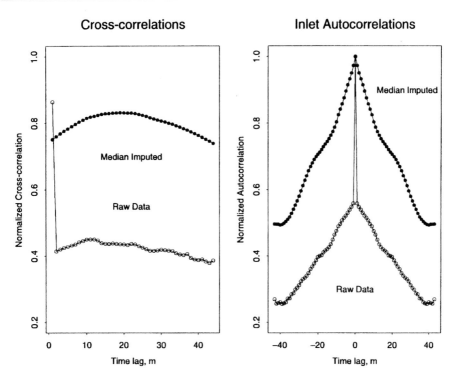

Figure 7.18. *Cross-correlations (left-hand plot) and inlet autocorrelations (right-hand plot) estimated from the raw and median-imputed storage tank dataset.*

(solid circles) computed from the modified dataset obtained by replacing the gross outliers in the original dataset with the median values of these data sequences. The dramatic difference in the appearance of these plots illustrates the consequences of these outliers. In particular, the result obtained from the median-imputed dataset exhibits a broad maximum at $k \sim 19$, reasonably consistent with the expectation that the material should spend about 16 hours in the storage tank. Further, the breadth of this maximum is consistent with the occurrence of significant mixing in the tank, a point discussed further below. In contrast, the results from the raw data exhibit a very pronounced, narrow maximum at $k = 0$. Unfortunately, this result also has a clear physical interpretation: material is spending very little time in the storage tank and, as a consequence, very little mixing is occurring, consistent with the extremely narrow peak seen in $\hat{\rho}_{xy}(m)$. This situation can arise in practice due to severe *fouling*, corresponding to the buildup of solid material in the tank, greatly reducing its effective volume. Acceptance of this hypothesis could lead to an unnecessary process shutdown to clean out the tank; as emphasized by English et al. (1998), this can be an extremely costly proposition.

The right-hand plot in Figure 7.18 shows the autocorrelation estimates $\hat{\rho}_{xx}(m)$ for the inlet data sequence $\{x_k\}$ plotted for $-43 \leq m \leq 43$ to emphasize the symmetry of the autocorrelation function (i.e., $\rho_{xx}(-m) = \rho_{xx}(m)$ for all m) and the fact that the maximum in $\rho_{xx}(m)$ is much more pronounced than the broad maximum seen in the cross-correlation estimates $\rho_{xy}(m)$. The fact that $\hat{\rho}_{xx}(m)$ exhibits a sharper maximum at $m = 0$ than $\hat{\rho}_{xy}(m)$ does at $m = d$ reflects the mixing that is occurring in the storage tank. Again, it is important

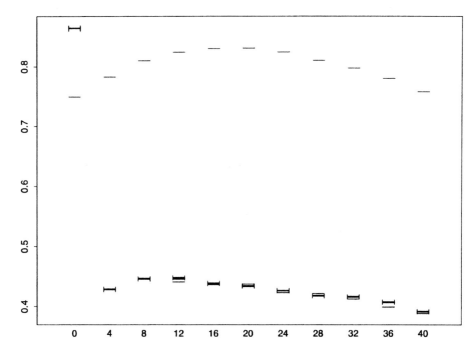

Figure 7.19. *Single deletion results for the storage tank cross-correlations.*

to use the median-imputed data to avoid serious outlier-induced distortions, as may be seen by comparing the estimates computed from the raw data (open circles) with those computed from the median-imputed data (solid circles).

Figure 7.19 shows the results obtained for a GSA comparison based on the leave-one-out sampling scheme described in Sec. 7.1.3 applied to the cross-correlation estimates $\hat{\rho}_{xy}(m)$. The boxplots summarize the cross-correlations $\hat{\rho}_{xy}(m)$ estimated for $m = 4J$, where $J = 0, 1, 2, \ldots, 10$. As in the scale characterization of the storage tank dataset presented in Sec. 7.3.1, these boxplots show very narrow ranges of variation except for a single outlying result that corresponds to the omission of the common-mode outlier pair from the inlet and outlet datasets. Note that these outlying responses give an excellent approximation to the cross-correlation function computed from the median-imputed data values shown in the left-hand plot in Figure 7.18, while the boxplots correspond quite well to the results computed from the raw data. The same basic description also applies to Figure 7.20, which shows the GSA comparisons for the estimated inlet autocorrelations. Since $\rho_{xx}(0) = 1$ for all data sequences $\{x_k\}$, deletion has no effect for this case, but for $m \neq 0$, a single outlier is evident in the leave-one-out deletion results, corresponding to the omission of the gross outlier from the inlet data sequence.

7.4   Comparison-based examples

The subset deletion strategy discussed in Secs. 7.1.3 and 7.3 makes what should be "small" changes in a dataset and looks for unusually large changes in the results, which are often indicative of the presence of data anomalies. The following discussion examines the com-

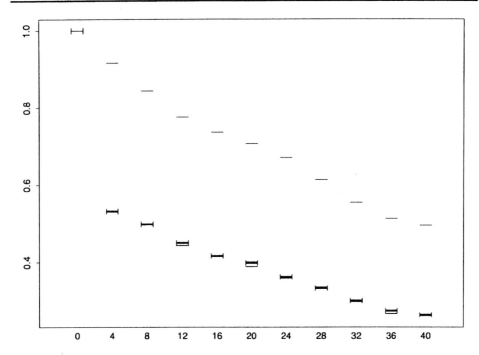

Figure 7.20. *Single deletion results for the inlet autocorrelations.*

parison strategy introduced in Sec. 7.1.4, which is based on the opposite notion: we make what should be "large" changes in the dataset and look for unusually small changes in the analysis results. As noted in Sec. 7.1.4, this sampling scheme is most appropriate when the models underlying the data analysis are highly structured. This point is illustrated in Sec. 7.4.1, which applies a comparison-based sampling scheme to the problem discussed in Sec. 7.3.2. Sec. 7.4.2 then extends this analysis to an outlier-resistant approach based on the rank correlations introduced in Chapter 2.

7.4.1 Correlation-destroying permutations

In the engineering and physics literature, a *white noise sequence* $\{x_k\}$ is a sequence of i.i.d. random variables, typically assumed to have zero mean and finite variance σ^2. It follows that the autocorrelation function $\rho_{xx}(m)$ for a white noise sequence is $\rho_{xx}(0) = 1$ and $\rho_{xx}(m) = 0$ for all $m \neq 0$. White noise sequences are highly irregular, reflecting the fact that x_k and x_{k+m} are statistically independent. In contrast, a *dependent* or *correlated* sequence $\{x_k\}$ is one for which $\rho_{xx}(m) \neq 0$ for one or more positive integers m. Intuitively, dependence generally implies that neighboring elements of the data sequence are somehow related, exhibiting a more predictable variation with k than white noise sequences do. If we randomly reorder a dependent data sequence, we destroy this relationship, an observation that provides the basis for the example considered here. Specifically, if $\{z_k\}$ is obtained by randomly reordering the dependent sequence $\{x_k\}$, we should observe $\rho_{xx}(m) \neq 0$ but $\rho_{zz}(m) \simeq 0$. Hence, the GSA comparison strategy compares the $\hat{\rho}_{xx}(m)$ estimates obtained

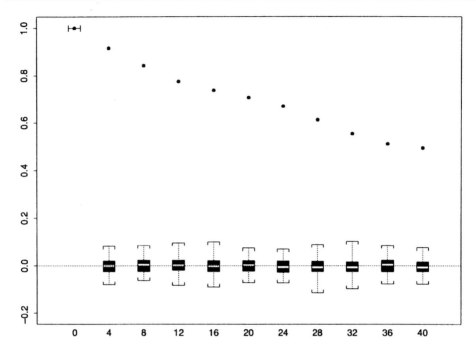

Figure 7.21. *Estimated autocorrelations for median-imputed storage tank inlet data (solid circles), with boxplot summaries of 200 random permutations.*

from the original data sequence with the results $\hat{\rho}_{zz}(m)$ obtained for a set of M independent random permutations of $\{x_k\}$. Large differences between the original and the randomly reordered results provide evidence in support of a nonzero correlation estimate $\hat{\rho}_{xx}(m)$, while small differences suggest that the true autocorrelations may be zero.

This idea is illustrated in Figure 7.21, which shows the results obtained for 200 random permutations of the median-imputed storage tank inlet dataset discussed in Secs. 7.3.1 and 7.3.2. Specifically, the solid circles in the plot represent the normalized autocorrelation estimates $\hat{\rho}_{xx}(m)$ computed from the median-imputed data sequence, while the boxplots summarize the results obtained from 200 independent randomizations of this sequence. The horizontal dashed line at $\rho_{xx}(m) = 0$ in this figure approximately coincides with the medians of all of these permutation values for $m > 0$. Further, the total range of all of these permutation values is approximately the same and is consistently small, on the order of ± 0.1. In contrast, the values of $\rho_{xx}(m)$ computed from the median-imputed data sequence all lie well outside the range of these permutations for all of the positive m values considered here. Based on these permutation values alone, we can conclude that the probability of observing the computed $\hat{\rho}_{xx}(m)$ values due to random chance is less than 1%. Further, the z-scores discussed in Sec. 7.1.4 associated with these $\hat{\rho}_{xx}(m)$ values are all very large (between $z \simeq 16$ and $z \simeq 33$), greatly strengthening the conclusion that significant correlations are present in this data sequence.

Figure 7.22 presents the corresponding results computed from the raw storage tank inlet data shown in the left-hand plot in Figure 7.15, rather than the median-imputed values. Although the normalized autocorrelation estimates $\hat{\rho}_{xx}(m)$ for $m > 0$ shown here are signifi-

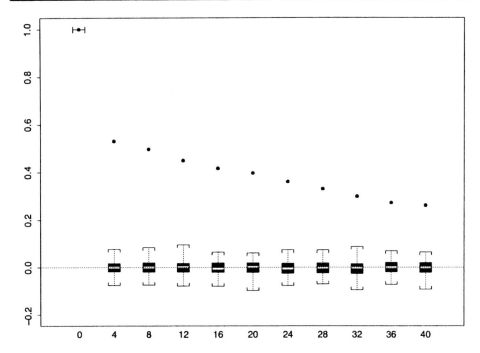

Figure 7.22. *Estimated autocorrelations for raw storage tank inlet data (solid circles), with boxplot summaries of* 200 *random permutations.*

cantly smaller in magnitude than those computed from the median-imputed data values, these correlations are still quite significant relative to the permutation values, which exhibit essentially the same range as before. The key point here is that, unlike the deletion-based sampling schemes discussed in Sec. 7.3.2, which could detect the presence of the gross outliers in the dataset, the comparison-based strategy described here cannot detect this data anomaly.

The permutation-based comparison strategy for assessing the significance of autocorrelation estimates extends directly to the case of cross-correlations. That is, since $\rho_{xy}(m)$ measures the degree of association between the sequences $\{x_k\}$ and $\{y_{k+m}\}$, applying random permutations to one or both of these sequences destroys this association and again provides a useful baseline for assessing significance. In fact, it follows directly from the expression for $\hat{\rho}_{xy}(m)$ that the effect of applying a random permutation π_1 to the sequence $\{x_k\}$ and a random permutation π_2 to the sequence $\{y_k\}$ is equivalent to applying the random permutation $\pi_3 = \pi_1^{-1} \cdot \pi_2$ to the sequence $\{y_k\}$. Consequently, we can randomize only one sequence in computing our comparison values, simplifying the computations somewhat.

The result obtained with this randomization strategy for the cross-correlations $\hat{\rho}_{xy}(m)$ estimated from the median-imputed storage tank data sequences is shown in Figure 7.23. As in the case of the inlet autocorrelations, note that the medians of the randomized correlation values are all approximately zero, consistent with our expectations. Similarly, the range of the 200 randomizations summarized in Figure 7.23 is again consistently small, typically on the order of ± 0.1 or less. As before, all of the correlations computed from the original data values lie well outside the range of these permutation results, implying statistical significance

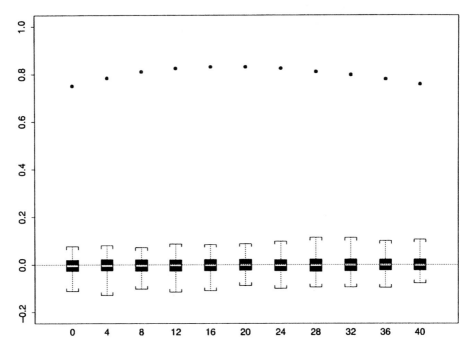

Figure 7.23. *Estimated cross-correlations for the median-imputed storage tank data (solid circles), with boxplot summaries of* 200 *random permutations.*

at the 1% level on the basis of the permutation ranks alone. Also, the z-scores are all on the order of 20, suggesting much greater significance (i.e., much smaller p values).

Finally, Figure 7.24 shows the normalized cross-correlations computed directly from the raw data. As before, the nonrandomized correlation values are generally smaller here than those for the median-imputed data, except for the case $m = 0$, which exhibits the maximum value for $\hat{\rho}_{xy}(m)$ computed from the raw data. In contrast to the autocorrelation results shown in Figure 7.22, however, the range of the permutation values obtained here is much larger for a few values of m, and the computed cross-correlations are *not* significant at the 1% level for these cases. Since these results differ from those shown in Figure 7.23 only with respect to the handling of the common-mode outlier pair, it is clear that these outliers are responsible for the differences. Here, the large differences in the range of the permutation results for $m = 8, 20, 24$, and 32 from all other results seem quite unusual and should probably make us suspicious that *something* bears further scrutiny.

7.4.2 Rank-based dynamic analysis

It was shown in Chapter 2 that the rank-based Spearman correlation coefficient exhibits a much lower sensitivity to outliers than the traditional product-moment correlation coefficient, and the following example illustrates that this advantage extends to dynamic correlation analyses. First, recall that $\rho_{xy}(m)$ represents the correlation coefficient between the data sequences $\{x_k\}$ and $\{y_{k+m}\}$. To obtain an outlier-resistant alternative to the estimator $\hat{\rho}_{xy}(m)$ discussed in Sec. 7.4.1, we replace the product-moment correlation coefficient with

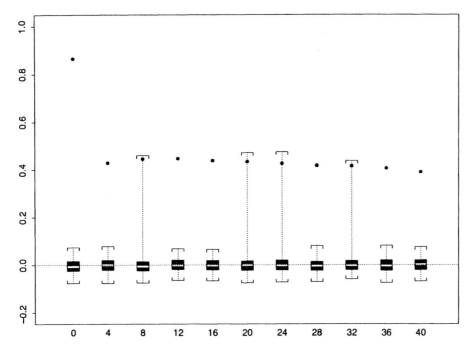

Figure 7.24. *Estimated cross-correlations for raw storage tank data (solid circles), with boxplot summaries of 200 random permutations.*

the Spearman rank correlation coefficient introduced in Chapter 2, giving

$$\rho_{xy}^{S}(m) = \frac{12}{N(N^2-1)} \sum_{k=1}^{N} \left(R_x(k) - \frac{N+1}{2} \right) \left(R_y(k+m) - \frac{N+1}{2} \right), \qquad (7.39)$$

where $R_x(k)$ is the rank of x_k in the rank-ordered list $\{x_{(i)}\}$ and $R_y(k+m)$ is the rank of y_{k+m} in the rank-ordered list $\{y_{(i)}\}$. As discussed in Chapter 2, this means that $R_x(k) = j$ if $x_k = x_{(j)}$, the jth smallest element in this rank-ordered sequence.

Figure 7.25 shows that, although $\rho_{xy}^{S}(m)$ is not the same as $\hat{\rho}_{xy}(m)$, these estimators often give approximately the same results for outlier-free data. The left-hand plot in Figure 7.25 shows three cross-correlation estimates for the storage tank data, two of which are the same as in Figure 7.18: the product-moment correlations $\hat{\rho}_{xy}(m)$ computed from the raw data are shown as open circles, while the values of $\hat{\rho}_{xy}(m)$ computed from the median-imputed datasets are shown as solid circles. The Spearman rank correlation estimates $\hat{\rho}_{xy}^{S}(m)$ defined in (7.39) *computed from the raw data* are shown as solid triangles, lying slightly below the estimates $\hat{\rho}_{xy}(m)$ computed from the median-imputed data. These last two results are barely discernable, and the results for $\rho_{xy}^{S}(m)$ computed from the median-imputed data are not shown here because they are completely indistinguishable from those computed from the raw data. The corresponding rank-based inlet autocorrelations $\rho_{xx}^{S}(m)$ are shown in the right-hand plot in Figure 7.25, again with the product-moment estimates $\hat{\rho}_{xx}(m)$ computed from the raw and median-imputed inlet data shown for comparison. Here,

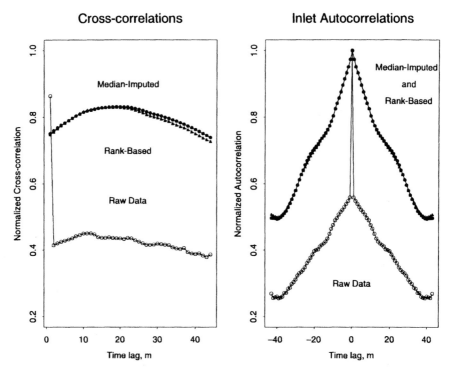

Figure 7.25. *Product-moment auto- and cross-correlations from raw and median-imputed data, with rank-based correlations from the raw data.*

the median-imputed estimates for $\hat{\rho}_{xx}(m)$ and the rank-based estimates $\rho^S_{xx}(m)$ computed from the raw data are almost entirely indistinguishable.

Permutation-based GSA comparison results for the rank-based autocorrelations $\rho^S_{xx}(m)$ computed from the raw storage tank inlet data are shown in Figure 7.26. The format of this figure is the same as that of Figures 7.21 and 7.22: the values for $\rho^S_{xx}(m)$ computed from the original dataset are shown as solid circles, while the boxplots summarize the corresponding estimates obtained from 200 random permutations of this data sequence. As in Figures 7.21 and 7.22, the median values of $\rho^S_{xx}(m)$ are approximately zero for all $m > 0$, a point emphasized by the horizontal dashed line at $\rho_{xx}(m) = 0$ in this plot. Also, the range of these randomization values is small, typically on the order of ± 0.1 or less. Hence, like their product-moment counterparts, the rank-based autocorrelations provide consistent evidence of correlations in the inlet data sequence, significant at the 1% level on the basis of permutation ranks alone. As in the previous inlet autocorrelation examples, the z-scores for these results are consistently large enough (between $z \sim 16$ and $z \sim 29$) to greatly strengthen this interpretation.

Figure 7.27 shows the corresponding permutation-based GSA comparison for the rank-based cross-correlations $\rho^S_{xy}(m)$ computed from the raw storage tank data sequences. These results are virtually identical to those in Figure 7.23, which shows the corresponding GSA comparisons for the product-moment cross-correlations $\hat{\rho}_{xy}(m)$ computed from the median-imputed data. Comparison of these results with those presented in Figure 7.24 for

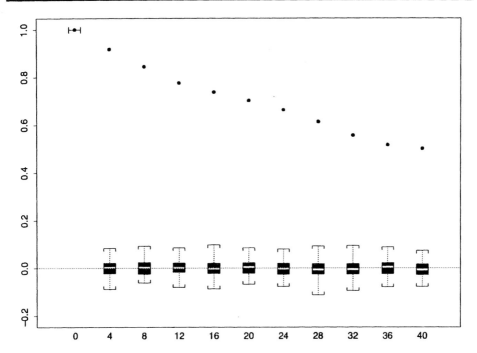

Figure 7.26. *Rank-based autocorrelation estimates for raw storage tank inlet data (solid circles), with boxplot summaries of 200 random permutations.*

$\hat{\rho}_{xy}(m)$ computed from the raw data emphasizes both the difference in outlier-sensitivity of the original estimates $\hat{\rho}_{xy}(m)$ and $\rho_{xy}^{S}(m)$ and the consequences of this difference for the randomization results. In particular, note that the unusual behavior of the permutation results seen in Figure 7.24 is not seen at all in the rank correlation results presented in Figure 7.27.

Overall, the results presented here and in Secs. 7.3.1, 7.3.2, and 7.4.1 have provided compelling evidence that the storage tank from which these datasets were collected exhibited an average residence time on the order of 19 hours, due to the maximum seen in the product-moment cross-correlations computed from the median-imputed data, that seen in the leave-one-out deletion diagnostic results for these cross-correlations, and that seen in the rank-based cross-correlations computed from either the raw or the median-imputed data sequences. In addition, the width of this broad maximum provides supporting evidence that the desired mixing was indeed occurring in the storage tank. The visually suspicious nature of the two common-mode outliers shown in Figure 7.15, their profound influence on the product-moment auto- and cross-correlations as seen in the leave-one-out deletion results presented in Sec. 7.3.2, and the plausible but highly unlikely interpretation attached to the $\hat{\rho}_{xy}(m)$ results computed from the raw data all lead us to declare these points as gross measurement errors and exclude them from our analysis.

7.5   Two systematic selection examples

As discussed in Sec. 7.1.5, the class of systematic selection strategies is a very broad one that typically combines auxiliary data or subject matter knowledge, multiple analysis results, and

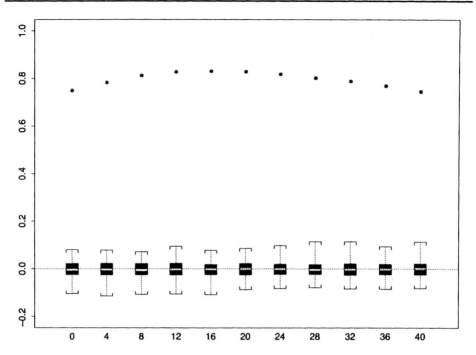

Figure 7.27. *Rank-based cross-correlation estimates for raw storage tank data (solid circles), with boxplot summaries of* 200 *random permutations.*

elements of the other sampling strategies discussed here. The following examples illustrate some of these points in two very different settings. The first example, discussed in Sec. 7.5.1, revisits the four industrial pressure data sequences discussed in Sec. 7.2.2, exploiting the fact that these four sequences were each sampled sequentially in time with a constant sampling rate. The second example is based on the real dataset described in Sec. 7.5.2, which consists of clinical data for 86 lung cancer patients. The analysis described there is based on the 12 variables included in this dataset for each patient and it illustrates a number of practical issues that arise in analyzing multivariable, mixed-type datasets.

7.5.1 Moving-window data characterizations

An important application of systematic data segmentation is the use of *moving-window characterizations*, an idea that is particularly important in the characterization of time-series but that also has other applications. For example, this idea plays an important role in the data-cleaning strategies described by Hernandez and Stolfo (1998) to support the merging of multiple databases. In the case of a time-series $\{x_k\}$, the sequence index k corresponds to a sampling time t_k, usually assumed to be of the form $t_k = t_0 + (k-1)T$, where $T > 0$ represents the constant time between successive data samples. The basic idea behind moving-window characterizations is to associate with each observation x_k in the sequence a *data window* $\mathbf{w}_k$ of fixed size:

$$\mathbf{w}_k = \{x_{k-J^-}, \ldots, x_{k-J^+}\}, \tag{7.40}$$

where $J^+ > J^-$ are integers. The moving-window data characterizations of interest here are computed from the data window $\mathbf{w}_k$ and are of the general form

$$y_k = \Phi(\mathbf{w}_k) = \Phi(x_{k-J^-}, \ldots, x_{k-J^+}). \tag{7.41}$$

In fact, particular choices of the function $\Phi(\cdot)$ in (7.41) define most of the nonlinear filters currently in common use in the field of digital signal processing (Astola and Kuosmanen, 1997; Pitas and Venetsanopoulos, 1990).

If $J^- \geq 0$, the data characterization y_k depends only on current and past values from the data sequence and is termed *causal*; the data characterization is termed *strictly causal* if $J^- > 0$, implying that y_k depends only on past values from the data sequence. Real-time data-processing applications may require causal or strictly causal data characterizations, but in all other settings, *noncausal* characterizations for which $J^- < 0$ have a number of practical advantages. For example, in the time-series data-cleaning applications discussed in Chapter 4, the use of noncausal data-cleaning filters permits an isolated spike at the current time instant k to be distinguished from the leading edge of a step change at time k. For this reason, the following examples consider only noncausal data characterizations. Further, these data characterizations are all based on *symmetric data windows* for which $J^- = -J^+$. Hence, (7.41) may be rewritten as

$$y_k = \Phi(x_{k-J}, \ldots, x_k, \ldots, x_{k+J}), \tag{7.42}$$

where $J > 0$ is a fixed *window half-width parameter* that defines the $(2J + 1)$-point moving data window on which the characterization is based.

Initially, the following examples consider *moving-window location estimators* based on the symmetric data window just described. These characterizations are defined by specifying a standard location estimator for the function $\Phi(\cdot)$ in (7.42). The simplest example is the *linear unweighted average filter* defined by

$$y_k = \frac{1}{2J+1} \sum_{j=-J}^{J} x_{k-j}. \tag{7.43}$$

Alternatively, taking $\Phi(\cdot)$ as the median value in the data window yields the *median filter* discussed in Chapter 4 in connection with the time-series data-cleaning problem. Finally, taking $\Phi(\cdot)$ to be the symmetric α-trimmed mean introduced in Chapter 1 yields the *moving-window trimmed mean* or *trimmed mean filter*. Recall that the symmetric α-trimmed mean includes as special cases both the unweighted average (for $\alpha = 0$) and the median (for $\alpha = 0.5$). The examples discussed below briefly examine some of the consequences of different choices of the symmetric trimming parameter α and the window half-width parameter J.

An important practical issue that arises in moving-window data characterizations is how to treat the ends of the data record. For example, suppose we have a data sequence $\{x_k\}$, where k ranges from 1 to N. In many applications (e.g., the time-series data-cleaning applications discussed in Chapter 4), we want a filtered data sequence $\{y_k\}$ that is the same length as the original data sequence $\{x_k\}$. For $k \leq J$, however, the moving data window $\mathbf{w}_k$ includes the data observation x_{k-J}, whose index is negative or zero. Similarly, for $k > N - J$, the symmetric window $\mathbf{w}_k$ includes the observation x_{k+J}, whose index is greater

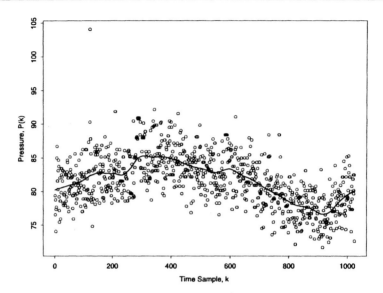

Figure 7.28. *Plot of the first industrial pressure data sequence (open circles) and the* supsmu *nonparametric trend estimate (solid line).*

than N. To overcome this difficulty, it is customary to form the *extended data sequence* $\{\tilde{x}_k\}$ defined for k between $-J+1$ and $N+J$ by

$$\tilde{x}_k = \begin{cases} x_1 & \text{for } k = -J+1, \dots, 0, \\ x_k & \text{for } k = 1, \dots, N, \\ x_N & \text{for } k = N+1, \dots, N+J. \end{cases} \tag{7.44}$$

Forming the data window $\mathbf{w}_k$ from this extended data sequence makes y_k well-defined for $k = 1, 2, \dots, N$. This strategy is adopted in all of the moving-window data characterizations considered here.

The four industrial pressure data sequences discussed in Sec. 7.2.2 provide a nice illustration of the simplicity and utility of moving-window data characterizations. Figure 7.28 shows the first pressure data sequence overlaid with a trend estimate obtained using the *supsmu* nonparametric scatterplot smoother (Härdle, 1990; Venables and Ripley, 2002). This scatterplot smoother is *not* a simple moving-window data characterization, but rather a complicated adaptive nonparametric procedure available in the S-PLUS software package (Insightful, 2001). It is considered here because it provides a useful standard of comparison for a variety of simple moving-window location estimation procedures. The essential notion is that nonparametric smoothing procedures such as *supsmu* and moving-window location estimation procedures both attempt to capture "intermediate-scale" data variations that are obscured in the original data sequence by short-term noise fluctuations.

The trend estimates obtained by four different smoothing procedures are compared in Figure 7.29. The upper left plot shows the results obtained with the adaptive *supsmu* procedure discussed above, using its default settings in the S-PLUS software package (Insightful, 2001). The upper right plot shows the results obtained with the *lowess* robust local regression procedure that is very popular in microarray data analysis, again using the default

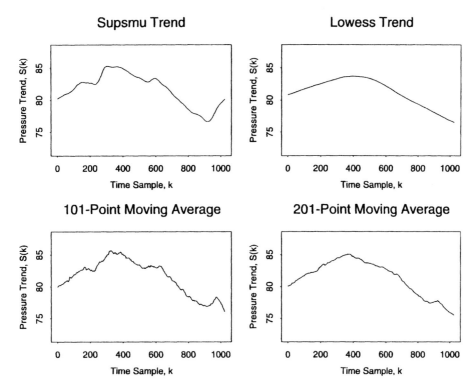

Figure 7.29. *A comparison of four trend estimates for the first industrial pressure data sequence.*

settings in the S-PLUS software package. This setting corresponds to using two thirds of the data in forming the local linear regression estimates on which the trend estimate is based ($f = 2/3$). It is clear from the comparison of these two plots that the *supsmu* trend estimate follows more of the local variations in the data sequence than the *lowess* trend estimate does, although this situation could be changed by reducing the smoothing parameter f in the *lowess* trend estimate. The objective here, however, is not to compare the performance of these scatterplot smoothers but rather to show that *roughly* comparable results may be obtained much more simply by using moving-window location estimators.

The two lower plots in Figure 7.29 show the results obtained for this same data sequence with two unweighted linear moving average filters. In the lower left plot, the window half-width parameter is $J = 50$, corresponding to a 101-point moving average. Note the general qualitative similarity of this result to the *supsmu* trend plotted above it: although the linear moving average trend estimate is not as smooth, it does exhibit the same general shape. The one notable exception occurs at the right end of the data record, where we see an artifact of the 50-point data extension used in implementing the moving-window average. Conversely, although the effects are not the same, nonparametric smoothers such as *supsmu* and *lowess* can also behave poorly near the ends of the data record (Simonoff, 1996, p. 142). The lower right plot in Figure 7.29 shows the consequences of increasing the window half-width parameter from $J = 50$ to $J = 100$, giving a 201-point linear moving

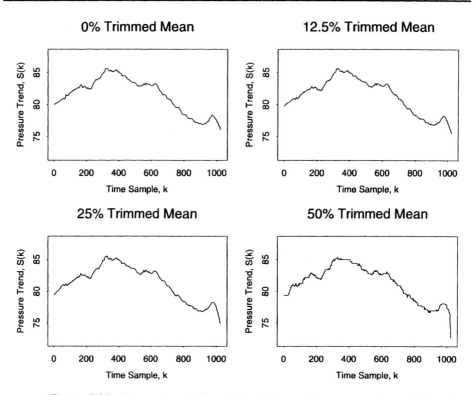

Figure 7.30. *Comparison of four different trimmed mean smoothers, all based on a* 101*-point moving data window.*

average filter. Because this filter is based on a wider data window, it captures fewer of the local features seen in the *supsmu* trend and more closely resembles the *lowess* trend estimate shown in the upper right plot. Again, the key point of this example is to illustrate that results *roughly* comparable to those obtained with complicated nonparametric smoothers such as *supsmu* and *lowess* can be obtained with simple moving-window procedures such as the unweighted linear average filter.

Figure 7.30 compares the results obtained by applying four different moving-window trimmed mean filters to this data sequence. In all cases, the half-width parameter is $J = 50$, resulting in a 101-point moving data window. The upper left plot shows the results for trimming parameter $\alpha = 0$, giving the unweighted linear average shown in the lower left plot in Figure 7.29. The upper right plot in Figure 7.30 shows the results for the symmetric 12.5% trimmed mean, while the bottom two plots show the results for the 25% symmetric trimmed mean, or *midmean* (lower left), and the 50% trimmed mean, corresponding to the median (lower right). The differences between the results obtained with these different trimmed means are a strong function of the dataset considered, as shown in Chapter 1. Here, the differences are very minor for the most part, although two points should be noted. First, the effects of the data sequence extension strategy on which these moving-window filters is based vary significantly with the trimming parameter α. This point may be seen most clearly by comparing the right and left ends of the plots for $\alpha = 0$ and $\alpha = 0.5$.

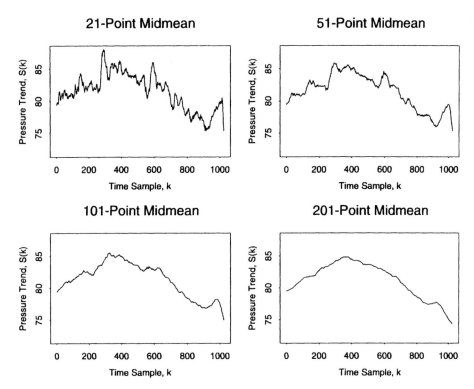

Figure 7.31. *Comparison of four midmean smoothers, based on different moving data window sizes.*

Second, careful comparison of the four results shown in Figure 7.30 reveals only very small differences between the detailed results for $\alpha = 0$, 0.125, and 0.25, but slightly larger differences for $\alpha = 0.5$. This result corresponds to the fact that the median filter—i.e., the moving-window trimmed mean with $\alpha = 0.5$—is known to introduce significant local distortion in a time-series, an important point discussed in Chapter 4.

The comparison of the two unweighted linear averages shown in the bottom plots in Figure 7.29 demonstrated that the intermediate-scale local variations seen in the filtered output depend on the width of the moving data window on which it is based. This point is emphasized more strongly in Figure 7.31, which compares the results obtained for the window half-width parameters $J = 10$, 25, 50, and 100, corresponding to moving data windows of 21, 51, 101, and 201 points, respectively. In all cases, the midmean filter ($\alpha = 0.25$) was applied to the first of the four industrial pressure data sequences. As expected, these results show that the trend estimate becomes smoother as J increases, since the number of samples included in the average on which the midmean is based increases with J, but the price paid for this increased smoothness is a loss of significant intermediate-scale smooth variation in the data. In particular, the 21-point moving data window used to obtain the results shown in the upper left plot is narrow enough to follow apparent cyclic variations in the data on the scale of ~ 50 samples. In contrast, the 201-point moving-window midmean trend shown in the lower right plot in Figure 7.31 can only capture long-term variations and

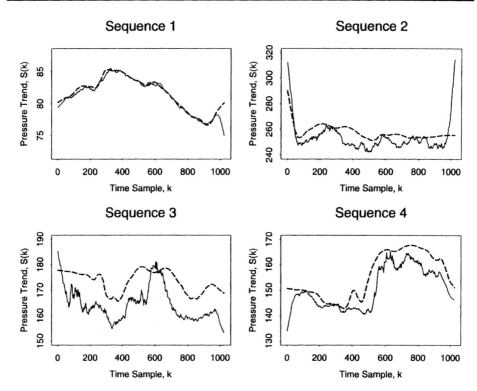

Figure 7.32. *Comparison of* supsmu *and moving midmean trend estimates for all four industrial pressure data sequences.*

is almost identical to the 201-point unweighted average shown in the lower right plot in Figure 7.29. Recall that these results were quite similar to those obtained with the *lowess* nonparametric smoother, which exhibited none of the intermediate-scale variations seen in the results obtained with the *supsmu* nonparametric smoother.

The results shown in Figure 7.32 compare the 101-point moving window midmeans (solid lines) with the corresponding *supsmu* trend estimates (dashed lines) for all four of the industrial pressure data sequences discussed in Sec. 7.2.2. Aside from the discrepancy at the right end of the data record, these trend estimates agree extremely well for Sequence 1, shown in the upper left plot in Figure 7.32. Although not as good, agreement is still quite reasonable for Sequences 2 and 4, again excluding the ends of the data record. The poorest agreement is seen here for Sequence 3, where the *supsmu* trend seems to be mostly about 5% larger than the midmean trend estimate. Even here, however, except for the segment between $k \sim 550$ and $k \sim 700$ and at the two ends of the data sequence, the two trend estimates generally track together reasonably well.

The key point of the preceding examples was to illustrate that, in the best cases, very simple moving-window location estimates can give data characteristics that are quite comparable with the trend estimates generated by very sophisticated adaptive nonparametric smoothers. The remainder of this discussion illustrates the following important corollary observation: other moving-window characterizations can be developed for situations where

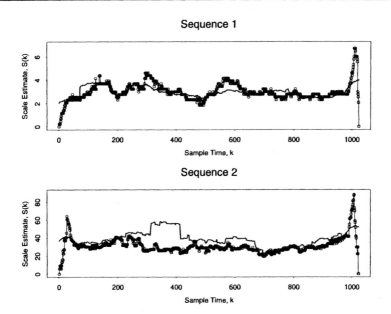

Figure 7.33. *Moving-window standard deviation and MAD scale estimates for industrial pressure data Sequences* 1 *and* 2.

alternative procedures analogous to *supsmu* and *lowess* smoothers are not available. In particular, the following examples consider some extensions of the moving-window location estimators just discussed to moving-window scale and skewness estimators.

The first example is that shown in Figure 7.33, which compares the usual standard deviation estimator with the MAD scale estimator introduced in Chapter 1. The upper plot shows the results obtained for the first industrial pressure data sequence, while the lower plot shows the results obtained for the second sequence. In all cases, the results were obtained using a 101-point moving data window, corresponding to the window half-width parameter $J = 50$, and the original data sequences were extended by J repetitions of the first and last point, as discussed above. In both plots, the moving-window standard deviation estimate is shown as the solid line, while the moving-window MAD scale estimate is shown as a thin line overlaid with open circles, often making it appear as a very heavy solid line due to the density of data points. As with the comparison of the *supsmu* and midmean trend estimates shown in the upper left plot in Figure 7.32, the results obtained for Sequence 1 in Figure 7.33 generally show excellent agreement between these two scale estimates. Notable exceptions occur at the ends of the data record, where the MAD scale estimate goes to zero. This behavior is a direct consequence of the fact that the first data point in the dataset appears $J + 1$ times out of $2J + 1$ points in the initial data window $\mathbf{w}_1$, meaning that the MAD scale estimate is identically zero for this data window due to the implosion phenomenon discussed in Chapter 3. The same argument applies to the last data point, and this effect is clearly seen in both plots in Figure 7.33.

Except for this effect, the agreement between the moving-window standard deviation and MAD scale estimates is also quite good for the second industrial pressure data sequence, shown in the lower plot in Figure 7.33. The sole exception to this statement occurs for the

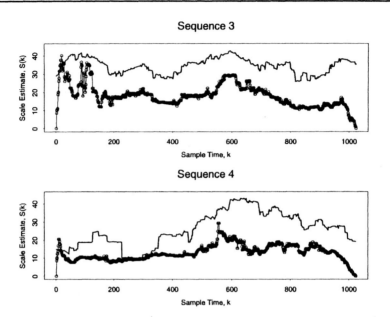

Figure 7.34. *Moving-window standard deviation and MAD scale estimates for industrial pressure data Sequences 3 and 4.*

data segment between $k \sim 300$ and $k \sim 400$, where the standard deviation is about twice the MAD scale estimate. Close examination of the original data sequence (the upper right plot in Figure 7.12, discussed in Sec. 7.2.2) suggests that it may be somewhat more variable for this range of data samples than the rest of the data sequence. The key point here is that the simple plot shown at the bottom of Figure 7.33 leads us more readily to focus on this segment of the dataset as possibly unusual than the plot of the data sequence itself does.

Figure 7.34 shows the analogous moving-window standard deviation and MAD scale estimates for the third and fourth industrial pressure data sequences discussed in Sec. 7.2.2. As in Figure 7.33, these results are based on a 101-point moving data window, and the standard deviation estimates are indicated with a solid line, while the MAD scale estimates are indicated as open circles overlaid on a thin line, generally appearing as a heavy solid line due to the density of points. For Sequence 3 (top plot), the standard deviation is almost always substantially larger than the MAD scale estimate. This result suggests that this data sequence is heavy-tailed and is distributionally more consistent than Sequence 2, where evidence for local variation between $k \sim 300$ and $k \sim 400$ was seen in Figure 7.33. Similar evidence for distributional variations with sample time k are seen for Sequence 4, as is clear from the bottom plot in Figure 7.34. Specifically, the standard deviation appears to be somewhat larger than the MAD scale estimate for $k \lesssim 200$, about equal between $k \sim 200$ and $k \sim 350$, and substantially larger for $k \gtrsim 350$ by an amount that depends on k. Comparing this result with the upper right plot in Figure 7.13 (Sec. 7.2.2), which shows the data sequence itself, strongly suggests a distributional change at $k \sim 350$, with the possibility of isolated outliers for $k \lesssim 200$. Taken together, these results suggest that it may be reasonable to divide the original data sequence into two subsequences for separate analysis, one for $1 \lesssim k \lesssim 350$ and the other for $350 \lesssim k \lesssim 1,000$.

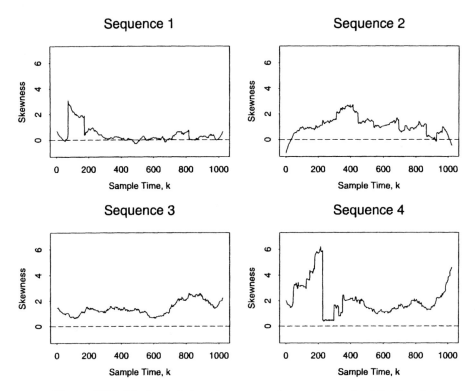

Figure 7.35. *Moving-window skewness estimates for each of the four industrial pressure data Sequences.*

Figure 7.35 shows the 101-point moving-window skewness estimate $\hat{\gamma}_k$ obtained for the four pressure data sequences. These results are all plotted on the same scale to facilitate comparison, and a horizontal dashed line at $\gamma = 0$ is included for reference. With the exception of the segment between $k \sim 80$ and $k \sim 180$, the results for Sequence 1 (upper left plot) show relatively little systematic variation with k and a small value for $\hat{\gamma}_k$, roughly consistent with the assumption of distributional symmetry. The anomalous segment between $k \sim 80$ and $k \sim 180$ is caused by the visually obvious outlier in the original dataset (upper left plot in Figure 7.12, discussed in Sec. 7.2.2), a point discussed further below. The moving-window skewness estimates for Sequence 2 (upper right plot) show more evidence of systematic variation with k and a generally larger skewness value, except near the ends of the data sequence. As with all of the other moving-window data characterizations considered here, the results near the ends of the sample are dominated by sequence extension artifacts. In particular, these artifacts are most significant at the ends of the sample, gradually diminishing as we move into the data sequence, and vanishing completely for $100 < k < 924$. Hence, they play no role in the maximum skewness feature seen between $k \sim 300$ and $k \sim 400$, consistent with the differences seen between the standard deviation and MAD scale estimates shown in the lower plot in Figure 7.33.

Moving-window skewness estimates $\hat{\gamma}_k$ for Sequence 3 (lower left plot) are consistently positive and exhibit significant variation with k, but these variations seem to be

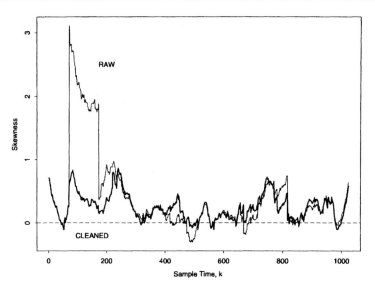

Figure 7.36. *Influence of data cleaning on the moving-window skewness estimates for Sequence* 1.

generally smaller and smoother than those seen for Sequence 2, consistent with the random subset skewness results presented in Sec. 7.2.2 for Sequences 2 and 3. Finally, the results shown in the lower right plot in Figure 7.35 for Sequence 4 exhibit the widest range of skewness values of any of the four sequences and the most pronounced dependence on the sample index k. As in the case of Sequence 2, however, these skewness results and the previously examined scale results suggest the same segmentation of the data sequence. Specifically, the most dramatic skewness variation—and the largest skewness estimates— occur for $k \lesssim 200$, while the sequence from $k \sim 200$ to $k \sim 350$ appears to have a distinct character with small skewness values. The skewness values for $k \gtrsim 350$ are again larger and generally consistent in value and character with those seen in Sequence 3. The possibility of isolated outliers for $k \lesssim 200$ noted above, together with the extreme sensitivity of skewness estimates to isolated outliers discussed in Chapter 1, suggests a possible explanation for the unusual behavior seen in this plot for $k \lesssim 200$.

This point is illustrated in Figure 7.36, which shows two moving-window skewness characterizations for Sequence 1. The first characterization, shown as the light line, is the 101-point moving-window skewness estimate presented in the upper left plot in Figure 7.35. The second characterization, shown as the dark line in Figure 7.36, is that obtained by applying this same moving-window skewness estimator to a cleaned version of Sequence 1. Specifically, the Hampel filter described in Chapter 4 with half-width parameter $K = 5$ and threshold parameter $t = 3$ was applied to Sequence 1 to remove isolated outliers. There are a number of differences between the two curves shown in Figure 7.36, but the most pronounced is that the anomalous peak between $k \sim 80$ and $k \sim 180$ in the original characterization is entirely absent in the corresponding characterization of the cleaned dataset. This observation clearly demonstrates that this anomalous feature in the raw data characterization is an outlier-induced artifact. This observation lends support to the idea that the anomalous behavior seen for $k \lesssim 200$ in the Sequence 4 skewness results may also be caused by outlier-induced artifacts. There, however, the issue is more complicated since Sequence 4 appears to be asymmetrically distributed. As noted in Chapter 2, the problem of dealing with outliers in asymmetric data sequences is a difficult one, discussed further in Chapter 8.

The key point of the examples presented here was to illustrate the simplicity, utility, and broad applicability of moving-window characterizations for time-series data sequences. This point was also illustrated in Chapter 4, where moving-window implementations of the univariate outlier detection procedures described in Chapter 3 were considered for time-series data-cleaning applications. In fact, moving-window data characterizations are potentially applicable whenever the sequence $\{x_k\}$ is indexed by a totally ordered sequence $\{k\}$ for which $j < k$ can be interpreted to mean "record x_j precedes record x_k" in some useful sense. This property of keys in a relational database provides the basis for the procedures discussed by Hernandez and Stolfo (1998) for the multiple database merge/purge problem.

7.5.2 The Michigan lung cancer dataset

The previous example illustrated some of the simple ways that knowledge of inherent structure—specifically, the time-sequential character of the data—can be exploited in analyzing data. The following example illustrates some of the options and challenges that present themselves when analyzing a composite dataset containing data values of different types, showing the kinds of insight that can be obtained through stratification, provided it is done in a useful way. This point is important in practice since the existence of large-scale black-box analysis procedures may tempt us to undertake a largely automated analysis of datasets with significant but possibly complicated structure, using universal approximation methods that take no account of this underlying structure. Much more informative and useful results can often be obtained with analyses that seek and exploit these heterogeneities, especially in the early exploratory stages.

The specific dataset considered here is one discussed by Beer et al. (2002) containing clinical data for 86 lung cancer (adenocarcinoma) patients, including a patient identifier, 2 variables related to a clustering result discussed by the authors, and 12 variables considered here. Of these, three are patient characteristics (age, gender, and smoking history), seven are tumor characteristics discussed in more detail below, and two characterize the patient's survival time and status at the end of the study. Two important features of this dataset are, first, that it includes binary, nominal, ordinal, and real data types, and, second, that one of the potentially most interesting variables (survival time) requires careful interpretation if we are to obtain meaningful results.

More specifically, the recorded survival times for the 86 patients in this dataset are plotted in Figure 7.37, most as open circles. In addition to these real-valued survival times, each patient is given a binary designation depending on whether he or she died during the course of the study or was still alive at the end of the study. For the 24 patients who died before the end of the study, these values represent their actual survival time from the date of their lung cancer surgeries until the date of their deaths. These survival times are indicated by solid circles in Figure 7.37. For the other 62 patients in the study, the reported survival times represent *lower bounds* on the patient's true survival time, since they were still alive at the end of the study. Consequently, the information content of these lower bounds is a function of their value: for the patient who was alive at the end of the study whose survival

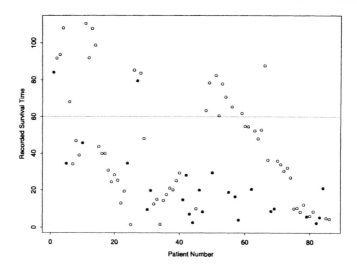

Figure 7.37. *Recorded survival times in the Michigan lung cancer dataset.*

time is recorded as 1.5 months, we really only know that this patient had an operation 1.5 months before the study ended and was not in such bad shape that he or she died in less than 1.5 months. Conversely, even if we do not know the patient's true survival time, but we know that it is longer than 60 months, then we can classify this patient as one who has survived longer than the 5-year milestone commonly used to assess how well a patient is doing. This time limit is shown as a horizontal dashed line in Figure 7.37, and it may be seen that of the 24 patients who died during the study, only two lived longer than this 60-month milestone, but both of these patients lived significantly beyond it (79.5 and 84.1 months, respectively). In fact, if we apply the Hampel identifier discussed in Chapter 3 to the survival times for this group of 24 patients, we identify these 2—and only these 2—as outliers. The remaining 22 patients in this group exhibit survival times between 2.4 and 45.8 months. Here, we define Group A as the set of 22 patients who died less than 60 months after their surgery and Group B as the 21 patients in the study who had survival times longer than 60 months, ranging from 60.5 to 110.6 months. Note that this group includes the 2 patients who died during the study but lived longer than 60 months, along with 19 others who were still alive at the end of the study but who had lived at least 60 months after their surgery. In the analysis that follows, we look for similarities and differences between these two groups.

The seven tumor characteristics include two genetic mutations and the five histopathology variables: *stage, tumor size, nodal invasiveness, type,* and *degree of differentiation.* Tumor stage is an ordinal variable, ranging from 1 for early-stage tumors to 4 for late-stage tumors; here, all tumors were either stage 1 or stage 3. Tumor size is another ordinal designation, again ranging from 1 to 4, and all four of these possible values are present in this dataset. Nodal status (invasiveness) is also an ordinal variable that assumes one of the three values 0, 1, and 2, and again, all of these possible values are present in this dataset. The tumor type classification is somewhat complicated. Ideally, the tumor type should be a nominal (i.e., unordered categorical) variable exhibiting one of four possible values: bronchial derived (BD), bronchial alveolar (BA), clear cell (CC), or papillary (PA). In this dataset,

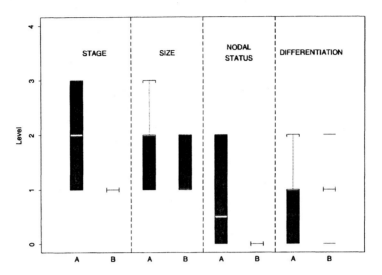

Figure 7.38. *Boxplot comparisons of four tumor characteristics for Group* A *(nonsurvivors) and Group* B *(long-term survivors).*

however, 50 of the 86 patients have tumor type BD, 14 have tumor type BA, and the remaining 22 have mixed or modified type classifications such as "BA/mucinous" (4 patients) or "BA/PA" (8 patients). Problems of this type may be handled in a number of different ways, each with its own set of advantages and disadvantages. For example, we could augment the number of values for this nominal variable from four to eight, enough to accommodate all of the distinct mixed or modified classes present. Alternatively, we could treat each of the four basic types (BA, BD, CC, and PA) as a separate binary variable, augmented with a fifth binary variable ("mucinous" or "not mucinous"), effectively increasing the number of type variables from one to five. A detailed exploration of these options is beyond the scope of this example, but the key points are, first, that "messy" categorical variables like this do often arise in practice, and, second, that they can be approached in a variety of different ways that generally lead to different analysis methods and results. Finally, the fifth tumor characteristic considered here is the degree of differentiation, which is an ordinal variable with three levels: "poor," "moderate," and "well." Again, as with tumor type, there is one example of a mixed characterization in the differentiation values included here: one case is designated "moderate/well." Because this variable is ordinal, however, this mixed characterization is easily handled: we assign the value 0 to "poor," the value 1 to "moderate," the value 2 to "well," and the value 1.5 to the single case designated "moderate/well."

Figure 7.38 presents boxplot summaries of four of the five tumor histopathology characteristics: stage, size, nodal status, and degree of differentiation. The fifth histopathology variable—tumor type—is not included in this summary because of the complications noted above in deciding how to represent it; this variable is examined separately below. Although boxplot summaries are not the best way of comparing highly quantized variables like these (i.e., nominal or ordinal variables that assume only a few possible values), the boxplot summaries presented in Figure 7.38 clearly show that the two patient groups considered here exhibit different ranges of variation, some of them markedly different. In particular,

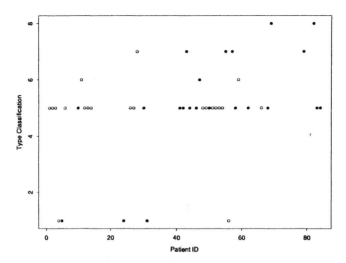

Figure 7.39. *Scatterplot summary of the eight augmented tumor type classifications by patient ID. Solid circles represent patients in Group* A *(nonsurvivors) and open circles represent patients in Group* B *(long-term survivors).*

note that stage and nodal status exhibit only their smallest possible values for the long-term survivors (Group B) and that tumor size Class 3 is only represented in the nonsurvivors (Group A). The situation with degree of differentiation is the least clear of the four variables considered here, suggesting that a more careful (i.e., sophisticated and/or formal) analysis of this variable's influence is necessary. Overall, it is clear from these boxplots that tumor stage and nodal status are extremely influential variables, a result that is neither new nor surprising (consistent with the known importance of early detection in treating cancer) but that nicely illustrates the practical advantages of a simple preliminary stratification-based analysis of highly structured composite datasets like the one considered here.

Figure 7.39 summarizes the tumor type classification data for Groups A and B using the extended eight-class representation discussed above. Only five of these classes are present in Groups A and B, corresponding to Types 1 (BA), 5 (BD), 6 (BD/CC), 7 (BD/PA), and 8 (BD/mucinous). In the 2 patient groups considered here, Type 8 (BD/mucinous) is fairly rare, occurring in only 2 cases out of 43, but both of these cases fall into the nonsurvivor patient group. Similarly, Type 7 (BD/PA) only occurs five times, but four of these five are from the nonsurvivor group. Types 1 (BA) and 6 (BD/CC) are also small but appear more evenly split between the two patient groups, and the largest class is Type 5 (BD), which is also fairly evenly split between Groups A and B. As with the degree of differentiation discussed above, to give more than these vague qualitative observations would require a more formal analysis, preferably with additional data.

Three binary variables are included in this dataset—gender, p53 mutation, and K-ras mutation—and these values are summarized in Table 7.2 for Groups A and B. To assess the difference between groups with respect to these binary variables, we can employ standard binary comparison methods (Collett, 2003, Sec. 2.3). Taking the specific example of gender, we begin by estimating the probability p_A that a patient in Group A is male and the probability p_B that a patient in Group B is male. These probabilities are simply estimated by the fraction

Group	Gender M/F	p53 +/−	K-ras +/−
A	10/12	5/17	13/9
B	9/12	4/17	10/10*

Table 7.2. *Summary of the three binary variables for patient Groups* A *and* B. **Note:** *The K-ras value was not reported for one of the patients in Group* B, *so the total number of observations for this variable is only* 20 *instead of* 21.

of male patients in each group, giving $\hat{p}_A = 0.455$ and $\hat{p}_B = 0.429$. Under the null hypothesis that there is no gender difference between groups, we can also estimate the probability p that a patient selected randomly from either group is male: this is simply the total fraction of male patients in the two groups together, giving $\hat{p} = 0.442$. To test the hypothesis that the two groups exhibit a significant difference with respect to gender, we can compute the test statistic (Collett, 2003, p. 33)

$$z = \frac{\hat{p}_A - \hat{p}_B}{\sqrt{\hat{p}(1 - \hat{p})\left[\frac{1}{N_A} + \frac{1}{N_B}\right]}}, \tag{7.45}$$

where N_A and N_B are the total numbers of patients in Groups A and B, respectively. This test statistic is based on the assumptions that, first, patient gender can be modelled as an independent binary random variable, and, second, the sample size is large enough for $\hat{p}_A - \hat{p}_B$ to have an approximate normal distribution. It has been suggested (McCullagh and Nelder, 1989, p. 104) that a binary probability estimate $\hat{p}$ will be approximately normally distributed if $N\hat{p}(1 - \hat{p}) \geq 2$. Since $N_A\hat{p}_A(1 - \hat{p}_A) \simeq 5.45$ and $N_B\hat{p}_B(1 - \hat{p}_B) \simeq 5.14$, it follows that the normal approximation should be reasonable here for $\hat{p}_A$ and $\hat{p}_B$, hence also for the difference $\hat{p}_A - \hat{p}_B$. The value of the test statistic z defined in (7.45) for the hypothesis of a gender difference between the two groups is $z \simeq 0.171$, which is too small in magnitude to support this hypothesis (the associated normal probability for the null hypothesis is $p \simeq 0.86$).

Analogous computations for the p53 mutation data shown in Table 7.2 indicate no significant differences between Groups A and B with respect to this binary variable, either. Specifically, the estimated probabilities that the p53 mutation status is positive for patients in the two groups are $\hat{p}_A = 0.227$ and $\hat{p}_B = 0.190$. In both cases, the rule of thumb $N\hat{p}(1 - \hat{p}) \geq 2$ is satisfied, supporting the use of the normal approximation, and the z-value associated with their difference is $z \simeq 0.298$, which has a probability under the null hypothesis of $p \simeq 0.77$.

Interpretation of the K-ras mutation data shown in Table 7.2 poses a different problem since this value is not reported for one of the patients in Group B. Hence, we cannot directly apply the analysis just described to this binary variable. Because there is only a single missing observation, however, we can adopt an extremely simple variation on the multiple imputation strategy for missing data discussed in Chapter 4. Specifically, we can compute the results we would obtain under the two possible values for this missing observation and compare the results: in favorable cases, we will draw the same conclusion whichever value the missing observation assumes. The estimated probability that K-ras mutation status is positive for Group A is $\hat{p}_A = 0.591$, implying $N_A\hat{p}_A(1 - \hat{p}_A) \simeq 5.32$,

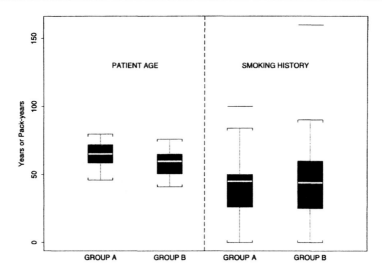

Figure 7.40. *Boxplot comparisons of age and smoking history for Group* A *(nonsurvivors) and Group* B *(long-term survivors).*

so the normal approximation should be reasonable. The estimated probability that K-ras mutation status is positive for Group B depends on whether we assume that the missing observation is positive or negative, leading to two estimated probabilities: $\hat{p}_B^- = 0.476$ and $\hat{p}_B^+ = 0.558$, both satisfying the conditions for the normal approximation to be reasonable. The z-values computed from (7.45) under these assumptions for the missing observation are $z^- \simeq 0.757$ and $z^+ \simeq 0.217$, neither of which indicates significant differences between Groups A and B with respect to K-ras mutation status (i.e., $p^- \simeq 0.45$ and $p^+ \simeq 0.83$).

Finally, Figure 7.40 presents boxplot summaries of the two real-valued patient characteristics in this dataset: age and smoking history. These boxplots compare age in years and smoking history in pack-years for Groups A and B. Although patients in Group B (the long-term survivors, median age 59.9 years) appear to be somewhat younger than those in Group A (the nonsurvivors, median age 65.3 years), these differences appear much less dramatic than those seen in the case of tumor stage and nodal status. Somewhat surprisingly, there appears to be no clear evidence for a difference between these groups with respect to smoking history (median values of 45 and 44 pack-years, respectively). Nevertheless, this observation is consistent with the results of Beer et al. (2002), who found smoking history to be only marginally significant in their analysis of this dataset.

Overall, the point of this example has been to illustrate the practical advantages of stratification for a composite dataset. The dataset considered here consisted of 15 variables, of which 12 were considered here. Two of these twelve variables (survival time and survival status) were used together to stratify the dataset into Groups A and B, and a preliminary analysis of the other ten variables was presented on the basis of this stratification. From these results, it appears that we can at least initially omit four variables from further consideration (gender, p53 mutation status, K-ras mutation status, and smoking history), focusing primarily on the four variables that appear most significant (patient age, tumor stage, tumor size, and nodal status). The importance of the remaining two variables (degree of differentiation and tumor type) is unclear and requires further examination.

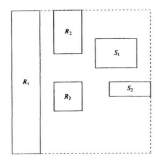

Chapter 8

Concluding Remarks and Open Questions

The primary objectives of this book have been twofold: first, to demonstrate the damaging effects of various data anomalies that arise in real datasets, and, second, to describe a number of strategies that have been found useful in dealing with these anomalies. This final chapter begins by summarizing observations from other authors in Sec. 8.1 that help to put these results into useful perspective relative to the problem of analyzing large datasets. Next, Sec. 8.2 briefly examines the role of prior knowledge, auxiliary data, and working assumptions in analyzing data, citing a recent paper by Dodge (1996) to illustrate a number of points. Finally, Sec. 8.3 examines some broad data analysis questions that appear to be open at present.

8.1 Analyzing large datasets

As noted in Chapter 1, the term "data mining" refers to the analysis of large datasets. While the meaning of "large" can vary widely between analysts and applications, two fundamental features are, first, that the analysis of "large" datasets requires highly automated, systematic procedures, and, second, that these datasets are virtually certain to contain data anomalies that can complicate this analysis significantly. Three examples discussed by Huber and Nagel (1996) provide a useful frame of reference: one was a pesticide application dataset containing over one gigabyte of data, another was a 900-megabyte dataset of hospitalization data from the former German Democratic Republic, and the third was a data analysis project called STREETMAN to support maintainence of approximately 700 kilometers of German highways. Although the size of the datasets involved in the third example is not given explicitly, motivation for the project was the fact that an earlier, related, project on road safety by a small engineering firm the authors worked with resulted in the generation of over 40,000 pages of charts and tables. Recognizing that this "analytical result" was unlikely to be useful to anyone led to the development of an interactive data analysis system, "which allows the user to quickly zoom into the relevant sections and also perform multivariate analysis of road parameters and then only generate hardcopy for the information really needed" (Huber and Nagel, 1996, p. 209).

   Based on their experience in analyzing these and other large datasets, Huber and Nagel (1996) describe three classes of data analysis problems. Class A problems correspond to

269

traditional confirmatory data analysis: analytical objectives are clearly formulated and a
dataset is then collected to support this analysis. Class B problems are typical of exploratory
analysis of historical data records: a dataset—often a very large one—is available for
analysis, but analysis objectives are often vague and/or only weakly related to the reasons the
dataset was originally acquired. Type C problems are typical of large software development
projects: analysis objectives are grand ("A system should be developed that solves *all*
problems"), and, while no datasets are yet available, data collection is typically underway
and cannot be influenced. The authors note that, in their experience, situations B and C
are much more common than situation A, but something approximating situation A must
be achieved before detailed analysis can begin. That is, analytical objectives must be
reasonably clear and a *useful* dataset must be obtained for the purposes of this analysis,
either by distilling it from a larger available dataset or by identifying critical data items that
are not available and making efforts to acquire them.

To support these applications, Huber and Nagel (1996) advocate *data-based proto-*
typing, which they describe as

> . . . *an experimental process with a large learning component: One continuously*
> *acquires new information about the data, in particular detail aspects and may*
> *experiment with heuristic methods and algorithms.*

Although the authors do not give an explicit prescription for data-based prototyping, their
general approach to it involves the following key ingredients:

1. visual data inspection,

2. data preparation,

3. analysis strategy/hypothesis formulation,

4. prototyping and scripts,

5. systematic analysis,

6. iteration,

7. custom software programming.

The authors strongly advocate initial visual examination of the data to detect obvious outliers,
missing data, or other important data integrity problems, and to begin to clarify analytical
objectives. Huber and Nagel note that they routinely examine 10,000 to 20,000 observations graphically, observing that simple visualization techniques such as scatterplots cease
to be useful for larger datasets, requiring sampling or other forms of data aggregation before
visual analysis. In view of these observations, it is important to recall the results of Marron,
Hernandez-Campos, and Smith (2002) discussed in Chapter 7: in some situations, apparently reasonable random sampling procedures can completely miss critically important data
features, suggesting the replacement or augmentation of random sampling with systematic
sampling procedures. The key point is that the subset selection ideas discussed in Chapter
7 may have a useful role to play in the visual analysis of large datasets.

Huber and Nagel (1996, p. 202) give the following description of data pretreatment:

Aside from the elimination of data entry and systematic errors, this step involves the assignment of standardized and unique names for variables and attributes, re-coding data to sensible value ranges, and assigning standardized missing values, etc.

This last point—the need for a standard representation for missing data values—was emphasized in Chapter 2, where it was noted that misinterpretation of missing values could cause outliers, disguised missing data, or misalignment errors. Huber and Nagel also note that "the effort needed for a careful data preparation is often underestimated," later citing an example of Schall (1993) involving preparation of California census data:

The entire process from designing the database to making new census data available in a production version can take up to nine months, depending on the size and complexity of the data.

Similar observations concerning the effort required for data preparation are made by Dasu and Johnson (2003, p. ix), who note,

In our experience, the tasks of exploratory data mining and data cleaning constitute 80% of the effort that determines 80% of the value of the ultimate data mining result.

Following careful initial visualization and data preparation, Huber and Nagel (1996) advocate formulating a detailed analysis strategy, *working in close collaboration with the end-users of the data.* More specifically, these authors note,

An important goal in this initial ad-hoc analysis is, to make hazy ideas precise, to structure and to modularize the analysis process in order to reduce complexity. Instead of lengthy discussions on whether or not to use a particular model or approach, one should try to apply them directly to the data. Only from the results can one really judge the usefulness of a particular approach and whether it merits further investigation and elaboration. It is often more constructive to try out a questionable method and let the person suggesting it decide to abandon it, than to try to argue on a theoretical basis.

Note that this last idea is one where the GSA framework described here can be particularly useful: simply include the questionable method as one of the GSA scenarios, along with one or more alternatives that are better founded theoretically.

Once a tentative analysis strategy has been formulated, Huber and Nagel (1996) strongly advocate "scripting" or interactively documenting subsequent analysis efforts to facilitate "trial and error" analyses that may require periodic backtracking. In fact, the authors note,

Experience shows that even very experienced data analysts are not capable of producing more than a few error-free analysis steps in a row (not due to typos!). Frequent plausibility checks at all intermediate levels are absolutely critical for producing correct final results.

Note the analogy between these results and those discussed in Chapter 2 in connection with software errors and those discussed in Chapter 4 in connection with externally noninformative variables.

The steps described up to this point represent the first four of the seven listed earlier. Huber and Nagel (1996) argue that it is only at the fifth step (systematic data analysis) that "the actual data analysis begins." In particular, it is only at this point that a typical Class B or C problem has been reduced approximately to a Class A problem where sophisticated analytical methods can be applied. As a specific example, the authors describe various aspects of the 900-megabyte hospitalization dataset mentioned earlier. Preliminary processing steps involved combining multiple records for the same individual, diagnosis, and year (e.g., arising from transfers between hospitals) and eliminating patient IDs to meet confidentiality requirements. Further reduction was still required to obtain a manageable dataset for analysis, which was accomplished by aggregating variables to ultimately obtain a contingency table with 2.3 million cells. The result was a 13.9-megabyte dataset that could be analyzed on a personal computer.

The final steps of the data-based prototyping procedure are iteration—an important component discussed briefly in Chapter 6 (Sec. 6.8.1)—and custom software development. Two points are important here. First, Huber and Nagel (1996) see little distinction between a large-scale data analysis effort and a software development project. This observation contradicts the desire often expressed to avoid software development in favor of using available packages, whether commercial or freeware. Certainly the use of available *modules* is to be encouraged—*provided they are known to be reliable*—but unless the original data analysis problem corresponds to one of the rare Class A problems for which the appropriate packaged solution already exists, the need for custom software development will almost certainly arise in any large-scale data analysis effort. The second important point emphasized by Huber and Nagel (1996, p. 204) is *"know when to stop."* In particular, the authors argue that once additions to a working prototype start becoming cosmetic in nature, it is time to produce the final version and move on to something else.

8.2   Prior knowledge, auxiliary data, and assumptions

One of the primary motivations for GSA is the fact that different methods applied to the same dataset can yield very different results. In difficult cases, it may not be at all apparent which—*if any*—of these results are reasonable. In practice, then, it is often necessary to appeal to prior knowledge, auxiliary data, and a careful examination of working assumptions to aid in interpreting these results. The following example provides a distressingly clear illustration of the need for these factors in a reasonable data analysis and the effort required to obtain additional information of this type in difficult cases.

Dodge (1996) gives a detailed discussion of a small industrial process operating dataset (21 observations of 4 variables each), published by Brownlee (1960) and widely adopted as a benchmark problem for comparing regression analysis methods. In fact, Dodge (1996) lists 60 specific regression models fit to this dataset by different authors over a period of 33 years using a very wide range of methods. All of these regression models have the same form:

$$\hat{y} = y_0 + a_1 x_1 + a_2 x_2 + a_3 x_3. \tag{8.1}$$

They are presented in increasing order of the constant term, from $y_0 = -43.9$ to $y_0 = -34.5$. The coefficient a_1 in these models is always positive, but it varies from 0.6861 to 0.9566, while the a_2 coefficient includes 1 negative value and 59 positive values, ranging from 0.357 to 1.312. The estimated a_3 coefficient is 0 for 2 models and negative for the other 58, varying between -0.153 and -0.005.

One of the relatively early analyses of this dataset was by Daniel and Wood (1971), who identified 4 of the 21 observations as possible outliers. Part of the reason for this conclusion was the working assumption that observations correspond to measurements made on successive days of process operation. Dodge (1996) calls this assumption seriously into question, a point discussed further below. In addition, Dodge (1996) also presents a summary of the outliers identified by 25 other analyses of this dataset. The results range from 1 author who concluded that there were no outliers in the dataset to 2 analyses using high-breakdown methods (specifically, LTS regression and the MCD outlier detection method discussed in Chapter 4) that each found 9 of the 21 observations to be anomalous. Overall, the combined results of these 26 analyses find only 5 of the 21 observations that all agree are *not* outliers.

Dodge (1996) presents the results of an impressively extensive search for additional information about the Brownlee dataset. Ultimately, he concludes that the 21 observations included in this dataset represent a subsample of a larger set of 139 observations. These observations appear to correspond to a time-series of measurements on an industrial process operating in 1943 and long since demolished. In addition, the available evidence strongly suggests that no measurements were made on certain days and duplicate measurements were made on other days. Since it is not known which 21 of the 139 observations were retained in Brownlee's published dataset, it is not possible to say whether the samples correspond to 21 successive days (as Daniel and Wood (1971) and others have assumed, in part for purposes of outlier detection); to 21 randomly selected, distinct days over several months; or to an unspecified number of replicate measurements taken from fewer than 21 distinct days. It is clear from Dodge's summary that the ultimate reasonableness of any of these regression models or outlier characterizations can depend strongly on these unknown (and now probably unknowable) factors.

Since it is not possible to even formulate a detailed quantitative data analysis strategy without invoking *some* working assumptions, the dependence of our results on the assumptions implied by the previous example raises two critical points. First, these working assumptions are often implicit, either buried deep within the validity requirements for a particular analysis method or unconsciously incorporated into the analysis by those who are at least somewhat familiar with the data source and how it *should* behave. Common examples of the first type of implicit assumption are normality and statistical independence, and a common example of the second type is the belief that "variable X cannot possibly be influential in this situation." One of the key points of this book has been to emphasize that assumptions of either type can be completely wrong. Hence, the second critical observation is that, while these assumptions may simplify initial analysis and *some* assumptions are necessary for any analysis, no *specific* assumption should be held to be inviolable. In fact, many practitioners ultimately adopt a healthy respect for Murphy's law ("anything that can go wrong will"), summarized in the more specific context of data analysis by the following advice from Dasu and Johnson (2003, p. 186):

Take NOTHING for granted. The data are never what they are supposed to be, even after they are "cleaned up." The schemas, layout, content, and nature of content are never completely known or documented and continue to change dynamically.

A significant practical corollary, then, is the importance of knowing *explicitly* what the key working assumptions are. In fact, the attempt to write down key working assumptions can be extremely educational, both in revealing unrecognized areas of ignorance and in uncovering basic disagreements in working assumptions. This latter point is particularly important in working with large datasets, where subject matter expertise, data storage and retrieval expertise, and data analysis expertise often reside with different individuals or groups of individuals.

8.3   Some open questions

While they do not make up complete list of such questions, the following subsections briefly discuss four important anomaly-related open questions in data analysis.

8.3.1   How prevalent are different types of data anomalies?

The question of how frequently the data anomalies discussed in this book arise in real datasets is not a mathematical one, but it does profoundly influence the development and application of anomaly-resistant analysis methods. Since the available literature on outliers and missing data is quite large, the following discussion mainly considers these two types of data anomalies. Little appears to have been written on misalignment errors, so it is difficult to assess their prevalence in real datasets. The results of a study on shift errors in standardized tests discussed in Sec. 8.3.4 suggest significant misalignment errors occur with a frequency of 1% to 2%, but it is not clear how application-specific this result is.

With regard to outliers, it is useful to divide historical developments into three periods: the era of single outlier detection, the era of robust estimators, and the era of high-breakdown estimators. While these designations are oversimplifications (and thus not entirely accurate), they do indicate the historical progression of the outlier literature from its focus on "one" to "some" to "many" outliers. Early work focused on the detection of a single outlier, typically in a small dataset, leading to ideas like the still-popular 3σ edit rule. The resulting techniques are sometimes effective in these situations, provided the dataset is not too small, as discussed in Chapter 3. Another class of techniques that is well suited to a single outlier or a few outliers in a dataset comprises the deletion strategies discussed in Chapter 7. Unfortunately, many techniques that work acceptably in this single outlier setting suffer badly from the masking effects discussed in Chapter 3. In the case of 0% breakdown procedures such as the 3σ edit rule or OLS regression, these effects can cause badly biased results that effectively hide all evidence of the outliers present in the dataset. Techniques such as M-estimators (Huber, 1981) are much better suited to these problems, provided the contamination levels are not too extreme. The basic idea behind these methods is to replace the squared-error measure on which OLS methods are based with alternative measures that impose smaller penalties on large errors, since it is the large penalties that squared-error criteria impose on outliers that are responsible for the bias in OLS methods. This class of methods includes a variety of specific methods (e.g., different alternatives to the squared-error measure) and extensions (e.g., generalized M-estimators to deal with contaminated predictor variables), and they remain quite useful in practice. As a specific example, one of the best available methods for cleaning contaminated time-series is the data cleaner of Martin and Thomson (1982) discussed in Chapter 4, which is based on generalized M-estimators.

The symmetric α-trimmed mean discussed in Chapter 1 provides a nice illustration of the interplay between contamination levels and computational methods. Taking $\alpha = 0$ gives the zero-breakdown arithmetic mean, which enjoys great historical acceptance and exhibits a number of desirable theoretical properties, as noted in Chapter 3. Increasing α improves the outlier-resistance, and various authors have advocated the trimmed mean with different values of α. For example, Lehmann (1983, p. 368) summarizes results from a number of authors and recommends $\alpha \sim 0.1$, while in their individual summaries in the Princeton Robustness Study, Hampel recommends "trimmed means which don't trim too little on either end" (as a specific example, the midmean, $\alpha = 0.25$) (Andrews et al., 1972, p. 240), while Huber recommends $\alpha \sim 0.1, 0.15,$ or 0.25 (Andrews et al., 1972, p. 254). The maximum possible value is $\alpha = 0.5$, reducing to the median, which exhibits a 50% breakdown point and the smallest possible asymptotic bias for contaminated normal distributions (Huber, 1981, p. 75). Such observations provide the motivation for the LMS procedures discussed by Rousseeuw and Leroy (1987, p. 14), based on the idea of replacing the SSE in the OLS formulation with the *median* of squared errors. Note that since minimizing the sum of squares is equivalent to minimizing the average squared error, this idea corresponds to the replacement of an outlier-sensitive mean with an outlier-resistant median. Strategies of this general type have led to the development of high-breakdown estimators with the maximum possible breakdown point of 50%.

The key point of this discussion is that the assumed contamination level has been responsible for a great deal of method development and it provides very useful guidance in choosing between the different analysis methods that are now available. Still, the question of what contamination level is realistic remains the subject of much debate in the robust statistics community. As a specific example, Huber (1993, p. 144) poses the question, "How high a breakdown point do we really need: 5%–10%–25%–50%?" and he reaches the following conclusion:

> *Contaminations between 1% and 10% are sufficiently common that a blind application of procedures with a breakdown point of less than 10% must be considered outright dangerous. But it is difficult to find a rational justification for a breakdown point higher than 25% if this should result in serious efficiency loss at the model, or in excessive computation time.*

Indeed, the computational burden associated with high-breakdown estimators is the cause of significant concern and much algorithmic effort, and this concern extends to recent developments involving depth-based regression. In particular, questions of computational feasibility were one of the key concerns raised by discussants of the depth-based regression paper of Rousseeuw and Hubert (1999). Huber (1993) also argues that if a dataset is highly contaminated, careful scrutiny by a subject matter expert may be preferable to the use of high-breakdown estimators. The difficulty in practice, however, is to be able to *detect* the possibility of high contamination levels in a dataset, particularly in the case of multivariable datasets. One possibility suggested by Huber is to describe highly contaminated datasets by mixture models, possibly involving more than two clusters, an idea that leads to the use of exploratory cluster analysis. Here again, however, methods are important, as some of the most popular clustering procedures (e.g., the k-means algorithm of MacQueen (1967)) are themselves highly outlier-sensitive (Ertöz, Steinbach, and Kumar, 2003). Some results in this direction have been recently reported by Santos-Pereira and Pires (2002) and Rocke and Woodruff (2002).

The question of what fraction of missing data to expect in real datasets is somewhat different from the outlier question, for at least two reasons. First, missing data *should* be easier to detect, although in the case of inadvertently or deliberately disguised missing data, this may not be the case. Second, while we can argue that 50% contamination represents a reasonable upper bound on outlier contamination levels (this follows directly from the informal definition of an outlier as a data point that is anomalous with respect to the majority of the data values), any fraction of observations between 0% and 100% is possible for missing data. In fact, the missing data level encountered in practice is strongly application-dependent and, as in the case of outliers, it largely determines the class of treatment methods that we can consider. For example, it was noted previously that the gene expression datasets considered by Dudoit and Fridlyand (2002) contained either no missing data values or 3.3% or 6.6% missing data values. In these last two cases, single imputation strategies were proposed for these missing data values. In survey sampling applications, much higher rates of missing data are typically reported: In the Dutch income survey discussed by Huisman (2000), one of the primary concerns was the development of multiple imputation strategies to deal with missing data levels as high as 60%. Further, it was noted in the discussion of noninformative variables presented in Chapter 4 that some responses may be almost entirely missing, forcing us to either omit them from our analysis altogether or seek computable surrogates as in the case of unmeasured or unmeasurable variables.

One point of potentially important similarity between outliers and missing data values is the issue of systematic patterns in these data values. In the case of missing data, systematic patterns may be indicative of nonignorable missing data effects, while in the case of outliers, patterns are related to the notion of dependence structure, a topic discussed briefly in Sec. 8.3.2.

8.3.2   How should outliers be modelled?

The comparison presented in Chapter 3 of the 3σ edit rule, the Hampel identifier, and the modified boxplot rule for outlier detection demonstrated clearly that the relative performance of these procedures depends strongly on the characteristics of the outliers. One important characteristic is their concentration, an issue discussed in detail in Sec. 8.3.1, but other characteristics are also extremely important, raising a number of key issues. In particular, it was clear from the results presented in Chapter 3 that the contaminated normal model advocated by Huber (1981), where outliers exhibit the same mean as the nominal data but larger variance, is much more subtle and more difficult to deal with than the point contamination model. The question of which—if either—of these models is more reasonable in practice is not clear. In addition, a number of more complex issues arise when we consider more realistic analytical settings. For example, while it is analytically useful to assume that outliers appear as i.i.d. sequences, violations of this assumption do occur and can be extremely significant in applications involving dynamic data characterization. In particular, the distinction between isolated and patchy outliers was discussed in Chapter 4, where it was shown to be extremely important in the problem of dynamic model order determination. Similarly, the influence of these distinctions on spectrum estimation has been discussed by Pearson (2001b). This point has also been noted by Davies and Gather (1993, p. 799), who explicitly raise the question of what a "reasonable outlier model" should be and express concern that "in almost all simulations in the literature the outliers are taken to be i.i.d. random variables." In contrast, they note that one of the real data examples they consider exhibits clear outliers (whose physical source is known) that are both non-Gaussian in distribution and highly dependent. Viewed in this light, the question of alternatives to i.i.d. random variable outlier models (especially Gaussian i.i.d. outlier models) is a challenging one, in part because the problem of describing dependence in the non-Gaussian setting is itself a challenging one (Kotz, Balakrishnan, and Johnson, 2000). Somewhat analogous considerations arise when dealing with associated outliers in several variables in multivariable datasets, as in the case of common-mode outliers discussed in Chapter 2.

It is worth noting that these considerations are somewhat analogous to the considerations that arise in dealing with missing data. In particular, note that the simplest missing data model is the *missing completely at random (MCAR)* model (McLachlan and Krishnan, 1997, p. 227), which assumes that the distribution of missing observations is independent of both the missing data values and all other observed variables. This model is highly analogous to the i.i.d. random variable model for outliers just described. An important relaxation of the MCAR model is the *missing at random (MAR)* (Rubin, 1987, p. 53) model, which allows the missing data distribution to depend on other, completely observed, variables, but not on the values of the missing observations. Both of these models are used to describe ignorable missing data, but the MAR model leads to a different class of imputation strategies. The case of nonignorable missing data allows for a wider range of systematic differences between missing and nonmissing data values, such as a dependence of the probability of missing observations on the values of those observations. For the problems of possibly nonignorable missing data and possibly dependent outliers, a promising avenue of investigation that appears to have been relatively little explored is the characterization of *patterns* of these anomalies in real datasets. In the case of missing data, such investigations could lead to useful new models for nonignorable missing data, and in the case of outliers, these investigations might lead to useful models for dependent outliers. Note that the general replacement outlier model discussed in Chapter 3 may be particularly useful in this regard since the indicator variable z_k appearing there characterizes each data point as being either a nominal or an anomalous data value. Hence, questions of statistical dependence in this model can be assessed in terms of dependent binary sequences, for which many results may be derived fairly easily.

8.3.3   How should asymmetry be handled?

The problem of detecting outliers in asymmetrically distributed datasets was first noted in Chapter 2 in connection with the industrial pressure dataset example and was subsequently revisited in Chapter 4 in connection with the performance of three different outlier detection procedures, one of which has at least limited ability to handle distributional asymmetry. Unfortunately, none of these three procedures appeared to give satisfactory results for this

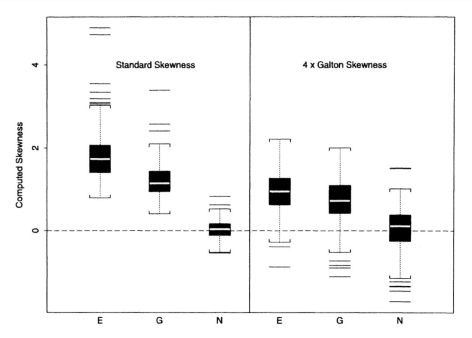

Figure 8.1. *Standard and Galton skewness measures estimated from samples of three different distributions: exponential (E), gamma (G), and normal (N).*

dataset. The general difficulty of the outlier detection problem in asymmetric situations was emphasized in the Princeton Robustness Study, which concluded with the following observation from J.W. Tukey (Andrews et al., 1972, p. 226):

> *We did a little about unsymmetric situations, but we were not able to agree, either between or within individuals, as to the criteria to be used.*

In practice, asymmetry poses several important problems, including the question just noted of how to detect outliers in the face of asymmetric nominal data, the question of how to characterize nominal data asymmetry when outliers are present, and the more general question of how to extend other forms of data analysis (e.g., regression analysis) to situations where asymmetry is pronounced.

The outlier-sensitivity of the standard moment-based skewness estimator $\hat{\gamma}_s$ was demonstrated in Chapter 1, where it was also shown that Galton's quantile-based skewness measure exhibited much-reduced outlier-sensitivity. Unfortunately, Galton's skewness measure also exhibits lower sensitivity to the underlying asymmetry of the nominal data sequence in the absence of outliers. This point is illustrated in Figure 8.1, which shows boxplots of both the standard–moment-based skewness estimate $\hat{\gamma}_s$ and Galton's skewness estimate $\hat{\gamma}_G$ for three distributions: the exponential distribution (E), the gamma distribution with shape parameter $\alpha = 2$ (G), and the Gaussian (normal) distribution (N). The probability density function for the gamma distribution is

$$p(x) = \frac{1}{\Gamma(\alpha)}\, x^{\alpha-1} e^{-x}, \tag{8.2}$$

where $\Gamma(\cdot)$ is the gamma function (Abramowitz and Stegun, 1972). This family includes the exponential distribution as a special case ($\alpha = 1$) and the normal distribution as a limiting case ($\alpha \to \infty$). The standard skewness measure for gamma-distributed random variables is

$$\gamma_s = \frac{2}{\sqrt{\alpha}}. \tag{8.3}$$

A comparably simple expression is not available for Galton's skewness measure, but γ_G is easily evaluated numerically from the quantiles of the gamma distribution for these examples, giving

E: exponential, $\gamma_G \simeq 0.262$;

G: gamma, $\alpha = 2$, $\gamma_G \simeq 0.172$;

N: normal $\Rightarrow$ symmetric $\Rightarrow \gamma_G = 0$.

The boxplots shown in Figure 8.1 compare the standard skewness estimate $\hat{\gamma}_s$ with Galton's skewness estimate, scaled by four to facilitate comparison. That is, since $\hat{\gamma}_G$ satisfies $-1 \leq \hat{\gamma}_G \leq 1$ while $\hat{\gamma}_s$ can assume any real value, direct comparison of the unscaled values obscures the distribution-dependence of $\hat{\gamma}_G$. Scaling the $\hat{\gamma}_G$ results by a factor of four in this example makes the natural ranges of variation (i.e., the widths of the central boxes) roughly comparable for the exponential distribution (E), making direct visual comparison of the results more meaningful. These comparisons illustrate the point noted above that $\hat{\gamma}_G$ is less sensitive to changes in the nominal data distribution than $\hat{\gamma}_s$ is.

It was noted in Chapter 2 that, for univariate data, a less restrictive alternative to the popular distributional symmetry assumption is unimodality. Also, for symmetric, unimodal distributions, the mean, median, and mode all coincide but they are generally all distinct for asymmetric distributions. Taken together, these two observations suggest the mode as an alternative location estimator that may remain useful for asymmetric unimodal distributions. Bickel (2002) has recently developed an outlier-resistant mode estimator that can serve as a basis both for location estimation in the presence of asymmetry and for skewness assessment. The underlying idea behind this estimator is the following. First, assume $F(x)$ is the cumulative distribution function associated with any unimodal density $p(x)$. Next, let w be any positive real number and define $\tilde{M}(w)$ as the value of M that maximizes

$$J(w) = F(M + w/2) - F(M - w/2). \tag{8.4}$$

Bickel (2002) then defines the *modal interval of width* w as the closed interval

$$I_w = [\tilde{M}(w) - w/2, \tilde{M}(w) + w/2], \tag{8.5}$$

and he notes that the mode M of the distribution lies in all modal intervals I_w. From this observation, it is clear that the mode is given by

$$M = \lim_{w \to 0} \tilde{M}(w). \tag{8.6}$$

Bickel (2002) describes a computable estimator $\tilde{M}$ based on this idea called the *half-range mode*, presenting a *Mathematica*® procedure for computing it that also handles mode estimates for multimodal distributions. Bickel (2002) also presents a detailed discussion of the robustness properties of this estimator and a simple extension to skewness characterization. Specifically, he defines the *modal skewness* as

$$\alpha = 1 - 2F(M), \tag{8.7}$$

where M is the mode of the distribution. Essentially, this skewness measure is based on the difference between the median $x^\dagger$ and the mode M. In particular, since $F(x^\dagger) = 1/2$ for any distribution, it follows that $\alpha = 0$ if $M = x^\dagger$, a situation that always holds for symmetric distributions. Similarly, if all data values are greater than or equal to the mode (e.g., in a J-shaped distribution such as the exponential distribution), it follows that $\alpha = +1$, while if all values are less than or equal to the mode, $\alpha = -1$. Estimating M using the half-range mode leads to the modal skewness estimator

$$\tilde{\alpha} = 1 - \frac{2\#(x < \tilde{M})}{N}, \tag{8.8}$$

where $\#(x < \tilde{M})$ is the number of values in a data sample of size N that are less than $\tilde{M}$ plus $1/2$ the number of samples that are equal to $\tilde{M}$.

Another important aspect of asymmetry is that symmetry assumptions often arise implicitly from the need to center the data. Hence, the use of a location estimate such as the mean or the median as the basis for this centering operation brings in a dependence on symmetry assumptions that is easy to overlook. Alternatively, it is sometimes possible to avoid this dependence by considering location-free data characterizations. Historically, perhaps the best-known of these characterizations is *Gini's mean difference* (Johnson, Kotz, and Balakrishnan, 1994, p. 3)

$$\hat{G} = \binom{N}{2}^{-1} \sum_{i=1}^{N} \sum_{j>i} |x_i - x_j|, \tag{8.9}$$

which attempts to estimate

$$G = E\{|x_i - x_j|\}, \tag{8.10}$$

where x_i and x_j are any two statistically independent samples from a continuous distribution. This quantity represents a measure of scale since it characterizes the distance between distinct random samples from the distribution. Because $\hat{G}$ is based on an average, it exhibits significant outlier-sensitivity, but Rousseeuw and Croux (1993) present a number of outlier-resistant alternatives, the simplest being

$$S = c \ \text{median}_i \ \{\text{median}_j \ \{|x_i - x_j|\}\}, \tag{8.11}$$

where taking $c = 1.1926$ makes S an unbiased estimate of the standard deviation σ for Gaussian data. The key point here is that both the statistic G and the estimators $\hat{G}$ and S are location-free: no estimate of the "center" of the distribution is required. Instead, these quantities attempt to characterize the density of points in a data sample. Two other data characterizations that do not depend on symmetry assumptions are the Spearman rank correlation coefficient discussed in Chapter 2 and the notion of regression depth (Rousseeuw

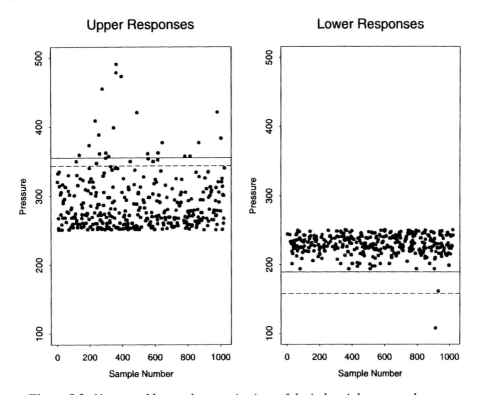

Figure 8.2. *Upper and lower characterizations of the industrial pressure dataset.*

and Hubert, 1999) discussed in Chapter 4. In both cases, these data characterizations exhibit invariance under certain monotone data transformations that can change distributional symmetry dramatically without having any effect on the computed result.

Conversely, another possible approach to dealing with distributional asymmetry for univariate data sequences is to explicitly address the asymmetry assumption, splitting the dataset into upper and lower parts and characterizing each part independently. Note that this idea is somewhat analogous to that of classification and regression trees described by Breiman et al. (1984). The simplest implementation of this strategy uses the median to split the dataset into two equal-sized subsets (i.e., the lower and upper halves of the data), although an alternative worth exploring would be to use the robust mode estimator of Bickel (2002) as the basis for this splitting. The consequences of the median-based splitting strategy for the asymmetric pressure data sequence considered in Chapters 2 and 4 are shown in Figure 8.2. Specifically, the left-hand plot shows those pressure values lying above the median, regarded as a distinct dataset, while the right-hand plot shows the corresponding pressure values lying below the median. In addition, two different outlier detection limits are shown for each of these datasets. The dashed line in each plot corresponds to the limit obtained for the Hampel identifier discussed in Chapter 3: in the upper response plot, this line corresponds to the median plus three times the MAD scale estimate *computed from the complete dataset*. Similarly, the dashed line in the lower response plot corresponds to the median minus three times this MAD scale estimate. The solid line in the left-hand plot (the upper responses) represents the upper Hampel identifier limit *computed only from the upper response data (i.e., the data values above the median)*. Similarly, the solid line in the right-hand plot (the lower responses) represents the lower Hampel identifier limit computed from the lower response data only. For the lower response data, the difference between these two outlier detection limits is both substantial and practically significant: the unmodified Hampel identifier only detects one of the two visually obvious outliers in this plot, while the modified Hampel identifier clearly detects both of them. Conversely, note that the modified Hampel identifier is *less* aggressive for the upper responses, declaring 26 points as upper outliers, as opposed to 36 upper outliers detected by the unmodified Hampel identifier. It is not clear that the approach taken here is the best one for problems of this type, but the results obtained do appear to be more satisfactory than those obtained from the original dataset using any of the methods discussed in Chapter 3. Further, it is interesting to note that the approach just described for the problem of outlier detection in the face of nominal data asymmetry takes a step in the direction of cluster analysis proposed by Huber (1993) for characterizing contaminated data. Specifically, the pressure dataset considered here illustrates the potential advantages of classifying data into three groups: nominal data values, upper outliers, and lower outliers.

Finally, note that one historically important approach to handling asymmetry is through the use of transformations. Frequently, the objective of these transformations is to make the distribution of the transformed data sequence approximately normal, hence approximately symmetric. A specific example is the use of the logarithmic transformation to improve the distributional character of measured intensities in the analysis of microarray data (Draghici, 2003, Sec. 12.2.1). This transformation is a member of the family of Box–Cox transformations (Atkinson, 1985; Atkinson and Riani, 2000; Box and Cox, 1964) defined by

$$T_\lambda\{x_k\} = \begin{cases} \dfrac{x_k^\lambda - 1}{\lambda \dot{x}^{\lambda-1}}, & \lambda \neq 0, \\[2ex] \dot{x} \log x_k, & \lambda = 0, \end{cases} \tag{8.12}$$

where $\dot{x}$ is the geometric mean of the observed sequence $\{x_k\}$. Note that this transformation is only applicable to sequences $\{x_k\}$ of positive real numbers. Other transformations, appropriate in other settings, are discussed by Atkinson (1985).

In contemplating the use of a transformation like the Box–Cox family, a key practical question is how the transformation parameter should be chosen. The approach advocated by Box and Cox (1964) is to cast the problem as one of maximum likelihood parameter estimation under the assumption that the transformed data sequence is an i.i.d. sequence of Gaussian random variables. Extensions of this idea to somewhat more general settings are discussed by Atkinson and Riani (2000, Chapter 4). A fundamental difficulty with this approach is that the presence of outliers in the original data sequence can severely bias our estimate of the transformation parameters, a point illustrated clearly in the three modified poison data examples discussed by Atkinson and Riani (2000, Secs. 4.5–4.7). As a consequence, just as in the analysis of OLS regression residuals discussed by Belsley, Kuh, and Welsch (1980), the resulting transformation can hide the outliers from the view of outlier detection procedures such as those discussed in Chapter 3. One practical alternative is that discussed in detail by Atkinson and Riani (2000, Chapter 4), which combines several Box–Cox transformations with the forward search strategy discussed in Chapter 4 (Sec. 4.4.3).

There, the basic idea is to construct a test statistic for the adequacy of each specific transformation considered, use highly robust estimation methods to find an outlier-free, small subset of the data, and monitor the test statistic as points are added back into the dataset. The observation of anomalous behavior as outliers are added back into the dataset can give an indication of their presence.

8.3.4   How should misalignments be detected?

The problem of misalignment of records in multivariable datasets was discussed at length in Chapter 2, and its practical severity was illustrated by the CAMDA normal mouse dataset discussed in Chapter 1. There, an apparent software error resulted in the misalignment of approximately 36% of the data values in a summary dataset obtained by combining several individual datasets. Analogous difficulties were seen in a second microarray dataset discussed in Chapter 2, where the presence of incomplete records in an Excel spreadsheet caused subsequent file read errors in an S-PLUS analysis procedure. The key point is that both of these sources—simple software errors and inconsistently handled missing data values—are sufficiently common problems that we can expect serious misalignment errors to arise regularly in practice. The practical difficulty is that, unlike with the simpler outlier detection problem, which has been studied for over a century, much less has been done in the area of systematic misalignment detection and correction procedures.

The treatment by Stivers et al. (2003) of the CAMDA normal mouse data misalignment problem provides some useful insight into the more general misalignment detection and treatment problem. Recall that the authors of this study performed a preliminary PCA to confirm certain basic expectations about the data (specifically, that the responses would fall into four groups, one for each of the three tissue samples considered and one for the common control mix). The fact that they did not obtain the expected result prompted them to search for the cause, which they ultimately determined to be a misalignment error. Two key observations here are, first, that PCA is a multivariate characterization, and, second, that the preliminary analysis was intended to confirm a gross structural feature that should otherwise have been of little inherent interest. The use of multivariate characterizations such as PCA, correlation, and regression analysis is essential because shift errors primarily influence the relationship between variables in a dataset rather than the distribution of data values themselves. Similarly, the preliminary use of simple "uninteresting" data characterizations is valuable in detecting misalignment errors and other subtle data anomalies because violations of simple forms of expected behavior are easier to see than violations of more complex forms of expected behavior. In addition, note that this same characterization was useful in assessing the quality of subsequent attempts to correct the problem even before its ultimate character was known.

Another example of misalignment anomalies is the problem of shift errors in manually recorded standardized examinations discussed by Skiena and Sumazin (2000). This problem arises when a student marks the intended answer for question q in the space corresponding to question $q + j$ for some $j \neq 0$, a problem that typically persists for several successive questions. These authors reported finding that 1% to 2% of the examinations they analyzed from SUNY Stony Brook contained probable shift errors. In addition, they reported finding that the problem of detecting shift errors depended on at least five factors: (1) the ability of the student, (2) the difficulty of the examination, (3) the incorrect shifted answers, (4) random guessing by the examinee, and (5) the pattern of the correct answers. To detect shift errors, the authors considered three approaches: a method based on dynamic programming that uses string alignment algorithms between a set of examination results and the answer key and two approaches based on probabilistic models. They conclude that the dynamic-programming approach tended to excessively compensate poorly performing students, so they prefer the two probability-based approaches. In both of these approaches, the examination results are first converted into a binary string, with 0 corresponding to each correct answer and 1 corresponding to each incorrect answer. These sequences are then characterized in terms of the probability $P(N, n, k, m)$ that a random binary string of length N with m zeros contains a patch of length n with at least k values equal to 1. Observed patches with low probability under this model are termed suspicious and subjected to further evaluation. For example, it is argued that detection and correction of shift errors should result in an increase in the examination score and not a decrease, and this is one criterion used in classifying suspicious patches. Results presented for real examination results with artificially introduced shifts clearly demonstrate that the probability of detecting these artificial shifts is a strong function of the detection algorithm used and the difficulty of the examination. In particular, detection results improved as more details were included in the probability model (e.g., the use of classwide scores to assess the difficulty gave better results than using only the individual student's score), and detection became more difficult as the difficulty of the examination increased. Both of these tendencies relate to the observation that errors in a patch of relatively easy questions are more suggestive of a shift error than the same errors in a patch of relatively difficult questions.

A particularly important feature of this last example is that it makes significant use of the binary sequence characterizing student responses: every recorded response can be uniquely classified as correct or incorrect based on the available data. The basic data quality question addressed by Skiena and Sumazin (2000) is whether the assumed identity mapping between the student's recorded answers and that student's *intended* answers is likely correct or not. It is certainly possible that suitable surrogates for this binary answer classification can be found for other classes of problems, but it is not obvious how often this will or will not be the case. In addition, it is also important to note that the results reported by Skiena and Sumazin (2000) improved as more detailed auxiliary knowledge was included in the detection procedure (e.g., difficulty of the examination questions, the observation that isolated strings of incorrect answers were less likely for high-scoring students than for low-scoring students). This point reinforces the conclusion drawn from the microarray study of Stivers et al. (2003) that application-specific auxiliary knowledge can be extremely useful in detecting data misalignments.

Finally, a special case of the data misalignment problem that arises in survey sampling has been considered by Hill (1993). In particular, Hill considered the problem of *skip sequencing* in surveys, a procedure commonly used to reduce the time required to complete a manual survey. The basic idea is to arrange questions in such a way that the need for answers to some questions depends on the answer given for specific previous questions (e.g., "if you answered 'no' to question 4, skip questions 5 through 9 and go on to question 10"). Hill notes,

> Although the savings afforded by skip sequencing may be considerable, they
> come at a cost in terms of data reliability, which may also be high, but which

No.	Question: Did you ...	I	R_1	R_2	R_3
1	... have a job? (if yes, go to 4)	Y	N	N	—
2	... spend time looking? (if yes, go to 5)	—	Y	N	Y
3	... want a job? (if yes, go to 5)	—	—	N	—
4	... have a job each week? (if yes, go to 10)	N	—	—	—
5	... receive unemployment compensation? (if yes, go to 10)	N	N	—	N
6	...				
	Number of induced errors:	—	2	4	2

Table 8.1. *Skip-sequencing example based on that presented by Hill* (1993).

*is seldom readily observable. The reason the losses in reliability may be high
is that sequencing acts to amplify error by transmitting it from one question to
subsequent questions—often* many *subsequent questions.*

To see how this contagion mechanism works, it is instructive to look at a simple example. Table 8.1 is based on an employment/unemployment survey discussed by Hill (1993), and it lists five questions with their associated skip-sequencing instructions. In the actual survey on which this example is based, a random sample of the original participants were chosen for reinterview, and the original and reinterview responses were compared. In Table 8.1, hypothetical interviewer (original) responses are listed in column I, and three possible reinterview responses are given in columns R_1, R_2, and R_3 to illustrate some of these survey error types. A *response error* is declared whenever the original response I differs from the reinterview response R_1, R_2, or R_3. Note that in the sequences R_1 and R_2, the response error in question 1 causes a different set of subsequent questions to be answered. When the same question is asked in both the original interview and the reinterview but only one answer is recorded, Hill refers to the result as a *sequencing error*. In cases like response sequences R_1 and R_2 where the sequencing error is due to the combined effects of a response error and the skip sequencing of the survey, Hill calls the result a *response-induced discrepancy*. The key point here is that both of the sequences R_1 and R_2 are internally consistent (i.e., consistent with the skip-sequencing structure of the survey), but the response error in question 1 leads to a different number of overall response errors in the survey, depending on the responses to subsequent questions. In particular, note that the response error in question 1 induces two additional response errors in response sequence R_1 (questions 2 and 4), while this response error induces four additional response errors in sequence R_2 (questions 2, 3, 4, and 5). Finally, response sequence R_3 exhibits what Hill calls a *spontaneous sequencing error* or a *procedural error:* the nonresponse to question 1 forces the interviewer to proceed to question 2 and follow the appropriate skip sequencing after that. Here, this initial nonresponse induces two more response errors (questions 2 and 4), which Hill calls a *procedurally induced discrepancy*. Hill notes that while spontaneous sequencing errors are often viewed as errors on the part of the interviewer (hence the alternative term *procedural error*), this situation also arises when a respondent is unwilling or unable to answer a question.

Because of the forward propagation of errors just described, Hill (1993) introduces what he calls a *discrete contagious regression model* in which response errors are clustered. The number of clusters is assumed to have a Poisson distribution (appropriate to rare events), and the number of errors n_e in each cluster is assumed to have an independent, modified Poisson distribution (specifically, $n_e - 1$ is assumed to have a Poisson distribution). Hill derives a maximum likelihood estimation procedure for this error model and uses it to analyze the results of the 1984 Survey of Income and Program Participation (SIPP) Reinterview Program, described in detail by Kalton, Hill, and Miller (1990). He finds that the discrete contagious regression model fits the SIPP data significantly better than the simpler Poisson error model appropriate to random response errors not induced by skip sequencing. In addition, Hill also finds that the number of induced response errors is a strong function of skip-sequence length (specifically, longer skip sequences give rise to more errors), and it also depends on characteristics (e.g., educational level, age, race, and gender) of both the interviewer and the respondent. In both this example and the example of sequence errors in examination responses considered by Skiena and Sumazin (2000), specialized approaches were developed for the misalignment problem that were adapted to the specific problem under consideration and that made significant use of auxiliary knowledge and problem-specific features. In other, more general, settings, the question of how best to detect such data misalignments appears to be largely open and of extreme practical importance.

Bibliography

Abramowitz, M., and Stegun, I. (1972). *Handbook of Mathematical Functions*. New York: Dover.

Aczél, J. (1966). *Lectures on Functional Equations and Their Applications*. New York: Academic Press.

Aczél, J. (1987). *A Short Course on Functional Equations*. Boston: D. Reidel.

Aczél, J. (1997). Bisymmetry and consistent aggregation: Historical review and recent results. In Marley, A., editor, *Choice, Decision, and Measurement: Essays in Honor of R. Duncan Luce*, pages 225–233. Lawrence Baum Associates, Mahwah, NJ.

Aczél, J., and Dhombres, J. (1989). *Functional Equations in Several Variables*. Cambridge, U.K.: Cambridge University Press.

Aczél, J., Gronau, D., and Schwaiger, J. (1994). Increasing solutions of the homogeneity equation and of similar equations. *J. Math. Anal. Appl.*, 182:436–464.

Aczél, J., and Maksa, G. (1996). Solution of the rectangular $m \times n$ generalized bisymmetry equation and of the problem of consistent aggregation. *J. Math. Anal. Appl.*, 203:104–126.

Adriaans, P., and Zantinge, D. (1996). *Data Mining*. Reading, MA: Addison–Wesley.

Aitchison, J. (1994). Principles of compositional data analysis. In Anderson, T., Fang, K., and Olkin, I., editors, *Multivariate Analysis and Its Applications*, pages 73–81. Hayward, CA: Institute of Mathematical Statistics.

Altman, D., and Bland, J. (1983). Measurement in medicine: The analysis of method comparison studies. *The Statistician*, 32:307–317.

Andrews, D., Bickel, P., Hampel, F., Huber, P., Rogers, W., and Tukey, J. (1972). *Robust Estimates of Location*. Princeton, NJ: Princeton University Press.

Anscombe, F., and Glynn, W. (1983). Distribution of the kurtosis statistic b_2 for normal samples. *Biometrika*, 70:227–234.

Astola, J., Heinonen, P., and Neuvo, Y. (1987). On root structures of median and median-type filters. *IEEE Trans. Signal Proc.*, 35:1,199–1,201.

Astola, J., and Kuosmanen, P. (1997). *Fundamentals of Nonlinear Digital Filtering*. Boca Raton, FL: CRC Press.

Atkinson, A. (1985). *Plots, Transformations and Regression*. New York: Oxford University Press.

Atkinson, A. (1991). Optimum design of experiments. In Hinkley, D., Reid, N., and Snell, E., editors, *Statistical Theory and Modelling*, Chapter 9. London: Chapman and Hall.

Atkinson, A. (1994). Fast very robust methods for the detection of multiple outliers. *J. Amer. Stat. Assoc.*, 89:1,329–1,339.

Atkinson, A., and Donev, A. (1992). *Optimum Experimental Designs*. New York: Oxford.

Atkinson, A., and Riani, M. (2000). *Robust Diagnostic Regression Analysis*. New York: Springer-Verlag.

Atkinson, A., Riani, M., and Cerioli, A. (2004). *Exploring Multivariate Data with the Forward Search*. New York, London: Springer-Verlag.

Baker, R. (2002). Future directions of membrane gas separation technology. *Ind. Eng. Chem. Res.*, 41:1,393–1,411.

Barcena, M., and Tusell, F. (2000). Tree-based algorithms for missing data imputation. In Bethlehem, J., and van der Heijden, P., editors, *Proc. 14th Symposium Computational Statistics, COMPSTAT 2000*, pages 193–198. Heidelberg: Physica-Verlag.

Barnett, V., and Lewis, T. (1994). *Outliers in Statistical Data*. New York: Wiley, 3rd edition.

Basilevsky, A. (1994). *Statistical Factor Analysis and Related Methods*. New York: Wiley.

Bassett, G. (1991). Equivariant, monotonic, 50% breakdown estimators. *Amer. Stat.*, 45:135–137.

Becker, C. (2000). The size of the largest nonidentifiable outlier as a performance criterion for multivariate outlier identification: The case of high-dimensional data. In Bethlehem, J., and van der Heijden, P., editors, *Proc. 14th Symposium Computational Statistics, COMPSTAT 2000*, pages 211–216. Heidelberg: Physica-Verlag.

Beer, D., Kardia, S., Huang, C.-C., Giordano, T., Levin, A., Misek, D., Lin, L., Chen, G., Gharib, T., Thomas, D., Lizyness, M., Kuick, R., Hayasaka, S., Taylor, J., Iannettoni, M., Orringer, M., and Hanash, S. (2002). Gene-expression profiles predict survival of patients with lung adenocarcinoma. *Nature Medicine*, 8:816–824.

Beizer, B. (1990). *Software Testing Techniques*. New York: Van Nostrand Reinhold.

Belsley, D. (1991). *Conditioning Diagnostics: Collinearity and Weak Data in Regression*. New York: Wiley.

Belsley, D., Kuh, E., and Welsch, R. (1980). *Regression Diagnostics*. New York: Wiley.

Berger, M. (1987). *Geometry* I. Berlin, New York: Springer-Verlag.

Bernaards, C. (2000). The influence of data generation and imputation methods on the bias of factor analysis of rating scale data. In Bethlehem, J., and van der Heijden, P., editors, *Proc. 14th Symposium Computational Statistics, COMPSTAT* 2000, pages 217–222. Heidelberg: Physica-Verlag.

Bhatia, R., and Davis, C. (2000). A better bound on the variance. *Amer. Math. Monthly*, 107:353–357.

Bickel, D. (2002). Robust estimators of the mode and skewness of continuous data. *Comput. Stat. Data Anal.*, 39:153–163.

Billingsley, P. (1986). *Probability and Measure*. New York: Wiley.

Bloomfield, P., and Steiger, W. (1983). *Least Absolute Deviations*. Cambridge: Birkhäuser Boston.

Bolshakova, N., and Azuaje, F. (2003). Cluster validation techniques for genome expression data. *Signal Processing*, 83:825–833.

Box, G., and Cox, D. (1964). An analysis of transformations. *J. Royal Stat. Assoc., Series B*, 26:211–243.

Box, G., Jenkins, G., and Reinsel, G. (1994). *Time Series Analysis*. Englewood Cliffs, NJ: Prentice–Hall, 3rd edition.

Breiman, L., Friedman, J., Olshen, R., and Stone, C. (1984). *Classification and Regression Trees*. Belmont, CA: Wadsworth and Brooks.

Brockwell, P., and Davis, R. (1991). *Time Series: Theory and Methods*. New York: Springer-Verlag.

Brownlee, K. (1960). *Statistical Theory and Methodology in Science and Engineering*. New York: Wiley.

Brualdi, R. (1999). *Introductory Combinatorics*. Upper Saddle River, NJ: Prentice–Hall, 3rd edition.

Bruce, A., and Martin, R. (1989). Leave-k-out diagnostics for time series. *J. Royal Stat. Soc., Series A*, 51:363–424.

Buzzigoli, L., and Giusti, A. (2000). Disclosure control on multi-way tables by means of the shuttle algorithm: Extensions and experiments. In Bethlehem, J., and van der Heijden, P., editors, *Proc. 14th Symposium Computational Statistics, COMPSTAT* 2000, pages 229–234. Heidelberg: Physica-Verlag.

Calder, W. (1996). *Size, Function, and Life History*. Mineola, NY: Dover.

Chatterjee, S., and Hadi, A. (1988). *Sensitivity Analysis in Linear Regression*. New York: Wiley.

Chave, A., and Thomson, D. (1989). Some comments on magnetotelluric response function estimation. *J. Geophys. Research*, 94:14,215–14,225.

Chave, A., Thomson, D., and Ander, M. (1987). On the robust estimation of power spectra, coherences, and transfer functions. *J. Geophys. Research*, 92:633–648.

Cios, K., Pedrycz, W., and Swiniarski, R. (1998). *Data Mining Methods for Knowledge Discovery*. Boston: Kluwer Academic.

Cochran, W. (1968). The effectiveness of adjustment by subclassification in removing bias in observational studies. *Biometrics*, 24:205–213.

Cohen, A. (1985). A bounding approach to calculating $\alpha^{1/p}$. *Computing*, 34:87–89.

Collett, D. (2003). *Modelling Binary Data*. Boca Raton, FL: Chapman and Hall, 3rd edition.

Conversano, C., and Cappelli, C. (2002). Missing data incremental imputation through tree based methods. In Härdle, W., and Rönz, B., editors, *Proc. 15th Symposium Computational Statistics, COMPSTAT* 2002, pages 455–460. Heidelberg: Physica-Verlag.

Corbellini, A. (2002). Clockwise bivariate boxplots. In Härdle, W., and Rönz, B., editors, *Proc. 15th Symposium Computational Statistics, COMPSTAT* 2002, pages 231–236, Berlin.

Cornell, J. (2002). *Experiments with Mixtures*. New York: Wiley, 3rd edition.

Croux, C., and Haesbroeck, G. (1999). Influence function and efficiency of the maximum covariance determinant scatter matrix estimator. *J. Multivariate Anal.*, 71:161–190.

D'Agostino, R., and Stephens, M., editors (1986). *Goodness-of-Fit Techniques*. New York: Marcel Dekker.

Daniel, C., and Wood, F. (1971). *Fitting Equations to Data*. New York: Wiley.

Dasu, T., and Johnson, T. (2003). *Exploratory Data Mining and Data Cleaning*. New York: Wiley.

Date, C. (2000). *An Introduction to Database Systems*. Reading, MA: Addison–Wesley, 7th edition.

Davies, L., and Gather, U. (1993). The identification of multiple outliers. *J. Amer. Stat. Assoc.*, 88:782–801.

Davis, H. (1962). *Introduction to Nonlinear Differential and Integral Equations*. New York: Dover.

Davison, A., and Hinkley, D. (1997). *Bootstrap Methods and Their Application*. Cambridge, U.K.: Cambridge University Press.

Day, W.H.E., and McMorris, F.R. (2003). *Axiomatic Consensus Theory in Group Choice and Biomathematics*. Philadelphia: SIAM.

Dehon, C., and Croux, C. (2002). Statistical inference for a robust measure of multiple correlation. In Härdle, W., and Rönz, B., editors, *Proc. 15th Symposium Computational Statistics, COMPSTAT* 2002, pages 557–562. Heidelberg: Physica-Verlag.

Denby, L., and Martin, R. (1979). Robust estimation of the first-order autoregressive parameter. *J. Amer. Stat. Assoc.*, 74:140–146.

Dodge, Y. (1996). The guinea pig of multiple regression. In Rieder, H., editor, *Robust Statistics, Data Analysis, and Computer Intensive Methods*, pages 91–117. New York: Springer-Verlag.

Dong, G., and Deshpande, K. (2001). Efficient mining of niches and set routines. In Cheung, D., Williams, G., and Li, Q., editors, *Advances in Knowledge Discovery and Data Mining*, pages 234–246. Berlin, New York: Springer-Verlag.

Donoho, D., and Huber, P. (1983). The notion of breakdown point. In Bickel, P., Doksum, K., and Hodges, J., editors, *A Festschrift for Erich L. Lehmann*, pages 157–184. Belmont, CA: Wadsworth.

Doyle III, F., Pearson, R., and Ogunnaike, B. (2002). *Identification and Control Using Volterra Models*. London, New York: Springer-Verlag.

Draghici, S. (2003). *Data Analysis Tools for DNA Microarrays*. Boca Raton, FL: Chapman and Hall/CRC.

Draper, D., Hodges, J., Mallows, C., and Pregibon, D. (1993). Exchangeability and data analysis. *J. Royal Stat. Soc., Series A*, 159:9–37.

Drummond, C., and Holte, R. (2003). C4.5, class imbalance, and cost sensitivity: Why under-sampling beats over-sampling. In *Proc. ICML-2003 Workshop: Learning with Imbalanced Data Sets* II, pages 1–8. Heidelberg: Physica-Verlag.

Dudoit, S., and Fridlyand, J. (2002). A prediction-based resampling method for estimating the number of clusters in a dataset. *Genome Biol.*, 3:research0036.1–0036.21.

Efron, B. (1982). *The Jackknife, the Bootstrap, and Other Resampling Plans*. Philadelphia: SIAM.

Efron, B., and Tibshirani, R. (1993). *An Introduction to the Bootstrap*. New York: Chapman and Hall.

Ellis, S.P. (2002). Fitting a line to three or four points on a plane. *SIAM Rev.*, 44:616–628.

Emerson, J. (1991). Graphical display as an aid to analysis. In Hoaglin, D., Mosteller, F., and Tukey, J., editors, *Fundamentals of Exploratory Analysis of Variance*, Chapter 8, pages 165–192. New York: Wiley.

English, T., Kaiser, L., Doyle, F., and Dhurjati, P. (1998). Analysis of post-upset plant data for fault detection. In *Proc. IFAC On-Line Fault Detection and Supervision in the Chemical Process Industries*, pages 353–358, Lyon, France.

Eriksson, L., Johnasson, E., Lindgren, F., Sjöström, M., and Wold, S. (2002). Megavariate analysis of hierarchical QSAR data. *J. Computer-Aided Molecular Design*, 16:711–726.

Ertöz, L., Steinbach, M., and Kumar, V. (2003). Finding clusters of different sizes, shapes, and densities in noisy, high dimensional data. In *Proc. 3rd SIAM Internat. Conf. Data Mining*, pages 47–58, San Francisco.

Filzmoser, P., Dehon, C., and Croux, C. (2000). Outlier resistant estimators for canonical correlation analysis. In Bethlehem, J., and van der Heijden, P., editors, *Proc. 14th Symposium Computational Statistics, COMPSTAT 2000*, pages 301–306. Heidelberg: Physica-Verlag.

Fox, A. (1972). Outliers in time series. *J. Royal Stat. Soc., Series* B, 34:350–363.

Gallagher, N., and Wise, G. (1981). A theoretical analysis of the properties of median filters. *IEEE Trans. Acoustics, Speech, Signal Proc.*, 29:1,136–1,141.

Garreau, J. (1981). *The Nine Nations of North America*. Boston: Houghton Mifflin.

Gibbons, J.D., Olkin, I., and Sobel, M. (1999). *Selecting and Ordering Populations: A New Statistical Methodology*. Philadelphia: SIAM.

Goldberg, A. (1976). The relevance of cosmopolitan/local orientations to professional values and behavior. *Sociol. Work Occupation*, 3:331–356.

Good, P. (2000). *Permutation Tests*. New York: Springer-Verlag, 2nd edition.

Gordon, A. (1999). *Classification*. Boca Raton, FL: Chapman and Hall/CRC, 2nd edition.

Govindarajulu, Z. (1999). *Elements of Sampling Theory and Methods*. Upper Saddle River, NJ: Prentice–Hall.

Gower, J., and Hand, D. (1996). *Biplots*. London, New York: Chapman and Hall.

Grimmett, G., and Stirzaker, D. (1982). *Probability and Random Processes*. New York: Oxford, 2nd edition.

Guckenheimer, J., and Holmes, P. (1983). *Nonlinear Oscillations, Dynamical Systems, and Bifurcations of Vector Fields*. New York: Springer-Verlag.

Haaser, N., and Sullivan, J. (1991). *Real Analysis*. New York: Dover.

Haavisto, P., Gabbouj, M., and Neuvo, Y. (1991). Median based idempotent filters. *J. Circuits, Systems, Computers*, 1:125–148.

Hajek, J., Sidak, Z., and Sen, P. (1999). *Theory of Rank Tests*. New York: Academic Press.

Hampel, F. (1985). The breakdown points of the mean combined with some rejection rules. *Technometrics*, 27:95–107.

Hansen, P., Jaumard, B., and Mladenovic, N. (1995). How to choose k entities among n. In Cox, I., Hansen, P., and Julesz, B., editors, *Partitioning Datasets*. Providence, RI: American Mathematical Society.

Hansen, P., and Mladenovic, N. (2002). Variable neighborhood search. In Glover, F., and Kochenagen, G., editors, *State-of-the-Art Handbook of Metaheuristics*. Norwell, MA: Kluwer.

Härdle, W. (1990). *Applied Nonparametric Regression*. Cambridge, New York: Cambridge University Press.

Hardy, G., Littlewood, J., and Polya, G. (1952). *Inequalities*. Cambridge, U.K.: Cambridge University Press, 2nd edition.

Healy, M., and Westmacott, M. (1956). Missing values in experiments analyzed on automatic computers. *Appl. Stat.*, 5:203–206.

Hendershot, R., Fu, Y., Snively, C., Lauterbach, J., Pearson, R., and Ogunnaike, B. (2003). Combined experimental and theoretical effort for rational design of novel catalytic materials. Paper 508b, presented at *AIChE Annual Meeting*, San Francisco.

Herbst, A., Ulfelder, H., and Poskanzer, D. (1971). Adenocarcinoma of the vagina: Association of maternal stilbestrol therapy with tumor appearance in young women. *New England J. Med.*, 284:878–881.

Hernandez, M., and Stolfo, S. (1998). Real-world data is dirty: Data cleansing and the merge/purge problem. *Data Mining and Knowledge Discovery*, 2:9–37.

Hettmansperger, T., and Sheather, S. (1992). A cautionary note on the method of least median squares. *Amer. Stat.*, 46:79–83.

Hill, D. (1993). Response and sequencing errors in surveys: A discrete contagious regression analysis. *J. Amer. Stat. Assoc.*, 88:775–781.

Hoaglin, D., Mosteller, F., and Tukey, J. (1991). *Fundamentals of Exploratory Analysis of Variance*. New York: Wiley.

Huber, P. (1981). *Robust Statistics*. New York: Wiley.

Huber, P. (1993). Projection pursuit and robustness. In Morgenthaler, S., Ronchetti, E., and Stahel, W., editors, *New Directions in Statistical Data Analysis and Robustness*, pages 139–146. Basel, Boston: Birkhäuser Verlag.

Huber, T., and Nagel, M. (1996). Data based prototyping. In Rieder, H., editor, *Robust Statistics, Data Analysis, and Computer Intensive Methods*, pages 197–213. New York: Springer-Verlag.

Hubert, L., Arabie, P., and Meulman, J. (2001). *Combinatorial Data Analysis: Optimization by Dynamic Programming*. Philadelphia: SIAM.

Huff, D. (1954). *How to Lie with Statistics*. New York: Norton. 43rd printing.

Huisman, M. (2000). Post-stratification to correct for nonresponse: Classification of zip code areas. In Bethlehem, J., and van der Heijden, P., editors, *Proc. 14th Symposium Computational Statistics, COMPSTAT 2000*, pages 325–330. Heidelberg: Physica-Verlag.

Insightful (2001). *S-PLUS 6 User's Guide*. Seattle: Insightful Corp.

Japkowicz, N., and Stephen, S. (2002). The class imbalance problem: A systematic study. *Intelligent Data Anal. J.*, 6:429–449.

Jobson, J. (1991). *Applied Multivariate Data Analysis, Vol. I: Regression and Experimental Design*. New York: Springer-Verlag.

Johnson, N., Kotz, S., and Balakrishnan, N. (1994). *Continuous Univariate Distributions*, volume 1. New York: Wiley.

Johnson, N., Kotz, S., and Balakrishnan, N. (1995). *Continuous Univariate Distributions*, volume 2. New York: Wiley.

Johnson, R., and Wichern, D. (1988). *Applied Multivariate Statistical Analysis*. Englewood Cliffs, NJ: Prentice–Hall.

Jörnsten, R., Vardi, Y., and Zhang, C.-H. (2002). A robust clustering method and visualization tool based on data depth. In Dodge, Y., editor, *Statistical Data Analysis Based on the L_1-Norm and Related Methods*, pages 1–14. Basel, Boston: Birkhäuser.

Kalton, G., Hill, D., and Miller, M. (1990). *The Seam Effect in Panel Surveys (SIPP Research Monograph No. 9011)*. Washington, DC: U.S. Census Bureau.

Kaner, C., Falk, J., and Nguyen, H. (1999). *Testing Computer Software*. New York: Wiley, 2nd edition.

Kaufman, L., and Rousseeuw, P. (1990). *Finding Groups in Data*. New York: Wiley.

Kerr, M., and Churchill, G. (2001). Bootstrapping cluster analysis: Assessing the reliability of conclusions from microarray experiments. *Proc. Nat. Acad. Sci.*, 98:8,961–8,965.

Klambauer, G. (1975). *Mathematical Analysis*. New York: Marcel Dekker.

Kooiman, P., Krose, A., and Ressen, R. (2000). Official statistics: An estimation strategy for the IT-era. In Bethlehem, J., and van der Heijden, P., editors, *Proc. 14th Symposium Computational Statistics, COMPSTAT 2000*, pages 15–26. Heidelberg: Physica-Verlag.

Kothapalli, R., Yoder, S., Mane, S., and Loughran Jr., T. (2002). Microarray results: How accurate are they? *BMC Bioinformatics*, 3:22.

Kotz, S., Balakrishnan, N., and Johnson, N. (2000). *Continuous Multivariate Distributions*, volume 1. New York: Wiley, 2nd edition.

Kreyszig, E. (1978). *Introductory Functional Analysis with Applications*. New York: Wiley.

Lehmann, E. (1983). *Theory of Point Estimation*. New York: Wiley.

Levitt, S., and Snyder Jr., J. (1997). The impact of federal spending on house election outcomes. *J. Political Economy*, 105:30–53.

Lipshutz, R., Morris, D., Chee, M., Hubbell, E., Kozal, M., Shah, N., Shen, N., Yang, R., and Fodor, S. (1995). Using oligonucleotide probe arrays to access genetic diversity. *Biotechniques*, 19:442–447.

Liu, R. (1990). On a notion of data depth based on random simplices. *Ann. Stat.*, 18:405–414.

Liu, R. (2003). Multivariate control charts: Hotelling T^2, data depth and beyond. In Khattree, R., and Rao, C., editors, *Handbook of Statistics: Statistics in Industry*, pages 573–593. Amsterdam: Elsevier.

Liu, R., Parelius, J., and Singh, K. (1999). Multivariate analysis by data depth. *Ann. Stat.*, 27:783–858.

MacQueen, J. (1967). Some methods for classification and analysis of multivariate observations. In Cam, L. L., and Neyman, J., editors, *5th Berkeley Symposium Math. Stat. Prob.*, volume 1, pages 281–297. Berkeley: University of California Press.

Mantegna, R., Ferrante, G., and Principato, F. (1999a). Experimental investigation of third and fourth moments of $1/f$ noise in microwave devices. In *Proc. 15th International Conf. Noise in Physical Systems and $1/f$ Fluctuations*, pages 439–441. London: Bentham Press.

Mantegna, R., Ferrante, G., and Principato, F. (1999b). Kurtosis experimental detection of electronic noise. In *Proc. 15th International Conf. Noise in Physical Systems and $1/f$ Fluctuations*, pages 442–445. London: Bentham Press.

Marden, J. (1995). *Analyzing and Modeling Rank Data*. London, New York: Chapman and Hall.

Marron, J., Hernandez-Campos, F., and Smith, F. (2002). Mice and elephant visualization of internet traffic. In Härdle, W., and Rönz, B., editors, *Proc. 15th Symposium Computational Statistics, COMPSTAT 2002*, pages 47–54. Heidelberg: Physica-Verlag.

Martin, J., and McClure, C. (1983). *Software Maintenance: The Problem and Its Solutions*. Englewood Cliffs, NJ: Prentice–Hall.

Martin, R., and Thomson, D. (1982). Robust-resistant spectrum estimation. *Proc. IEEE*, 70:1,097–1,114.

Martin, R., and Yohai, V. (1986). Influence functionals for time-series. *Ann. Stat.*, 14:781–785.

McClure, R. (1985). private communication, DuPont Company.

McCullagh, P., and Nelder, J. (1989). *Generalized Linear Models*. London, New York: Chapman and Hall, 2nd edition.

McLachlan, G., and Bashford, K. (1988). *Mixture Models*. New York: Marcel Dekker.

McLachlan, G., and Krishnan, T. (1997). *The EM Algorithm and Extensions*. New York: Wiley.

Milanese, M., Norton, J., Piet-Lahanier, H., and Walter, E. (1996). *Bounding Approaches to System Identification*. New York: Plenum Press.

Miller, A. (1990). *Subset Selection in Regression*. London, New York: Chapman and Hall.

Mitrinovic, D., Pecaric, J., and Fink, A. (1993). *Classical and New Inequalities in Analysis*. Dordrecht, Boston: Kluwer Academic.

Moore, R.E. (1979). *Methods and Applications of Interval Analysis*. Philadelphia: SIAM.

Morgenthaler, S. (2002). Weights and fragments. In Härdle, W., and Rönz, B., editors, *Proc. 15th Symposium Computational Statistics, COMPSTAT 2002*, pages 629–634. Heidelberg: Physica-Verlag.

Nodes, T., and Gallagher, N. (1982). Median filters: Some modifications and their properties. *IEEE Trans. Acoustics Speech Signal Proc.*, 30:739–746.

Papadimitriou, C., and Steiglitz, K. (1982). *Combinatorial Optimization: Algorithms and Complexity*. Englewood Cliffs, NJ: Prentice–Hall.

Papoulis, A. (1965). *Probability, Random Variables, and Stochastic Processes*. New York: McGraw–Hill.

Pearl, J. (1984). *Heuristics: Intelligent Search Strategies for Computer Problem Solving*. Reading, MA: Addison–Wesley.

Pearson, R.K. (1988). Block-sequential algorithms for set-theoretic estimation. *SIAM J. Matrix Anal. Appl.*, 9:513–527.

Pearson, R. (1999). *Discrete-Time Dynamic Models*. New York: Oxford.

Pearson, R. (2001a). Exploring process data. *J. Process Control*, 11:179–194.

Pearson, R. (2001b). Outliers in process modeling and identification. *IEEE Trans. Control System Tech.*, 10:55–63.

Pearson, R., Gonye, G., and Schwaber, J. (2003). Imbalanced clustering of microarray time-series. In *Proc. ICML-2003 Workshop: Learning with Imbalanced Data Sets* II, pages 65–72. Heidelberg: Physica-Verlag.

Pearson, R.K., Lähdesmäki, H., Huttunen, H., and Yli-Harja, O. (2003). Detecting periodicity in nonideal datasets. In *Proc. 3rd SIAM Internat. Conf. Data Mining*, pages 274–278. Philadelphia: SIAM.

Pearson, R.K., Zylkin, T., Schwaber, J.S., and Gonye, G.E. (2004). Quantitative evaluation of clustering results using computational negative controls. In *Proc. 4th SIAM Internat. Conf. Data Mining*, pages 188–199, Philadelphia: SIAM.

Pison, G., and Van Aelst, S. (2002). Analyzing data with robust multivariate methods and diagnostic plots. In Härdle, W., and Rönz, B., editors, *Proc. 15th Symposium Computational Statistics, COMPSTAT 2002*, pages 165–170. Heidelberg: Physica-Verlag.

Pitas, I., and Venetsanopoulos, A. (1990). *Nonlinear Digital Filters*. Boston: Kluwer Academic.

Port, S. (1994). *Theoretical Probability for Applications*. New York: Wiley.

Priestley, M. (1981). *Spectral Analysis and Time Series*. London, New York: Academic Press.

Pritchard, C., Hsu, L., Delrow, J., and Nelson, P. (2001). Project normal: Defining normal variance in mouse gene expression. *Proc. Nat. Acad. Sci.*, 98:13,266–13,271.

Qin, S. and Badgwell, T. (2000). An overview of nonlinear model predictive control applications. In Allgöwer, F. and Zheng, A., editors, *Nonlinear Model Predictive Control*, pages 369–392. Boston: Birkhäuser.

Rahman, N. (1972). *Practical Exercises in Probability and Statistics*. London: Griffin.

Ranganath, G. (1992). Materials with negative Poisson's ratio. *Current Sci.*, 63:160–163.

Rässler, S. (2002). *Statistical Matching*. New York: Springer-Verlag.

Riedel, K., Sidorenko, A., and Thomson, D. (1994). Spectral estimation of plasma fluctuations. I. Comparison of methods. *Phys. Plasmas*, 1:485–500.

Riordan, J. (2002). *Introduction to Combinatorial Analysis*. Mineola, NY: Dover.

Robertson, D. (2000). Improving Statistics Canada's cell suppression software (CONFID). In Bethlehem, J., and van der Heijden, P., editors, *Proc. 14th Symposium Computational Statistics, COMPSTAT* 2000, pages 403–408. Heidelberg: Physica-Verlag.

Rockafellar, T. (1970). *Convex Analysis*. Princeton, NJ: Princeton University Press.

Rocke, D., and Woodruff, D. (2002). Computational connections between robust multivariate analysis and clustering. In Härdle, W., and Rönz, B., editors, *Proc. 15th Symposium Computational Statistics, COMPSTAT* 2002, pages 255–260. Heidelberg: Physica-Verlag.

Rohatgi, V., and Szekely, G. (1989). Sharp inequalities between skewness and kurtosis. *Stat. Probab. Lett.*, 8:297–299.

Rosenbaum, P. (1970). *Observational Studies*. New York: Springer-Verlag, 2nd edition.

Roth, V., Lange, T., Braun, M., and Buhmann, J. (2002). A resampling approach to cluster validation. In Härdle, W., and Rönz, B., editors, *Proc. 15th Symposium Computational Statistics, COMPSTAT* 2002, pages 123–128. Heidelberg: Physica-Verlag.

Rousseeuw, P. (1984). Least median of squares. *J. Amer. Stat. Assoc.*, 79:871–880.

Rousseeuw, P. (1994). Unconventional features of positive-breakdown estimators. *Stat. Probab. Lett.*, 19:417–431.

Rousseeuw, P., and Croux, C. (1993). Alternatives to the median absolute deviation. *J. Amer. Stat. Assoc.*, 88:1,273–1,283.

Rousseeuw, P., and Hubert, M. (1999). Regression depth (with discussion). *J. Amer. Stat. Assoc.*, 4:388–433.

Rousseeuw, P., and Leroy, A. (1987). *Robust Regression and Outlier Detection.* New York: Wiley.

Rousseeuw, P., Ruts, I., and Tukey, W. (1999). The bagplot: A bivariate boxplot. *Amer. Statistician*, 53:382–387.

Rousseeuw, P., and Van Driessen, K. (1999). A fast algorithm for the minimum covariance determinant estimator. *Technometrics*, 41:212–223.

Rousseeuw, P., and Van Driessen, K. (2000). A fast algorithm for highly robust regression in data mining. In Bethlehem, J., and van der Heijden, P., editors, *Proc. 14th Symposium Computational Statistics, COMPSTAT 2000*, pages 421–426. Heidelberg: Physica-Verlag.

Rousseeuw, P., and Van Zomeron, B. (1990). Unmasking multivariate outliers and leverage points. *J. Amer. Stat. Assoc.*, 85:633–651.

Rowe, N.C. (1988). Absolute bounds on the mean and standard deviation of transformed data for constant-sign-derivative transformations. *SIAM J. Sci. Stat. Comput.*, 9:1,098–1,113.

Rubin, D. (1987). *Multiple Imputation for Nonresponse in Surveys.* New York: Wiley.

Rubin, D. (2000). The broad role of multiple imputation in statistical science. In Bethlehem, J., and van der Heijden, P., editors, *Proc. 14th Symposium Computational Statistics, COMPSTAT 2000*, pages 3–14. Heidelberg: Physica-Verlag.

Sahai, H., and Ageel, M. (2000). *The Analysis of Variance: Fixed, Random, and Mixed Models.* Boston: Birkhäuser.

Santos-Pereira, C., and Pires, A. (2002). Detection of outliers in multivariate data: A method based on clustering and robust estimators. In Härdle, W., and Rönz, B., editors, *Proc. 15th Symposium Computational Statistics, COMPSTAT 2002*, pages 291–296. Heidelberg: Physica-Verlag.

Särndal, C.-E., Swensson, B., and Wretman, J. (1992). *Model Assisted Survey Sampling.* New York: Springer-Verlag.

Schall, M. (1993). Easy access to census data. *Stat. Comput. Graphics*, 4:7–8.

Schena, M., Shalon, D., Davis, R., and Brown, P. (1995). Quantitative monitoring of gene expression patterns with a complementary DNA microarray. *Science*, 270:467–470.

Schweppe, F. (1973). *Uncertain Dynamic Systems.* Englewood Cliffs, NJ: Prentice–Hall.

Senkan, S. (2001). Combinatorial heterogeneous catalysis—A new path in an old field. *Angew. Chem. Internat. Ed.*, 40:312–329.

Shao, J., and Wu, C. (1989). A general theory for jackknife variance estimation. *Ann. Stat.*, 17:1,176–1,197.

Simonoff, J. (1996). *Smoothing Methods in Statistics*. New York: Springer-Verlag.

Singer, J. (1991). Types of factors and their structural layouts. In Hoaglin, D., Mosteller, F., and Tukey, J., editors, *Fundamentals of Exploratory Analysis of Variance*, Chapter 4, pages 50–71. New York: Wiley.

Skiena, S., and Sumazin, P. (2000). Shift error detection in standardized exams. In Giancarlo, R., and Sankoff, D., editors, *Combinatorial Pattern Matching (LNCS 1848)*, pages 264–276. Berlin, New York: Springer-Verlag.

Spearman, C. (1904). The proof and measurement of association between two things. *Amer. J. Psychol.*, 15:72–101.

Stivers, D., Wang, J., Rosner, G., and Coombes, K. (2003). Organ-specific differences in gene expression and UniGene annotations describing source material. In Johnson, K.F. and Lin, S.M., editors, *Methods of Microarray Data Analysis III: Papers from CAMDA'02*, pages 59–72. Boston: Kluwer.

Strehl, A., Ghosh, J., and Moody, R. (2000). Impact of similarity measures on web-page clustering. In *Proc. AAAI-2000: Workshop of Artificial Intelligence for Web Search*, pages 58–64. Menlo Park, CA: AAAI Press.

Tanur, J. (1992). Samples and surveys. In Hoaglin, D., and Moore, D., editors, *Perspectives on Contemporary Statistics*, Chapter 4, pages 55–70. Washington, DC: Mathematical Association of America.

Thompson, S. (2002). *Sampling*. New York: Wiley, 2nd edition.

Thomson, D. (1990). Quadratic-inverse spectrum estimates: Applications to palaeoclimatology. *Philos. Trans. Royal Soc. London, Series* A, 332:539–597.

Thomson, D. (1995). Signal processing challenges in climate data: Global temperature and CO_2. In *Proc. 1995 Internat. Conf. Acoustics Speech Signal Proc.*, pages 2,821–2,824. New York: IEEE.

Tian, X., Vardi, Y., and Zhang, C.-H. (2002). L_1-depth, depth relative to a model, and robust regression. In Dodge, Y., editor, *Statistical Data Analysis Based on the L_1-Norm and Related Methods*, pages 285–299. Basel, Boston: Birkhäuser.

Tukey, J. (1977). *Exploratory Data Analysis*. Reading, MA: Addison–Wesley.

van Lint, J., and Wilson, R. (1992). *A Course in Combinatorics*. Cambridge, U.K., New York: Cambridge University Press.

Vardi, Y., and Zhang, C.-H. (2000). The multivariate L_1-median and associated data depth. *Proc. Nat. Acad. Sci.*, 97:1,423–1,426.

Venables, W., and Ripley, B. (2002). *Modern Applied Statistics with S*. New York: Springer-Verlag.

Verboven, S., and Hubert, M. (2002). Robust principal components regression. In Härdle, W., and Rönz, B., editors, *Proc. 15th Symposium Computational Statistics, COMPSTAT 2002*, pages 515–520. Heidelberg: Physica-Verlag.

Wall, L., Christiansen, T., and Orwant, J. (2000). *Programming Perl*. Beijing, Cambridge, MA: O'Reilly and Associates, 3rd edition.

Weihs, C. (1995). Canonical discriminant analysis: Comparison of resampling methods and convex-hull approximation. In Krzanowski, W., editor, *Recent Advances in Descriptive Multivariate Analysis*, Chapter 3, pages 34–50. New York: Oxford.

Weiss, M. (1988). *The Clustering of America*. New York: Harper and Row.

Willems, G., Pison, G., Rousseeuw, P., and Van Aelst, S. (2002). A Hotelling test based on MCD. In Härdle, W., and Rönz, B., editors, *Proc. 15th Symposium Computational Statistics, COMPSTAT 2002*, pages 117–122. Heidelberg: Physica-Verlag.

Wright, T. (1884). *A Treatise on the Adjustment of Observations by the Method of Least Squares*. New York: Van Nostrand.

Yin, L., Yang, R., Gabbouj, M., and Neuvo, Y. (1996). Weighted median filters: A tutorial. *IEEE Trans. Circuits Systems—II: Analog Digital Signal Proc.*, 43:157–192.

Zhong, S., and Ghosh, J. (2003). Scalable, balanced, model-based clustering. In *Proc. 3rd SIAM Internat. Conf. Data Mining*, pages 71–82. Philadelphia: SIAM.

Ziegler, G. (1995). *Lectures on Polytopes*. New York: Springer-Verlag.

Index

3σ edit rule, 23, 70, 73–76, 88, 274
Akaike information criterion (AIC), 114
autocorrelation, 8, 241
auxiliary knowledge, 138–139, 222

bagplot, 204
balanced, 186
binary variable, 266–268
biplots, 205
bootstrap, 208, 210
    moving blocks, 210
boxplot, 26, 178, 193
    asymmetric outlier rule, 78
    clockwise bivariate, 205
    definition and illustration, 4–7
    outlier rule, 70, 73, 77–78, 88
    symmetric outlier rule, 78
breakdown
    definition, 19
    finite sample, 76
    how high?, 275
    kurtosis estimator, 20
    masking, 76
    maximum possible, 19
    mean, 20
    median, 19
    swamping, 77

caliper, 179
canonical correlation analysis (CCA), 130
chaos, 168
cluster analysis, 97, 174, 183, 192, 230–231, 276
    balanced, 231
collinearity, 58, 97–100
    definition, 11

computational negative controls (CNC), 219, 244–251
constraints, 58–60
contamination
    definition, 19
    typical, 19
continuity
    absolute, 194
convex
    function, 163
    polytope, 169
correlation coefficient, 196
    overlapping subsets, 212–213
    product-moment, 47–48
    Spearman rank, 50–51, 197, 248, 280
    zero, 165
covariance matrix
    definition, 48
    indefinite, 108
cross-correlation, 241–244
    rank-based, 248–251
crossing, 187

data-based prototyping, 270
data depth, 134–138, 228
data distribution
    asymmetric, 36, 90, 277–283
    beta, 232
    chi-square (χ_p^2), 129
    exponential, 278
    gamma, 194, 278
    Gaussian (normal), 74, 219, 278
    Student's t, 233
    uniform, 167, 194
    unimodal, 36
dataset
    Brownlee, 272

301

dataset (*cont.*)
 CAMDA normal mouse, 16–17, 24, 54, 138–139, 283
 catalyst, 87–88
 flow rate, 88–90
 industrial pressure, 90–91, 235–237, 254–263
 Michigan lung cancer, 263–268
 microarray, 1, 2, 37–39, 95–96, 126
 storage tank, 237–251
DataSpheres, 228
deadzone nonlinearity, 65
deletion diagnostics, 30, 213–217, 241, 244, 274
 successive, 216
descriptor, 26, 178, 179, 192–193
 figure-of-merit, 192, 199–201
distance-distance plot, 129
dotplot, 193

empirical quantiles, 5
equivariant, 155
 affine, 156
 regression, 156
 scale, 156
exact fit property (EFP), 141
exchangeability, 25, 32, 178–180, 199, 219
expectation maximization (EM) algorithm, 203
experimental design, 188–190
extended data sequence, 254
extreme studentized deviation (ESD), 74

forward search, 133
fouling, 243
function
 differentiable, 151, 157
functional equation, 144–159
 bisymmetry, 154
 Cauchy's basic, 144
 Cauchy's exponential, 145
 Cauchy's logarithmic, 145
 Cauchy's power, 146

Galton's skewness measure, 196, 278
 definition, 44
 outlier-sensitivity, 44
general position, 156, 158
generalized sensitivity analysis (GSA), 25–31, 177–201
giant magnetostriction, 13
Gini's mean difference, 280
gross errors, 33, 52–53

Hampel filter, 122–124
 iterative, 202
Hampel identifier, 24, 35, 70, 73, 76–77, 88
hard saturation nonlinearity, 64
heuristic, 177
homogeneity, 134, 144, 147–149, 151
 generalized, 147
 order c, 147
 order zero, 149
 positive, 147
Hotelling's T^2 statistic, 129

ideal quantizer, 64
idempotent, 9, 60, 62–66, 118, 120
implosion, 77
imputation, 23, 60
 cold-deck, 105
 hot-deck, 105
 mean, 103
 multiple, 105–108, 276
 single, 103–105, 276
inequality, 159–166
 arithmetic-geometric mean (AGM), 154, 161–162
 Cauchy–Schwarz, 160
 Chebyshev, 159
 Jensen, 163
interquartile distance (IQD)
 comparisons, 29–30
 definition, 7, 24
 outlier-sensitivity, 43
interval arithmetic, 168
inward testing procedures, 202

jackknife, 214–215

kurtosis
    beta distribution, 232
    breakdown point, 20
    definition, 5
    estimator, 5
    lower bound, 18, 232
    outlier-sensitivity, 18
    Student's t, 234
    variability, 232–235

leptokurtic, 233
Literary Digest, 61
location-invariance, 149–152
lowess smoother, 223, 254

MA plot, 37, 126
Mahalanobis distance, 39, 128–131
    definition, 47
Mann–Whitney test, 46
Martin–Thomson data cleaner, 115, 275
masking, 74, 274
mean
    arithmetic, 154, 157, 161–162
    bounds, 163–166
    generalized, 161
    geometric, 154, 161–162
    harmonic, 154, 162, 165
    outlier-sensitivity, 20, 41–43
    quasi-arithmetic, 154
    quasilinear, 154–155, 161
    versus median, 20–23
    zero breakdown, 20
median
    breakdown, 19
    characterization, 157
    definition, 5
    deletion-sensitivity, 21
    multivariate, 134–138
    outlier-sensitivity, 43
    smallest bias, 275
    versus mean, 20–23
median absolute deviation (MAD)
    comparisons, 29–30
    definition, 24

median filter, 117
    center-weighted (CWMF), 118–122,
        187
metaheuristic, 177, 178
mice and elephants, 211
microarray, 1, 2, 16–17, 37, 54
midmean, 28, 256, 275
minimum covariance determinant (MCD),
    128
minimum volume ellipsoid (MVE), 131
Minkowski addition, 168
misalignment
    CAMDA dataset, 16–17, 25
    caused by missing data, 55
    caused by software errors, 56
    causes, 54–58
    consequences, 9–11
    definition, 9
    detection, 283–286
    prevalence, 274
missing data
    coded, 33, 71
    definition, 7
    disguised, 8, 33, 60, 71
    from file merging, 66–67
    ignorable, 7, 60
    imputation, *see* imputation
    missing at random (MAR), 277
    missing completely at random (MCAR),
        277
    modelled as zero, 26
    nonignorable, 7, 52, 60–61, 102, 103,
        106, 276, 277
    representation, 61, 271
    treatment strategies, 60, 102–110
modal skewness, 280
mode estimator, 279
modified R^2 statistic, 134
monotone missingness, 107
moving-window characterizations, 252–
    263

nesting, 187
niche, 16
noise, 96–97
    versus anomalies, 33

nominal variable, 264
nonadditivity model, 229
noninformative variable, 25, 93–102, 276
    application-specific, 95
    external, 94
    inherent, 94
nonlinear digital filters, 117, 202
nonsampling errors, 52
norm, 179
nulls, 61–63

Occam's hatchet, 98
Occam's razor, 98
order statistics
    definition, 5
ordinal variable, 264
outlier
    common mode, 53, 237, 277
    definition, 2, 23
    detection, 23, 69–91
    good, 13–16
    isolated, 112, 277
    lower, 36
    multivariate, 3, 9, 24, 37–40, 124–138
    orientation, 39
    patchy, 112, 119, 277
    sources, 52–53
    time-series, 40, 110–124
    univariate, 2, 3, 9, 11, 23–24, 34–37, 69–91
    upper, 36
outlier model
    additive, 70, 115
    contaminated normal, 72, 79
    discrete mixture, 71
    point contamination, 71
    Poisson, 112
    replacement, 71
    slippage, 73
    univariate, 70–73
outlier-sensitivity
    Galton's skewness measure, 44
    interquartile distance (IQD), 43
    kurtosis, 18
    Mann–Whitney test, 46

    mean, 20, 41–43
    median, 43
    skewness, 43
    t-test, 45
    variance, 43
oversampling, 231

permutation invariance, 151, 154, 157
platykurtic, 232
plug flow model, 242
Poisson's ratio, 13
Preface, ix
Princeton Robustness Study, 20, 73, 152, 194, 275, 278
principal components analysis (PCA), 130, 205
principal component regression (PCR), 130
pseudonorm, 158
pyramids, 228

quantile-quantile (Q-Q) plot, 194–195, 219, 220, 235

random subsets, 26, 208–212, 238
    disjoint, 208–209
    limitations, 270
ranking populations, 228
regression
    comparisons, 272
    depth-based, 137–138
    iteratively reweighted least squares, 201
    least median of squares (LMS), 22, 275
    M-estimators, 274
    ordinary least squares (OLS), 98–102, 188–189, 215, 274
    set-theoretic, 169
relational database, 57, 95
resistant, 25
root mean square (RMS), 120
root sequence, 115, 118–120

sampling
    Bernoulli, 224

sampling (*cont.*)
    cluster, 230
    importance, 211
    model-based, 223
    Poisson, 225
    probability proportional-to-size, 225
    random with replacement, 208
    random without replacement, 208
    scheme, 26, 178, 190–191
    sequential, 230
    stratified, 225
    subset-based, 178, 207–268
    systematic, 223
sampling bias, 60
scenario, 25, 178, 180–186
set-valued variables, 108, 166–172
shift errors, 283
silhouette coefficient, 97, 192
skewness
    definition, 42
    industrial pressure dataset, 235
    outlier-sensitivity, 43
software errors, 56–58, 272
stampede phenomena, 65
standard deviation
    bounds, 163–166
    comparisons, 29–30
starburst plot, 204

stick-slip phenomena, 65
stratification, 186–188, 225–230
stratification principle, 228
subdistributive, 169
subscenario, 28, 186–190
supsmu smoother, 254
swamping, 77

t-test, 45, 129
three-valued logic, 61–63
trimmed mean, 275
    comparisons, 27–29, 186
    definition, 27
trimmed mean filter, 253

undersampling, 231
unknown-but-bounded, *see* set-valued
    variables
unmeasurable variable, 108–110, 276

vague problems, 177
variance
    outlier-sensitivity, 43
volcano plot, 45–47

white noise, 245

z-score, 220–222, 246, 248, 250